BLUE GUIDE

ROME

Alta Macadam

Somerset Books • London
WW Norton • New York

Blue Guide Rome
Ninth edition

Published by Blue Guides Limited, a Somerset Books Company
49–51 Causton St, London SW1P 4AT
www.blueguides.com
'Blue Guide' is a registered trademark

ISBN 1–905131–11–9

A CIP catalogue record of this book is available from the British Library.

Published in the United States of America by
WW Norton and Company, Inc.
500 Fifth Avenue, New York, NY 10110
USA ISBN 0–393–32887–2

Cover: Top: Ippolito Caffi: *The Roman Forum* (Museo di Roma, Archivio Fotografico)
Bottom: 15th-century *Annunciation*, in the Pantheon (photo: Róbert Szabó Benke)
Title page: Detail of a drinking fountain (photo: Róbert Szabó Benke)
Spine: Statue of Castor, Piazza del Campidoglio (photo: Róbert Szabó Benke)

All other acknowledgements, photo credits and copyright information are given
on p. 624, which forms part of this copyright page.

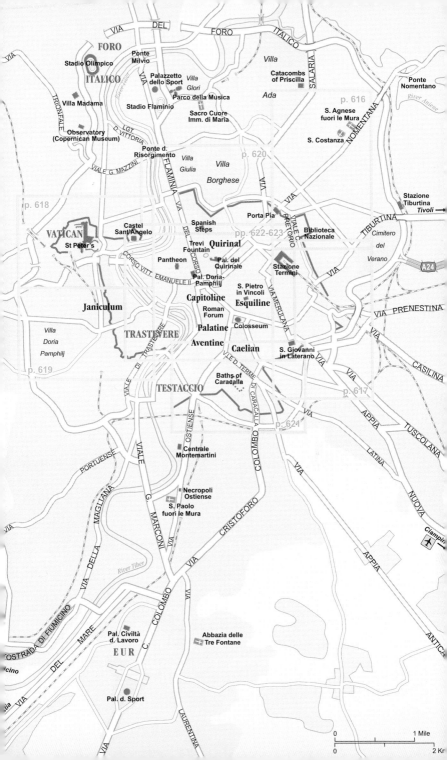

CONTENTS

PRACTICAL INFORMATION

About the author
Alta Macadam has been a writer of Blue Guides since 1970. She lives with her Italian family in Florence, where she has been associated with the Bargello museum, the Alinari photo archive, Harvard University at Villa I Tatti, and New York University at Villa La Pietra. Her *Americans in Florence* was published by Giunti in Florence in 2003. As author of the Blue Guides to Florence, Venice, Tuscany and Umbria, she travels extensively in Italy every year to revise new editions of the books.

About the contributors
Nigel McGilchrist (N.McG.) was educated at Winchester and Oxford. He is an art historian who has lived in the Mediterranean—Italy, Greece and Turkey—for over twenty-five years, working for a period for the Italian Ministry of Arts and then for six years as Director of the Anglo-Italian Institute in Rome. He has taught at the University of Rome, for the University of Massachusetts, and was for seven years Dean of European Studies for a consortium of American universities. He lectures widely in art and archaeology at museums and institutions in Europe and the United States, and lives near Orvieto.

Charles Freeman (C.F.) is a freelance academic historian with a long-standing interest in Italy and the Mediterranean. His *Egypt, Greece and Rome, Civilizations of the Ancient Mediterranean* (second edition, Oxford University Press, 2004) is widely used as an introductory textbook to the ancient world. His most recent book, *The Horses of St.Mark's* (Little Brown, 2004), is a study of the famous horses through their history in Constantinople and Venice. He leads study tours of Italy for the Historical Association and has recently been elected a Fellow of the Royal Society of Arts.

Mark Roberts (M.R.) joined the staff of the British Institute of Florence in 1977, and was Librarian from 1980 to 1999. He has translated many art historical works for Pannini of Modena and other Italian publishers, and has written a guide to the street-names of Florence (Coppini, 2001). For New York University he has put in order the Harold Acton papers at the Villa La Pietra. He lives at Badia a Passignano with his wife and family.

Thanks are also due to Professor Peter Fidler of the University of Innsbruck and Brigitte Winkler-Komar for consultation on the architecture of the Baroque.

INTRODUCTION

Rome is one of the most celebrated cities of the world, and ever since her greatest days as the centre of the Roman Empire—and later as the home of the Roman Catholic Church—has had a role of the first importance in European history. The Eternal City was the *Caput Mundi* in the Roman era: from here law and the liberal arts and sciences radiated to the furthest reaches of the Empire, which covered the whole of the known western world. Ancient Rome, with a population of over one million, was built over the famous Seven Hills on the left bank of the Tiber. The walls built to defend it by the Emperor Aurelian in the 3rd century AD still defined the urban limits of the city in the late 19th century, and it was only in the 1940s that the population began to reach (and supersede) that of ancient Rome.

The city today preserves numerous magnificent Roman buildings. Some of these are very well preserved—such as the Pantheon and Colosseum—while others are picturesque ruins in the very centre of town. The Vatican, in the part of the city which from the 9th century onwards became the stronghold of the popes, has, since 1929, been the smallest independent state in the world. Amongst Rome's many churches there are still a number which preserve their early Christian mosaics, as well as those from the splendid Baroque period, with masterpieces by Bernini and Borromini.

Superb collections of ancient Greek and Roman sculpture can be seen in the Capitoline museums as well as the Vatican, where the Sistine Chapel with Michelangelo's frescoes and Raphael's *stanze* can also be admired. There are still some fine private patrician collections of paintings.

No visitor can fail to notice the abundance of water in Rome, brought to it by aqueduct since ancient Roman times from springs many miles away. Almost every piazza has a lovely fountain and there are numerous street fountains known as *nasoni* ('hooked nose', from the shape of the tap), which provide a continuous flow of drinking water for everyone. A special feature of the city are its numerous fine parks including the huge Villa Borghese in its very centre. The distinctive atmosphere of Rome is perhaps best perceived today in the elegant streets around Piazza di Spagna, as well as in Piazza Navona, Campo dei Fiori, around the Pantheon and in Trastevere.

Many restoration projects and new excavations are at present under way. The recent creation of the regional park around the wonderful Via Appia Antica was a triumph for the conservationists who had long battled to preserve it.

For centuries Rome has been visited by pilgrims and travellers; today mass tourism has arrived (over three million people see the Sistine Chapel every year). You are strongly advised to spend time exploring the quieter streets and squares and the smaller museums and palaces as well as the world-famous sights of this beautiful city.

HISTORICAL SKETCH

by Charles Freeman

Rome the city, as both image and symbol, has penetrated so many layers of consciousness that an historical introduction can only scratch the surface. First, as capital of an extraordinary empire, which stretched from Britain to the Euphrates, it evoked a mass of different allegiances and meanings which lingered on, often in fresh or revived forms, long after its fall in the 5th century. Then, out of the Dark Ages, the city emerged as the capital of western Christendom, a spiritual focus which became global as Roman Catholicism spread to every continent. Since 1870, Rome has been a national capital, and there have been new challenges and tensions as the city sought to bring unity to a country where local loyalties have always been strong.

Within the city itself every period of history has been shaped by the past and has often deliberately echoed it. Classical architecture has been copied or adapted, often brilliantly, for the churches and palaces of Christian Rome (even reusing ancient materials) while the Roman empire was invoked in the bombastic rhetoric and territorial ambition of Mussolini. Getting to know Rome—insofar as that can ever be achieved—depends as much on understanding these moods and resonances as on knowing its buildings and streets. 'As the wave of memories flows in', writes the novelist Italo Calvino, 'the city soaks up like a sponge and expands'.

Origins of the city

The historian Livy (59 BC–AD 17) summed up the advantages of Rome's position. 'Not without reason did gods and men choose this spot for the site of our city—the salubrious hills, the river to bring us produce from the inland regions, and seaborne commerce from abroad, the sea itself, near enough for convenience yet not so near as to bring danger from foreign fleets, our situation in the very heart of Italy—all these advantages make it of all places in the world the best for a city destined to grow great.' Rome lay on an ancient salt route, which ran inland from the coast, at its crossing of the river Tiber in the centre of the fertile plain of Latium. There was higher ground close to the crossing. The Seven Hills of Rome, as they are traditionally listed, are all on the east bank. Four of these, the Quirinal, Viminal, Esquiline and Caelian, are in fact outcrops of higher land divided by the courses of ancient streams while the Capitoline, Palatine and Aventine stand on their own closer to the river. On the west bank, there is the long ridge of the Janiculum with the Vatican hill immediately to the northwest of it. This high ground allowed escape for early settlers from the marshy and often flooded land between the Capitoline and Palatine hills (the future site of the Roman Forum) and the larger floodplain north of the Capitoline where the river swept round in an extended bend. Livy omitted to note the persistent problems of flooding, which were only solved by the building of embankments along the Tiber at the end of the 19th century.

In its earliest days, between 1000 and 750 BC, Rome was only one of many settlements on the plain of Latium. Its founding by Romulus is traditionally dated at 753 BC. The Romulus myth is much later than this, but the date itself is plausible: urban growth in Italy was certainly being stimulated in the 8th century through contacts between traders from Greece and the native peoples of Etruria to the north. Although early inscriptions show that the Romans were always Latin speaking, the city was something of a frontier town open to both Greek and Etruscan influences.

Very recently it has been announced that a 'royal palace' dating from this period has been found in the Roman Forum (*see p. 80*). This can all be linked to early traditions that there were 'kings' of Rome acclaimed by the local population. At least two of these kings are said to have been Etruscans, and they brought with them models of city life from Etruria (themselves heavily influenced by Greek examples) as well as religious and military rituals. The last 'king' of Rome was the Etruscan Tarquinius Superbus (credited with building the temple of Jupiter on the Capitoline Hill). His son is said to have raped Lucretia, the wife of a Roman aristocrat. She committed suicide as the result of her dishonour, and Tarquinius was driven out by a Roman counter-attack, led by a certain Brutus. The traditional date, which seems close to the historical record, is 509 BC. A republican government was now put in place, and a suspicion of any form of tyrannical power lasted throughout its 500-year history.

The early Republic

The chief magistrates of the new Republic were two consuls elected for one year. Their chief duty was to lead the Roman armies. They were supported by more junior magistrates, among them the praetors, who administered the law and stood in for the consuls when these were away on campaign; the quaestors who dealt with the city's finances; and the censors who kept the official list of citizens (with the right of 'censuring' any whose behaviour was unworthy). These were all elected posts, and an ambitious man would work his way up from a junior magistracy to the top. After their term of office senior magistrates retired to the senate; and although this had little formal power, it became a repository of wisdom and experience that proved influential in the making of foreign policy and the supervision of the city. The magistrates were elected by councils of citizens. What was remarkable about Rome, certainly in comparison with the cities of Greece, was her generosity in granting citizenship. Even freed slaves received it automatically, as did most Italian communities who allied with Rome. Citizens could vote, if they could reach Rome, and received legal protection, but had to offer military service and pay *tributum*, a property tax, in return. This was the secret of Rome's success. Every victory was followed by the bringing of a mass of new citizens who could be recruited to serve in the armies and so bring on new victories. The cult of victory ran deep in the city's psyche. Spoils were brought into the city, dedications made to the city's gods, new temples built by successful generals (at least 14 are known from before 290) and an impetus for expansion sustained. No one was likely to be elected to a magistracy unless he had first proved his worth in war. (The exception which proved the rule was the brilliant 1st-century BC orator Cicero, who talked his way to power.)

Imperial expansion

The city inexorably expanded its power. In 396 came an important victory over the major Etruscan city of *Veii*; then a series of gruelling wars saw triumph over the Latin peoples (338 BC) and over a combined alliance of central Italian tribes at *Sentinum* in 296. The rigours of yearly campaigns in the rugged terrain of the Apennines gave the Romans a tenacity which was never lost. In the 280s Roman expansion moved south, to the decaying Greek cities of southern Italy. In conquering them, Rome came into conflict with the Carthaginian empire, which dominated the western Mediterranean. The two Punic Wars were more taxing than anything Rome had faced before and an invasion of Italy by Hannibal (218) brought her close to collapse. Hannibal was eventually defeated in 202. These hard-won wars left Rome with enormous confidence; a navy, which she had built from scratch; and control of Sicily, parts of Spain and north Africa. Troublesome Celtic tribes who had supported Hannibal in northern Italy were now suppressed and colonies of Roman citizens were imposed between them. The punishment of Philip V of Macedon who had supported Hannibal now extended Rome's grasp into Greece, and by the middle of the 2nd century BC, the whole peninsula had succumbed.

The impact of these sudden conquests on Rome was profound. A mass of booty was brought into the city in triumph. Much of it was Greek, and carried with it connotations of luxury and sybaritic living. Many traditional Romans looked back to earlier days, when the frugal, hard-working citizens had been tied to the land. Their ideal was Cincinnatus (c. 460 BC), who had left his farm to defend the early republic, then returned to it as soon as the war was over. Now the grander families were building fine houses (the Palatine Hill was a favourite spot), employing a mass of slaves on their estates around Rome (and thus undermining the traditional economy of the peasant farmers) and flaunting Greek rather than Roman culture. In Rome itself the process can be seen in the city's building materials. Early Rome had been built in tufa, a volcanic rock which hardens with exposure. There are many kinds, and the Romans gradually discovered the more hardwearing varieties, notably the blue-grey *peperino*, used from the 2nd century BC. By the 1st century BC a much harder white limestone, travertine, was being extracted from quarries east of Rome. Still an important building material in the city today, it allowed more detailed and enduring carving than the easily weathered tufa. However, the most coveted building material, for Romans as it had been for Greeks, was now marble. The earliest known marble building in Rome was a temple to Jupiter Stator (Jupiter the Saviour) in 146 BC. There was marble in Italy (at Carrara, its mines first exploited about 50 BC) but most had to come form further afield: Greece (Parian, the finest, and Pentelic, the marble used for the Parthenon), Turkey, Egypt and other parts of north Africa. By the 1st century BC, the wealthier Romans were beginning to import coloured marbles for their homes, as thresholds, wall coverings and columns. With the integration of Egypt into the empire by Augustus (30 BC) a mass of new marbles were to be discovered in the Nile valley and eastern desert (including the purple porphyry which became a symbol of imperial power), and vast columns were shaped and then shipped back to the capital. One of the fascinations of visiting Rome is to see these many marbles recycled.

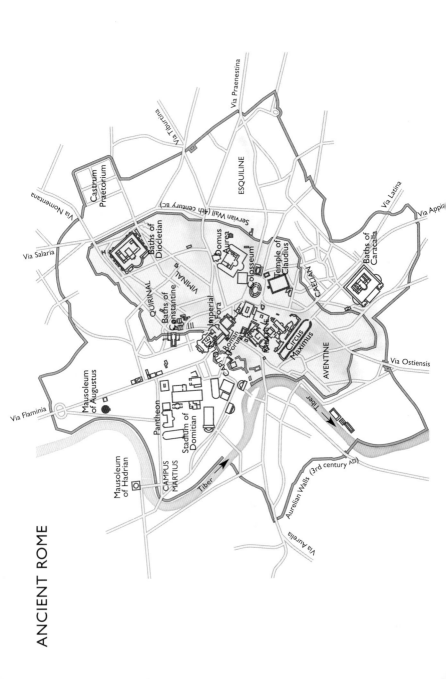

ANCIENT ROME

Civil war: Pompey and Caesar

By the end of the 2nd century BC there was increasing popular unrest in Rome. The city had expanded so fast that its water and food supplies were vulnerable, there was land hunger in Latium and all the time conscripts had to be found for the defence of the empire. Attempts to redistribute land in favour of the poor were quashed by an intransigent senate, and respect for this ancient institution plummeted. Eventually the traditional constraints on the consuls, which required them to retire after their terms of office, were subverted by a brilliant general, Marius, who got himself re-elected as consul from year to year, raised his own armies (the restriction of recruitment to property-holders had had to be abolished) and fought off Rome's enemies in North Africa and the Italian borders. He had set a precedent. By the 50s BC two brilliant generals, Pompey the Great and Julius Caesar, were using commands—Pompey in Asia, Caesar in Gaul—to build up prestige, wealth, and loyal troops. They showered their wealth on Rome, the support of whose citizens was vital if their power was to be maintained at the centre. The focus for their building projects was the Campus Martius which, with its propensity to flood, was still undeveloped. Pompey built Rome's first stone theatre, a semicircle of steps surmounted by a temple to Venus Victrix (its shape can still be traced in the way Via Biscione curves into Piazza Paradiso; *map p. 308*). Caesar also built a theatre, but his immediate ambition was to construct a marble-coated voting enclosure. It echoed his claims to be the voice of the citizens against the magnates of the senate.

An eventual showdown between Pompey and Caesar led, after a civil war fought across the empire, to the triumph of Caesar. Returning to Rome in 46, he continued his benevolence to the city. The Forum, traditionally the centre of political life, had been ravaged by unrest—even the senate house had been burned down in one riot. Caesar seized his chance to restore the area, rebuilding porticoes, temples (including one to himself), basilicas and rostra for public speaking. He went further in creating a completely new Forum, immediately to the north of the existing one and close to a new senate house. Yet his position was ambiguous. He had been granted a dictatorship—traditionally a short-term appointment during emergencies but in his case extended for life—and he seemed increasingly seduced by the trappings of power. There were still members of the senatorial aristocracy who clung to the ancient republican ideal of *libertas* and many feared Caesar would adopt the dreaded title of *rex*. Led by Brutus, the descendant of the Brutus who had overthrown tyranny in 509, the conspirators surrounded Caesar as he was walking to business in the portico which fronted Pompey's theatre and stabbed him to death (March 44). However, when it was discovered that Caesar had left money and his gardens to the citizens of Rome in his will, Brutus and his co-conspirator Cassius were forced to flee the city.

The assassination of Caesar might have been the moment when the Roman empire collapsed, especially when Caesar's nephew, Octavian (whom he adopted as his son in his will) and Mark Antony, Caesar's fellow consul and close supporter, fell out and there was renewed civil war. At the Battle of Actium (31 BC), Octavian triumphed over the combined forces of Mark Antony and the Egyptian queen Cleopatra. The victory brought Egypt—and with it immense wealth—into the empire.

The early Empire

The glorification of Rome by Augustus (*see p. 120*) established the city as the imperial showpiece. Rome took on a mass of new symbolic meanings, and temples to the 'goddess' Roma became commonplace in the empire. The emperor Claudius (AD 41–54) was pragmatic and far-seeing. He realized that the survival of the city, whose population may now have been as high as one million, depended on efficient supplies of food and water. Two of Rome's greatest aqueducts, the Acqua Claudia (providing 184,000 cubic metres of water a day) and the Anio Novus (providing 190,000 cubic metres) were completed during his reign. Claudius also improved the grain supply. An estimated 200,000 tonnes of grain a year were needed, and it was brought in from southern Italy, Sicily, North Africa and above all Egypt, much of it coming into Rome via the port of Ostia. Even so the good order of the city was always precarious. The emperor had his personal Praetorian Guard, and there was also a city prefect with his own forces of law and order. Local government was centred on 14 'regions' set up by Augustus. Each had a magistrate chosen by lot and deputies usually chosen from freedmen, who welcomed the status. Their duties included care of local shrines, fire-watching and the maintenance of clean streets. Fire was the greatest threat to the city and Augustus organized a force of 7,000 nightwatchmen who were divided into smaller groups which were each responsible for two regions. They could deal immediately with residential fires and had the right to check that water buckets were kept on the upper floors of the *insulae*, the tenement blocks in which the mass of citizens lived. Even so fires quickly got out of hand: six major ones are recorded between 15 and 54 AD before the devastation of 64. Augustus' own house was destroyed by one in AD 3. The continuous supply of fresh water was also a priority, and a workforce of slaves was kept permanently working on the aqueducts.

Rome remained a city of extraordinary contrasts. The public areas, the old Forum and the great Imperial Fora built alongside it, the Capitoline hill and the Palatine, now the home of the emperors, were staggering in their magnificence. They were continually rebuilt and maintained and embellished with propaganda buildings such as the triumphal arches celebrating imperial victories over Rome's enemies. Yet among all this marble magnificence the mass of the population lived in poverty in the *insulae*. The higher the floor in a tenement, the more tenants were crammed into it, and the building thus became vulnerable to collapse. Political life was quiet as the emperors had displaced the popular assemblies, although there were still honorary posts such as the consulship and provincial governorships worth fighting over. In his *Annals* and *Histories*, the historian Tacitus provides a brilliant picture of a city where political life has atrophied and all depends on the will of the emperor.

The extravagance and megalomania of Nero ended in his suicide (69 AD). His successor, Vespasian, was more sensitive to the needs of the population. He built the Colosseum, one of the great achievements of Roman architecture, for the provision of mass entertainment. This entertainment was always brutal, featuring slaughter for slaughter's sake, and often grotesque, with strange combinations of animals and men set in conflict with each other, but it sucked in the energies of a restless populace

Trajan (*see p. 117*) and Hadrian (117–138) were great benefactors of the city, even though Hadrian spent much of his reign wandering the empire. His successor Antoninus Pius (138–161) stayed in Rome, 'like a spider in the centre of a web', as one observer put it. This is often seen as the moment when the empire reached its height and when the identification between the name of Rome and its empire became complete. 'All nations look to the majesty of Rome', the Greek orator Aelius Aristides enthused in a panegyric to the empire in 150 AD. 'You have made the word "Roman" apply not to a city but to a universal people ... You no longer classify mankind into Greek or barbarian—you have redivided mankind into Romans and non-Romans ...'

Barbarian incursions

However, the skies were clouding. From the mid-2nd century on increasing threats to the empire from barbarian tribes on the northern borders and a revived empire of Persia in the east forced conscientious emperors to spend much of their time on campaign. Marcus Aurelius (161–80) was able to celebrate his triumphs in Rome and leave a column detailing his exploits there, but much of his reign was spent dutifully repelling raids along the Danube. Septimius Severus (193–211) spent a short time in the city (his triumphal arch celebrating a victory over the Parthians remains in the Forum) but campaigns took him from the Persian border to Britain, where he died in 211.

The century that followed almost saw the collapse of the empire as barbarian raids reached ever deeper within the empire and emperor followed emperor in a desperate search for stability. It was a sign of the times that one of the more effective emperors, Aurelian (270–75), felt impelled to create a massive set of walls for Rome, large parts of which still stand (*see p. 338*).

The empire was saved by the Balkan general Diocletian (284–305), who reorganized it under the tetrarchy of two senior emperors (the *Augusti*) aided by two junior ones (the Caesars) and restored stability. Diocletian had little time for Rome—he was busy constructing alternative imperial 'capitals' closer to the borders—and he only visited it once, in 303. However, he gave the city some form of recognition by rebuilding much of the Forum after a fire and constructing the greatest set of baths the pampered city had yet seen. After his abdication Maxentius, the son of one of his generals, seized Italy. He was generous to Rome, building one of the most stunning of the Roman vaulted basilicas at the edge of the Forum as well as another circus for chariot racing beside the Via Appia. He met his end in 312 at the Battle of the Milvian Bridge (Ponte Milvio; *see p. 551*), which crosses the Tiber just north of Rome. His antagonist was Constantine, son of one of Diocletian's Caesars. Constantine entered Rome in triumph and the senate acquiesced by granting the new ruler an impressive triumphal arch next to the Colosseum. Constantine completed Maxentius' basilica and had a vast seated statue of himself placed in one of its halls. (Fragments of it, including the head, still exist; *see p. 39*). He then restored the Circus Maximus and followed the imperial tradition of commissioning yet another set of baths. This all suggested a conventional emperor seeking to buy the support of his capital city: but it was only a façade. Constantine was about to alter the Roman way of life for ever.

Constantine and the new world order

Constantine announced that his victory over Maxentius was a sign of the favour of the Christian god. It was an astonishing revelation. The Christians were still only a small part of the city's population and they had kept a low profile. No more than 25 Christian meeting places are recorded from before 312, and it is clear that these were modest buildings. Christian burials had taken place in underground passageways cut into tufa rock around the city (although the earliest catacombs, from the 1st century BC, were in fact Jewish). In what must be one of the most important moments in western economic and architectural history, Constantine decided to shower the Christian community with vast, opulently decorated basilica buildings as if their God were equal to those pagan deities he was replacing. The earliest basilicas, San Giovanni in Laterano and the neighbouring Santa Croce in Gerusalemme, were both built on imperial property. The first St Peter's, built over the traditional burial place of Peter on the Vatican Hill, may also have been on an imperial estate. Constantine was sensitive to a city which was still overwhelmingly pagan, and while the interiors of these basilicas were beautifully decorated (it has been estimated that the cost of the gold for the apse of San Giovanni in Laterano would have supported 12,000 poor for a year) the exteriors were kept plain. The bishops of Rome were nevertheless well supplied with estates and material resources. 'Enriched by the gifts of matrons, they ride in carriages, dress splendidly and outdo kings in the lavishness of their table', was the comment of the historian Ammianus Marcellinus in the 380s. By the end of the 4th century most of the aristocratic families of the city had converted, and a Roman identity for the Church was confirmed when Bishop Damasus transferred the liturgy from Greek to Latin in the 380s.

The world around Rome, meanwhile, was crumbling. The stretched Roman armies were finding it more and more difficult to deal with barbarian raids and the emperors had to compromise by allowing the invaders to settle within the empire in return for paying taxes. No emperor after Constantine lived in Rome. Constantine's successors had preferred Milan, and Constantine himself had created another glittering capital, Constantinople, in the east. When the young emperor Honorius moved down to the well protected city of Ravenna in 402, he left his generals to negotiate with Alaric, the leader of the Goths who were threatening Italy. After negotiations broke down, Alaric attacked Rome. The Goths were Christians and many treasures were saved by being gathered in St Peter's, but mansions were ransacked and the Forum looted. Even though the 'sack' only lasted three days, the impact on the empire was profound. As far away as Bethlehem the Christian scholar Jerome recorded his shock and bewilderment at the news. The image of Rome as the inviolable *urbs sacra*—a name given it by Caracalla—was destroyed for ever.

The papacy and medieval Rome

Among those who were stunned by the news of the sack of Rome was the great Christian theologian Augustine. In his *The City of God*, however, he gives his own gloss on events: the true City of God is the city in heaven. Rome, with its dependence on the pagan gods, had been bound to fall and the sack was therefore not to be mourned. This view was to be influential for a thousand years, until the Renaissance restored an awareness of the achievements of the Classical city and its civilization.

The disintegration of the Western Empire allowed the more ambitious bishops of Rome to become prominent. Leo I ('the Great', 440–61) stressed his position as a direct legal heir of Peter, thus finding new grounds for affirming the pre-eminence of the bishops of Rome, an authority which he asserted with confidence over his fellow western primates. When Attila and his Huns invaded Italy in 452, it was said that a personal confrontation by Leo forced him to withdraw. (Over a thousand years later Raphael recreated the scene in the Vatican for the Medici pope Leo X.) Less than 15 years later, in 476, the last emperor, Romulus Augustulus, abdicated, bringing the Western Empire to an end.

Decay set in in the next century. First there was a collapse in the Mediterranean economy (one account tells of the road between Rome and Ostia, once bustling with activity, being now covered in grass). A city such as Rome could never be sustained from its own resources, and the population began to shrink. More dramatic was the attempt by the eastern (Byzantine) emperor Justinian to recapture Italy for the empire. His general Belisarius entered Rome in 536, but protracted campaigns against the Ostrogoths led to the city being besieged, captured and recaptured. The aqueducts were cut and the population scattered—perhaps only 30,000 remained by the middle of the century. One Gothic leader massacred 300 children from senatorial families whom he had gathered as hostages, and the senate is heard of for the last time in 580. By the end of the century Rome was nominally back under the control of the Byzantine empire, but a new set of invaders, the Lombards, now held most of northern Italy. Refugees fled south, swelling the population of Rome to some 90,000, but the city was still a shadow of what it had been; churches and monasteries circled a decaying core. The collapse of drainage schemes on the plain appears to have led to the spread of malaria. (The disease was not to be eliminated until the 20th century.)

It was at this desperate moment that one of the great figures of Roman history, Gregory the Great (590–604), founder of the medieval papacy, appears. Gregory was the son of a former city prefect and he cared deeply for the people of his city. Instead of building new churches, he reorganized the papal estates so that they could feed the poor. As a pastor he was moderate, toning down the harsh asceticism of earlier Church leaders and endorsing the balanced monastic rule of St Benedict, of whom he was a great admirer. At the same time he refused to compromise on papal authority. While he accepted doctrines laid down by earlier church councils, he was adamant that 'without the authority and consent of the apostolic see [Rome] none of the matters transacted by a council has any binding force'.

Gradually the Church began infiltrating the historic centre. Patrician mansions were converted into monasteries, a hall from the Forum of Vespasian had taken on a new role as a church dedicated to two eastern saints, Cosmas and Damian (*see p. 125*). For a time pagan temples remained taboo areas, haunted by the malign powers of the pagan gods, but in 609 the Pantheon was made into a church dedicated to the Virgin Mary. The city was given new life through its relics, not only of Sts Peter and Paul, but of other early

Roman martyrs (the remains of whom were brought into the city from the catacombs in cartloads) as well as imports such as the *titulus* of the True Cross, to be seen (then as now) in Santa Croce. So began the history of Rome as a centre for pilgrimages. In 660 a monk from Ireland writes of sharing a hostel with pilgrims from Egypt, Palestine, Greece and even southern Russia.

Though the bishops of Rome had traditionally claimed supremacy over all the bishops of Christendom, this was clearly untenable when Rome was so isolated. The Goths, who had succeeded the imperial authorities in much of western Europe, were not even Catholic (they clung to what was now termed the Arian heresy, in which Jesus was seen as a lesser creation of God the Father). It took some time before Catholic rulers emerged in France and Spain so that with Ireland and England (which Gregory the Great had converted) a wider Catholic community was gradually consolidated in Europe. Within Italy itself the popes were consolidating control over their own estates in central and southern Italy and Sicily and were increasingly seen as the key figures in mediations between the Byzantine empire and the Lombards. Strong links between the empire and the papacy were retained—in fact 11 out of 13 popes between 678 and 752 were Syrian or Greek. However, disputes over doctrine, conflict over the relative powers of emperors and popes in spiritual matters, and the weakening of the Byzantine empire as Islam gained sway in the 7th century could only strengthen the papacy as an independent force. When the Byzantine emperor Leo III launched a campaign against religious images (726), the popes refused to join in and, in retaliation, actually encouraged the worship of icons in Rome.

In the late 8th century, the West reasserted itself. It happened unexpectedly. In 751 the Lombards captured Ravenna, the seat of the Byzantine exarch, thus eliminating Byzantine control in Italy. Pope Stephen II (752–70) saw his chance to ask Pepin the Short, King of the Franks, for support against further Lombard expansion. Pepin and his successor Charles, later Charlemagne, defeated the Lombards and Charles took the crown of Lombardy (774). The papacy thus regained some of its old estates in the north, but was now dependent on Frankish military power. When a struggle over the papacy broke out in 795, the elected pope, Leo III, sought Charlemagne's help in resisting his opponents and on Christmas Day 800 he crowned Charlemagne as Roman Emperor in St Peter's. It was a clear throwback to the past. Charlemagne even took 'Augustus' as one of his titles and was spoken of as 'the new Constantine'. In a now lost mosaic in a hall of Leo III in the Lateran, the Apostle Peter was shown on a throne with Charlemagne kneeling on one side and Leo on the other. What was left unresolved, however, was which of the two, emperor or pope, had power over the other.

Popes and Holy Roman Emperors

The next three centuries were dominated by a power struggle between popes and emperors for ultimate spiritual and temporal jurisdiction. In 824 Charlemagne's grandson Lothar proclaimed in his *Constitutio Romana* that emperor and pope were to share judicial functions over the city and that the people of Rome had to swear allegiance to the emperor. The election of a pope had to be confirmed by the emperor. This went directly against the popes' view of their role which they elaborated from a document, the so-called *Donation of Constantine*, which purported to show a transfer of imperial power by Constantine to the pope of his day, Sylvester (in the Chapel of St Sylvester in the church of the Quattro Coronati, Constantine is shown giving his imperial crown to Sylvester, 1246). The struggle intensified when the Carolingian house disintegrated and it was a German, Otto of Saxony, who came to Rome in 962 to be crowned by the pope, only to impose a pope of his own choosing. The conflicts which followed were bitter, but slowly an accretion of papal power is discernible. A council held in the Lateran in 1059 reserved the election of a new pope to the cardinals, the procedure which is still followed today. This removed the process from the direct influence of the emperors and the powerful families of Rome, unless—as was often to happen—they had cardinals of their own. At the same time the papacy gradually increased its control over the patchwork of estates, ancient duchies and cities in central Italy, the so-called Patrimony of St Peter. In 1122 an agreement between Pope Calixtus II and the emperor Henry V, the Concordat of Worms, was in essence a recognition of the spiritual supremacy of the pope even over temporal rulers.

Dissent and schism

In Rome itself the memories of an ancient republic based on the Capitoline Hill had never vanished. They were taken up by an expanding class of professionals, lawyers attached to papal administration, craftsmen and agricultural entrepreneurs who instigated a popular revolt against the supremacy of the popes and the noble families in 1143. The insurgents 'assembled on the Capitol and, desiring to renew the ancient dignity of the city, again set up the senate'. They appealed to the emperors, who refused to support them, but their persistence eventually led to the popes agreeing to recognize a communal government. In 1188 the representatives of the city were given the right to make peace and war and to receive a share in papal revenues. The most outstanding pope of the period, Innocent III (1198–1216), in fact managed to achieve control over the appointment of the *senatore*, the chief executive of the city, whom he normally chose from a leading noble family. He consolidated the papacy with a vastly improved bureaucracy in the curia, or papal court. He built few churches but many public buildings including, after he had been disturbed by a dream in which fishermen dredged up the bodies of dead children from the Tiber, the Ospedale di Santo Spirito for foundlings and the sick. From Rome Innocent reached throughout Europe, claiming the right to intervene in disputed imperial elections, to combat heresy with force and to launch crusades (the notorious Fourth Crusade, which sacked Constantinople in 1204, took place in his reign). This was the climax of the medieval papacy. The 13th century saw the arrival of the Dominicans and the Franciscans and in Santa Maria Minerva, Rome has one of its very few Gothic churches, modelled on the Dominican church in Florence, Santa Maria Novella. Influences from the north were clearly still suspect, however, and when the Franciscans took over and rebuilt the church of Santa Maria in Aracoeli on the Capitoline Hill from 1250, they chose the more traditional Romanesque style.

The end of the 13th century saw an outburst of new cultural and artistic activity, fostered by the popes, notably Nicholas IV (1288–92), and sustained by competitive showmanship from the city's cardinals. Many of Rome's churches were opulently redecorated. Tombs became more splendid and all the accoutrements of clerical life more gorgeous. Artists, including Cimabue and Giotto, were drawn southwards to Rome. The great new apse mosaic of the *Coronation of the Virgin* in Santa Maria Maggiore by Iacopo Torriti is perhaps the finest survivor from these years, which culminated in the announcement by pope Boniface VIII that 1300 would be a Holy Year, the first so proclaimed. An estimated two million pilgrims flocked to the city from throughout Christian Europe, bringing welcome amounts of offerings with them. (Accounts of this successful enterprise included a nice vignette of two clerics armed with rakes constantly sweeping away the coins around the altar of San Paolo.)

Despite the improved spiritual and temporal power of the papacy, it was still vulnerable to outside forces. Pope Clement V, elected in 1305, found himself under such strong influence from France that he was forced to moved the papal court to Avignon (*see p. 265*). It remained there until 1377, but even then the return of the papacy to Rome was marked by the crippling dispute of the Great Schism and it was not until 1420 that papal control was resumed in Rome. As one anonymous cleric noted, 'Rome without a pope is like a woman without a husband'. The city atrophied in the popes' absence, being reduced at one point to a mere 17,000 inhabitants. (Florence at this time had some 90,000, Venice a possible 100,000.) This was an unsettled time. Rome was, in theory, divided into 14 regions, as it had been in Augustus' time. Yet these divisions were made meaningless by the dominance of warring local families, whose power ranged across traditional boundaries. The Colonna lorded it over the Quirinal and Esquiline hills (and later appropriated the Mausoleum of Augustus). There were the Corsi on the Capitoline Hill and the Frangipani on the Palatine, with control of both the Colosseum and the Circus Maximus. The Pierleoni were dominant on the Isola Tiberina and Trastevere. The ruins of ancient Rome, such as still stood, were converted into fortresses and palaces, while a mass of towers (the 13th-century Torre delle Milizie near Trajan's market is a surviving example) acted as symbols of prestige and the readiness to defend territory.

Frustration with aristocratic infighting led to the most interesting event of the 14th century, the popular uprising masterminded by Cola di Rienzo in 1347. This man, an unbalanced opportunist of poor birth (it was typical of him that he claimed to be the illegitimate son of an emperor), was steeped in memories of the ancient Roman republic and having travelled to Avignon, he persuaded the pope that papal authority exercised through himself as a representative of the people needed to be asserted against the nobility of the city. Back in Rome, he took over the Capitol and in a wild but inspiring speech declared himself 'Illustrious Redeemer of the Holy Roman Republic'. Hatred of the fractious nobility was so great that for a short period Cola was triumphant. However, he was clearly unbalanced and extravagant claims that he was restoring the Roman Empire on behalf of himself and the pope soon lost him papal support. Despite a victory of his troops over the forces raised by the nobility, his increasingly tyrannical behaviour and a declaration by the embarrassed pope that he was a heretic led to his support slipping away. He was eventually clubbed to death by the mob in 1354. This bizarre episode showed, however, that ancient memories of the Roman Republic still lingered in the city: they were to reappear, in less dramatic form, in years to come.

Renaissance Rome

The years in Avignon (1308–77) and the Great Schism which followed it were eventually settled with the election of Martin V, from the ancient—but often turbulent—family of the Colonna, in 1417. When Martin arrived in Rome in 1420 he found it so 'dilapidated and deserted that it bore hardly any resemblance to a city ... Houses had fallen into ruins, churches had collapsed and whole quarters were abandoned'. It was the achievement of the popes who followed Martin to transform that desolate and fragmented place, which still bristled with its medieval towers, into a showpiece of Renaissance and Baroque art.

Papal Rome had two focuses. The ancient seat of the papacy remained San Giovanni in Laterano, whose basilica was the cathedral of Rome. The Lateran, however, had no link to the foundations of Christianity. It was to the Vatican Hill that pilgrims flocked to worship at the shrine over the supposed burial place of St Peter, and the core of the city's resident population remained in the Borgo, the immediate neighbourhood of St Peter's, and the warren of medieval streets covering the former Campus Martius. Nicholas V (1447–55) decided to move to the Vatican. By doing so he strengthened the direct relationship of the papacy with St Peter's, while in times of trouble popes could enjoy the protection of the river, the walls built by Leo IV in the 9th century and the Castel Sant'Angelo (formerly the mausoleum of Hadrian). With the election of each pope, a *sacro possesso* was celebrated with a grand procession from the Vatican across the Capitoline Hill, and down past the Colosseum to the Lateran.

The aim of the 15th-century popes was to create a city which reflected the spiritual and temporal power of the papacy as well as being accessible to the mass of pilgrims. The Holy Year of 1450 showed just how unsuitable the city was for large crowds when some 200 pilgrims drowned after a panic on the narrow Ponte Sant'Angelo. To relieve the pressure on the river crossing, Sixtus IV (1471–84) constructed the first bridge since antiquity, the Ponte Sisto (1475), together with a new street, the Via Lungara, connecting it with the Vatican.

Sixtus, in fact, was compared to Augustus for his mass of building projects, 'opening up and measuring out streets in accordance with the dignity of the empire', as one inscription put it. Pilgrims were greeted as they entered through the Porta del Popolo with the grand façade of his Santa Maria del Popolo, the first church in Rome with a dome. (Brunelleschi's great dome for Florence cathedral had been completed a few years before.) It was Sixtus who built the Sistine Chapel, for his own private use and for the papal elections, which are still held there. Near to the Vatican he rebuilt Innocent III's decaying Ospedale di Santo Spirito, transforming it into one of the largest hospital complexes of its day. Sixtus also moved a collection of ancient bronzes which had accumulated around the Lateran palace to the Capitol, where they formed the core of the

Capitoline museums. Perhaps his most enduring legacy was his decision to allow clergy to pass on any palaces they had built for themselves to their families, even if they had used Church money to do so.

These projects were possible because of the underlying wealth of the papacy. It enjoyed the the fruits of its own territory, which stretched across central Italy, in addition to an immense income from indulgences, from taxes on foreign churches, from special collections and the sale of offices. The Medici pope Leo X sold some 1,200 posts. The control of the popes over this wealth was absolute: at the death of Martin V, the papal treasury had to be retrieved from the Colonna's family palace. Some popes, for instance the Borgia Alexander VI, who had six illegitimate sons and a much-loved daughter, Lucrezia, to cater for, scattered it on their families; others on the glorification of the city. At the opposite extreme, the Venetian envoy complained of the austere Paul IV (1555–59): 'Life at court is mean ... The clergy have withdrawn from every sort of pleasures ... the state of things has been the ruin of artisans and merchants', a reminder that even though more spiritual Christians may have been shocked by papal excess, it did bring employment. Nevertheless, it meant that the ancient tradition of Rome as a city whose citizens lived off handouts was perpetuated and the mass of the population—judging from the anonymous notes which were left, in time-honoured tradition, by the statue of Pasquino (*see p. 281*)—showed a healthy cynicism about their clerical masters. 'We have done the Carafa, the Medici and the Farnese families', sighed one wag on the accession of the Borghese pope Paul V in 1605, 'now we have to enrich the Borghese'.

Yet the pope had also to show theological and political skills if he was to keep peace in the Church and maintain his position among the secular rulers of Europe. The fall of Constantinople to the Ottoman Turks in 1453, and continued Ottoman expansion through the Mediterranean and into central Europe, provided another challenge. In 1494 the wider political context within which the papacy operated was transformed when the rising nations of Spain and France began casting their eyes on the vulnerable and scattered Italian city states. In that year the French king Charles VIII marched down through Italy to claim the Kingdom of Naples. He forced his way into the centre of Rome while Alexander VI cowered in the Castel Sant'Angelo. After this humiliation, it was little wonder that Alexander's successor, Julius II (1503–13), founded his own army, the Swiss Guard (which since 1806 has been only a papal bodyguard), and led them into northern Italy where he humbled Venice and then France and even enlarged the Papal States.

Julius, born Giuliano della Rovere and a nephew of Sixtus IV, was the *papa terribile*, tempestuous and uncompromising. Against the impassioned opposition of traditionalists, he announced he would tear down and rebuild St Peter's. His architect was Donato Bramante, who had already ushered in the Renaissance to Rome with his charming Tempietto (*see pp. 388–89*). With Michelangelo diverted from work on a grandiose tomb for Julius to the repainting of the ceiling of the Sistine chapel and Raphael at work in the papal apartments, this was an extraordinary moment in the history of European art.

The Reformation and the Sack of Rome

The worldliness of the papacy finally faced the challenge of Martin Luther not over art or luxury, but over the sale of indulgences. Leo X excommunicated the rebel monk in 1521, but papal control over medieval Christendom began to fragment as the Reformation caught hold. To make matters worse, Pope Clement VII (1523–34), like Leo X a member of the powerful Florentine Medici family, unwisely became entangled in politics. His backing of the French against the Emperor Charles V led to Charles sending his troops towards Rome after families such as the Colonna offered him active support. Charles' troops were joined by a band of Lutherans, who were eager to wreak revenge on the anti-Christ, as the pope was now dubbed by his enemies. Out of the control of their commanders, they stormed into the city in May 1527. While Clement took refuge in the Castel Sant'Angelo and then had to flee north, the city was ransacked. Even the sick of the Ospedale di Santo Spirito were slaughtered in the mayhem, which one estimate suggests took 12,000 lives. The Vatican palace was only saved because one of the invaders' commanders protected it against his own men. When Clement, who was blamed for the disaster, finally made his way back, four fifths of the city was considered uninhabitable, trade was at a standstill and there were still unburied bodies among the rubble. 'Rome is finished', wrote one observer. Michelangelo returned to the city to complete the Sistine Chapel but the pessimism of his *Last Judgement* (*see pp. 444–45*) provided a strong contrast with the vitality and exuberance of the ceiling he had painted in happier times.

Yet amazingly, Rome was to revive. Clement's successor was the Farnese Paul III (1534–49), who was determined to restore some grandeur in the city, not least in the Palazzo Farnese, which he ordered to be enlarged as befitted the new status of his family. While Alexander VI and Clement VII had used the Castel Sant'Angelo as a refuge, Paul ordered new comfortable apartments to be installed there for everyday use. Bizarrely, in the frescoes with which they were decorated he linked himself, Alessandro Farnese, to Alexander the Great, a reminder of just how complex were the interactions between Renaissance and Christian present and Classical past. There was a real sense of a reconnection of Rome with its ancient roots. When the alarming news came that Charles V was on his way to Rome from the south (he had been fighting the Turks in Tunisia), Paul turned the situation to his advantage by laying on an imperial triumph. A route was cut through the city which echoed that of ancient times. The emperor entered along the Via Appia, passed the ruins of the Baths of Caracalla (from which Paul was busily looting statuary for his palace) and then processed through three triumphal arches: those of Constantine, Titus and Septimius Severus. Homage was paid to Trajan's Column before the imperial cavalcade made for the Vatican, where Charles dutifully kissed the papal foot. Some sort of redress had been made for the events of 1527.

Rome and the Counter-Reformation

The greatest challenge facing Paul was the reformation of the Church in the face of the inroads of Protestantism. (Henry VIII of England made his break with Rome during Paul's papacy.) It was Paul who called the Council of Trent (1545–63), which reformulated traditional Catholicism in such a way that it could offer an effective response to its enemies. In Rome he tightened papal control over dissidents by setting up the Inquisition (1542); and in founding the Society of Jesus (1540) under the ascetic Ignatius Loyola, Paul created an intellectual battering ram for the Church. It was Farnese money which was to finance the great Jesuit church of the Gesù (1568–75), whose opulent decoration shows how overpowering emotional impact was central to the Counter-Reformation fightback. (The Council of Trent in fact went so far as to insist that religious art should play on the emotions of the believer.)

The most obsessive of the Counter-Reformation popes was the austere Paul IV (1555–59). Narrow and impetuous, he made a disastrous alliance with France against Spain, which led to the defeat of papal troops. It was only a generous peace which preserved the Papal States. He set up the Index of Prohibited Books and alienated all by his parsimony—which did not, however, extend to his own family, many of whom shamelessly exploited his nepotism.The citizens of Rome liked money to be spent on them and their city rather than on the worthless hangers-on of the papal family of the day and they showed their true feelings at Paul's death by sacking the Inquisition buildings and releasing their prisoners. Paul's successor, Pius IV (1559–65), took note and began spending on the city again.

Renaissance Rome was to be brought to fruition by five years of intense activity by Sixtus V (1585–90). Sixtus, who had spent his early years as a swineherd in the Marche, appeared so sickly at the papal conclave that he won election as a stop-gap pope. Once elected, he emerged with a will of iron and a fixed plan to transform Rome, especially by encouraging settlement in the sparsely populated east of the city. (The French essayist Montaigne had noted in 1581 how desolate this area was.) He hit on the happy idea of re-erecting the Egyptian obelisks—most of which had been brought to Rome by Augustus sixteen hundred years before—at focal points in the city, especially to help pilgrims find their way around the streets. Sixtus' favourite church was Santa Maria Maggiore (he was to be buried there), and it acted as a hub for a new set of broad radiating streets. They were well received because coaches were just coming into fashion, and needed space to move. More welcome to the mass of citizens must have been Sixtus' restoration of a 3rd-century AD aqueduct (known as the Acqua Felice after Sixtus' Christian name) so that a supply of fresh water could now be piped to 27 fountains in the city.

By the time Sixtus died, in 1590, the scholar Pompeo Ugonio was able to write that Rome is 'permeated with the light of peace, augmented with wider streets, adorned with buildings, refreshed by fountains, implanted with massive obelisks reaching to the highest heavens... Wheresoever Rome turns, she sees herself restored to a new golden age abounding with justice, fortitude, vigilance, liberality, magnificence...'. This was certainly an exaggeration. Behind the façade of magnificence Rome, now with a population of 110,000, was still a city of gross inequality and simmering unrest. Sixtus had launched campaigns against the mass of prostitutes and beggars who thronged the streets; in 1604 a famine led to rioting against the unpopular Aldobrandini pope Clement VIII (1592–1605). Ancient tensions between the French and Spanish communities were another focus for conflict. It seems a fitting backdrop to the turbulent life of the painter Caravaggio, who arrived in the city for the first time in 1592. Yet the trouble below the surface was effectively masked by a new outburst of building which was to transform central Rome into the city we recognize today.

Baroque Rome

The great façade of St Peter's is emblazoned not with any biblical quotation but the name of Camillo Borghese, Pope Paul V, who completed it in 1614. The Borghese were a self-made family, originally from Siena, who had worked their way up through the papal administration, and Camillo emerged as a compromise candidate from the enclave of 1605. Paul spent lavishly, not only on St Peter's, but on the papal palace on the Quirinal. If Sixtus is remembered for his obelisks, Paul is remembered for his fountains. He rebuilt an aqueduct of Trajan so that fresh water now entered Rome on the Janiculum Hill, bubbling into a fountain in the form of a triumphal arch (the Acqua Paola). From there it flowed downhill into Trastevere and across the Ponte Sisto to feed the fountains in front of Palazzo Farnese. Another branch was diverted to the Vatican fountains.

The two themes which run through 17th-century Rome, the Rome of the Baroque, are the consolidation of the grand family palaces as the centre of a glittering cultural and social life and, secondly, the contribution of a man who did more than any pope to create the public ambience of the city: the architect and sculptor Gian Lorenzo Bernini.

Grand society in Rome centred on those families lucky enough to secure the papacy. In the first half of the century, these were, notably, the Borghese (Paul V) and Barberini (Urban VIII). Paul V's nephew Scipione Borghese acquired enough wealth to become one of the great art collectors of the city: some of his acquisitions are still on view in the villa he built in the Borghese gardens. The relations of Urban VIII did even better. They amassed a fortune so large that it was estimated to be 12 times the size of the annual income of the Papal States. Much of the wealth of these families was ploughed into their palaces. The Borghese acquired so much land for theirs they were able to create a piazza in front of it. The Barberini took advantage of the comparative emptiness of the Quirinal Hill to plan an H-shaped palazzo with separate wings for the secular and clerical sides of the family.

Perhaps the finest architectural achievement of this century was the completion of St Peter's under the patronage of the Chigi pope, Alexander VII (1655–67). His architect, Gian Lorenzo Bernini, had already enjoyed a glittering career. A consummate courtier and the favourite of Urban VIII, he had created sculptures of an emotionally charged but technically accomplished classicism, as well as fountains, tombs, palaces (including parts of the Palazzo Barberini), chapels, and his most important church, Sant'Andrea al Quirinale, begun in 1658. Inside St Peter's he was to raise the majestic bronze baldacchino over the central altar and create the brilliantly composed Cathedra of St Peter in the apse. Yet it was his sweeping colonnade, its arms reaching into the piazza to embrace the world of Christendom, that completed the magnificence of St Peter's.

reality of revolutionary France, dreamed of the overthrow of the papal autocracy and the creation of a united Italy. The Church stood firm, and outbursts of disorder in the Papal States in 1831 were crushed when the new reactionary pope, Gregory XVI (1831–46), called in Austrian troops to support him. Gregory's successor, Pius IX appeared more open to change, however, not least in his acceptance of gas lighting and railways. His apparent readiness to foster some form of unity among the Italian states aroused great enthusiasm. It might be possible, many thought, for Italy to be brought together under his benevolent care.

It was not to be. In early 1848 revolutions spread throughout Italy, from Sicily and Naples in the south to Venice and Milan in the north. To the enormous disappointment of his supporters, Pius disowned them. The reaction in Rome was such that he was forced to accept a constitutional government in the city but even this was swept away in November and the pope was forced to flee to Naples. His attempts from there to demand the submission of 'the rebels' on pain of excommunication only led to a vote by an elected city assembly to bring papal rule to an end and declare a Roman Republic (February 1849). The messianic Italian nationalist Giuseppe Mazzini then declared that 'Rome, by the design of Providence, and as the People have divined, is the Eternal City to which is entrusted the mission of disseminating the word which will unite the world'. Then there arrived, at the head of an unkempt collection of guerrilla troops, Giuseppe Garibaldi, the charismatic revolutionary leader who had already been sentenced to death once for his part in an insurrection on behalf of 'Young Italy'. He had spent his exile in South America joining in local revolutions, and it was his luck to return to Italy in 1848, just when there was a cause adapted to his talents.

By 1849, however, the revolutions which had spread throughout Europe were losing their vigour and the forces of reaction were gathering strength. Pius IX found an ally in the new French President—later emperor—Louis Napoleon, the nephew of Napoleon Bonaparte. Louis Napoleon was anxious to secure the support of the French clergy and present the restoration of Austrian influence in Italy, and he saw his chance to do this by offering military help to Pius to regain his kingdom. A French army was dispatched to Rome and arrived ready to attack the city in April. Hectic preparations were made in Rome's defence, and Garibaldi and his followers managed to repulse some of the French attacks which came from the west, from the higher ground of the Janiculum Hill. The streets which slope down into Trastevere from the church of San Pietro in Montorio on the hill still seem haunted by the skirmishing which took place here. The city fell, however. French troops entered it on 3 July 1849.

Pius returned in 1850, but his survival depended on the French garrison which remained in the city. The movement for Italian unity was now led by the Kingdom of Piedmont and Sardinia whose chief minister, Camillo Cavour, masterminded the removal of Austrian control of northern Italy. By 1861 the Papal States were lost to the new Kingdom of Italy and its monarch Vittorio Emanuele II. Papal control of Rome, all that was left of its territories, remained precarious, and Pius' instinct was to show no sympathy with the forces of change. In the papal encyclical of 1864, *Quanta Cura*, he condemned religious freedom and any idea that 'the pope should reconcile himself to and agree with progress, liberalism and modern civilization'. His spiritual authority might prevail; his temporal could not. Only two months later, under the pressure from the Franco-Prussian war, the French withdrew their garrison from Rome and Italian troops occupied the city. The Kingdom of Italy, with its capital now in Rome, was proclaimed in 1871.

Rome, the secular capital

Italian troops entered Rome near Michelangelo's Porta Pia on the 20th September, 1870 and the Via Pia was renamed Via XX Settembre in memory of the event. Pius refused to recognize the regime which had taken his territory, and never again set foot outside the Vatican.

Rome now needed to be converted into a modern capital city. It is astonishing when looking at old maps to see how underpopulated the area within the old Aurelian Walls remained. Even in 1871 the population, at 212,000, was only just over a fifth of what it had been in Classical times. Rome was still a city close to the surrounding Campagna (old photographs show shepherds with their flocks by the gates of the city) with virtually no industry of its own other than simple craftmanship. Now it had to be transformed into a capital with ministries, law courts and a palace for royalty: the Quirinal Palace was expropriated for them from the papacy. Emile Zola in his *Rome* (1896) speaks of 'the blood of Augustus rushing to the brain of these last-comers' (the Italian Government), urging them to a renewed desire to make Rome stately and great. There was a mass of new building in the western part of the city with grand new streets such as the Via Nazionale and the Via Cavour. Another new street, the Corso Vittorio Emanuele, ran up through the Campus Martius district to meet a new bridge Ponte Vittorio Emanuele (1911), so creating a completely new east–west axis. With the population rising fast, to 432,000 by 1891 and 660,000 by 1921, there was inevitably a great deal of scope for speculation, especially through the acquisition and conversion of former Church buildings.

Although the archaeological core of the city, from the Capitol to the ruins of the Baths of Caracalla, was made into a preserved zone, the rest of Rome was not so lucky and the carving up of the gardens of the Villa Ludovisi, now under the present-day Via del Tritone, caused an international outcry. Large numbers of apartment blocks for the expanding civil service took their place. Meanwhile the government's secular identity was affirmed through statues to Cola di Rienzo, by the Capitol, and Giordano Bruno, burned by the Church for heresy in 1600, in the Campo dei Fiori where the execution took place, and—perhaps most provocative of all—a Piazza del Risorgimento (the movement for Italian unity) alongside the walls of the Vatican (1921).

If the needs of the new Italian government (and the speculators who came its wake) predominated in the period before the First World War, after the war it was the ambitions of one man, Benito Mussolini, whose march on Rome in 1922 had led to an unexpected collapse of the Italian government, which took their place. 'Rome must be a city worthy of its glory, and that glory must be revivified tirelessly to pass on as the legacy of the Fascist era to generations to come,' he opined in 1924. For Mussolini Rome was there to be used as the backdrop for his imperialist fantasies. His desire to highlight the Classical monuments of the past by isolating them (the Mausoleum of Augustus is a good example) went hand in hand with his ambition to create 'the monumental Rome of the 20th century'. Central to his plans was to open Rome to the sea again. From the Piazza Venezia, the Via dei Fori Imperiali was cut through the ancient Fora—destroying buildings and important archaeological evidence for the imperial Rome which Mussolini idealized as it did so—towards the Via del Mare.

Mussolini did solve one outstanding problem: the uneasy relationship between the papacy and Italian state. Here was a nation made up largely of Catholics whose spiritual head, the pope, refused to recognize the very state to which they were supposed to give secular allegiance. Despite some tough talking between the representatives of Pius XI and Mussolini, the Lateran Pact of February 1929 produced a workable conclusion. The Vatican City was recognized as an independent state whose citizens were exempt from Fascist law. In return the pope accepted that the territorial losses of the 19th century were irrevocable—with financial compensation to be paid. Church authority over marriages and religious education within Italy was recognized. Mussolini is 'the man whom providence has sent us', said Pius XI, and it was indeed the Church which gained the long-term benefit of the pact.

Rome suffered little in the Second World War and in films such as Fellini's *La Dolce Vita* (1960) it acquired an image of carefree amorality. Yet there were deep-rooted problems facing the city, not least in how to deal with its future shape and identity. No city able to host the Olympics (1960), the Second Vatican Council (1962–65) and the World Cup (1990) could be considered moribund, but there was a feeling in the 1970s of life in Rome becoming out of control, not least through the proliferation of traffic which clogged the medieval streets and harmed its monuments. Piazzas pleasant to linger in in the 1960s became forbidding at night in the 1970s as Italy's political situation deteriorated. Perhaps the lowest point was the discovery of the murdered body of the prime minister, Aldo Moro, in the boot of a car in the Via Caetani in 1978. Throughout the 1980s the discrepancy grew between the urbane and often civilized façade of Italian life and a chaotic and unregulated cronyism behind the scenes. Umberto Bossi's Northern League, founded in 1989, was able to portray the unwieldy bureaucracy and high taxation of Rome's politicians as an unhappy contrast with the energies of the entrepreneurial north.

A turning point seems to have come with the decision, in 1993, to appoint a directly elected mayor. The first incumbent, Francesco Rutelli (1993–2001), gave new energy to the city. Vigorous attempts to cut traffic and the opening up of pedestrian areas allowed the centre to breathe again. Collections of the city's Classical art which had lingered for decades in storerooms were now at last displayed. The efficiency with which the Rome transport system dealt with the millions of pilgrims coming to the lying-in-state of Pope John Paul II in April 2005 was a mark of how far things have come. However, a recent warning that at least one of the city's most prestigious monuments, the Castel Sant'Angelo, is in desperate need of a full restoration, is a reminder that Rome's rich and complex heritage will always need continuing care.

POPES & THE PAPACY

by Mark Roberts

The word pope (*papa* in Latin and Italian) is a childish diminutive of 'father', and was originally applied to the clergy in general; it is still used of ordinary priests by the Greeks, but in the West quite early on it was restricted to bishops. By the Middle Ages only the Bishop of Rome called himself pope, and in 1073 Gregory VII strictly forbade anyone else to do so.

The Bishop of Rome, according to Catholic teaching, is the successor of St Peter the Prince of the Apostles, and is the vicar (or representative) of Christ on earth, the visible head, in other words, of the Church. This teaching is based on a famous passage in St Matthew's Gospel (*16, 13–20*), describing the encounter between Jesus and his disciples at Caesarea Philippi. Jesus had asked them 'Whom do you say that I am?', and Simon Peter alone had replied that Jesus was the Christ, son of the living God. Jesus then said to him: 'Thou art Peter, and upon this Rock I will build my Church ... and I will give to thee the keys of the kingdom of heaven'. The popes' claims to spiritual authority (the 'Petrine claims') are based on these very words of Christ, which are written in huge Roman capitals, two metres high, around the inside of the dome of St Peter's.

As well as being Bishop of Rome, the pope is styled Metropolitan Archbishop of the Roman Province, Primate of Italy and the adjacent islands, Patriarch of the West, and head of the Universal Church. He is also called *Pontifex Maximus* (the 'supreme bridge-builder', a title borrowed from Roman antiquity; it was used by the emperors, but originally referred to the head of a college of priests, who was seen as building a bridge between earth and heaven), and—more humbly—*Servus servorum Dei*, the servant of the servants of God. In case some of the grander titles should go to his head, the new pope was reminded of his mortality during the ceremony of his coronation, when a quantity of tow was ignited by a kneeling priest. As the tow burned to ashes, the priest sang *Beatissime pater, sic transit gloria mundi* ('most holy father, even thus passes all earthly glory'). However, the present pope and his two predecessors have chosen not to be crowned at all: the last papal coronation was Paul VI's in 1963.

The pope is elected by the cardinals, who are in a sense the clergy of Rome, and who form the Sacred College. The complicated rules for the conclave (from the Latin *conclave*, properly a chamber that can be closed with one key) were laid down in 1274 by Gregory X, though they have been altered several times since. The rules were designed to ensure that the election should not be unnecessarily delayed, should not be precipitated, should be free from any kind of external pressure. After the death of the pope, all the cardinals are summoned to the conclave, which is to begin on the tenth day following his decease. The election must be held in whatever city the pope dies, not necessarily Rome. On the tenth day a Mass of the Holy Spirit is sung, and the cardinals form a procession and proceed to the conclave, where apartments have been prepared for them separated by wooden partitions. On the first day crowds of people swarm in and out, but in the evening everyone is compelled to leave ('*Extra omnes!*'), except for the cardinals and their authorized servants, who are known as conclavists. All the doors are bricked up except one, which is locked and carefully guarded. After three days, according to Gregory's rules, the supply of food was to be restricted, and if a further five days elapsed without an election only bread, water and wine could be sent in. Voting takes place twice a day. The practice of burning the ballot papers, so as to indicate by the colour of the smoke whether or not a pope has been chosen, would seem to be no older than the 20th century. The requisite two-thirds majority is generally obtained fairly quickly, though in 1799 the cardinals took three months to make up their minds.

Attempts were often made to influence the result. As recently as 1903, the Austrian government used its veto to exclude the candidature of Cardinal Rampolla, thought to be anti-Austrian; Pius X, elected instead, immediately abolished the power of veto.

A winning candidate must be formally asked by the Cardinal Chamberlain whether he accepts the papacy. Sometimes he is very reluctant to do so: the infirm Leo XII, in 1823, pointed to his poor swollen legs, and said 'Do not insist, you are electing a corpse'. Sometimes he is rather pleased: Benedict XIV, in 1740, said 'Do you want a saint or a politician? Elect someone else. Do you want a good fellow (*un buon uomo*)? Very well then, elect me'.

John Paul II altered the rules so that the physical separation of the voting cardinals is no longer insisted upon: in 2005 they were put up in comparative comfort at the newly built Domus Sanctae Marthae inside the Vatican, although the voting sessions still took place in the Sistine Chapel.

Once he has accepted, and has chosen his name, the new pontiff is dressed in one of three different-sized outfits. The Cardinal Chamberlain makes the announcement to the waiting crowds: *Annuntio vobis gaudium magnum, habemus papam*; and for the first time the new pope gives his blessing *Urbi et orbi*, to the City and to the world.

Early popes are shown wearing a bishop's mitre, and sometimes the *pallium*, a circlet of white wool worn on the shoulders, worked with six purple crosses. The pope not only wears the *pallium* himself, he also sends it to patriarchs, primates and archbishops; it is woven from the fleeces of two lambs blessed in the church of Sant'Agnese fuori le Mura on St Agnes' Day (this ceremony, accompanied by the gentle bleating of the flower-garlanded lambs, still takes place every year on 21st January).

The triple crown, or papal tiara, has not been worn since the time of Paul VI (1978). In any case it was not a liturgical head-covering, and was never worn at Mass. Its form developed over several centuries. Nicholas I (858–67) is said to have been the first to unite the princely crown with the episcopal mitre. One coronet, around the lower edge, appears in art in the 12th century. Boniface VIII is said to have added a second crown, probably to symbolize the double monarchy—spiritual and temporal—which he claimed in his famous bull, *Unam sanctam*, of 1302, asserting the papacy's claim to be the only source of God-given authority, which kings must obey and to which royal power is merely ministerial. A third coronet was added in the early 14th century, either by Benedict IX or by Clement V, and the whole tiara was enlarged into its characteristic melon shape; it had a small cross on the top and two lappets at the back.

The triple crown has often been taken by commentators to symbolize the pope's threefold authority as Prophet, Priest and King, in other words his doctrinal, ministerial and jurisdictional powers. The doctrinal authority, or *Magisterium*, includes all the rights and privileges necessary for teaching divine revelation and for guarding the deposits of faith, and is held to be protected by 'Infallibility'. This teaching, defined by Pius IX in 1870, maintains that the pope's pronouncements on faith or morals, when made *ex cathedra* (from the throne, in other words addressed to the whole Church), are necessarily free from error. The ministerial authority involves, among other things, the appointment of cardinals, so that over a long pontificate a pope is able to pack the Sacred College with those *ab eo creati*, appointed by himself. The jurisdictional authority is very extensive, and is held to be 'full, ordinary and immediate' over the entire Church.

The other great papal symbol is the crossed keys, always part of the pope's coat of arms. The scene of the *traditio clavium*, or handing over of the keys, is familiar in art, and represents the power of binding and loosing, of locking and unlocking, given by Christ to St Peter and his successors at Caesarea Philippi. Perugino's fresco in the Sistine Chapel shows this scene, and so does Raphael's tapestry made for the same place (now in the Vatican museums).

For much of their history the popes have been temporal sovereigns as well as heads of the Church. They ruled over the Papal States, or 'Patrimony of St Peter'. This papal monarchy came to a dramatic end during the pontificate of Pius IX, in 1870, when King Vittorio Emanuele invaded the papal dominions: Pius refused to accept the settlement offered, and he and his successors became known as 'the prisoner of the Vatican', right up until the Concordat with Mussolini in 1929 (*see p. 30*). The pope now rules—as absolute monarch—over a tiny kingdom consisting only of the 109 acres of the Vatican City plus a few extra-territorial dependencies such as the Lateran and Castel Gandolfo. He has his own radio station and post office, so as to ensure freedom of communication with the outside world.

CAPITOLINE HILL

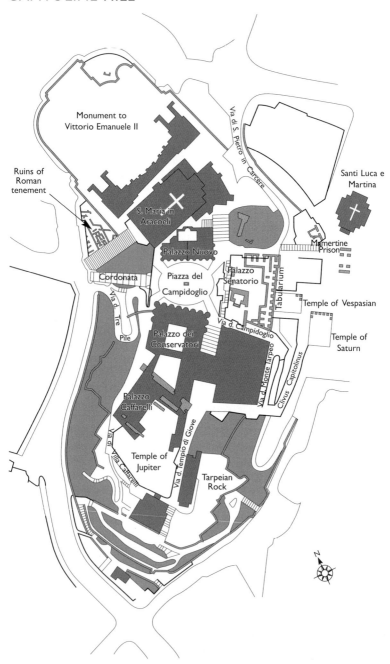

Monument to Vittorio Emanuele II

Ruins of Roman tenement

S. Maria in Aracoeli

Santi Luca e Martina

Via di S. Pietro in Carcere

Palazzo Nuovo

Mamertine Prison

Cordonata

Piazza del Campidoglio

Palazzo Senatorio

Tabularium

Temple of Vespasian

Via d. Tre Pile

Via d. Campidoglio

Temple of Saturn

Palazzo dei Conservatori

Via d. Monte Tarpeo

Clivus Capitolinus

Palazzo Caffarelli

Via di Villa Caffarelli

Temple of Jupiter

Via d. Tempio di Giove

Tarpeian Rock

N

THE CAPITOLINE HILL

The Capitoline Hill (*Campidoglio*), in the heart of the city (*map p. 622, 3C*), is the best place to start a visit to Rome. It was of the first importance in the city's early history, and today it preserves its ancient feeling of pride combined with a sense of intimate elegance. In the little piazza created by Michelangelo on the very summit of the hill, around the splendid equestrian monument to Marcus Aurelius, stand the town hall of Rome and the Capitoline museums, with the city's superb collections of Classical sculpture—the arrangement still reflects their history as the oldest public collection in the world. There are delightful peaceful gardens off the quiet street which encircles the top of the hill, from which there are superb views of the city and of the Roman Forum.

HISTORY OF THE CAPITOLINE HILL

The smallest of the seven hills of Rome, the Capitoline Hill is nevertheless the most important. It was the political and religious centre of ancient Rome, and since the end of the 11th century of the modern era it has been the seat of the civic government of the city.

On its southern summit (the *Capitolium*) stood the Temple of Jupiter Optimus Maximus Capitolinus, remains of which still exist. This was the most venerated temple in Rome, since 'the best and greatest of all Jupiters' was regarded as the city's special protector. The northern summit of the hill was occupied by the Arx, or citadel of Rome: incredibly, the authorities allowed this area to be altered at the end of the 19th century by the construction of the monument to King Vittorio Emanuele II. During a siege by the Gauls in 390 BC the Capitolium was saved from a night attack by the honking of the sacred geese of Juno that were kept here, which alerted the Romans to the danger. In 343 BC a temple was erected in honour of Juno Moneta; the name came to be connected with the mint later established here (and hence our word 'money'). In the Middle Ages the church of Aracoeli on this summit was the meeting-place of the Roman Council.

Approaches

At one time the hill was accessible only from the Roman Forum but since the 16th century the main buildings have been made to face north, in conformity with the direction of the modern development of the city. There are three approaches from Piazza d'Aracoeli. (The ruins here are of a Roman tenement house built in the 2nd century AD and over four storeys high. It is particularly interesting as one of the few remains found in Rome itself of a service building with shops on the ground floor and simple living-

Replica of the Classical bronze statue of Marcus Aurelius, in the centre of Piazza del Campidoglio.

quarters above.) Beyond, a long flight of steps mounts to the church of Santa Maria in Aracoeli, and on the right Via delle Tre Pile (a road opened for carriages in 1873) winds up past a fragment of Archaic tufa wall. In the middle the stepped ramp known as the **Cordonata**, designed by Michelangelo and modified around 1578 by Giacomo della Porta, provides the easiest way up the hill. At its foot are two Egyptian lions in black granite veined with red, dating from the Ptolemaic period (3rd century BC), that were formerly in the Temple of Isis which once stood near the Pantheon. The water they now blow from their mouths (except in winter) comes from the Acqua Felice, an aqueduct which was constructed to provide water for the hill in the late 16th century (*see p. 37*). In the garden halfway up on the left stands a rather sinister little 19th-century statue of Cola di Rienzo in a cowl. This was set up in 1887 to mark the spot where the popular hero was killed in 1354, after he had led a successful rebellion against the warring barons of Rome during the absence of the popes in Avignon, and had been proclaimed 'tribune' of a 'Holy Roman Republic' in 1347. He addressed the assembly in the church of Santa Maria in Aracoeli here and 'ruled' from the Campidoglio, but his ambition to recreate a glorious period of republican governance modelled on ancient Rome only lasted a matter of months since the populace turned against him and he was killed by the mob, who decided to side with the nobility. He was considered a romantic figure in the 19th century, when his utopian ideas of an empire led by the 'people' met with particular favour, and an opera by Wagner was based on his life.

Flanking the top of the steps are colossal sculptures of the twin heroes Castor and Pollux (known as the Dioscuri; *see p. 77*) with their horses. They are much restored late Roman works that were found in the 16th century in the Ghetto (where a temple to them once stood). Beside them on the balustrade are two Roman sculptures modelled on the enemy arms and armour which used to be displayed as trophies in triumphs held in honour of victorious generals after battle. They have been known for centuries as the 'Trophies of Marius', since it was traditionally thought that they depicted the war booty of General Marius after his victory over Germanic tribes in 101 BC, but in fact they date from the time of Domitian (late 1st century AD). The statues of the Emperor Constantine and his son Constantine II come from the Baths of Constantine, and the two columns were the first and seventh milestones of the Via Appia.

PIAZZA DEL CAMPIDOGLIO

At the top of the ramp is Piazza del Campidoglio, a superb piece of town planning by Michelangelo. Michelangelo was called on in 1538 by Pope Paul III, who decided it was time to elevate the appearance of this spot to reflect its importance as the historical centre of the city. Michelangelo had just been made a citizen of Rome, and was already working for the same pope on his huge fresco of the *Last Judgement* in the Sistine Chapel. The resulting piazza is surrounded on three sides by stately palaces, and the balustrade defines its open end. It is one of the most pleasing spaces in Rome, with the feel at once of an intimate courtyard and a terrace above the city. The attractive pavement was given its novel oval star design (also by Michelangelo) to give prominence to the famous **gilded bronze statue of Marcus Aurelius**, which Paul III had ordered to be moved here from the Lateran Hill. The small and elegant base is also Michelangelo's work. The statue has been displayed under cover since its restoration (*see p. 47*); it was replaced here by a disappointing copy in 1997. The sculpture of the horse and rider appears time and again in medieval representations of the city, and it is first documented in the 10th century when it was believed to represent the Christian emperor Constantine the Great. It is thought to have stood on the Lateran Hill as early as 782 and was certainly there by the 10th century, and it was greatly admired, together with other Classical bronzes, throughout the Middle Ages. On a visit to Rome in 1873 Henry James commented, 'I doubt if any statue of King or captain in the public places of the world has more to commend it to the general heart'.

At the back of the piazza is Palazzo Senatorio and on the left is Palazzo Nuovo. Facing it on the right is the **Palazzo dei Conservatori**, where the governing magistrates of the city carried out their administrative duties from the mid-14th century onwards, though they exercised effective power for only some hundred years, since Nicholas V saw to it that the papacy took control of the city in the middle of the following century, when he had the palace rebuilt. The present building was designed by Michelangelo (*see p. 39*). The Palazzo Nuovo opposite, also designed by Michelangelo, was not built until the mid-17th century.

THE CAPITOLINE MUSEUMS

Open 9am–8pm. Closed Mon; T: 06 3996 7800. Ticket office in Palazzo dei Conservatori. The ticket includes entrance to all the sculpture galleries in the Palazzo Nuovo and Palazzo dei Conservatori, as well as the Tabularium and the paintings collection in the Pinacoteca. There is a café on the delightful roof terrace of Palazzo Clementino, with splendid views.

NB: An important collection of Classical sculptures, part of the Capitoline Museums and formerly exhibited here, is now splendidly displayed at the Centrale Montemartini, described on p. 471ff, and should on no account be missed (combined ticket valid for one week).

The collections housed in Palazzo Nuovo and Palazzo dei Conservatori (with the adjoining Palazzi Clementino and Caffarelli) are grouped under the comprehensive title of the Musei Capitolini, famous for their magnificent Roman sculptures. Founded in 1471, they constitute the oldest public collection in the world.

HISTORY OF THE COLLECTIONS

In 1471 Pope Sixtus IV made over to the people of Rome a valuable group of bronzes (including the famous *Spinario* and the She-wolf of Rome, still exhibited here), which were deposited in Palazzo dei Conservatori. This nucleus was later enriched with finds made in Rome and by various acquisitions, notably the collection of Cardinal Alessandro Albani in 1733. A second museum was opened in 1876, and in 1925 the Museo Mussolini (also known as the Museo Nuovo) was opened on the ground floor of Palazzo Caffarelli adjoining Palazzo dei Conservatori. The superb contents of these two museums, closed to the public in 1984, are now permanently displayed at the Centrale Montemartini.

The Pinacoteca Capitolina was founded in the mid-18th century with the collections of Prince Gilberto Pio of Savoy and Cardinal Sacchetti. In the 19th century it lost some of its treasures to the Vatican Picture Gallery and to the Accademia di San Luca. It was later enriched by the Cini bequest, which included ceramics and some interesting 14th–15th-century paintings from the Sterbini collection.

The museums retain their old-fashioned intimate arrangement and provide a wonderful introduction to Classical sculpture, not only because they contain numerous masterpieces, but also because they illustrate the way these have been presented for centuries to travellers. The hospitable rooms are rarely over-crowded and have an atmosphere all their own, especially in the evening when they are illuminated solely by magnificent chandeliers. You can get face to face with the famous Roman busts, displayed in serried ranks on marble shelves. The memorable atmosphere is very special—quite different from the crowded Vatican museums, or the chilly displays of the state collection of Roman sculpture in Palazzo Massimo alle Terme.

The tunnel which connects the two buildings has been reopened so that remarkable remains of the Tabularium beneath Palazzo Senatorio can once again be visited. Since excavations during restoration work brought to light more of the Temple of Jupiter Capitolinus (*see below*) and Bronze Age sepulchres, part of Palazzo Caffarelli is still closed to the public. When it reopens these excavations will be visible, and a new pavilion, designed by Carlo Aymonino, will display the original statue of Marcus Aurelius, and probably also other large sculptures at present kept in the Sala degli Orazi e Curiazi.

PALAZZO DEI CONSERVATORI

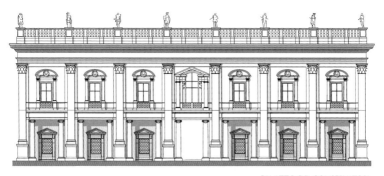

PALAZZO DEI CONSERVATORI

This beautifully proportioned building by Michelangelo has a very unusual design with Ionic columns supporting architraves (rather than the more usual arches) to form an open loggia below, and handsome windows with coupled columns on the *piano nobile*, below a prominent entablature with a balcony. The two storeys are united by columns, which rise from the ground as far as the entablature, the earliest example of the giant order being used in secular architecture to add to its sense of dignified grandeur. The building contains the Appartamento dei Conservatori on the first floor, and the Pinacoteca on the second. Considerable remains of the 6th-century BC Temple of Jupiter Capitolinus are incorporated into the building, and more of the temple is at present being excavated, soon to be visible to the public.

Courtyard

In the courtyard are fragments of a **colossal seated statue of Constantine the Great**, including the head, hand and feet, which were found in the Basilica of Maxentius in the Forum (*see p. 81*) in 1486 and which have been displayed here since then. It was about 12m high (but the apse above it was twice that height) and the body of the statue would have been made in wood probably covered with bronze. The forefinger is raised apparently to hold a sceptre. This is the best-known portrait of the emperor, with his staring hooded eyes and hooked nose, which would have been made all the more imposing when it was crowned with a diadem. Despite the huge dimensions, the anatomical details of the arms and feet are carefully portrayed. Opposite are reliefs representing the provinces subject to Rome, which once decorated the interior of the cella of Hadrian's Temple in Piazza di Pietra (*see p. 154*): many of these were places visited by the emperor himself. Above is a fragment of the huge inscription from the arch erected in AD 51 on Via Lata (now the Corso) to celebrate the conquest of Britain by Claudius. Beneath the portico is a seated statue of a female divinity given the attributes of the goddess Roma, flanked by two colossal statues of barbarian captives in rare grey marble, all three acquired by Clement XI in 1720 from the famous Cesi collection of ancient Roman sculpture formed in the 16th century. They had been the centrepiece of the garden statuary outside their palace in the Borgo district (mostly destroyed to make way for Bernini's colonnade in front of St Peter's).

Stairs and first-floor landing

Stairs lead up past three splendid large **reliefs from a triumphal arch** set up to celebrate Marcus Aurelius in 176 after his military victory over the Sarmatian and German tribes. He is shown in the act of conquest accompanied by Roman soldiers, dispensing clemency to prisoners kneeling at the foot of his horse. The second panel depicts the emperor in his triumphal procession up the Capitoline Hill, transported in his quadriga with the symbolic figure of Victory above and preceded by a trumpeter. The third panel shows the emperor burning incense in a tripod before sacrificing, while the bull, above the heads of the crowd, looks on, unaware of his fate. The scene takes place in front of the Temple of Jupiter Capitolinus (remains of which can still be seen nearby; *see p. 46*), the most detailed representation we have of this famous sanctuary.

On the first-floor landing is a relief from another demolished arch across the Via Lata (the Arco di Portogallo). Hadrian is shown standing on a podium with figures representing the Senate (behind him) and the Roman *popolo* (the handsome young man holding out his hand to the emperor) and the scene apparently records Hadrian's distribution of charity to the poor children of Rome (represented by the child at the foot of the podium). The seated statue of Charles of Anjou is by **Arnolfo di Cambio** or his workshop, and was made for the nearby church of Santa Maria in Aracoeli c. 1270 when Charles, King of Sicily, was ruler of Rome and the papacy. Arnolfo, a Florentine, produced numerous beautiful sculptural monuments for churches in Rome in the last quarter of the 13th century, aided by several assistants. As the Classical lines of this statue show, he was clearly influenced by ancient Roman sculpture.

Appartamento dei Conservatori

These rooms were decorated in the 16th century and later with scenes of Roman history. They have fine carved ceilings and marble doors, and are adorned with sculptures.

Sala degli Orazi e Curiazi: The room is frescoed with scenes depicting episodes in the early history of Rome by the prolific Roman painter Giuseppe Cesari, always known as Cavaliere d'Arpino, who carried out numerous decorations in Rome in the early 17th century and in whose workshop Caravaggio first studied. From the 16th century onwards statues of popes were set up in this room in acknowledgement of papal power in the city: but today just two statues face each other at either end of the room—Urban VIII (*see p. 421*), a marble studio work begun by **Bernini**, and Urban's successor Innocent X (*see p. 421*), a bronze by **Alessandro Algardi**, executed some ten years later. It is interesting to compare the work of these two great rival sculptors who were at work in Rome during the same period.

It was in this room in 1957 that the Treaty of Rome, the foundation of the European Economic Community, was signed by Italy, Belgium, France, West Germany, Luxembourg and Holland. In 2004 the constitution of Europe was ratified here by 25 member states of the European Union.

Some **important Roman bronzes**, destined to be exhibited in a new pavilion in Palazzo Caffarelli, are also exhibited here. The colossal cult statue of Hercules in gilded bronze was found in the time of Sixtus IV near the circular temple of Hercules Victor at the foot of this hill. It is derived from a Greek bronze. The colossal bronze head is thought to be a portrait of Constantine (showing him as an older man than his portrait in the courtyard below), and the hand and globe probably came from the same statue. The provenance of the head is unrecorded although we know it was outside the Lateran palace in 1200.

(II) Sala dei Capitani: This room has colourful frescoes of scenes in Roman history as recounted by Livy, by Tommaso Laureti (dating from 1594). At this time too statues of contemporary generals (*capitani*) who served the pontifical state, all of them members of Roman patrician families, were installed here, amusingly dressed as ancient Romans. The memorial to Virginio Cesarini has a portrait attributed either to Bernini or to Duquesnoy, the Flemish sculptor who moved to Rome in the early 17th century, collaborated with Bernini on the decoration of St Peter's, and became well known for his statuary. Next to it Carlo Barberini (brother of Pope Urban VIII) is celebrated by a full-length Roman statue restored by Alessandro Algardi, who added the cloak (and it was given its portrait head by Bernini). Others, including Tommaso Rospigliosi, with a typical 17th-century hair-do, are by **Ercole Ferrata**, who succeeded Bernini and Algardi as one of the most influential sculptors active in Rome in the late 17th century.

(III) Sala dei Trionfi: The most famous of the bronzes presented to the Conservatori by Sixtus IV in the 15th century are exhibited here. In the middle is the celebrated ***Spinario***, a sculpture of a boy plucking a thorn from his foot, formerly known as the *Fedele Capitolino*, because it was thought to be the portrait of Marcius, a Roman messenger who pressed on with his mission even though tortured by the thorn. It is a delicate Hellenistic composition in the eclectic style, probably dating from the 1st century BC. It is one of the most famous antique works and was much copied in the Renaissance. Also here is a superb bronze head, with striking eyes, known as **Brutus**. Since it shows Etruscan, Greek and Roman influences, its date is still disputed by scholars (between the 4th and 1st centuries BC), but it is one of the earliest bronze portraits known (the bust was added much later).

There is also an exquisite statue of a boy shown as if taking part in a religious ceremony (he would have held a cup for ritual libations in his hand): it dates from the 1st century AD.

The painted frieze illustrates a triumphal procession on its way up the Capitol hill in 167 BC, as described by Plutarch. On the wall hangs a very fine painting of the battle between Alexander the Great and Darius by **Pietro da Cortona** (*see p. 223*), on a monumental scale despite its small dimensions (and dominated by one of Cortona's characteristic bright blue skies).

(IV) Sala della Lupa: The famous **She-wolf of Rome**, shown baring her teeth as she turns towards us in fear, has been displayed here since at least the 16th century. For centuries the most famous piece of sculpture in the entire city, it originally stood on the Capitoline Hill and may be the figure that was struck by lightning in 65 BC, when the hind feet are said to have been damaged. It was taken to the Lateran Palace some time in the Middle Ages. It is thought to be an Etruscan bronze of the late 6th or early 5th century BC, probably belonging to the school of Vulca, a sculptor from *Veii* (Veio, just outside Rome). The figures of

the twins Romulus and Remus were added by Antonio Pollaiolo c. 1509, and the wolf has been the symbol of Rome since the story or myth of the city's foundation by Romulus, who was saved from starvation together with his brother Remus by being suckled by a she-wolf.

On the walls are displayed fragments of the **Fasti**, records of Roman magistrates and of triumphs of the great captains of Rome in the period of 13 BC–AD 12, removed from the inner walls of the Arch of Augustus in the Forum, and given a frame designed by Michelangelo.

(V) Sala delle Oche: The room is named after the two exquisite little antique bronzes of 'geese' (more probably ducks) displayed here on either side of a bust of Isis. The marble head of Medusa is a little-known work by **Bernini** showing the Greek monster who had snakes instead of hair, with her terrible eyes mercifully closed. The bronze **bust of Michelangelo** is one of several versions of the most famous portrait of the great artist by his close friend Daniele da Volterra who, being with him when he died in Rome, made this from his death mask.

(VI) Sala delle Aquile: This room is named after two Roman eagles on *cipollino* columns and also here is a Roman sculpture of Diana of Ephesus.

(VII–IX) *Sometimes closed*: In the first room is a bust of Hadrian in rare Egyptian alabaster.

(X) Sala degli Arazzi: This room is decorated with tapestries made in Rome, one of them based on the painting of

Romulus and Remus by Rubens in the Pinacoteca upstairs. The very well preserved half-length **portrait of Commodus** shows the vain emperor in the guise of Hercules: a lion-skin bonnet encircles his curly hair and is tied at his chest, and he holds a club and the apples of the Hesperides. The symbolism continues in the seemingly fragile carvings below, the orb and the cornucopia represent the empire, and the shield and kneeling Amazons (only one of which survives) the conquered. This must have been a public monument exalting the immortality of the emperor, and was made even more elaborate by the addition of two tritons in adoration on either side (remains of which are preserved here). The group was discovered on the Esquiline Hill at the end of the 19th century, and despite the fact that the emperor appears to us today rather ludicrous and anything but 'Classical', it is recognized as a masterpiece of marble carving.

(XI) Sala di Annibale: The earliest frescoes in the palace are in this room. Dating from the early 16th century, they illustrate the Punic Wars, with Hannibal firmly seated on his elephant. The room also boasts the oldest ceiling in the palace (1519). A beautiful bronze vase bears an inscription which records that it was the gift of King Mithridates VI to a gymnastic association. This dates it to the 1st century BC and it must have been part of the booty from a war in Pontus in northern Asia Minor, when either Sulla or Pompey defeated Mithridates.

(XII) Cappella: Decorated with frescoes and stuccoes in 1578, it also has a *Madonna and Child with Angels*, attributed to Andrea d'Assisi, an Umbrian painter of the late 15th century known as L'Ingegno.

Palazzo Clementino and Café: Stairs lead to an upper floor, where a few rooms have recently been opened, decorated with more Roman sculptures. The *Medagliere*, a rich collection of Roman, medieval and modern coins and medals founded in 1872, is displayed in modern showcases and very well labelled.

Beside the café is a delightful terrace with a wonderful view.

(XIII–XV) Sale dei Fasti Moderni: These three small rooms (*closed for restoration*) contain lists of the chief magistrates of Rome since 1640.

Second-floor landing

On the landing is another relief from the Arco di Portogallo showing the solemn seated figure of Hadrian below his wife Sabina (who predeceased him in 136 or 137), who is being borne aloft by an allegorical female figure with huge, beautifully carved wings, carrying a torch. The two splendid marble intarsia panels of a bull attacked by a tigress were found on the Esquiline Hill. They are virtually all that remains of a basilica known to have been built there in the 4th century AD by a consul named Junius Bassus. It had its walls entirely decorated with *opus sectile*. It is interesting to note that the tradition of producing mosaics in marble and precious stones continued in Rome throughout the

Middle Ages, and that when these panels were discovered in the 15th century, Roman artists came to emulate them. The taste for precious marble intarsia led to the founding of the famous workshop of the *pietre dure* in Florence.

Pinacoteca Capitolina

This gallery of paintings was founded in 1749 by Benedict XIV with the help of his Secretary of State Cardinal Silvio Valenti Gonzaga, a famous collector. It is particularly important for its 16th–18th-century Italian and foreign works. The Emilian School, with Ferrara, is well represented. Its most precious possessions are two paintings by Caravaggio. Since the labelling is good, only a few masterpieces have been described below.

Room II: An *Annunciation*, by Garofalo, the leading painter in Ferrara in the early 16th century, is displayed here.

Room III: Works by the Venetian school including a *Portrait of a Lady as St Margaret* by Girolamo Savoldo, and others by more famous painters of the same period: Palma Vecchio (*Woman Taken in Adultery*), Veronese (*Rape of Europa*) and Titian (*Baptism of Christ*, an early work).

Room VI: Works by the Bolognese School, including the Carracci (the *Head of a Boy* is a very fine early work by Ludovico) and Guido Reni (*St Sebastian*, *Cleopatra* and *Anima Beata*).

Room VII: This large room is named after the huge canvas of *St Petronilla* by Guercino, which was formerly in St Peter's. Four other works by the same artist are displayed here. The *Gipsy Fortune-teller* is one of the most delightful early works by **Caravaggio** (another version of it is in the Louvre). It shows the artist's typical mastery of light, and the clothes and head-dresses are

superbly painted (in a style which recalls Venetian masters such as Giorgione and Titian). The expressions of the two young protagonists are a perfect mixture of timidity, affection, and a sense of fun. The soldier is evidently the same model as the man who stood for one of the most prominent figures in the *Calling of St Matthew* in the church of San Luigi dei Francesi (*see p. 287*). Beside this is displayed one of a number of paintings by Caravaggio of St John the Baptist (a replica of which is in the Galleria Doria Pamphilj). Dating from 1602, the handsome young saint is portrayed in a pose which echoes one of Michelangelo's *ignudi* on the Sistine Chapel ceiling and the iconography is totally innovative— with a mountain sheep complete with horns instead of the traditional meek lamb. The painting of *Romulus and Remus Fed by the She-wolf* by Rubens was finished by pupils.

Room VIII: The room is named after **Pietro da Cortona**; represented here are a number of fine works by him (including the *Rape of the Sabines*).

Guido Reni: *St Sebastian* (1617–18). Oscar Wilde called this 'the most beautiful of all paintings'. Sebastian was martyred in Rome; his body is said to have been thrown into the Cloaca Maxima.

the cuirass, dating from the 1st century AD. It was found in the 16th century in the Imperial Fora, so it is thought that it stood outside the Temple of Mars Ultor. On the right are three small rooms not always open: sculptures here include the sepulchral monument of a master-mason, decorated with carvings of his tools, and a colossal double sarcophagus, a splendid work of the 2nd century AD, with portraits of the deceased couple reclining on the lid and beautiful reliefs representing the story of Achilles.

First floor

Galleria: This hall retains its splendid 18th-century display of statues, busts and inscriptions, where the aesthetic arrangement rather than the pieces themselves is of interest. At the top of the stairs the decorative krater of the 1st century AD rests on a very fine well-head from Hadrian's Villa at Tivoli, with archaistic decoration representing the procession of the 12 gods (*Dii Consentes*), the most famous of the Roman deities (*see p. 66*). When the colossal statue of Hercules was restored by Alessandro Algardi he altered it (perhaps unintentionally) to show the hero slaying the Hydra, instead of capturing the Hind. *Cupid as an Archer* is a good copy of a celebrated Greek work by Lysippus, and another famous Greek masterpiece (the *Discobolus* of Myron; *see p. 241*) is recorded in the *Discus Thrower*—but only the torso survives (the rest is a late 17th-century restoration, when the statue was altered to represent a fighting gladiator). Outside Room II is a statue of *Leda with the Swan*, a replica of a work attributed to Timotheos, another Greek master (4th century BC).

(II) Sala delle Colombe: Named after the exquisite small **mosaic of four doves** at a fountain, found in Hadrian's villa at Tivoli, inspired by a work of a famous mosaicist called Sosias, who was at work in Pergamon in the 2nd century BC, when it was one of the most beautiful of all Greek cities and had a famous school of sculptors. The other mosaic here, which depicts two striking theatrical masks, is probably of the same date. In a showcase below the windows is the *Tabula Iliaca*, a fragment of a plaque with miniature reliefs illustrating Homer's *Iliad* (1st century AD).

In the centre of the room is a charming little **statue of a young girl protecting a dove**, a Roman copy of a Hellenistic work of the 2nd century BC (the snake is a later restoration). This is one of the most engaging statues in the museum.

Some 80 Roman busts decorate the walls (well labelled) and on a child's sarcophagus are two heads of infants, a rarity in Roman portraiture.

Outside the door, in the Galleria, is a statue of a **drunken old woman**, apparently seated on the floor clutching a wine flask, typical of Hellenistic realist sculpture, and for long one of the most famous pieces in the museum. Near the door into Room VI, displayed opposite each other, are two colossal heads of female divinities; the one of Aphrodite is perhaps a Hellenistic original.

The *Capitoline Venus*, one of the most famous nude female figures of Antiquity.

a temple on Cnidos, and one of the most famous of all Greek statues. The goddess is shown having just removed her clothes before taking a purifying bath and, taken by surprise, she attempts to cover her nudity with her hands. For centuries it has been one of the most famous statues in the city. It is thought to be the statue admired by Master Gregory in the late 12th or early 13th century: in his *Meraviglie di Roma* he describes how he went back to see her no fewer than three times during his stay in the city, thoroughly seduced by her modesty. In 1835 a much later visitor to Rome, the French painter Ingres, complained that he was not admitted to see the statue since the prudish pope had locked her away because of her nudity; he tells us that Gregory XVI had also attached 'enormous vine leaves' to other sculptures on public display.

(IV) Sala degli Imperatori: Here is a splendid display of Roman Imperial busts, interesting as portraits of some of the most famous figures of Roman history. They are arranged chronologically, starting on the top shelf in the far corner by the door into Room V. Two very fine **portraits of Augustus** (one showing him wearing a wreath of myrtle) flank a portrait of his wife Livia. In the next corner is a portrait of his daughter Agrippina the Elder. This beautiful lady suffered a tragic fate: she married Germanicus, a successful and charismatic commander, but who died young in Antioch. Their son, Caligula, was to succeed Tiberius as emperor, but on the death of Germanicus, Tiberius banished Agrippina and she starved to death. (*The description continues on p. 52.*)

(III) Gabinetto della Venere: Off the far end of the Galleria, this room displays the celebrated **Capitoline Venus** (*pictured above*), found in the 17th century in a house near San Vitale and purchased by Benedict XIV in 1752. A superbly modelled statue of Parian marble, and extremely well preserved, it is a Roman replica of a Hellenistic original. It is thought to be derived from the *Aphrodite* made by the great sculptor Praxiteles for

(*The description continues on p. 52.*)

ROMAN STATUES & PORTRAITURE

Roman cities were filled with statues to an extent which would be unimaginable today. One estimate is that Rome had some two million at the height of its glory. They would be found in temples, lining the Fora, gracing public buildings, in gardens, and not least in private collections. The orator Cicero prided himself on the quality of his collection of original Greek statues and his letters are full of references to recent purchases. For the cultured elite a favourite theme was busts of Greek poets and philosophers—and many of the finest survivors are gathered in the Sala dei Filosofi in the Palazzo Nuovo (*see overleaf*). For Roman connoisseurs the most prestigious statues were Greek from the Classical period (480–323 BC). A good example, now displayed in the Centrale Montemartini (*see p. 473*), is the 5th-century BC pediment believed to come from a temple to Athena in the Greek city of Eretria. It was adapted to fit the temple dedicated to Apollo near the Theatre of Marcellus in the 1st century BC. Many of these early sculptures were looted during the Roman conquest of Greece, while in the 1st century AD the emperor Nero is supposed to have shipped 500 statues from Delphi alone after its oracle criticized him for murdering his mother. If original statues were not available, copies would be made. Hadrian reconstructed whole temples and porticoes from his favourite monuments of the Greek world in his villa at Tivoli.

The original media were bronze and marble (and occasionally gold or silver), although almost all the bronze statues have vanished. They were easier to carry off than marble, and also vulnerable to being melted down for other uses. In Rome the fine equestrian statue of Marcus Aurelius (*see p. 47*) shows the quality of what has been lost. Many marble statues are in fact copies of bronze originals—often a tell-tale strut or support records the transfer to the less tensile material. The problem for art historians is that these statues are very difficult to date. Most of the best-known statues in the Roman collections have been argued over for centuries. For instance, the famous *Laocoön* (*see p. 455*) has been dated as early as the 4th century BC and as late as the 1st century AD. Is it a Greek original or a Roman original? A direct Roman copy of a Greek original or a Roman adaptation of a Greek original? Recently one scholar has even suggested it might be a deliberate forgery made by Michelangelo. The complexity of these problems can be shown in the famous *Prima Porta* statue of Augustus in the Vatican (*see p. 452*). It appears to be a marble copy of a bronze original which some suggest may have stood in a temple to Athena in Pergamon. (A statue base which fits has been discovered there.) Although the original was contemporary with the copy (just after 20 BC), Augustus affects the style of a Greek Classical hero of the 5th century BC (as shown in the pose, proportions of the body and the hair) while his breastplate is designed to show off his victory over the Parthians as bringing peace and prosperity to the Empire. Other insignia emphasize his divine descent, via Julius

Caesar, from the goddess Venus. The whole is a culmination of his successful rule as the blessed of the gods.

Within this plethora of styles and influences, it is possible to pick out a distinctive Roman art, typically expressed in a 'warts and all' portrait bust. Even here the influences are many. The Etruscans contributed a fine tradition of carefully observed bronzes—the Capitoline She-wolf (*see p. 42*) is a marvellous example—while funerary reliefs with the faces of the dead looking forward can be traced back to other pre-Roman cultures. The opulent Greek cities of southern Italy, conquered by the Romans in the 3rd century BC, were another influence, particularly in sculpture of the Hellenistic period (after 323 BC) when there was a concentration on themes of everyday life. (A good example is the copy, from a Greek original of the 3rd century BC, of a drunken old woman; *see p. 48*.) All this provides a model for realism typical of Roman art but which does not in itself explain the popularity of the portrait bust. This may have originated with the practice of taking death masks of aristocratic Romans which were then made into busts to be carried in the family's funeral processions (see the statue of a man carrying the portrait busts of his ancestors in the Montemartini display; *p. 472*). Many of these busts were, of course, of older men, but it is clear too that the Romans preferred to show themselves off as elder statesmen, full of worldly experience. A magnificent early example, especially rare because it is in bronze, is the bust of Junius Brutus (*see p. 42*), the first Roman consul (an attribution which is not very secure), in the Palazzo dei Conservatori, dating probably from the 4th or 3rd century BC.

The Sala degli Imperatori in the Palazzo Nuovo (*see pp. 49/52*) shows the development in style from the time of Augustus to the late 4th century. Augustus is concerned with images which can be recognized throughout the empire and so his model is Greek Classicism. By the end of the 1st century the Flavian emperors, anxious to restore contact with the people after the megalomanic excesses of Nero, show themselves as down-to-earth men (although the 'honeycomb' hairstyles of their womenfolk are more extravagant). The emperor Hadrian sets a new tone by wearing a beard, as if he were a philosopher rather than emperor. One of the most bizarre presentations of an emperor is the late 2nd-century Commodus' representation of himself as Hercules (in the Sala degli Arazzi in the Palazzo dei Conservatori; *see p. 43*).

In the 3rd century the pressures began to build, and the emperors' faces show the challenges they faced from constant barbarian attack and political turmoil, as with the bust of Trajan Decius in the collection (*see overleaf*). By the 4th century a further development has taken place. The empire is now calmer but the emperors have removed themselves from the people. The colossal statue of Constantine in the courtyard of the Palazzo dei Conservatori represents the return to idealism: the emperor now transcends human life. We are on the way to the distanced and semi-divine rulers of the Byzantine world.   C.F.

Displayed on a pedestal is **Marcus Aurelius** as a handsome boy in his teens, long before he became emperor; the bust on the top shelf on the opposite wall (third from the right) shows him at least 30 years later as a much older man, now with a beard, when he had already been worn down by the cares of state. It is interesting to note that it was only with Marcus Aurelius that Roman portraiture began to depict psychological concerns in the faces of her great leaders. This is well illustrated in the very fine portrait on the shelf below the later bust, that of a much less well-known emperor, **Decius** (who adopted 'Trajan' as his first name), who ruled for just three years from 249 to 251, but apparently long enough to give him the worried expression with which he is shown here. Displayed on a pedestal is an unknown lady of the late Flavian period (late 1st century), with a splendid head-dress— one of the most beautiful of all the portrait busts in the museum. In the centre is a beautiful seated figure of Helen, mother of Constantine, inspired by a Greek statue by Pheidias.

(V) Sala dei Filosofi: Here is another splendid display of Roman busts, this time of **Greek philosophers and poets**, although only some of them are securely identified. On the lower shelf on the right wall is Pythagoras, the famous mathematician, shown with his characteristic cap, next to three portraits sometimes identified as Homer or the poet Hesiod, who was probably his near contemporary. The great philosopher Socrates, about whom we know perhaps more than about any other figure in Greek history, is shown with a turned-up

nose and protruding eyeballs. Above are two portraits thought to show the elderly playwright Euripides, and two of an old man with his mouth slightly open, sometimes identified as Democritus, famous for his great wisdom, who is known to have died at a ripe old age. Here there are also more portraits of Sophocles. On the lower shelf in the corner opposite the windows is a very fine large bust of Cicero, in his toga. The double portrait portrays the Athenian philosopher Epicurus with his pupil Metrodorus. On the last wall Homer is shown as a blind bard.

(VI) Salone: The room was sumptuously decorated in the late 17th and early 18th centuries to display more very fine Roman sculpture. Arranged in the centre are pieces in dark marble: the figure in green basalt shows Hercules as an infant: dating from the 3rd century AD, its huge dimensions make this an ugly piece, particularly because of the oddness of portraying a child as a colossus. Much more graceful, and beautifully proportioned, are the **pair of Centaurs**, which were found in Hadrian's Villa at Tivoli, and are signed by Aristeas and Papias from Asia Minor, known to have worked as copyists of Greek masterpieces and who may have come to work in Rome when Hadrian was emperor. The statues around the walls include *Apollo*, which is a Roman copy of an Archaic Greek work, the stylization of which reveals its early date (just before the Classical period). Very different in spirit is the frightened old woman, an extremely expressive work from the Hellenistic period, some two centuries later. It was probably part of a statuary group. The huntsman holding up a dead hare is an example of how Roman sculptors often mixed styles—the body is from the late Archaic period, while the head is a portrait from the 3rd century AD.

The **Wounded Amazon** is signed by the copyist Sosicles: her wound is only just suggested, close to her left hand. There are a number of other statues in Rome of wounded Amazons derived from 5th-century originals by Pheidias and Polyclitus—the survivors of the famous battle between the Greeks and Amazons, these hefty ladies lived in a distant country and had the habit of killing their male offspring. Their legend has, indeed, been the subject of numerous works of art over the centuries, because their warlike nature contrasted with the once accepted stereotype of the woman who sat at home.

(VII) Sala del Fauno: The room is named after the delightful Imperial-era statue of the **Laughing Silenus**, in red marble, derived from a Hellenistic bronze, displayed in the centre. The room was decorated in the 18th century with Roman brick stamps and inscriptions, including the end of a decree by which the Roman people and Senate conferred certain powers on the emperor Vespasian. It is inscribed on a bronze plaque, and although only fragmentary, is of great importance to historians, who have attempted through this document to determine whether by this law the emperor was given new sovereign powers, or whether this merely consolidated his position by reference to his eight predecessors. The text was used in the 14th century by Cola di Rienzo (*see p. 36*) in an attempt to demonstrate the

greatness and the rights of the citizens of Rome. Claiming that Boniface VIII had hidden it away beneath an altar, Rienzo had it installed inside San Giovanni in Laterano for all to see. The two statues of young boys displayed here show one with a goose and the other with a mask (both copies of Hellenistic works).

(VIII) Sala del Gladiatore: The **Dying Gaul**, an exquisitely modelled figure of a moustached Celtic warrior who sits mortally wounded on the ground, dominates this room. It was discovered in 1622 near the Villa Ludovisi and is a copy from the Roman period of one of the bronze statues dedicated at Pergamon by Attalus I in commemoration of his victories over the Gauls (239 BC). The statue was formerly called the 'Dying Gladiator'—'butcher'd to make a Roman holiday', in Byron's phrase—and has been one of the most famous statues in Rome since the 19th century. It was beautifully restored in 1986 when the position of the right arm, altered in a 17th century restoration, was corrected.

The statue of the **Resting Satyr** shows a handsome and confident youth languishing against a tree trunk, a good replica of a beautifully composed original by Praxiteles, found in Hadrian's villa. It seems this was one of the Greek statues most admired by the Romans since some 70 copies of it are known. This is the 'Marble Faun' of Nathaniel Hawthorne's novel, the entire opening chapter of which takes place in this room, which today, some 150 years later, has the same statues 'still shining in the undiminished majesty and beauty of their ideal life'. Hawthorne goes on to give a detailed description of the Satyr

admiral Marcantonio Colonna who was given a 'Triumph' in the church modelled on those given on this hill to the victorious emperors and generals of ancient Rome (*see p. 106*). In the sea battle Colonna had led the papal troops who, combined with the Venetian fleet, had overcome the 'infidel'. The church, hung with pretty chandeliers, has a large number of very fine sepulchral monuments.

West wall: The tomb of a cardinal, with a reclining effigy (1465), is one of numerous fine tombs in the city by the 15th-century Lugano-born sculptor Andrea Bregno. (There is another monument, to a member of the Savelli family, by his school in the apse of the church.) Beside it (set up on end against the west wall in the 19th century to try to preserve it) is the pavement tomb of the archdeacon Giovanni Crivelli, signed by **Donatello** (1432): it is easy to miss and so worn that perhaps it is only by observing the feet that you can appreciate that this is indeed the work of this famous sculptor. It was probably made in Florence, together with the only other work by Donatello in Rome, a ciborium now in the museum of St Peter's (*see p. 417*), since Donatello spent almost all his long life in his native city. However, it is known that in the very first years of the 15th century he visited Rome with his close friend Brunelleschi to study the ancient Classical art, which was to have such a fundamental influence on his work.

The tomb of the astronomer Lodovico Grato Margani was designed in the 16th century and is a studio production by Andrea Sansovino, although the figure of Christ is by Sansovino himself. There is another funerary monument by Sansovino, a Tuscan sculptor and architect who worked in Rome in the first years of the 16th century, on the left of the south door.

South aisle: The first chapel is entirely decorated with delightful frescoes of the life of St Bernardino by **Pinturicchio** (c. 1486), who was much influenced by Perugino, and was at work with him at this time on some of the frescoes on the lower walls of the Sistine Chapel. It was in the Vatican that he carried out perhaps his most beautiful frescoes: those in the Appartamento Borgia. While in Rome he visited the Domus Aurea (where his signature can still be seen), which was rediscovered at that time. He often copied the grotesques he saw in the vaults. He was an extremely skilled fresco painter, and most of his works have survived in a wonderful state of preservation.

In the last chapel in this aisle are fragments of **frescoes by Pietro Cavallini**, discovered at the end of the 20th century. They include, on the altar wall, a lovely *Madonna and Child with two Saints* and on either side very damaged scenes of buildings, and *Christ between two Angels*. These are extremely important examples of Roman art of the late 13th and early 14th centuries, only very little of which survives. In the tympanum above the exterior of the south door there is a mosaic of the *Madonna and two Angels*, thought to be by the school of Cavallini.

Crossing: On the pilasters facing the high altar are two beautiful marble ambones from the earlier church, decorated by the **Cosmati** around the year 1200. The beautiful tomb in the north transept of Cardinal Matteo di Acquasparta (d. 1302) is another Cosmati work, incorporating a fresco by Pietro Cavallini.

COSMATI & THE 'COSMATESQUE'

Pre-Renaissance architecture all over Europe set great store by fine decorative embellishment. In Rome, and the area around the city, a particularly beautiful kind of decorative revetment, referred to as Cosmati work, was developed in the 12th and 13th centuries, which made use of abandoned and excavated ancient Roman coloured marble to create new and original designs. In part, it grew out of the Imperial Roman passion for *opus sectile* (fine polychrome marble and stone inlay), a tradition which had been transmitted through Byzantium and the areas of its influence, in particular in southern Italy. The characteristic of Cosmati work is the inlay into a plain marble slab of small triangles, squares and other shapes of cut porphyry, coloured marble, semi-precious stone and gold glass, in bold concentric, intertwined, or rhythmically varying geometric designs. These patterns also had a practical purpose when used on the pavements of churches: they divided and mapped the floor into regular areas which facilitated the choreographing of processions on feast-days. San Clemente, Santa Maria Maggiore and Santa Maria in Cosmedin are other good places to admire this effect.

The term 'Cosmati', comes from two craftsmen, both called Cosmas, whose names are inscribed in some of their works; but it is used to refer to several families and generations of largely anonymous craftsmen who worked in this exquisite decorative manner, and who flourished for over a century from c. 1140. Their work is principally concentrated in Rome and its province, but the fashion spread rapidly, to centres as distant as London (see, for example, Edward the Confessor's monument in Westminster Abbey). Inspired perhaps by the descriptions in *Revelation 21* of the walls and pavements of the New Jerusalem, it must have appeared to those who commissioned the works as a symbolically appropriate embellishment for floors, as well as for pulpits, screens, thrones, tombs, doorways and even whole cloisters. Cosmati work is elegant and durable, and its liveliness and beauty are particularly enhanced by the illumination of flickering candles and oil-lamps.   N.McG.

South transept: The Savelli Chapel contains 14th-century family tombs: that of Luca on the left, which incorporates a 3rd-century Roman sarcophagus, is attributed to the great sculptor Arnolfo di Cambio, while that on the right, of Luca's wife Vana, includes an effigy of their son, Pope Honorius IV (who died in 1287, the same year as his mother). In the chapel to the right of the Chapel of the Holy Sacrament there is a beautiful small 13th-century mosaic: the *Madonna between St John the Baptist and St Francis*.

High altar: Over the altar is the *Madonna d'Aracoeli*, a tiny painting thought to be a very early work (attributed by some to a 10th-century master).

North transept: In the centre is a little circular 17th-century temple with eight marble columns above a Cosmatesque altar on which is depicted the legend of the founding of the church (*see p. 55 above*). The remains of an earlier altar and Roman masonry were found beneath this, as well as a carved 12th-century sandalwood coffer containing relics of St Helen (preserved in the Franciscan convent). To the right is the entrance to the **Cappella del Santissimo Bambino** (built at the end of the 19th century when alterations had to be made to the church when the Monument to Vittorio Emanuele II was under construction), where there is a popular devotional image of the Infant Christ, covered in jewels. Reputed to have been carved from the wood of an olive tree from the Garden of Gethsemane, this has been greatly venerated since it was solemnly crowned by the pope in 1897. It was particularly famous for its miraculous powers in the 19th and 20th centuries when it used to be carried (in a carriage provided by the Torlonia) to the bedsides of the sick. It receives letters from all over the world and it is a Christmas tradition for children to recite little poems in front of its crib. Since it was stolen in 1994 it has had to be replaced by a copy.

THE TARPEIAN ROCK

The rest of the Capitoline Hill is interesting to explore, although at the time of writing some of the gardens were closed for replanting. Via di Monte Tarpeo leads to Via del Tempio di Giove, at the top of which, enclosed by a modern wall and very much below the level of the road, are the remains of the eastern corner of the façade of the Temple of Jupiter Optimus Maximus Capitolinus (*see p. 46*). From the peaceful gardens here there is an extensive view of Rome to the south and southeast.

The precipice below is thought to be the **Tarpeian Rock** (although it has also been suggested that this was on the north side of the hill). It seems that the entire hill was once known as the *Rupe Tarpea*, and Milton, in *Paradise Regained*, referred to it thus:

> *The Tarpeian rock, the citadel*
> *of great and glorious Rome, queen of the earth...*

Legend relates that in the very earliest days of Rome, the founders, anxious to increase the population, invited the neighbouring Sabines to a party telling them to bring with them their daughters and sisters, and while the male guests were intent on enjoying games organized for their benefit, the women were 'raped' and locked up on the Capitoline Hill. But the key of the fortress was unwisely entrusted to Tarpeia, who betrayed Rome by opening the doors to the Sabine men. However, the Sabines nobly disapproved of her traitorous behaviour and instead of being grateful, they promptly killed her. Ever afterwards, during the days of ancient Rome, traitors who were condemned to death were apparently flung from this rock. Its notorious fame has endured to this day in the imagination of visitors, even if so little is known about it, and the place tends to be ignored by modern scholars; over the centuries it was often mentioned by poets, and the 'Rape of the Sabines' became a favourite subject for painters and sculptors in Europe from the 16th century onwards. It typically fired the Romantic imagination of Byron in *Childe Harold's Pilgrimage*:

> *The steep*
> *Tarpeian, fittest goal of treason's race,*
> *The promontory whence the traitor's leap*
> *Cured all ambition'.*

The delightful quiet road continues past a little 19th-century temple to the edge of the hill and then turns right under an arch to skirt the side of the hill above gardens and paths which descend to its foot. In front of the 16th-century Palazzo Caffarelli (with an entrance to the café in the Musei Capitolini and the museum offices) a recently restored little garden with pleasant places to sit provides another splendid panorama of Rome, this time towards St Peter's.

THE ROMAN FORUM

The Roman Forum (*map p. 623, 3D*) is one of the most evocative places in Rome. Its ruins stand in the centre of the modern city as a romantic testament to her past greatness. This was the heart of ancient Rome, and almost every event of importance in the city's development, from the time of the kings through the Republican and Imperial eras to the Middle Ages, is reflected here. Many buildings survive from those times, some with columns or vaults still standing, others only identified by their foundations. The huge paving stones of Rome's most important ancient road, the Sacra Via, are still visible here and pass the well preserved triumphal arches dedicated to Titus and Septimius Severus.

Planning a visit

Open 8.30–dusk; T: 06 3996700. Free entrance (you need an admission ticket for the Palatine; see p. 85). The Forum can become crowded; it is best to visit as soon as it opens. You should allow at least half a day for a complete visit. In summer the Forum is occasionally floodlit at night and tours are available; for information call the number above.

The description below begins at the entrance on Via di Monte Tarpeo from the Capitoline Hill along the Clivus Capitolinus, the ancient road which connected the hill with the Forum. There are few signs in the Forum, and only some of the buildings are discreetly labelled with marble plaques. This makes the ruins all the more romantic to visit, but means that their history and original appearance can only be fully appreciated by studying the plan and description below. Although there are no refreshments available in the Forum, there are a number of drinking fountains with a constant supply of Rome's particularly fresh water.

History of the Roman Forum

The site of the Forum was originally a marshy valley lying between the Capitoline and Palatine Hills. In the Iron Age it was used as a necropolis. During the period of the last of the six kings of Rome—traditionally considered to have succeeded Romulus—the area was first paved as a market place (*forum*) c. 625 BC. The Etruscan king Servius Tullius (578–535 BC) made the area habitable by channelling its stagnant waters into a huge drain called the Cloaca Maxima. The first monuments of the Forum also date from the period of the kings.

The original Forum was a rectangle bounded on the north and south by two rows of shops (*tabernae*) approximately on the line of the Basilica Emilia to the north and

The Roman Forum, with the columns of the Temple of Saturn on the right, the Temple of Vespasian on the left, and the Arch of Septimius Severus beyond.

64

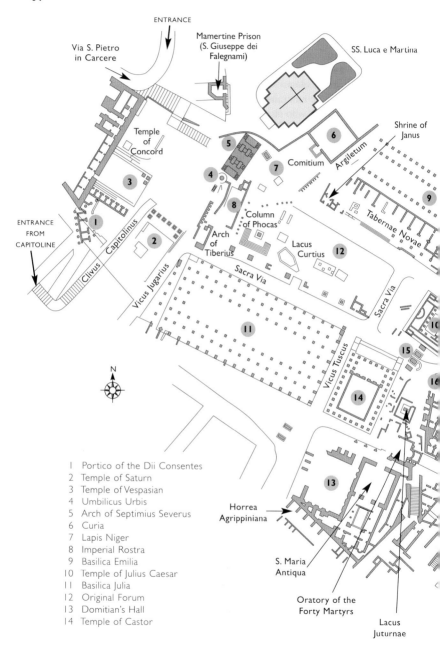

ENTRANCE

Via S. Pietro
in Carcere

Mamertine Prison
(S. Giuseppe dei
Falegnami)

SS. Luca e Martina

Temple
of
Concord

Shrine of
Janus

5

6

Comitium

Argiletum

7

3

4

9

ENTRANCE
FROM
CAPITOLINE

8

Column
of Phocas

Tabernae Novae

Capitolinus

Arch
of
Tiberius

Lacus
Curtius

12

2

Clivus

Vicus Jugarius

Sacra Via

Sacra Via

11

Vicus Tuscus

15

16

N

14

10

13

Horrea
Agrippiniana

1 Portico of the Dii Consentes
2 Temple of Saturn
3 Temple of Vespasian
4 Umbilicus Urbis
5 Arch of Septimius Severus
6 Curia
7 Lapis Niger
8 Imperial Rostra
9 Basilica Emilia
10 Temple of Julius Caesar
11 Basilica Julia
12 Original Forum
13 Domitian's Hall
14 Temple of Castor

S. Maria
Antiqua

Oratory of the
Forty Martyrs

Lacus
Juturnae

THE ROMAN FORUM

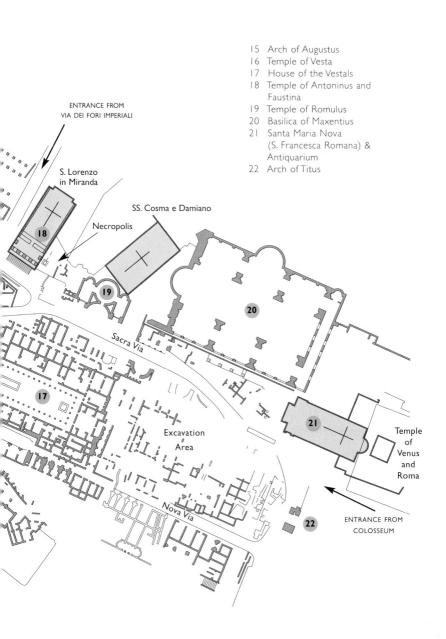

This cult originated with the Etruscans, who recognized six male and six female deities, who assisted Jupiter in directing his thunderbolts. The Romans came to identify these gods with the great Greek gods: Jupiter (Zeus), Neptune (Poseidon), Mars (Ares), Apollo (also called Apollo by the Greeks), Vulcan (Hephaistos), Mercury (Hermes), Juno (Hera), Minerva (Athena), Diana (Artemis), Venus (Aphrodite), Vesta (Hestia), and Ceres (Demeter).

The portico was reconstructed in 1858. Beyond, on the side of the Capitol Hill, you can see the mighty wall of the Tabularium (*described on p. 46*) with Palazzo Senatorio towering above. On the right is an area of new excavations, where a deposit of ex-votos from the Archaic period, probably connected with an ancient cult of Saturn, has been found, and an interesting 12th-century district of the city has been revealed.

2 Eight columns, nearly 11m high, with part of the entablature, survive of the pronaos of the **Temple of Saturn**, raised on a high podium. Six columns in grey granite are in front: the other two, in red granite, are at the sides. The Ionic capitals were added in a 5th-century restoration. This was one of the most ancient sanctuaries in the Forum, which may have been inaugurated in 498 BC in honour of the mythical god-king of Italy, whose reign was the fabled Golden Age. There is still some mystery about this ancient deity, whose name suggests he was the god of sowing, but who is sometimes also associated with the Kronos of Greek mythology. The 'Saturnalia' was the most important day of festivities in the Roman year when temporary free-dom was given to slaves and presents were exchanged, and it was always celebrated here on 17th December: it later came to be associated with New Year's Day and Christmas. The temple was rebuilt, after several previous reconstructions, by Lucius Munatius Plancus in the year of his consulship, 42 BC, and the columns we see today survive from this time. It was again restored after fires in 283 and c. 400 AD. The temple was the state treasury, where gold and silver ingots and coined metal were kept. The treasury itself (*aerarium*) was a room east of the narrow stairway of the temple: the holes for the lock can still be seen.

3 On the other side of the Clivus Capitolinus are three high columns, all that remains of the hexastyle pronaos of the sumptuous and elegant **Temple of Vespasian** erected at the foot of the Tabularium staircase by his sons Titus and Domitian after his death in AD 79. The front part of the basement has recently been excavated.

Next to it is the site of the **Temple of Concord**. This was a reconstruction by Tiberius (7 BC–AD 10) of a sanctuary which traditionally was thought to have been built in 366 BC by Camillus, a famous military leader and politician in early Roman history, to commemorate the concordat between the patricians and the plebeians. Instead it is probable that the temple was built for the first time in 218 BC. It was then rebuilt in 121 BC with the consent of the consul Lucius Opimius after the murder of the plebeian Gracchus. But it did anything but symbolize concord: Gracchus, a great reformer who was twice elected tribune, had tried to undermine the authority of the senate by uniting the *plebs* with the *equites* (members of the business community) and lost his life in a riot provoked by Opimius and the senate. He is also remembered for his far-sighted—but unsuccessful—attempt to extend Roman citizenship to Latins and Italians. The temple became a museum and gallery of paintings and sculptures by famous Greek artists. Only the pavement remains *in situ*; part of the frieze is in the Tabularium.

4 Close to the triumphal arch is a cylindrical construction in brick, the **Umbilicus Urbis** (?2nd century BC), supposed to mark the centre (the *umbilicus* or navel) of the city, and hence of the known world. In front of it is a quadrangular area protected by a roof, thought to be an **Altar of Saturn**, dating from before the 6th century BC. Two trees grew here in Republican times, a lotus and a cypress, said to be older than the city itself. Beside this is the site of the **Miliarium Aureum** ('golden milestone'), a bronze-covered column set up by Augustus as the symbolic starting-point of all the roads of the empire, with the distance from Rome to the chief cities engraved in gold letters on its base. Ever since there has been a familiar saying that 'all roads lead to Rome'. There was a *curator viarum*, an official whose duty it was to oversee the upkeep of the roads in recognition of the fact that they were of such fundamental importance to the smooth running of the empire.

5 One of the most moving moments in the visit to the Forum is walking beneath the triple **Arch of Septimius Severus**, which has survived its 1,800 years remarkably well. It is nearly 21m high and over 23m wide, and entirely faced with marble. Erected in AD 203 in honour of the tenth anniversary of that emperor's accession, it was dedicated by the senate and the people to Severus and his sons Caracalla and Geta in memory of their military victories, notably in Parthia (present-day Iran; *see p. 121*). The name of Severus' elder son, Geta, who was murdered by Caracalla in 212, was replaced by an inscription in praise of Caracalla and his father, but the holes made for the original letters are still visible. On the well-proportioned arch the four large reliefs depict scenes from the two Parthian campaigns: in the small friezes are symbolic Oriental figures paying homage to Rome, and at the bases of the columns are captive barbarians. A small interior staircase led up to the four chambers of the attic.

Just beyond the arch, on the left, is a conspicuous **marble base for an equestrian statue** with a dedicatory inscription to the emperor Constantius II. He was the youngest of Constantine the Great's three sons (the others confusingly named Constantine II and Constans). Constantine left the Empire to all three of them on his death in 337. The inscription records Constantius' victory in 352/3 over Magnentius, who had usurped his position for a few years. On the right is a large **marble column base**, with reliefs showing a procession of senators and scenes of sacrifice (it was provided with a modern brick plinth at the end of the 20th century). This is the only one left of five original bases which bore columns set up here by the Emperor Diocletian. As the inscription *Caesarum Decennalia Feliciter* records, they celebrated the felicitous tenth anniversary in AD 303 (the year of Diocletian's first visit to Rome) of the rule of the famous tetrarchy instituted by Diocletian, which made provision for four co-rulers. This was designed to increase the stability of the empire: Diocletian and Galerius conducted campaigns in the east, while Maximian and Constantius Chlorus brought the western provinces under their rule.

6 On the left is the most impressive and conspicuous building in the entire Forum, the **Curia Senatus** (or *Curia Julia*), the senate house. Replacing the original *Curia Hostilia* said to have been built by Tullus Hostilius, traditionally held to be the third king of Rome (673–642 BC), it was begun by Sulla in 80 BC and rebuilt after a fire by Julius Caesar in 44 BC. Fifteen years after Caesar's death it was completed by Augustus, who dedicated a statue of Victory in the interior. The present building dates from the time of Domitian and was restored by Diocletian after a fire in 283. In 630 it was converted into the church of Sant'Adriano. In 1935–39 it was restored to the form it had under Diocletian.

The lower part of the brick façade was originally covered with marble and the upper courses with stucco. A simple pediment with travertine corbels crowns the building; it was originally preceded by a portico. The existing doors are copies of the originals, removed by Alexander VII in the 17th century to San Giovanni in Laterano where they still—incredibly enough—serve as the main entrance to the basilica (an example of the famous 'plundering' of the ancient

buildings in the Forum, which in fact probably saved these historic works from destruction in later centuries).

The remarkable interior (*the doors are usually open unless there are exhibitions in progress*), 27m long, 18m wide and 21m high, has a beautiful green-and-maroon pavement in *opus sectile*: it has been so well preserved because it was found beneath the floor of the church. The three broad marble-faced steps on the two long sides provided seats for some 300 senators. At the end, by the president's tribune, is a brick base, which may have supported the golden statue of Victory presented by Augustus. It was this statue which was the subject of the famous controversy in the 4th century when the Christians (aided by St Ambrose) decided it should be removed after Gratian had forbidden pagan worship in 382. The great orator Symmachus (who became consul in 391) eloquently spoke out in its defence, asking what did it matter by which knowledge each of us reaches the Truth, declaring that it was surely not possible to reach such a sublime Mystery by a single route.

The side walls with niches were partly faced with marble. The porphyry statue of Hadrian or Trajan exhibited here, dating from the 1st or 2nd century AD, was found in excavations behind the building at the end of the 20th century.

Also exhibited here are the **Plutei of Trajan**, or *Anaglypha Traiani*, two finely sculptured balustrades or parapets, found in the Forum in 1872 between the Comitium and the Column of Phocas. Both their date and original location are uncertain. On the outer faces (visible from the doorway) are scenes showing emperors carrying out public duties: the first (on the left) appears to represent an emperor burning the registers of outstanding death duties, an event which took place in 118, during Hadrian's reign; in the second (on the right) an emperor standing on a rostra with a statue of Trajan is receiving the thanks of a mother for the founding of an orphanage. The architectural backgrounds systematically depict the buildings on the west, south and east sides of the Forum (from the right of the first panel to the left of the second): the Temple of Vespasian, an arch without decoration, the Temple of Saturn, the Vicus Jugarius, and the arcades of the Basilica Julia (continued on the second panel), followed by an interval which may represent the Vicus Tuscus, then the Temple of Castor and Rostra of the Temple of Julius Caesar on which the emperor is standing and, at the end, his attendants mounting the ramp of the Rostra through the Arch of Augustus. On both sides the statue of Marsyas is depicted beside the sacred fig tree (*see p. 76*). On the inner faces (not visible from the doorway) are depicted the animals used as offerings during public sacrifices (*suovetaurilia*): a boar, a ram and a bull.

In recent excavations behind the Curia, remains of the Augustan building have come to light. Two doors at the rear end opened into a columned portico of the Forum of Caesar (*see p. 121*), providing an entrance from the old Republican Forum to the new Imperial one. Connected to the Curia was the *Secretarium Senatus* used by a tribunal set up in the late Empire to judge senators.

In front of the Curia building was the area of the **Comitium**, the place where the *Comitia Curiata*, representing the 30 districts or *curiae* into which the city was politically divided, met to record their votes. The earliest political activity of the Republic took place here. During the Empire the Comitium was restricted to the space between the Curia and the Lapis Niger (*see below*); under the Republic the area was much larger.

7 A pavement in black marble, protected by upright marble slabs and a modern iron fence, which marks the site of the **Lapis Niger** and the oldest relics of the Forum, can be seen here. The Lapis Niger ('Black Stone') was a pavement of black marble laid to indicate a sacred spot. This was traditionally taken to be the site of the tomb of Romulus, or of Faustulus, the shepherd who found the infants Romulus and Remus, or of Hostus Hostilius, father of the third king of Rome: but is now identified as the ancient sanctuary of Vulcan, known as the Vulcanal. Below ground level (reached by a flight of iron steps; *now unfortunately kept closed*) are a truncated column, possibly the base for a statue, an altar and a square stele with inscriptions on all four sides. These provide the most ancient example of the Latin language (probably mid-6th century BC) and seem to refer to a *lex sacra* (holy law) warning against profaning a holy place. In the space between the pavement and the monuments, bronze and terracotta statuettes and fragments of 6th-century vases were found (now exhibited in the Baths of Diocletian; *see p. 232*), mixed with profuse ashes indicating a great sacrifice.

ROMAN GODS & THEIR WORSHIP

The relationship between the Romans and their gods was a very powerful one. From the earliest history of the city it was believed that the community should participate in a variety of rituals which would win the support of the gods. These rituals had to be followed exactly and all involved some kind of sacrifice. Surviving religious calendars suggest that there were at least 40 major festivals in Rome, celebrating the changing seasons of the year or important moments in the evolution of the state. Indeed, religion was so closely tied up with the needs of the state that priesthoods were often political offices.

The Roman gods themselves have their roots deep in the earliest history of Italy. So Jupiter, the sky god, is found in different forms in most Italic (pre-Roman) societies, as is Mars, the god of war. Among female deities Juno is an ancient goddess of fertility. With a strong Greek presence in southern Italy from the 8th century BC, Roman equivalents of Greek divinities appear, such as Venus for Aphrodite and Ceres for Demeter. Minerva, an ancient Italian goddess of handicrafts, becomes associated with Athena. Dionysus, the god of wine and sexual abandon, emerges, via the Greek cities of southern Italy, as the Roman Bacchus—but his rites were so wild that the senate banned them in 186 BC. His worship survived in a more restrained form. Some Greek gods were directly transferred to Rome. So Apollo, whose attributes included the ending of plagues, was introduced specifically for that purpose in Rome in 433 BC. Asclepios, the god of healing, was 'summoned' to Rome for the same reason in 291 BC and as Aesculapius was given a temple on Isola Tiberina (where a hospital stands to this day). The Etruscans too had an important influence on Roman religion. It was the Etruscan kings who founded the great Temple of Jupiter, on the Capitoline Hill (it was dedicated to the triad of Jupiter, Juno and Minerva in the first year of the Republic) and who introduced the ritual of the Triumph, which ended with sacrifice at its steps. Books of prophecies by a Sibyl (whose origins are unknown) were reputedly brought to Rome by one of the Etruscan kings and were consulted at times of crisis. The Sybilline Books became so intimately connected with the city that even Christians consulted them for prophecies of the coming of their faith to Rome.

Although new festivals could appear, the most ancient were virtually impossible to eradicate. The Lupercalia (15th February), associated with fertility, probably predates the foundation of Rome but was still being celebrated (to the disgust of Christians) as late as AD 494. The ancient rituals of the state were clung to with intense conservatism and any sensible emperor respected them. However, the Romans would never have ruled an empire of so many cultures without a readiness to innovate, adapt and compromise. By the 1st century BC the Greek practice of offering cult worship to leaders had spread to Rome. Julius Caesar appears to have been offered a temple and his own priesthood in Rome itself, although this offended traditionalists. He was accepted as a god only after his death, as were Augustus and other 'good' emperors such as Trajan. The linking of an emperor to the 'goddess' Roma, in a temple dedicated, say, to Augustus and Roma, became an important feature of Roman imperialism. However, it remained essential for an emperor not to claim divinity during his lifetime. Domitian was assassinated in 96 after he had insisted on being addressed as 'Lord God', as was the emperor Marcus Aurelius Antoninus (218–22) when he unwisely took on the name and cult of the Syrian sun god Elagabalus. By the end of the 3rd century emperors were linking themselves closely to traditional gods such as Jupiter or Hercules, and they would elevate themselves above their people as if the chosen god's patronage had given them a semi-divine status while they were still alive.

The cosmopolitan nature of Rome can be seen in the wide range of foreign cults which were accepted into the city. Cybele, the great mother goddess of Anatolia, known to the Romans as *Magna Mater*, was brought to Rome in 205 and a temple exotically served by oriental priests was built to her cult on the Palatine Hill. A large temple to the Egyptian goddess Isis was built near the existing church of Santa Maria sopra Minerva in the 1st century AD (an obelisk found on the site stands on Bernini's charming elephant in the square outside the church). The cult of Mithras from Persia was also enormously popular (*see p. 515*).

In the long run, of course, it was the Christian community, first attested in the 1st century, which was to become the most dominant of these foreign cults. The Christians actively denigrated existing Roman religion, and their refusal to sacrifice to the traditional gods made them the target of persecution; motivated, it would appear, by the ancient fear of losing the support of Rome's gods. The motives for Constantine's adoption of Christianity are difficult to fathom, but his transference of immense imperial resources into church-building was revolutionary. At first the new foundations (largely on the burial sites of martyrs outside the city walls) did not threaten the ancient pagan centre of Rome, but in a *cause célèbre* of the 380s, the church forced the removal of the ancient winged statue of Victory from the senate house (*see p. 68*). Power now shifted to the Church. The Christian scholar Jerome captures the changing mood of the next few years well: 'The golden Capitol now falls into disrepair; dust and cobwebs cover all Rome's temples. The city shakes on its foundations, and a stream of people hurries, past half-fallen shrines, to the tombs of the martyrs'. Even if ancient pagan festivities continued for some time, Rome was nominally a Christian city.

The office of *pontifex maximus* has a long and interesting history. In republican Rome it was an office to be competed over, and Julius Caesar's election to the office in 63 was an important moment in his political career. Under Augustus its power and status were absorbed by the emperor and every emperor held the title until the Christian emperor Gratian (375–83). In the 15th century the popes took it as one of their titles: '*pont. max.*' follows the names of popes on public inscriptions.

C.F.

Excavations to the east of the Lapis Niger have revealed some remains of the **Republican Rostra**, dating partly from 338 BC and partly (the curved front and steps) from the period of Sulla, who became dictator in 81 BC.

In front of a small group of trees you can see the paved **Argiletum**, once one of the Forum's busiest streets, which leads north between the Curia building and the west end of the Basilica Emilia.

It originally continued north to the district of the Subura, a poor and unsavoury part of town, haunt of thieves and prostitutes, and described by Juvenal as home to 'the thousand perils of a savage city'. The area to the north is still being excavated: the Macellum, a market building paved in *peperino* and surrounded by columns, built in the late 3rd or early 2nd century BC, has recently been unearthed.

THE HEART OF THE FORUM

The open space to the south was the original Forum. As the meeting-place of the whole population and a market place, it was kept free of obstructions in Republican days (up to 31 BC). All important ceremonies and public meetings took place here. The Forum was where all the main religious festivals were held, where political offenders were executed, and where the funerals of important people took place. During the Empire (27 BC–AD 395) the Forum lost its original character, and new buildings encroached on the area. It remained merely an official centre, and was to a great extent replaced by the new Imperial Fora (*see p. 112*). The few columns and monuments which survive in the area of the Forum are best seen from the further side (*described on pp. 76–77 below*).

8 To the right of the Arch of Septimius Severus are the ruins—now mostly a mound of rubble and brick arches—of the **Imperial Rostra**, or orators' tribune, which was placed facing the Forum. Speakers would address the crowd from here, and it was here that magistrates' edicts, legal decisions and official communications were published. The Rostra was brought from its original site in front of the Curia during Caesar's restoration. It is 3m high, 24m long and 12m deep. The original structure, of very early date, was decorated with *rostra*, the iron prows of the ships captured at the battle of Antium (modern Anzio) in 338 BC, when Rome finally subjugated the Volsci,

who had formerly controlled the territory in southern Latium. On the platform rose columns surmounted by commemorative statues, and its parapet was probably decorated with the sculptured Plutei of Trajan (*see p. 68 above*). At the north end was the Rostra Vandalica, an extension of the 5th century AD; the modern name is taken from an inscription commemorating a naval victory over the Vandals in 470.

The Rostra was famously profaned by the Emperor Augustus' sensual daughter Julia, who used it at night for her notorious carnal encounters. Despairing of her incorrigible ways, Augustus eventually exiled her to the island of Pandateria.

9 A path of dirt and ancient paving stones continues east between the area of the Forum on the right and a row of shops, the **Tabernae Novae**, on the left, still well preserved. These used to stand under a two-storeyed portico of the **Basilica Emilia**, which was restored during the late Empire, and whose scant remains lie to the north. The basilica was built by the censors Marcus Aemilius Lepidus and Marcus Fulvius Nobilior in 179 BC, restored by members of the Aemilia *gens*—including another Marcus Aemilius Lepidus—in 78 BC and rebuilt in the time of Julius Caesar. It was again rebuilt in AD 22 after a fire and nearly destroyed by another fire during Alaric the Goth's sack of Rome in 410. Much of this ancient building was demolished during the Renaissance in order to reuse its marble.

It comprised a vast rectangular hall 70m by 29m, divided by columns into a central nave and aisles, single on the south side and double on the north. It was paved in coloured marble slabs. Basilicas were important buildings, used for public administration and as law courts: they were usually extremely large, roofed halls with aisles supported by columns and ending at one end in an apse. Their plan was adopted in Christian architecture for the earliest churches. Of this basilica only some broken marble columns and part of its marble paving are left, but enough to show its original plan. At the end nearest the Curia (*not at present accessible*) are some mottled columns, and the covered remains of its fine pavement, in coloured marble, in which are embedded some coins that fused with the bronze roof-decorations during the fire of 410 AD. At the opposite end, visible from the path which leads up to the gate on the Via dei Fori Imperiali, casts of fragments of a frieze of the Republican era have been assembled below the terrace.

The path in front of the Tabernae Novae passes the presumed site of the **Shrine of Janus**, the bronze doors of which were closed only in peace-time, which is said to have occurred only three times in the history of Rome. Just beyond was the Shrine of Venus Cloacina, which stood on the point where a great drain of the Cloaca Maxima (*see p. 77*) entered the Forum. At the far end three granite columns dating from the time of the late Empire have been set up in front of the shops, and a large dedicatory inscription from the senate in 2 BC to Lucius Ceasar, grandson and adopted son of Augustus, which probably once decorated a triumphal arch dedicated to him and his brother Gaius.

10 A curved wall protected by a roof is all that remains of the **Temple of Julius Caesar**, the site of which marks the eastern limit of the original Forum. The body of Julius Caesar was brought to the Forum after his assassination on the Ides of March in 44 BC, and it was probably here that his body was cremated and his will read by Mark Antony. The temple was dedicated by Augustus in 29 BC in honour of *Divus Julius* (the 'Divine' Julius Caesar). Tiberius gave a funeral oration here over Augustus' own body before it was buried in his mausoleum (*see p. 550*) in AD 14.

staged an impressive parade in front of the temple. It had three *cellae* and a deep pronaos, built on a high podium, and was restored after 200 BC. It was reconstructed by the consul Metellus Dalmaticus in 117 BC, when a tribune for orators was installed, and, according to Cicero, it was also used by money-changers. This temple was destroyed by fire in 14 or 9 BC, and the present building was inaugurated by Tiberius during the reign of Augustus (AD 6).

Peripteral in plan, and approximately 26m by c. 40m in area, the temple had eight Corinthian columns at either end and 11 at the sides. The wide pronaos, excavated in 1982–85, was approached by a flight of steps. The three remaining columns, which are 12.5m high and have a beautifully proportioned entablature, date from the time of Tiberius. The twins are usually depicted as giants with white chargers: the most famous statues of them are on the Quirinal Hill (*see p. 212*) and another pair are on the balustrade of Piazza del Campidoglio (*see p. 37*).

15 To the left of the Temple of Castor the paving of the old road which once ran through the **Arch of Augustus** has been uncovered. Only the foundations of this triumphal arch remain: it had a central arch flanked by lower and narrower side passages surmounted by pediments. Excavations here at the end of the 20th century have dated it to 20 BC, after the standards captured by the Parthians (*see p. 121*) had been returned. The consular and triumphal registers known as the *Fasti Capitolini* (*see p. 42*), which date from this period, may have belonged to the arch. Another, single, triumphal arch is known to have been erected by Augustus in another part of the Forum in 30 BC to commemorate his victory over Antony and Cleopatra at Actium two years earlier.

Beyond the fence here are the remains of the restored shrine of the **Lacus Juturnae** (Pool of Juturna), closely connected to the story of the Dioscuri. Juturna, the nymph of healing waters, was venerated in connection with the springs here, which were of great importance in the time of the Republic. In the 4th century, fittingly enough, this became the seat of the city's water administration.

THE RELIGIOUS CENTRE OF THE FORUM

The reconstructed remains of the Temple of Vesta are conspicuous here, as well as the considerable remains of the House of the Vestals.

16 A number of columns on high bases support a fragment of entablature, as well as part of the curving cella wall of the **Temple of Vesta**. This temple was a circular edifice of 20 Corinthian columns, its design recalling the form of the huts used by the Latin people, traces of which have been found on the Palatine and elsewhere in Rome. The first temple on this site was possibly made, like these, of straw and wood. The temple was burned down several times, notably during Nero's fire of AD 64 and in 191. It was rebuilt as often, the last time by Septimius Severus and his wife, Julia Domna. It was closed by Theodosius and was in ruins by the 8th century. The circular basement surmounted by tufa blocks and some architectural fragments survived until 1930, when it was partially reconstructed.

Here the Vestals guarded the sacred fire and Vesta, goddess of the hearth, protected it. In the interior was an *adytum*, or secret place, containing the *Palladium*, a statue of Pallas Athena supposedly taken from Troy by Aeneas. No one was allowed inside the adytum except the Vestals and the *pontifex maximus*, and its contents were never shown. The *Palladium* was an object of the highest veneration, as the safety of the city depended on its preservation. When the Emperor Elagabalus tried to steal it, the Vestals are supposed to have substituted another statue, keeping the cult statue of Vesta in a small shrine near the entrance to the House of the Vestals.

THE VESTAL VIRGINS

The task of the Vestals, the virgin priestesses of Vesta, was to keep the fire that symbolized the perpetuity of the state constantly alight: its extinction was the most fearful of all prodigies, as it implied the end of Rome. The origin of the cult is supposed to go back to Numa Pompilius, second king of Rome, or even to Aeneas, who brought the eternal fire of Vesta from Troy, together with the images of the *penates* (household gods).

There were six Vestals, who were chosen by the king, and later, during the Republic and Empire, by the *pontifex maximus*, a post held by the emperor himself. Girls between six and ten years of age from patrician families could be candidates. After her election, a Vestal lived in the House of the Vestals for 30 years: ten learning her duties, ten performing them and ten teaching novices. During this period she was bound by the vow of chastity. At the end of the 30 years she was free to return to the world and even to marry. The senior Vestal was called *vestalis maxima* or *virgo maxima*. If a Vestal let the sacred fire go out, she was whipped by the *pontifex maximus*, who then had to rekindle the fire by the friction of two pieces of wood from a *felix arbor* (propitious tree).

The Vestals' other duties included making offerings to Vesta, sprinkling her shrine daily with water from the Egerian fountain, assisting at the consecration of temples and other public ceremonies, and guarding the *Palladium* (*see above*). Maintained at the public expense, they had many privileges, such as an exalted order of precedence and the right of intercession. Wills—including the emperor's—and treaties were entrusted to their keeping. If a Vestal broke her vow of chastity, however, she was immured alive in the *Campus Sceleratus*, the present Piazza Indipendenza (*map p. 623, 1F*) and the man was publicly flogged to death in the Forum.

17 The **House of the Vestals** was immediately east of the temple (*not accessible, but partly visible beyond a fence; the best view of it is from the Palatine Hill*). A charming rose garden is planted in its ruined courtyard. The house seems too large for just six Vestals, and part of it may have been reserved for the *pontifex maximus*, whose official seat during the Republican era was in the Regia (*see below*). It dates from Republican times, but was rebuilt after the fire of Nero in AD 64, and was last restored by Septimius Severus.

The spacious courtyard, 61m long and 20m wide, has three ponds in it, irregularly spaced and unequal in size. The central pond was once partly covered by an octagonal structure of unknown purpose. The statue-bases and statues of Vestals date from the 3rd century AD onwards. A two-storey portico surrounded the courtyard, off which are the remains of numerous rooms (some of which had more than two storeys) including a dining room and kitchen, and a mill.

Between the Temple of Vesta and the huge Temple of Antoninus and Faustina was the site of the **Regia**, identified only by very scanty remains, although excavations are in progress here. This was traditionally supposed to be the palace of Numa Pompilius, the second king of Rome, and the official headquarters of the *pontifex maximus*. Primitive huts, similar to those on the Palatine (*see p. 97*) were found here, and the earliest permanent construction excavated dates from the 7th century BC. The edifice, known to have been rebuilt by a consul named Domitius Calvinus after a fire in 36 BC, retained its 6th-century form over the centuries: the elegance of its architecture can be seen from the few scattered fragments here. The Regia may have been the depository of state archives and of the *Annales Maximi*, written by the *pontifex maximus*. It also included the Sacrarium of Mars, with the *ancilia* (sacred shields), and the Chapel of Ops, goddess of harvests (and thus of plenty). The foundations of a triumphal arch, erected in 121 BC by the censor and military commander Quintus Fabius Maximus Allobrogicus to span the Sacra Via, have been discovered at the southeast corner of the Regia.

THE EASTERN PART OF THE FORUM

18 The Sacra Via continues beneath the huge **Temple of Antoninus and Faustina**, one of the best-preserved temples in the Forum, complete with its pronaos of ten huge columns above a flight of steps. This was a famous temple of Imperial Rome, which the Senate dedicated to the memory of the Empress Faustina after her death in AD 141.

When her husband, the Emperor Antoninus Pius, died 20 years later, the temple received its double dedication. The pronaos, which has monolithic Corinthian columns (17m high) in *cipollino*, six in front and two on either side, is preceded by a (reconstructed) flight of steps. The architrave and frieze of vases and candelabra between griffins, and the side walls of the cella, of *peperino* blocks originally faced with marble, also survive. Sculptures, including a female torso, have been placed in the pronaos.

The temple was converted into the church of San Lorenzo in Miranda (*closed to the public*) before the 12th century, and given a Baroque façade in 1602. The dedication to St Lawrence may commemorate the trial of the saint, which is thought to have taken place in this temple before his martyrdom in 258. Famous as one of the earliest Christian martyrs, Lawrence is frequently portrayed in Christian art being burned alive on a gridiron. His death seems to have signalled an important moment in Rome for the advance of Christianity and decline of pagan worship.

The Sacra Via continues east (note the pretty drain-cover in the paving) past an **Archaic necropolis**, discovered in 1902. This was the cemetery of the ancient inhabitants of the Esquiline or of the original settlement on the Palatine, and dates back to the early Iron Age, before the date of the traditional foundation of Rome. Tombs were found for both cremations—with ashes in urns surrounded by tomb furniture, in small circular pits—and for burials—either in tufa sarcophagi, hollowed-out tree trunks or trenches lined with tufa slabs.

From here the Sacra Via begins to ascend the low ridge of the Velia, which connected the Palatine Hill with the Esquiline. On either side of the road are the ruins of private houses and shops, some under cover.

19 On the left is the so-called **Temple of Romulus** (the interior can be seen from the church of Santi Cosma e Damiano; *see p. 125*), a well preserved 4th-century building with a curving pronaos in which two porphyry columns supporting an architrave taken from some other building flank the doorway, which still preserves its splendid original bronze doors, a remarkable survival from ancient Rome. This was formerly thought to have been a temple dedicated to Romulus, son of Maxentius, who died in AD 309, but it has recently been suggested that it may instead have been a temple of Jupiter, or the audience hall of the city prefect. It is a circular building built of brick and covered by a cupola flanked by two rectangular rooms with apses, each originally preceded by two *cipollino* columns (only those on the right survive). It was converted in the 6th century into the church of Santi Cosma e Damiano, the temple serving as a vestibule.

20 Beyond a medieval portico on the left of the road, an old shady path with huge ancient paving stones leads up left, and left again, to the amazing remains of the huge **Basilica of Maxentius** (also called the Basilica of Constantine, and the Basilica Nova), which dominates the Forum. The three vast barrel-vaulted niches—20.5m wide, 17.5m deep and 24.5m high—are one of the largest and most impressive examples of Roman architecture to have survived anywhere. The skill and audacity of their design inspired many Renaissance builders, and it is said that Michelangelo studied them closely when he was planning the dome of St Peter's. They formed just the north aisle of the basilica which was begun by Maxentius (AD 306–10) and completed by Constantine who considerably modified the original plan, after he had defeated Maxentius in the famous Battle of the Milvian Bridge (see p. 15).

This enormous building was a rectangle 100m long and 65m wide, divided into a nave and two aisles by massive piers supported by buttresses. As first planned, it had a single apse on the west side. Against the central piers were eight Corinthian columns 14.5m high; the only survivor was moved by Paul V in the 17th century to Piazza Santa Maria Maggiore, where it still stands. The original entrance was from a side road to the east; on the south side Constantine added a portico with four porphyry columns (which partly survive), which opened onto the Sacra Via. The basilica was used as the seat of the city prefects, and, in the 4th century AD, of the *Secretarium Senatus*, the tribunal which heard cases against senators, formerly connected to the Curia (see p. 68). In the middle of the north wall Constantine built a second apse, which was shut off from the rest of the building by a colonnaded balustrade; here the tribunal probably held its sittings.

The interior walls, decorated with niches, were faced with marble below and with stucco above. The arches of the groin-vaulted nave, whose huge blocks have fallen to the ground, were 35m high and had a radius of nearly 20m. Parts of a spiral staircase leading to the roof can also be seen on the ground, having collapsed in an earthquake. A tunnel was built under the northwest corner of the basilica for a thoroughfare which had been blocked by its construction. The entrance to the tunnel, walled up since 1566, can still be seen. In 1487

a colossal statue of Constantine was found in the west apse, fragments of which are now in the courtyard of Palazzo dei Conservatori (see p. 39). The bronze plaques from the roof were removed in 626 by Pope Honorius I to be used for the old basilica of St Peter's.

21 On the ascent to the Arch of Titus is the church of Santa Francesca Romana, or Santa Maria Nova (entered from Via dei Fori Imperiali; *described on p. 125*). The former convent of this church is now the seat of the Forum and Palatine excavation offices and contains the **Antiquarium of the Forum**, a small collection of finds made in the Forum by Giacomo Boni in 1900 and in successive campaigns in the early 20th century. Although it has been kept in a neglected state for many years, it has an extraordinary atmosphere, preserving its charming old-fashioned arrangement with only a few labels here and there and engravings of the excavations. One of the rooms looks into the impressive cella of the Temple of Venus and Roma (see p. 103), which can be seen from nowhere else. It is ironic that the most important archaeological site in Italy should have one of its most abandoned museums.

22 Dominating the summit of the Sacra Via is the well preserved **Arch of Titus**, presumably erected by Domitian just after the death of Titus in AD 81 in honour of the victories of Titus and Vespasian in the Judaean War, which ended with the sack of Jerusalem in AD 70. In the Middle Ages the Frangipani family incorporated the arch into one of their castles, but the encroaching buildings were partly removed by Sixtus IV

Imperial troops carry spoils from the temple at Jerusalem, captured in AD 70. Detail of a relief on the Arch of Titus.

(1471–84) and finally demolished in 1821. The arch was dismantled and then restored by Giuseppe Valadier, who used travertine instead of marble to repair the damaged parts so that they are easily distinguishable.

The beautiful, perfectly-proportioned single archway with Composite columns is covered with Pentelic marble. The two splendid reliefs inside are very worn. One of them shows the goddess Roma guiding the Imperial quadriga with Titus and the winged figure of Victory; and the other shows a triumphal procession bringing the war booty from Jerusalem, which includes the altar of Solomon's Temple decorated with trumpets, and the seven-branched golden candlestick (or Menorah), the symbol of Judaism. In the centre of the panelled vault is the Apotheosis of Titus, showing the deified Emperor mounted on an eagle. On the exterior frieze is another procession in which the symbolic figure of the vanquished Jordan is carried on a stretcher.

On the right of the Sacra Via there is now a large open space with just two olive trees, which covers recent excavations. From here there is a good view of the Forum towards the Capitoline Hill.

THE SLOPES OF THE PALATINE

In this area are scattered ruins, among which are remains of a large portico, the vestibule to the Domus Aurea of Nero (see p. 107). Evidence was also discovered here of the destruction of numerous buildings by Nero for this huge palace which invaded the centre of the Roman city, extending from the Oppian and Caelian Hills across the Velia to the Palatine.

Domitian reused the portico when he built the *Horrea Piperataria*, a bazaar for oriental goods, pepper and spices, to the north of the Sacra Via. Later, the area to the south also became commercialized, as part of a general plan of the Flavians to reinstal public edifices in this area after the death of Nero. Domitian's building was finally destroyed in 284, when the Basilica of Maxentius was built. A small circular base with a relief of a maenad and an inscription recording its restoration by Antoninus Pius (originals in the Antiquarium), close to the Sacra Via, may be the remains of a Sanctuary of Bacchus.

The site of the Archaic walls

A large area on the northern slopes of the Palatine between the Nova Via and the Sacra Via, from west of the Arch of Titus as far as the House of the Vestals, has been excavated since 1985 beneath the visible remains of *horrea*, large warehouses on several floors. The building nearest the House of the Vestals probably dates in its present form from the time of Hadrian. The larger building to the east may be the *Horreum Vespasiani*, a market which fronted the *Horrea Piperataria*. A row of shops against the Palatine Hill is prominent: almost in the centre a well-preserved vaulted edifice can be seen, beside which steps led up to the Nova Via and the upper floors.

The most important result of the excavations in this area so far has been the discovery of Archaic walls on three levels: the oldest traces date from 730–675 BC, when Romulus is thought to have founded Rome; above these was a wall in red tufa defended by a ditch (675–600 BC). The latest wall may have been part of the boundary defences of the first city—which was roughly rectangular in shape and hence known as *Roma Quadrata*—dating from the time of Servius Tullius (530–520 BC). It was constructed with large blocks of red tufa. Subsequent levels have shown interesting remains of at least four Archaic houses and at least four Republican houses, one of which, facing the Clivus Palatinus, may eventually be opened to the public.

On the Nova Via, which runs parallel with the Sacra Via along the southern slope of the Palatine Hill, is the ticket office and entrance to the Palatine (*described in the following chapter*).

THE PALATINE HILL

The Palatine Hill, to the south of and above the Roman Forum (*map p. 623, 3–4D*), is a beautiful park containing impressive ancient ruins. It was here that the primitive city was founded, and splendid Imperial palaces were later built over its slopes, so that the word Palatine came to be synonymous with the palace of the emperor (and hence the word 'palace'). The gardens are nicely kept, with a profusion of wild flowers and fine trees, and are inhabited by many birds (and cats). There are wonderful views from the edge of the hill. Remarkably isolated from the traffic-ridden streets at the foot of the hill, the Palatine is one of the most romantic and charming spots in the centre of the city.

Open 9–1hr before sunset. Ticket includes admission to the Palatine Museum and the Colosseum. For the Archaeological Card, see p. 568. The entrances to the Palatine are in the Roman Forum off the Nova Via, and on Via San Gregorio (see plan on pp. 88–89).

Of the areas normally kept locked, the House of Livia, the House of the Griffins, and the House of Marcus Aemilius Scaurus can only be seen by appointment (T: 06 3996 7700). The House of Augustus was closed at the time of writing. The Aula Isiaca and Loggia Stati Mattei are usually opened on request at the Palatine Museum. There are excellent tours of these sites on certain days throughout the year: see their programme. Several of the more interesting sites are apt to be fenced off because of fresh excavations or damage of some kind.

LEGENDS ATTACHED TO THE HILL

According to tradition the hill was settled from Greece. Sixty years before the Trojan War (traditional date 1184 BC) Evander, son of Hermes and an Arcadian nymph, led a colony from Pallantion in Arcadia, and built a town at the foot of a hill near the Tiber, naming it after his native village. Aeneas, who escaped from burning Troy after the Trojan War, sailed to Italy, and according to Virgil was welcomed here by Evander. Some Classical authors give another explanation of the name *Palatium*: that it is derived from Pales, the goddess of flocks and shepherds, whose festival was celebrated on 21st April, the day on which the city of Rome is said to have been founded by Romulus and Remus in 754 or 753 BC.

According to tradition the twins were found on the hill by the shepherd Faustulus, and the cave where they were nursed by the she-wolf was located at its foot. When they grew up and decided to found a new city, they contested its site, Remus advocating the Aventine and Romulus the Palatine. It was decided that the first to see a flight of birds as an omen would be given the choice, and when 12 vultures flew over the Palatine Romulus was given the honour of naming the city. After killing his brother, he became the first king of Rome.

HISTORY OF THE PALATINE

Recent research suggests the hill was inhabited sporadically by the Late Bronze Age (13th–12th centuries BC), and traces of occupation going back to the 9th century BC have been discovered during excavations. The earliest Palaeolithic material has been found in the area of the Temple of Victory (near the Temple of Cybele) and at the northern foot of the hill.

Some time after its foundation, the city was surrounded by a strong wall forming an approximate rectangle, hence the name *Roma Quadrata*. Three gates were provided in the walls: the *Porta Mugonia* on the northeast and the *Porta Romanula* on the northwest (neither of these has yet been identified), and the Scalae Caci (which may have been identified in recent excavations) at the southwest corner overlooking the valley of the Circus Maximus. The northern slopes of the Palatine, in the area nearest to the Forum, were for centuries considered one of the most prestigious residential districts. During the Republic many prominent citizens lived here, including the great orator and writer Cicero, the statesman and philosopher Quintus Lutatius Catulus, the orators Crassus and Hortensius, the demagogue Publius Clodius and the triumvir Antony. Remains of some of these residences have recently been unearthed. Augustus, who was born on the Palatine, acquired the house of Hortensius and enlarged it. His new buildings included the renowned Temple of Apollo, with Greek and Latin libraries attached. Part of his palace has also been excavated. The example of Augustus was followed by later emperors, whose residences became more and more magnificent, and the Palatine tended to become an imperial reserve.

In ancient times the central summit was called the *Palatium*. It sloped down towards the *Forum Boarium* (cattle market) and the Tiber, with a hillside called the Germalus (now occupied by the Farnese Gardens) looking towards the Capitoline. The Velia, a second, lower summit, was connected with the Esquiline by a saddle through the Roman Forum. The intervening hollows were filled in by successive constructions in the Imperial era. The whole of the Palatium itself was reserved for the constructions of the Palace of the Flavian emperors (now called the Palace of Domitian), which comprised the official palace, the emperor's residence and the stadium. To provide a water supply, Domitian extended the Acqua Claudia from the Caelian Hill to the Palatine.

Odoacer, first king of Italy after the extinction of the Western Empire in 476, lived on the Palatine; so for a time did Theodoric, King of the Ostrogoths, who ruled Italy from 493 to 526. The hill later became a residence of the representatives of the Eastern Empire. From time to time it was favoured by the popes, and some churches were built here. In the course of time, after a period of devastation, the Frangipani and other noble families erected their castles over the ruins. In the 16th century most of the Germalus was laid out as a villa for the Farnese.

Excavations

Systematic excavations were started about 1724 by Francesco Bianchini, shortly after Duke Francis I of Bourbon-Parma had inherited the Farnese Gardens. Little more was done in a scientific way until 1860; in that year the gardens were bought by Napoleon III, who entrusted the direction of the excavations to Pietro Rosa, an extremely skilled archaeologist who preserved the finds by founding the Palatine Museum. He continued his work after 1870 when the Palatine was acquired by the Italian Government. In 1907 the Germalus was explored, and later Giacomo Boni worked on the buildings below the Domus Flavia of the Palace of Domitian. Between the two world wars Alfonso Bartoli carried out research under the Domus Augustana of the same palace and elsewhere, and brought to light much information about the earliest inhabitants. In the 1960s important work was done in the House of Augustus, and the adjacent Temple of Apollo was identified. Excavations have been in progress since 1985 on the lower northern slopes of the hill, beneath the Domus Tiberiana, on the southwest corner of the hill in the area of the Temple of Cybele, and near the Vigna Barberini.

Approaches

The usual approach to the hill is from the Roman Forum. The ticket office is on the Nova Via, the ancient road which runs parallel to and above the Sacra Via in the Roman Forum, along the southern slopes of the Palatine. It provided a means of communication between the Forum and the buildings on the Palatine. The visible remains probably date from the Flavian period, but at the point where it crosses the Clivus Palatinus, recent excavations have revealed paving which seems to date from the Republican era. There are considerable ruins of shops and buildings which faced onto the road. A Republican house, close to it and facing the Clivus Palatinus, was excavated in 1985. With some 50 bedrooms it is thought that it may have been the servants' quarters attached to the House of Marcus Aemilius Scaurus (*admission by appointment only; see p. 85*). He was a quaestor (an official who had judicial and financial powers) under Pompey, whose former wife he married, and may have lived here in 58 BC before he fell into disgrace and was exiled in 52 BC. His residence is mentioned frequently by Roman writers as being the most splendid on the hill in the Republican era.

THE WESTERN PALATINE

Farnese Gardens and Domus Tiberiana

Monumental steps with a nymphaeum and a water cascade lead up from the Nova Via through the **Farnese Gardens** ⓵ , laid out by Vignola in the middle of the 16th century for Cardinal Alessandro Farnese, grandson of Paul III. They extended from the level of the Forum, then much higher, to the slopes of the Germalus; the various terraced levels were united by flights of steps. Vignola's work was completed by Girolamo Rainaldi at the beginning of the 17th century. Above another terrace with a fountain stand the twin pavilions of the aviary, on the highest level of the gardens, overlooking the Forum.

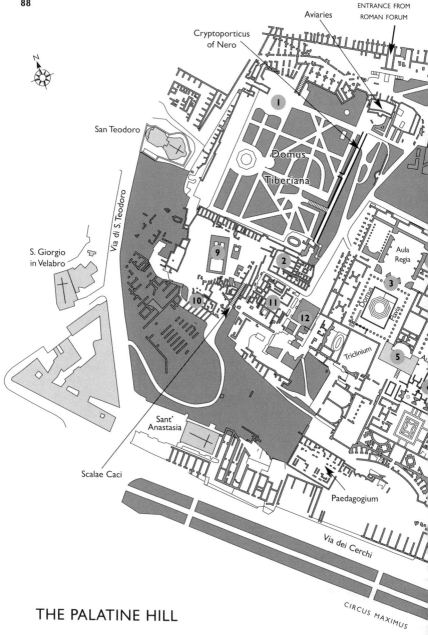

ENTRANCE FROM
ROMAN FORUM

Aviaries

Cryptoporticus
of Nero

San Teodoro

Via di S. Teodoro

S. Giorgio
in Velabro

Domus
Tiberiana

Aula
Regia

Domus Flavia

Triclinium

Sant'
Anastasia

Scalae Caci

Paedagogium

Via dei Cerchi

CIRCUS MAXIMUS

THE PALATINE HILL

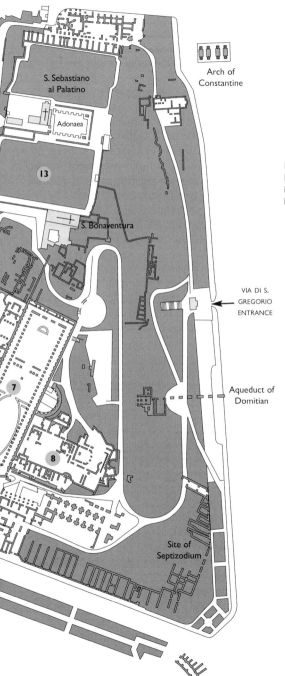

Arch of
Constantine

S. Sebastiano
al Palatino

Adonaea

13

S. Bonaventura

VIA DI S.
GREGORIO
ENTRANCE

Aqueduct of
Domitian

7

8

Site of
Septizodium

1   Farnese Gardens
2   House of Livia
3   Palace of Domitian
4   House of the Griffins
    & Lararium
5   Museo Palatino
6   Loggia Stati Mattei
7   Stadium
8   Domus Severiana
9   Temple of Cybele
10 House of Romulus
11 House of Augustus
12 Temple of Apollo
13 Vigna Barberini

Detail of vault frescoes on the Palatine attributed to the Roman painter Fabullus, who worked for Nero in the 1st century AD.

but more probably another room used for public ceremonies, or a guardroom protecting the main entrance to the palace. Beneath this is the earlier House of the Griffins (*described opposite; admission only by appointment*). To the west is the Basilica Jovis, divided by two rows of columns of *giallo antico*; it has an apse at the further end, closed by a marble screen. This may have been used as an auditorium, for political and administrative meetings. A flight of steps (*no admission*) connects the basilica to the cryptoporticus in the Farnese Gardens. A portico of *cipollino* columns, also on the north, may have served as a loggia.

The triclinium

To the south of the peristyle is the triclinium, or banqueting hall. It has an apse reached by a high step; in this was placed the table where the emperor dined. The hall was paved with coloured marbles, which are well preserved in the apse. Leading out of the hall on either side was a court with an oval fountain. Around the fountain on the west side, which is also well preserved, is a magnificent pavement in *opus sectile* belonging to the earlier Domus Transitoria of Nero. The conspicuous pavilion here was constructed by the Farnese in the 16th century as part of their gardens: the double loggia looking northwest has painted decorations attributed to the Zuccari brothers, prolific artists who decorated many buildings in Rome and were often given commissions by the Farnese family. A staircase (*no admission*) leads down from the triclinium to a court beneath it with a partly restored nymphaeum, decorated with rare marbles, which was also part of Nero's palace; the exquisite mid-1st-century AD frescoes from the vault, attributed to Fabullus (*illustrated above*), have been detached and are now exhibited in the Palatine Museum.

The Domus Augustana

Behind the triclinium is a row of partly-restored columns belonging to the Flavian palace. Further south are two rooms with apses, once thought to be Domitian's reconstruction of the Greek and Latin libraries of the Temple of Apollo nearby, but now considered to be reception rooms used by Augustus for legates.

Behind and to the east of the Palatine Museum are the remains of another part of the Palace of Domitian, which was the private residence of the emperor, the Domus Augustana or 'the Augustus'. It was built on two levels with two peristyles, one on the upper level and one much lower. On the upper level, only the bases of the columns of the open peristyle, in front and to the east of the Palatine Museum building, and various small rooms survive. A path leads to the southwest edge of the hill between the museum and the triclinium, from where there is a splendid view of another court (*closed to the public*), some 10m below ground level, in the middle of which is a large basin with a quadrangular shrine. Numerous living-rooms and fountain courts can be seen here. A doorway in the bottom wall leads to the exedra of the palace overlooking the Circus Maximus; this was originally decorated with a colonnade.

House of the Griffins

The House of the Griffins **4** (*only shown by appointment; T: 06 3996 7700*) is named after the two griffins in stucco which decorate a lunette in one of the rooms. This is the oldest Republican building preserved on the Palatine (2nd or 1st century BC). Its wall paintings are in the second Pompeian style (1st century BC; *see p. 90 above*). The house is on two levels, the decorations being on the lower level. Of the several rooms reached by a steep staircase, the large hall is the best preserved. In the centre of a mosaic floor there is an *opus sectile* pavement. The mural paintings simulate three planes of different depth, while the columns imitate various marbles. Round the top of the room runs a cornice and the ceiling is stuccoed.

Museo Palatino

Roughly in the centre of the hill is a former convent building, now home to the Palatine Museum **5**. The museum (*same opening times as the Palatine Hill*) houses material from excavations here. The collection was founded in the mid-19th century and was moved to its present building in 1868. Since 1997 it has been beautifully displayed and well labelled, and includes material from the most recent excavations of the earliest settlements on the hill, as well as Roman wall decorations and frescoes, stucco, marble intarsia and sculptures.

Ground floor: The earliest prehistoric hut villages (9th–8th centuries BC) found on the hill are well illustrated here; finds from the area near the Temple of Victory include Palaeolithic artefacts and two exquisite terracotta heads of Zeus and Apollo (3rd century BC).

Upper floors: The rooms here are dedicated to the period of the Emperors. The beautiful painted terracotta panels (38–28 BC; *example illustrated overleaf*) with reliefs of paired figures were found in the area of the House of Augustus and Temple of Apollo, and the three black marble herms, are now identified as part of the series of the 50 Danaids which decorated the temple portico. These were the daughters of Danaus who, according to a complicated Egyptian myth, were ordered by their father to kill their Egyptian husbands on their

Terracotta panel showing Apollo and Hercules contesting possession of the sacred tripod at Delphi, symbol of Apollo's lordship of the sanctuary. When the Oracle failed to respond to Hercules he tried to seize the tripod, but Apollo defended it. Zeus intervened to separate his two sons by hurling a thunderbolt between them.

wedding day, and were sent to Hades and condemned to carry leaking jars of water. Some scholars think that the two fragments from a colossal statue of Apollo might be the famous Greek original by Skopas (360 BC), which is known to have been in this temple. There are also fragments of wall paintings (1st century BC) one of which shows Apollo with his lyre. Beautiful marble intarsia pavements and exquisite frescoes of Homeric subjects all come from Nero's Domus Transitoria, found beneath the triclinium of the Palace of Domitian (54 AD).

There are also marble intarsia panels which were once wall decorations, two busts of Nero, a beautiful head of Agrippina, daughter of Marcus Aurelius (mid-1st century AD), and a graffiti caricature of the Crucifixion which shows a young man standing before a cross on which hangs a figure with the head of an ass. The blasphemous inscription in Greek reads 'Alexamenos worships his god'.

The last room has a fine display of statues, including a Greek original, and a graceful statuette of a Satyr turning round to look at his tail, a Roman copy of a Hellenistic bronze. The headless seated statue of Cybele from her temple is also kept here.

The Aula Isiaca

Close to the museum building is the **Loggia Stati Mattei** **6** (*usually opened on request at the museum*), a winter loggia formerly part of the Villa Mattei, built in 1520 with a vault decorated with grotesques on a white background by the circle of Baldassare Peruzzi, clearly showing the influence of Raphael. The *tondi* with the Signs of the Zodiac were detached in 1846 and ended up in the Metropolitan Museum of Art in New York: the museum has recently generously returned them here. The frescoes from the walls found their way to St Petersburg at the same time and are still in the Hermitage.

The loggia now overlooks a room which contains murals detached in 1966 from the **Aula Isiaca** (Hall of Isis) beneath the Basilica Jovis of the Palace of Domitian. This was a large rectangular hall with an apse at one end, erected in the Republican era and modified probably under Caligula, and dedicated to the cult of Isis. The fantastic architectural paintings, with Egyptian motifs, were painted just before the edict of 21 BC banning the worship of Isis, but their style was much in vogue at this time after Octavian's victory over Antony and Cleopatra at Actium. They were discovered in 1724 and were copied in the same century by Francesco Bartoli. His watercolours of them (when they were in much better condition) are preserved in the Topham Collection at Eton College in England.

THE EASTERN PALATINE

The eastern part of the Palace of Domitian, well below ground level, is the so-called **Stadium** **7**, which most scholars now believe was a garden occasionally used as a hippodrome. There is a splendid view of it from above, although there is no admission to the ground level. It is a huge enclosure 160m long, with a series of rooms at the north end and a curved wall at the south. The interior had a two-storeyed portico with engaged columns covering a wide ambulatory or cloister. The arena has a semicircular construction at either end, presumably once supporting a *meta* (turning-post). In the centre are two rows of piers of a late-Empire portico. Towards the south are the remains of an oval construction inserted in the early Middle Ages which blocked the curved end. Columns of granite and *cipollino*, Tuscan, Corinthian and Composite capitals, and fragments of a marble altar with figures of divinities now lie on the ground. In the middle of the east wall is a wide exedra shaped like an apse, of two storeys, and approached from the outside by a curved corridor: this is traditionally identified as an imperial box, used by the emperor when he commanded the races and athletic contests here.

East of the stadium (and hardly visible from the fence) was the so-called **Domus Severiana** **8**, which was built over a foundation formed by enlarging the southern corner of the hill by means of enormous substructures that extended almost as far as the Circus Maximus. The scant remains include part of the Baths of Septimius Severus. To the north (near the exit onto Via di San Gregorio) is the aqueduct built by Domitian to provide water for his palace; it was an extension of the Acqua Claudia which ran from the Caelian Hill to the Palatine. The aqueduct was restored by Septimius Severus.

To the south is the site of the imperial box built by Septimius Severus, from which he could watch the contests in the Circus Maximus (*see p. 325*). In the extreme southeastern corner of the Palatine is the site of the **Septizodium** (also called the Septizonium), also built by Septimius Severus in AD 203, a richly-decorated building intended to impress visitors to Rome arriving by the Via Appia. Renaissance drawings show that it had three floors, each decorated with columns. The ornamental façade, some 90m long, was divided vertically into seven zones (hence the name of the building), the number corresponding either to that of the known planets or to the days of the week. During a crisis between the papacy and the Emperor Frederick II at a conclave in 1241, Matteo Orsini, a Roman baron who, as senator, had taken control of the government of the city, imprisoned 12 cardinals here. He forced them to elect Pope Celestine IV, but the new pope died, as did three of the cardinals as a result of their confinement. Apparently already falling down at that time, the building was finally totally demolished by Domenico Fontana by order of Sixtus VI in 1588–89, and the columns and blocks of marble and travertine were reused in various buildings in the city. Recent excavations here have revealed its plan.

The buildings on the southern edge of the hill can only be seen from a distance, from Via dei Cerchi or the Circus Maximus. They include the Severian arches, the south end of the stadium, the exedra of the Domus Augustana and, halfway down the hill, the Paedagogium (2nd or 1st century AD) supposed to have been a training-school for the court pages.

THE SOUTHWESTERN PALATINE

NB: The southwestern part of the hill is at present closed during excavations and restorations. Nevertheless, some very important monuments, including the Temple of Cybele, the site of the hut village, and the House of Augustus, are on this part of the hill, and therefore are outlined below.

The **Temple of Cybele**, the *Magna Mater* **9** , very ruined, stands on a mound covered by a thicket of dark ilex trees. It was consecrated in 191 BC. Just to the east of the temple, on lower ground and under cover, are the remains of the **Temple of Victory**, one of the earliest temples so far found on the hill, built in 294 BC. Between the two temples is the base of a much smaller temple, recently identified as the Temple of Victory Virgo dedicated by Marcus Porcius Cato (Cato the Elder) in 193 BC. Cato was well known for his wise politics while serving as censor, and is also famous for his writings.

The area on the southwestern edge of the hill is the most ancient part of the Palatine, and excavations have been in progress here since 1978. Traces of a wall of tufa and the site of the **Scalae Caci**, one of the three gates of *Roma Quadrata* (*see p. 86*) have been found. The gate is named after Cacus, a giant monster, which, according to legend had his den in the *Forum Boarium* at the foot of the hill and terrified the populace by his pillaging. It was only when he dared to steal the cattle which had belonged to the monster Geryon, and which Hercules had obtained as one of his Twelve Labours, that he was finally put to death by the Greek hero. Also here are holes and channels in the tufa marking the site of a **hut village** of the Early Iron Age (9th century BC). It is known that the Lupercal was also in this part of the hill, although traces of it have not yet been found. This was the cave sanctuary of the she-wolf connected with the legend of Romulus and Remus and sacred to Rome. There was an altar here which was surrounded by a grove sacred to the god Lupercus. This was the site of the annual festival of the Lupercalia, held on 15th February, when the priests of the god, the *luperci*, dressed in goatskins, processed around the hill whipping whomever they met. (It was believed that the castigation of women encouraged fertility.) The Latin *februarius* means purification and expiation. A hut at the top of the Scalae Caci near the Temple of Mater Matuta is known as the **House of Romulus 10**: it was restored periodically and up until the 4th century AD was mentioned as being the hut that belonged to the shepherd Faustulus who found the legendary twins and brought them up.

Nearby is the **House of Augustus 11**, Rome's first emperor, who was born in his father's house on the other side of the Palatine Hill. He acquired the orator Hortensius' house in 23 BC, and incorporated it into his new palace after 36 BC. The house was reconstructed by the emperor (at public expense) after a fire in 3 AD, and includes his private quarters as well as rooms for public ceremonies, and two libraries. The wall paintings which have been found here are of great interest. They date from 25 BC–AD 25 and are remarkable for their vivid colour (mostly red, yellow and black), intricate designs, including architectural and theatrical motifs, and refined figure studies. There is also a charming frieze of pine-cones. Considerable fragments of the stuccoed vaults and pavements of marble inlay have also survived. There is a nymphaeum decorated with shells, and an exquisite little *studiolo*, beautifully restored, which has the most refined decoration so far found in the house.

After a building of the late Republican era was found beneath them, the ruins to the southeast of the House of Augustus were identified as the famous **Temple of Apollo 12** initiated by Augustus in 36 BC and dedicated eight years later, after the Battle of Actium. A corridor, which is thought to have connected the temple to the house, has

The Colosseum has been an emblem of Rome's eternity for centuries. The Venerable Bede (c. 673–735) quotes a prophecy made by Anglo-Saxon pilgrims: 'While the Colisaeus stands, Rome shall stand; when the Colisaeus falls, Rome shall fall; when Rome falls, the world shall fall'.

HISTORY OF THE COLOSSEUM

The amphitheatre, begun by Vespasian in AD 70 on the site of the lake in the gardens of Nero's Domus Aurea, was completed by Titus ten years later. The expense was in part covered by the sale of war booty. The inaugural festival lasted 100 days, during which many gladiators and 5,000 wild beasts were killed.

The gladiatorial combats and wild animal hunts (*venationes*) which took place in the Colosseum throughout the Imperial period were very popular forms of entertainment, and grand ceremonies and processions preceded them. Gladiators, who were mostly prisoners of war, slaves or condemned convicts, fought man to man in single combat, and it was only when one was killed that the other was declared winner. The spectacles with wild animals included crocodiles, lions, elephants and tigers shipped to Rome for the purpose. The arena was also sometimes flooded for mock sea-battles (*naumachiae*). Gladiatorial combats were suppressed in the 5th century and fights with wild beasts in AD 523.

The amphitheatre was restored after a fire in 217 under Alexander Severus and in 248 the thousandth anniversary of the foundation of Rome was celebrated here. The damage from an earthquake in 443 was probably repaired by Theodosius II and Valentinian III. The building was again shaken by earthquakes in 1231 and 1349. It was converted into a castle by the Roman aristocratic families of the Frangipani and the Annibaldi.

In 1312 the Colosseum was presented to the senate and people of Rome by the Emperor Henry VII. By the 15th century it had become a quarry for building material. Its travertine was used during the construction of Palazzo di Venezia and Palazzo della Cancelleria. Other parts of the building were reused in St Peter's and Palazzo Barberini. However, in 1749 Benedict XIV dedicated the Colosseum to the Passion of Jesus and pronounced it sanctified by the blood of martyrs, although there is no historical basis for the tradition that Christians were killed in the arena.

At the end of the 19th century the Colosseum was freed from obstructive buildings and undergrowth, and the structures beneath the arena were uncovered. Further clearances were carried out after the construction in 1933 of Via dei Fori Imperiali. The Colosseum is again undergoing a long process of restoration and study expected to take many years, based on a detailed elevation, the first ever made of the whole building. Since the time of Paul VI the pope has visited the Colosseum on Good Friday to re-enact the Passion of Christ Carrying the Cross (the *Via Crucis*), televised throughout the world.

The Exterior

The exterior is roughly 189m long, 156m wide and 48–50m high (the total circumference measuring 545m). It is built of travertine outside and of brick-faced concrete and tufa in the interior. The travertine blocks were originally held together with iron clamps; these were torn out in the Middle Ages but their sockets are still conspicuous. The mighty exterior wall, which supports the complicated interior, has four storeys. The lower three have rows of arches decorated with engaged columns of the three orders superimposed: Tuscan Doric on the lowest, Ionic in the middle and Corinthian on the top. The fourth storey, dating from the restoration of Alexander Severus, has no arches but is articulated by slender Corinthian pilasters. The projecting corbels supported 240 wooden poles which, when inserted through the holes in the cornice, protruded above the top of the building to support an awning which gave protection to the audience (*see p. 102 below*). Statues originally occupied the arches of the second and third storeys.

All 80 arches on the ground floor were numbered and served as entrance arches. The numbered arches led to the concentric vaulted corridors giving access to the staircases. Spectators entered the arch which corresponded to their ticket numbers, ascended the appropriate staircase and found their seat in the cavea by means of one of numerous passages. There were also four main entrances at the ends of the diameters of the ellipse, situated northeast, southeast, southwest and northwest. That on the northeast (between arches XXXVIII and XXXIX), which was without a cornice and was wider than the others, opened into a hall decorated with stuccoes; this was reserved for the emperor. Outside the southern end of the Colosseum excavations have recently revealed an entrance constructed by Commodus.

Admiration for the ruins

The Colosseum was particularly admired by 19th-century travellers to Rome because of its romantic ruined state. Lord Byron dedicates many stanzas of *Childe Harold's Pilgrimage* (Canto IV, 1818) to this 'vast and wondrous monument ... a ruin—yet what ruin!'. Dickens in 1846 declared: 'It is the most impressive, the most stately, the most solemn, grand, majestic, mournful sight, conceivable. Never, in its bloodiest prime, can the sight of the gigantic Coliseum, full and running over with the lustiest life, have moved one heart, as it must move all who look upon it now, a ruin. God be thanked: a ruin!'. Augustus Hare was disgusted by the 'tidying up' of the Colosseum in 1882 and the eradication of its 'marvellous flora' (in fact, the monument used to be covered with an extraordinary variety of plants and flowers, some of them unknown elsewhere in Rome).

The Interior

Though more than two-thirds of the original masonry has been removed, the magnificence of the interior of the amphitheatre, which could probably hold more than 50,000

TRIUMPHS

The original Triumph was a way of allowing a Roman general to celebrate victory without giving him lasting political dominance. The elaborate ritual appears to be Etruscan in origin, adopted by the Roman Republic after the expulsion of the kings in 509 BC. Once a major battle had been won (so many generals applied for triumphs that it was later stipulated that 5,000 of the enemy had to have been killed in a victory which effectively brought a war to an end) the victor gathered his troops, captives and booty outside the walls of Rome. Behind the general stood a slave who held a laurel wreath over his head and who reminded him continually of his mortality. Dressed as the god Jupiter for the day, and riding in a four-horse chariot (four horses were always a symbol of heroic status), the general led the procession into the city through the *Porta Carmentalis*, winding its way along the major public spaces so as many citizens as possible could see it. Finally it would enter the Forum and move along the Sacra Via and up to the Temple of Jupiter on the Capitoline Hill, where the general would place his wreath and sacrifice to the gods. His prisoners were led away for execution. After his day of triumph a general was supposed to retire from active political life, but by the end of the republic, powerful men such as Pompey the Great and Julius Caesar were subverting the rules and a Triumph proved a stepping stone to permanent power.

After the fall of the Republic (27 BC), only emperors were able to celebrate full-scale Triumphs, although victorious generals could be granted triumphal insignia. As there was by now no question of a Triumph leading to political quiescence, it could be recorded in permanent form in a triumphal arch. In the Roman Forum the arches erected to commemorate the victory of Titus over Jerusalem (erected after his death, in AD 81), of Septimius Severus over the Parthians (erected in AD 203) and of Constantine over the rival emperor Maxentius at the Milvian Bridge (erected in 315) survive from the 34 recorded in the city. On Titus' arch reliefs show the emperor enjoying his triumph with the booty from the temple at Jerusalem carried in procession with him. In the Capitoline Museum there is a fine relief of the emperor Marcus Aurelius in a triumph of AD 176. Other arches were scattered through the western empire, especially in Italy, Africa and Gaul.

Triumphal arches were traditionally surmounted by a four-horse chariot, sometimes with the emperor inside (all have long since disappeared). In 1797 the French general Napoleon Bonaparte seized Rome. He saw himself as the heir of the Roman conquerors of the past, and like them wished to carry off plunder. Many of the city's finest Classical statues were transported to Paris, where they entered the city in a triumphal procession. Napoleon constructed two triumphal arches: the Arc du Triomphe and the Arc du Carrousel. On the latter he placed the only surviving quadriga from the ancient world, the four horses of St Mark's (returned to Venice after his downfall).   C.F.

THE OPPIAN HILL
Map p. 623, 3E

The Oppian Hill, just northeast of the Colosseum, is one of the four summits of the Esquiline and was one of the Seven Hills (*Septimontium*) of primitive Rome. On its slopes is the Parco Oppio, a public garden that has recently been replanted, which contains the famous Domus Aurea.

Scattered remains of the huge **Baths of Trajan**, built after a fire in 104 by Apollodorus of Damascus and inaugurated in 109, can been seen throughout the Parco Oppio. Their design was taken as a model by later builders of Imperial baths. The conspicuous ruins include an exedra which was decorated as a nymphaeum, and a hall with two apses. Beneath a building thought to have been a library, a remarkable Roman fresco of a city was discovered in 1998 (*not yet open to the public*). Between Via Terme di Traiano and Viale del Monte Oppio (well below ground-level) is a nymphaeum on a basilican plan, probably part of Nero's Domus Aurea, restored by Trajan.

Entrance to the so-called **Sette Sale** (*map p. 623, 3F*) is at 2 Via Terme di Traiano (*admission by appointment; T: 06 6710 3819*). This remarkable large vaulted building with nine sections is in fact the reservoir of the Baths of Trajan. Excavations have shown that a house was built above the reservoir in the 4th century. The famous sculpture of the *Laocoön*, now in the Vatican museums (*see p. 455*), was discovered in 1506 in a vineyard near the Sette Sale. Hardly anything remains of the smaller Baths of Titus, which occupied the southwest corner of the Oppian Hill.

At the bottom of the hill, on the east side of the Colosseum and between Via Labicana and Via San Giovanni in Laterano are remains of the **Ludus Magnus** (*map p. 623, 3E*), the principal training-school for gladiators, constructed by Domitian. Part of the curved wall of a miniature amphitheatre used for practice can be seen.

DOMUS AUREA

Open 9–7.45. Closed Tues; T: 06 3996 7700. Accompanied visits enter every 15mins, and the tour takes about 45mins. NB: It is necessary to book a visit. Often the best way is to do so on the spot at the entrance; visitors not in a group can often go in directly or shortly after-wards. The entrance is in the public park on the Oppian Hill above Via Labicana, on a path called Viale Domus Aurea.

History of the Domus Aurea

This was once a huge palace, built by Nero and called his 'Golden House'. The extensive ruins of one wing are now open to the public, extremely important for their architecture as well as the remains of the fresco and stucco decorations.

Nero already had one palace, the Domus Transitoria on the Palatine, which was destroyed in the fire of AD 64. Even before its destruction he had planned to build another, the Domus Aurea, in the heart of the city. With its outbuildings and gardens, buildings to the north. In the opinion of ancient writers these constructions made up a monumental group unequalled in the world.

Important excavations are being carried out in the eastern and southern parts of the Forum, formerly covered by roads and public gardens, and scholars have redrawn the plan of the entire area (*see plan on p. 118*).

Santa Maria di Loreto and the Nome di Maria

At the west end of Via dei Fori Imperiali, opposite the corner of the Vittorio Emanuele II monument, two little domed churches, of similar design but different date, flank Trajan's Column. The first, Santa Maria di Loreto (*map p. 622, 2C*), by Antonio da Sangallo the Younger, with a lantern by Giacomo del Duca (1582), is a fine 16th-century building (*closed at the time of writing*). It contains an altarpiece on a gold ground attributed to Marco Palmezzano, and four female statues including *St Susanna* (a little-known saint who was martyred under Diocletian; *see p. 236*) shown pointing towards the altar and dressed as a Roman Vestal, by the Flemish-born Baroque sculptor François Duquesnoy (1630). Duquesnoy came from a family of sculptors (his father was the creator of the *Manneken-pis*). Though recognition came to him, he nevertheless suffered from bouts of insanity, and his family was a troubled one (his brother was sentenced to death for committing a profane act in church). Nevertheless this statue, standing in Classical *contrapposto*, with a supple grace and exquisitely executed drapery, carries with it a mood of serene calm and modesty.

The second church, dedicated to the Nome di Maria, is one of just two churches in the city by the little-known architect Antonio Dérizet, who had the good taste in 1738 to match the much earlier church. The *Madonna and Child* over the high altar may date from the 13th century.

Trajan's Column

The original entrance to the Forum may have been here, close to Trajan's Column. The Column, still almost intact and carefully restored in 1980–88, is generally considered to be the masterpiece of Roman sculptural art. It was dedicated to Trajan by Hadrian in memory of his conquest of the Dacians, the inhabitants of what is now Romania. Around the column shaft winds a spiral frieze 200m long and between 0.89m and 1.25m high, with some 2,500 figures in relief illustrating in detail the various phases of Trajan's remarkable military achievements in the Dacian campaigns (101–02 and 105–06). The carving was carried out in less than four years by an unknown Roman master and his workshop. The scenes show the Emperor himself as well as his soldiers and those of the enemy, both always depicted with great delicacy and intent on showing the dignity of the defeated as well as the victors. Numerous naturalistic details include plants and animals. It is presumed that the column could originally be seen from the neighbouring buildings, which surrounded it on various levels: from ground-level it is now more difficult to appreciate the beautiful details of the carving with the naked eye. Casts of each panel (made before restoration) are kept in the Museo della Civiltà Romana (*see p. 541*).

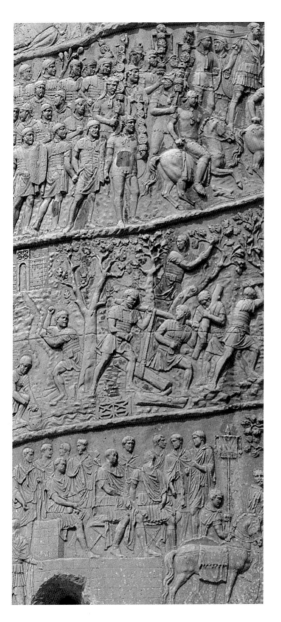

Detail from Trajan's Column, one of the great masterpieces of Roman sculptural art.

The column, 100 Roman feet (29.7m) high, is constructed in a series of marble drums. An internal spiral stair of 185 steps (*no admission*) ascends to the top of the Doric capital on which the statue of Trajan—replaced by St Peter in 1588—once stood. (The idea of a statue surmounting the column gave the model for the adulation of later heroes, such as Nelson in Trafalgar Square in London.) The ashes of the emperor, who died in Cilicia (in modern-day Turkey) in 117, and of his wife Plotina, were enclosed in a golden urn and placed in a vault below the column. Trajan was the first and probably the only emperor to be buried in the centre of the city. An inscription at the base has been taken to indicate that the top of the column reached to the original ground level, thus giving an idea of the colossal excavations necessary for the construction of the forum.

On the left and right of the column were two twin edifices, sometimes identified as libraries, which had at least three storeys (so it seems that the details of the carving on the column would have been easily visible from them).

Basilica Ulpia

Behind the column are fragments of colossal grey granite columns, one with its marble Corinthian capital, some of the largest ever found in Rome, and now thought to have belonged to the monumental entrance. Beyond, crossing the entire site, are the extensive remains of the **Basilica Ulpia** (Trajan's family name was Ulpius), dedicated to the administration of justice, and the largest in Rome. Like all basilicas, it was once roofed with bronze tiles, and may have been some 50m high. It was divided by colonnades into a nave and four aisles: some of the columns of this area of the inner colonnade are still standing (the rest of it is under the modern roads). The back entrance, with two doors, was here, but it was originally approached from the other side (from the open forum) where traces of three doors have been found. Part of the pavement in coloured marbles has survived, as has a fragment of the entablature, with reliefs of scenes of sacrifice.

On each short side was an extensive apse or portico; the north portico was found under Palazzo Roccagiovine beside Via Magnanapoli. It conforms to the semicircular shape of the markets. In the Middle Ages the portico was stripped of its precious marbles: all that survives are the remains of three steps of *giallo antico*, a column base, traces of the polychrome marble pavement and a column of the apse. Behind the portico part of the wall of the enclosure is visible. The site of the south portico is under Via dei Fori Imperiali, where excavations are in progress.

Forum and Markets of Trajan

On the lower ground and stretching beyond the modern raised walkway which now crosses the site, extends the area of the open **Forum of Trajan**, itself in the form of a rectangular piazza (which covered some 9,000 square metres), with a portico and exedra on each of the long sides. In the centre but towards the lower end was a colossal equestrian statue of Trajan, the travertine base of which was found during excavations in 1999. It seems there was a monumental arch beyond this, adjoining the Forum of Augustus, once thought to have been the main entrance. The site of the Temple of Trajan has not so far been located. To the north of the forum and virtually adjoining it rises the huge semicircle of the Markets of Trajan.

Since most of the area of the Forum of Trajan is at present closed, from the site of the Basilica an iron walkway descends to a passageway on the left which gives access to the **Markets of Trajan**. These were built before the forum, at the beginning of the 2nd century AD, and consisted of 150 individual shops used for general trading, built in a huge semicircle of three superimposed rows with arcaded fronts, set in to the slopes of the Quirinal. The semicircle ends on either side in a well-preserved apsidal hall. The apsidal buildings on the second floor have survived almost intact. A conspicuous remnant of a wall of huge tufa blocks shows where the area of the markets ended and the Forum began, thus making a distinct division between the commercial and sacred areas. At the other (far right) end of the markets a very high wall dating from the period of Domitian can be seen, with, at the top, a 15th-century loggia which belonged to the Casa dei Cavalieri di Rodi, ancient seat of the Roman priorate of the Order of the Knights of St John of Jerusalem (*see p. 545*).

The Emperor Trajan (ruled AD 98–117)

Trajan is often seen as the ideal Roman emperor. He was born in Spain, probably in 53, and made his way up through military campaigns in Syria, Spain and Germany until the elderly emperor Nerva adopted him as his son and thus made his succession as emperor inevitable. It was a good example of the way talent could be rewarded, and Trajan more than repaid the compliment. He was a stable and restrained man, always scrupulous in his dealings with the powerful senatorial class and his provincial governors, and built up a reputation for administrative competence. Pliny praised him for being open to all petitioners and giving replies quickly, and the correspondence between the two, when Pliny was governor of Bithynia, is full of practical common sense. Trajan's humanity was shown through schemes to help impoverished and abandoned children. Gregory the Great even said that Trajan deserved to be admitted to heaven as an honorary Christian.

Like all successful Roman emperors Trajan knew the importance of military victories, and his campaigns were wildly popular. The most successful in the early 2nd century were against the Dacians who, under their king Decabalus, threatened the empire from north of the Danube. When they were finally subdued (105–06) and Decabalus's palace sacked, there was immense booty to be brought back to Rome. The victory was celebrated with 123 days of games, after which Trajan set about building a massive Forum alongside that of Augustus, with porticoes, libraries, a vast basilica and eventually a huge temple constructed by his successor Hadrian to the now deified emperor. When the emperor Constantius visited the Forum in 357, the historian Ammianus Marcellinus described how 'the emperor stood transfixed with astonishment, surveying the gigantic fabric around him. ... Its grandeur defies description and can never again be approached by mortal men'. At its heart stood, then as now, a 30-metre column with reliefs showing the Dacian campaign. Yet there was a practical side to Trajan, and he appreciated that vast buildings did not in themselves provide for the needs of Rome's citizens. So, even before he had built the Forum, Trajan had constructed his great market complex, 150 shops on three levels in the hillside, to the east of the existing Fora; had created a canal to stop the Tiber flooding; and rebuilt the port of Ostia.

In his later years Trajan headed east. There had been peace with the Parthian empire for 150 years, but the emperor may have feared revived enmity (or, as ancient sources suggest, he may have been searching for even greater glorification). There were more astonishing victories and Trajan marched through Mesopotamia, adding it as a province of the empire before arriving at the Persian Gulf in 116. Here news of revolts behind him forced him to give up and he died the next year, always regretful that he had not equalled the conquests of Alexander. His popularity back in Rome remained intact and in later years the senate used to greet a new emperor with the words 'May you be even luckier than Augustus and even better than Trajan'.   C.F.

IMPERIAL FORA
(RECONSTRUCTION OF THE SITE)

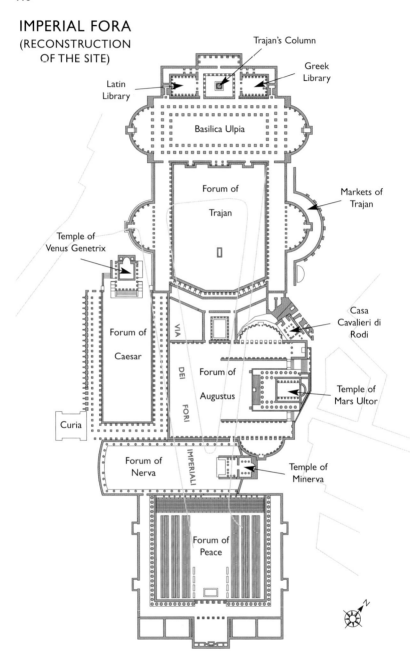

Trajan's Column

Greek Library

Latin Library

Basilica Ulpia

Forum of Trajan

Markets of Trajan

Temple of Venus Genetrix

Casa Cavalieri di Rodi

Forum of Caesar

VIA

Forum of Augustus

Temple of Mars Ultor

DEI

Curia

FORI

Forum of Nerva

IMPERIALI

Temple of Minerva

Forum of Peace

N

Other parts of the very well-preserved markets are not at present visible while major work is in progress to convert them into a museum illustrating the history of the Imperial Fora. These include a rectangular hall of two storeys, with six shops on each floor, with an upper storey with a large covered hall which may have served as a bazaar, and the ancient paved road, the Via Biberatica, which passed in front of the markets.

Behind the markets the crenellated summit of the **Torre delle Milizie** (*closed for many years*) can be seen. Thought to date from the mid-13th century and still a conspicuous feature in the skyline of Rome since it is one of the highest buildings in the centre of the city, it was on the edge of this part of the medieval city and so would have been visible from miles around. It acquired its lean after an earthquake in 1348 and may have belonged to the Conti, the same family who owned the other even earlier tower in this district (*see p. 124*)—they are among the most important civic medieval buildings to have survived in the city. In 1914 the Torre delle Milizie was restored and isolated from the convent of Santa Caterina by Antonio Muñoz, an architect who showed great skill in restoration projects in the city at this time (best known for the work he carried out on the church of Santa Sabina; *see p. 328*). It originally had three storeys: two of these survive.

FORUM OF AUGUSTUS

Adjoining the Forum of Trajan is the Forum of Augustus, built to commemorate the victory of Philippi (42 BC). It was dedicated to Mars Ultor (the 'Avenger'; at the battle Caesar's assassins, Cassius and Brutus, were defeated). It can be seen from the raised walkways which cross Trajan's Forum and pass right in front of the Temple of Mars Ultor, providing an excellent view of it. The Forum of Augustus itself is still being excavated and is partly covered by Via dei Fori Imperiali.

Temple of Mars Ultor

The forum was dominated by the octastyle Temple of Mars Ultor, which has columns on three sides, dedicated in 2 BC when Augustus was named '*Pater Patriae*'. It had a large pronaos and an apsidal cella. Three tall fluted columns with Corinthian capitals supporting an architrave, at the end of the right flank, are still standing. A broad flight of very high steps ascends to the capacious pronaos where four of the eight Corinthian columns in front (the two middle and the two end ones) have been partly reconstructed from antique fragments. The effect of undue width in the cella was lessened by a colonnade on either side, and here are stepped bases of statues (probably of Mars, Venus and the *Divus Julius*). Behind is the curve of the large apse.

This was one of the most honoured temples throughout the Empire, and as a centre of solemn ceremonies and the Imperial sanctuary, it became a museum of art and housed miscellaneous relics, including the sword of Julius Caesar. Also kept here were the Roman standards which had been lost to the Parthians in a war in 54 BC in which Crassus and his son died and the Roman army suffered a humiliating defeat. Caesar

The Emperor Augustus (ruled 27 BC–AD 14)

Octavian, known to history by his title *Augustus*, 'the revered one', was one of the most remarkable figures in Roman history and certainly the most influential. Emerging as the adopted son of Julius Caesar, he exploited his position ruthlessly as the Republic collapsed after Caesar's assassination. He cooperated at first with Mark Antony but the rivalry between them soon turned to open conflict. Mark Antony, who had taken command of the empire in the east, allowed himself to become entangled with the ever-opportunistic Cleopatra, and this enabled Octavian to brand them both as enemies of Rome. In 31 BC at the Battle of Actium their navy was routed and both committed suicide in Egypt.

Back in Rome, now enriched with the wealth of Egypt and backed by a large army, Octavian could easily have become a dictator. However, that was not his way. Despite the ruthlessness of his youth, he now showed himself to be measured and balanced. His favourite god Apollo was, after all, the god of reason. Knowing that the senate was desperate for respect and peace, he disbanded his army and let the senate acquiesce in his growing influence. His title, *Augustus*, was awarded him in 27 BC and he gradually absorbed other ancient republican titles too, as if the old political system were still intact. Behind this façade he was spending his booty fast. He claimed to have restored no fewer than 82 temples in Rome. He completed the Forum of Caesar and then embarked on a massive one of his own, centred on a temple to Mars Ultor: Mars as the avenger of his adoptive father's murder. Statues of the heroes of Rome's past lined the porticoes and led up to a great bronze of himself in a four-horse chariot. Other statues played on ancient traditions: Augustus appears as military commander, youthful hero or veiled priest as circumstances dictated. They were distributed throughout the empire—one estimate is that there were originally between 30,000 and 50,000 in total. One notable legacy of Augustus in Rome is the large number of obelisks, which he brought back from Egypt. By the time his projects were complete, he could rightly boast that he had made Rome into a city of marble.

The empire prospered under Augustus' steady control: poets such as Virgil and Horace praised his rule and there was no challenge to his growing influence. Further recognition of his success came in in 9 BC when the senate dedicated the *Ara Pacis*, the Altar of Peace, to him after he had returned from campaigns in Spain and Gaul. (In its reconstructed form it stands close to a massive mausoleum Augustus had created for himself and his family in 28 BC.) In 2 BC he was granted the honorary title *Pater Patriae*, father of the fatherland, an honour which left him deeply moved. Still his reign continued, although by now Augustus was ailing. He died in AD 14, and it was observed at his cremation that his body had been seen ascending through the smoke towards heaven. The senate forthwith decreed that he should be ranked as a god. By now the Republic had been irrevocably transformed into an empire, and emperors ruled it for the rest of its history.   C.F.

had planned to lead a campaign to Parthia (accompanied by Octavian; Augustus' name before he became emperor) in 44 BC just before his murder, but it was not until 24 years later that Augustus achieved their surrender, signifying a temporary reconciliation with the Parthians and the establishment of a Roman protectorate in what is now Iran. However, they remained a continuous threat to the stability of the Roman empire and numerous campaigns were organized against them by Trajan, Marcus Aurelius and Septimius Severus' sons: their well-organized army (with its formidable horsemen) was in effect the only one able to offer serious resistance to the empire up until the 3rd century, before the Parthian empire fell to the Sasanids, and the Persians took over as Rome's arch enemies.

The high wall behind, some 30m high and still partly standing, was built to isolate the Forum of Augustus from the Subura, which was a crowded, insalubrious residential district of ancient Rome. On the ground between the surviving columns of the temple and the right-hand portico are numerous interesting architectural fragments (others are preserved in the Casa dei Cavalieri di Rodi; *see p. 545*).

The temple was surrounded by a portico raised on three steps (as in Caesar's Forum) which enclosed a large piazza in the centre of which there was a statue of Augustus in a triumphal chariot. On either side of the temple the three marble steps survive which led up to the porticoes where there were rectangular niches (the remains of some of which can still be seen) decorated by Augustus with statues of his ancestors (members of the Julian clan) and Roman heroes from Aeneas to Republican days. The left portico has an extension at the north end where you can still see part of a large hall which was big enough to contain a colossal statue of Augustus (probably some 12m high): the base remains (and it has the sriking imprint of one of its huge feet, although this, and the beautiful pavement made from different coloured marbles, cannot be seen from this distance away). It has been discovered that the white marble slabs which decorated the walls were painted with bright blue and red festoons.

Large semicircular apses (or exedrae) decorated the exteriors of the two porticoes but these were almost completely destroyed during the Renaissance for their marble. The southwestern area of the Forum, where there must have been two more exedrae—which scholars now think could have belonged to a covered basilica—has not yet been fully exposed and excavations continue.

FORUM OF CAESAR

On the other side of Via dei Fori Imperiali, near the Vittorio Emanuele II monument, the steep Via di San Pietro in Carcere diverges right to climb above the Mamertine Prison (*described below*) to the Capitoline. Here, well beneath the level of the road, the remains of part of the Forum of Caesar, which was the first of the Imperial Fora, can be seen. Recent excavations have shown that Caesar created an entrance to it from the Roman Forum (behind the Curia building; *see p. 69*). The forum was completed by Augustus.

Temple of Venus Genetrix

The focal point of the new Forum was the Temple of Venus Genetrix, the most important building erected in the city by Julius Caesar, who claimed descent from the goddess. 'Genetrix' was not one of the Venus' known manifestations; instead it was an attribute given by Caesar designating her as the one who gave birth to his family (although it has also been suggested that Caesar intended a double meaning with the epithet, wanting also to claim Venus as the mother of the Roman people as a whole). The temple's high base remains (although it has lost its marble facing) and on top of it three of its fluted Corinthian columns have been re-erected. The temple was dedicated in 46 BC, two years after Caesar's decisive defeat of Pompey at the battle of Pharsalus (after which Pompey fled from Thessaly to Egypt where he was stabbed to death on his arrival). In front of the temple stood an equestrian statue of Caesar. Works of art by well-known contemporary artists including a statue of the goddess by Arcesilaus (his best-known sculpture), and two pictures of Ajax and of Medea by Timomachus of Byzantium were exhibited inside. Next to a statue of Julius Caesar stood a gilded bronze statue of Cleopatra, who had lived in Rome for a while with Caesar, as his mistress and mother of his son, at the time when the temple was dedicated. It is thought that Augustus plundered the statue in Egypt after his famous defeat of Antony and Cleopatra at Actium, and erected it here as a spoil of war.

Cassius Dio, who was twice consul under Commodus and Alexander Severus, and wrote a history of Rome from the earliest times up until his own day (2nd century AD), vividly imagined the scene at the dedication of the temple by Caesar: '...when the people had finished dinner, Caesar entered his Forum shod with slippers and garlanded with flowers of all kinds. From there he continued home, escorted by almost the whole population, and by elephants bearing torches'. Cassius goes on to state categorically that this Forum was more beautiful than the Roman Forum.

The Forum itself was an open piazza which was surrounded on three sides by two rows of columns raised on three steps and paved in white marble. Well below the level of the temple the three steps of the southwestern colonnade can clearly be seen, and most of the columns are still standing. Behind them are remains of *tabernae*, or shops, on two floors. Trajan rebuilt the temple and Forum and added the Basilica Argentaria, or exchange building, as well as a large heated public lavatory (*forica*), remains of which survive above the shops. Recent excavations, which are still in progress, have also revealed various strata of a medieval district of the city built above the ancient ruins.

Mamertine Prison

From Via di San Pietro in Carcere (*marked on the plan on p. 64*), a well preserved stretch of the Clivus Argentarius, the Roman road which ran between the Capitoline and the Quirinal hills, is still open to pedestrians. Lined with the remains of shops where the money-lenders of the ancient city congregated, and a nymphaeum dating from the time of Trajan, it descends to the dark little church of San Giuseppe dei Falegnami, built in 1598 above the Carcere Mamertino or the **Mamertine Prison** (*open 9–5*). Known as the *Tullianum*, this is thought originally to have been a cistern, like those at Tusculum and other Etruscan cities. On the lower level the form of a round building that may have had a tholos, or conical dome, which could date it as early as the 6th century BC, can be seen. A spring still exists in the floor. In Roman times the building was used as a dungeon for criminals and captives awaiting execution. According to Christian tradition, St Peter and St Paul were also imprisoned here, and even if in the Middle Ages the building was consecrated as San Pietro in Carcere, it has for centuries retained its grim memories as the most ancient prison in the city. The Gemonian Steps close by were also associated with death, about which stories abounded of people being flung down them, or corpses being exhibited for ridicule.

Opposite is the handsome church of **Santi Luca e Martina** (*usually closed*), probably founded in the 7th century by Honorius I. It was rebuilt in 1640 by the painter and architect Pietro da Cortona (*see p. 223*), who is buried here, and it is considered his early masterpiece, partly on a centralized Greek-cross plan, although the two storeys, the upper dedicated to St Luke and the lower to St Martina, have an original and complex design. The façade, built of travertine, and the dome are particularly fine. In the upper church there is a marble statue of Martina, the little-known titular saint, said to have been martyred under Alexander Severus in 228. This was made in 1635 by a minor sculptor, Niccolò Menghini, the year after a sarcophagus thought to contain her remains was found near here in the Roman Forum. The lower church is reached by a staircase to the left of the high altar. Here there is a tabernacle by Pietro da Cortona, and the side chapel, with a pretty scallop motif, has a fine terracotta group of three saints by Alessandro Algardi (who also carved the bas-relief of the *Deposition* in the vestibule).

FORUM OF NERVA

A terrace adjoining the Forum of Caesar provides a fine view of the extensive area of new excavations in the southwestern part of the Forum of Nerva: the view from here is dominated by the rear of the Curia building in the Roman Forum and the church of Santi Luca e Martina. Begun by Domitian, this Forum was completed after his assassination by his successor Nerva in AD 97, during a very brief rule of less than two years marked by enlightened and humanitarian government. It was also called the *Forum Transitorium* because it led into Vespasian's earlier Temple of Peace and was traversed by the Argiletum, the street that led from the Roman Forum to the Subura district (*see p. 72*). From the terrace can be seen the large marble slabs which provided the paving of the Forum and part of the Cloaca Maxima drain (*see p. 77*). The excavations carried out in 1991–97 have revealed clear evidence of the various uses of this land over the centuries: traces of Republican houses destroyed in the fire of AD 64 have been found here, as well as medieval and 16th-century dwellings. A sewage conduit laid in the 15th century was also discovered, and this has been restored and now serves to connect the new excavations with those done in the 1930s on the other side of Via dei Fori Imperiali, adjoining the Forum of Augustus. This includes the massive basement of the **Temple of Minerva**, which rose in the centre of the Forum and was still standing at the beginning of the 17th century, when it was pulled down by Paul V to provide marble for the fountain of the Acqua Paola on the Janiculum.

Beside the railing on the other side of Via dei Fori Imperiali are two enormous Corinthian columns in purple and white marble, which have survived over the centuries from the colonnade on the northeast side of the temple, and have always been known affectionately by the Romans as the *Colonnacce*. In the attic between the columns is a **high-relief of Minerva**, after an original of the school of Skopas. In the rich frieze of the entablature Minerva (Athena) is seen teaching the arts of sewing and weaving and punishing Arachne, the Lydian girl who excelled at weaving and dared to challenge the goddess. In front of the Colonnacce is another section of the Argiletum, which was repaved in the 9th century when it was still one of the busiest roads in the city. Near here is the base of the massive Torre dei Conti, all that remains of a great tower erected above one of the exedrae of the Temple of Peace probably after 1198 by Riccardo dei Conti, brother of Innocent III, as part of a fortified residence. It was damaged by an earthquake in 1348 and reduced to its present state by Urban VIII in the 17th century. It is to be restored as a museum.

FORUM (TEMPLE) OF PEACE

To the east of the Forum of Nerva extended the Temple of Peace, also called the Forum of Peace or Forum of Vespasian, built with the spoils of the Jewish War by Vespasian and inaugurated in AD 75 to commemorate peace at the end of the civil wars which followed the death of Nero. Until excavations were begun here in the 1990s little was known of the plan of this area. So far the central portion and part of the western corner have been uncovered, but since excavations are still in progress it is at present very difficult to get a clear picture. During the Republican era there was a large food market (*macellum*) on this site, which was destroyed in the fire of 64 AD. The temple was preceded by a large piazza which it now seems was really a garden decorated with six low brick walls, on the top of which water constantly flowed along marble channels, beside which over 30 flower-pots have been found which apparently contained 'Gallic' roses. On three sides of the piazza there was a portico above marble steps (part of the one at the southwest side can be seen), and these were decorated on two sides with quadrangular exedrae (one of which is preserved beneath the Torre dei Conti). A rectangular hall flanking the temple, probably a library used to house the city plans and public property registers, had one of its walls decorated with the *Forma Urbis*, a famous plan of the ancient city commissioned by Septimius Severus between 205 and 208. It was carved in some 150 marble blocks which made up a detailed map (showing public buildings, streets, etc all marked with their names) about 18m by 13m in overall size, today considered the most important document for our knowledge of the topography of the Roman city. The first fragments of it were found here in 1562, and another 24 pieces were unearthed in 1999. Though the most important pieces are not on pubic display, a part of it can be seen in the Crypta Balbi (*see p. 134*).

SANTI COSMA E DAMIANO

Map p. 623, 3D

Usually open 9–12 & 4–6.

This large hall, probably once a library, was converted in 527 by St Felix IV into the church of **Santi Cosma e Damiano**, dedicated to two brothers from Cilicia who were miraculous healers (they are now the patron saints of doctors). The beautiful mosaics commissioned by St Felix survive on the triumphal arch and in the apse and include the saint himself holding a model of his church. The splendid mosaics inspired other such decoration in early Christian churches in Rome, especially in the 9th century. The detail is astonishing, and the style of expression more personal than the static mosaics of the later Byzantine tradition. On the triumphal arch is the *Lamb Enthroned*, surrounded by seven candlesticks, four angels and the symbols of two Evangelists. In the apse are St Cosmas and St Damian being presented to Christ at His Second Coming by St Peter and St Paul; St Theodore (on the right); and St Felix IV (on the left, restored). There are also mosaics of palms (symbols of life and of victory over death) and the phoenix (symbol of the Resurrection). Below the word *Iordanes* is the Lamb on a mount from which four rivers, symbolizing the Gospels, flow; 12 other lambs represent the Apostles, with Bethlehem and Jerusalem on either side.

At the west end a huge window was installed in 2000 to provide a view of a remarkably well preserved circular Roman temple, the so-called Temple of Romulus in the Roman Forum (*see p. 81*), which served as a vestibule to the church up until the end of the 19th century. The original bronze doors can also be seen.

The church was rebuilt in 1632, when the pavement was added to make it a two-storeyed building, and the frescoes and painted altarpieces mostly date from that time. On the Baroque high altar is a 13th-century *Madonna and Child*, and in the first chapel in the right aisle is an unusual fresco of Christ on the Cross wearing a crown, which may also date from the 13th century. It seems to be derived from the *Volto Santo* in Lucca, (an ancient wooden likeness of Christ which is still a famous devotional image), and was probably repainted in the 17th century by an artist from that Tuscan city.

In a domed Roman vestibule off the early-17th century cloister, decorated with a fountain and palm trees, is part of an 18th-century Neapolitan *presepio* (crib). The models and figures in wood, terracotta and porcelain are of exceptionally fine workmanship.

SANTA MARIA NOVA

Map p. 623, 3D

Open 9.30–12.30 & 3 or 3.30–5 or 7.

Adjoining the Basilica of Maxentius, and reached by a flight of steps from Via dei Fori Imperiali, or by a short road from Piazza del Colosseo, is the church of Santa Maria Nova or Santa Francesca Romana. It stands on the summit of the Velia and encroaches on the Temple of Venus and Roma (*see p. 103*); a fine stretch of ancient Roman road

is conspicuous on the approach to the west door. The church incorporates an Oratory of St Peter and St Paul built by Paul I (757–67) in the west portico of the Temple of Venus and Roma. In 847, after grave structural damage to the church of Santa Maria Antiqua in the Roman Forum, that church was abandoned and the diaconate was transferred to the oratory, which became Santa Maria Nova. The church was enlarged and the apse mosaic and campanile added before it was consecrated anew in 1161. The façade, designed by Carlo Lombardi, was added during his reconstruction in 1615.

St Francesca Romana (1384–1440)—Francesca Buzzi, wife of Lorenzo Ponziani—founded the Congregation of Oblates here in 1421, and joined it herself after her husband's death in 1436. Canonized in 1608, she is the patron saint of motorists, and on her festival (9th March) the street between the church and the Colosseum is congested with cars lining up for a blessing. The painter Gentile da Fabriano was buried in the church in 1428. The former conventual buildings now contain the excavation offices and Antiquarium of the Roman Forum.

There is a restored Cosmatesque pavement in the raised east end. In the vestibule of the side entrance (right) are the tombs of Cardinal Marino Bulcani (d. 1394) and of Antonio da Rio (or Rido), castellan of Castel Sant'Angelo (c. 1450). In the south transept are the tomb of Gregory XI by Pier Paolo Olivieri, set up in 1585 by the Roman people in honour of the pope who had restored the seat of the papacy to Rome from Avignon in 1377. Let into the south wall behind grilles are two flagstones from the Sacra Via which supposedly show the imprint of the knees of St Peter, made as the saint knelt to pray for the punishment of Simon Magus, who was demonstrating his wizardry by flying. The legendary site of Simon's consequent fall is in the neighbourhood. From here stairs lead down to the crypt with the body of St Francesca Romana, and a 17th-century bas-relief of her with an angel. The confessio, an early work by Bernini, has a marble group of the same subject (1866).

In the apse are beautiful mosaics of the *Madonna and Saints* (probably completed in 1161), and on either side, statues of angels of the school of Bernini. Above the altar is a 12th-century *Madonna and Child*, detached in 1950 from another painting found beneath it. The earlier painting, a very large and beautifully-painted *Virgin and Child*, which may have come from Santa Maria Antiqua, is now kept in the sacristy (*for admission, ring at the convent outside, no. 4*). Probably dating from the end of the 6th century (it was already described as 'an ancient image' by the middle of the 8th), it is one of the most ancient Christian paintings in existence. It belongs to the type known as *Glykophilousa*, from the Greek for 'sweet love', and shows the Madonna embracing the Child with her arm, as the Child reaches up to caress her face. Also here are fragments of medieval frescoes, and early 16th-century paintings (attributed to Perino del Vaga) of Paul III and Reginald Pole, whom the pope made cardinal after his refusal to condone Henry VIII's divorce.

Christ at His Second Coming, in the apse of Santi Cosma e Damiano, depicted with beard and scroll, echoing earlier, Classical philosopher/orator models.

Museo del Risorgimento

Open 9.30–5.30; T: 06 6780664; www.risorgimento.it. Entrance in Via di San Pietro in Carcere (on the left of the monument as you face it).
The agitated period of the Risorgimento, literally the 'resurgence', the political renaissance of Italy, shared with much of the rest of Europe the ideals of liberty and independence, to be achieved through revolution. While the military leader Giuseppe Garibaldi was the most famous and charismatic supporter of the cause, Camillo Cavour was the prime mover of Italian political autonomy and a republic was proclaimed by an elected assembly in Rome under the guidance of Giuseppe Mazzini. This museum was founded in 1906 but not opened until the 1970s. It was reopened in 2000 and is very well arranged (with explanations also in English) to illustrate the Risorgimento itself, as well as the First World War, after which Italy made substantial territorial gains from Austria-Hungary (notably the South Tyrol). Stairs, hung with prints, lead up past a small theatre where fascinating early films (*Film Luce*) of the First World War are shown. Up more stairs is a grand rectangular room with mementoes of Garibaldi, Mazzini and Cavour. In the long curving corridor, with busts of war heroes, are various well-labelled sections on moments of historic significance in Italian history from 1848 onwards. The second rectangular room at the other end of the corridor is devoted to the First World War. Exhibitions are often held in other parts of the building.

PALAZZO DI VENEZIA
Map p. 622, 2C

Across Piazza Venezia is the battlemented Palazzo di Venezia, the first great Renaissance palace in Rome. The famous architects Giuliano da Maiano, Bernardo Rossellino and Leon Battista Alberti have all been suggested as its architect, but it has recently been attributed to the little-known Francesco del Borgo. The palace was begun in 1455, enlarged in 1464 and finally finished in the 16th century. It was built, partly of stone from the Colosseum, for the Venetian cardinal Pietro Barbo, afterwards Paul II (1464–71), the first of the great High Renaissance popes. Barbo is said to have built the palace in order to view the horse races in the Corso. He used it as a papal residence and rebuilt the church of San Marco here, providing it with a loggia for papal benedictions. The palace was often occupied as such even after Pius IV (1559–65) gave it to the Venetian Republic for its embassy. Charles VIII of France stayed here after entering Rome with 20,000 soldiers in 1494. From 1797 (when Venice was ceded to Austria by Napoleon) until 1915 it was the seat of the Austrian ambassador to the Vatican. In 1917 Italy resumed possession and the palace was restored. During the Fascist regime it was occupied by Mussolini, who made the Sala del Mappamondo his office. Some of his most famous speeches were made from the balcony overlooking Piazza Venezia.

The door on Piazza Venezia is finely carved and attributed to Giuliano da Maiano. The picturesque inner courtyard (*together with the garden it can usually be visited on Sat and*

Sun at 11.30), with its tall palm trees, has a large, unfinished 15th-century loggia on two sides, of beautiful proportions. The fountain dates from 1730.

Adjoining the palace and facing the Via and Piazza di San Marco is the Palazzetto di Venezia (c. 1467). This was originally in Piazza Venezia, but was moved to its present position in 1911 because it obstructed the view of the Vittorio Emanuele II monument.

Museo del Palazzo di Venezia

Open 9–7; closed Mon; T: 06 6999 4318. The State Rooms are open only for exhibitions. Entrance in Via del Plebiscito (ticket office on the first floor).

The Museo del Palazzo di Venezia is the city's museum of decorative arts, with ivories, majolica, church silver and terracottas, as well as paintings, wood sculptures and bronzes, but it is one of the least visited musuems in the city. It occupies several of the papal apartments in Palazzo di Venezia, and many rooms in the Palazzetto di Venezia.

First Floor

A monumental staircase by Luigi Marangoni (1930) leads to the first floor. Here is the loggia with early medieval architectural fragments, off which there is a room which displays a sculptured female head of Nike, thought to be an original Greek work dating from the late 5th century BC. To the left is the Appartamento Cibo, the residence of the Cardinals of San Marco, with some good ceilings and colourful floors, where mostly 15th- and 16th-century paintings (including the Sterbini collection) are arranged by Italian regional schools (the Veneto, Emilia Romagna, Lazio, Umbria and the Marche).

Room 1: Highlights include an exquisite early 14th-century diptych by an artist named from this work, the Maestro del Dittico Sterbini, and a double portrait attributed to Giorgione.

Room 3: Two fine wood statues of the Magi, from the Marche, date from the 14th century. The painted Crucifix and fragment of the *Head of the Redeemer* are both by 13th-century artists working in Rome. The *Madonna of Acuto* (a little town in southern Lazio), an early 13th-century wood polychrome seated statue, is the earliest known work of its kind.

Rooms 4 and 5: 14th- and 15th-century paintings by artists of the Tuscan school include a fresco fragment of the *Head of the Redeemer* by Benozzo Gozzoli.

Room 6: 17th- and 18th-century works and a bust of Innocent X by Alessandro Algardi (in terracotta, but skilfully painted white to look like marble), and a gilded terracotta group of the *Baptism of Christ*, also by Algardi (acquired in 2004).

Room 7 (Salone Altoviti): The ceiling *grottesche* are attributed to Vasari.

Room 8: Here are displayed charming pastel portraits (17th–19th centuries).

Room 11: This is the long corridor, which connects these apartments to the Palazzetto di Venezia. It has a splendid view of the delightful courtyard. A representative collection of Italian ceramics with examples from all the main work-

Rooms 9–11: Here are shown architectural fragments found on the site including a very fine huge Corinthian capital, probably once part of the theatre, and a model of the site. Part of the wall of the Roman cryptoporticus can be seen in the last room.

Second Floor

The sections on the second floor, mostly in a large hall with a fine wood roof, illustrate the general history of Rome in the Middle Ages (from the 5th–10th centuries).

Room 1: Divided into two sections, the room displays household objects, including cutlery and kitchen utensils from various sites in the city, 4th–6th-century jewellery, some 6th-century ceramics found recently in the House of the Vestals in the Roman Forum, oil lamps, glass, and coins. In the second section are finds from tombs in the city from the 5th–8th centuries.

Room 2: The display is devoted to the Byzantine period, with 7th-century lead seals found on this site, ceramics, tools, jewellery, and lamps.

Room 3: Interesting 7th–9th-century frescoes detached from a building below the church of Santa Maria in Via Lata (*see p. 151*) on the Corso.

Room 4: Exhibits here are related to papal Rome from the 8th century onwards. These include commemorative inscriptions, 8th- and 9th-century architectural fragments from Roman churches, and pilgrims' phials (made out of lead, terracotta or glass). These phials were sold at sacred shrines and contained the oil which was used to illuminate holy relics and which was considered to have miraculous powers. The last part of the hall is devoted to the economic life of the city in the Middle Ages, with coins, and a rare (reconstructed) bishop's throne dating from the 9th century, decorated in incised bone, found on this site.

Room 5: On the platform above are medieval finds from the area of the Imperial Fora and Roman Forum, which prove these areas were still densely inhabited in medieval times.

The (rather uninteresting) Roman remains below ground level are shown by a custodian. Excavations continue on this site, and so far the exedra in the centre of the Balbi cryptoporticus and a Mithraeum (*for the cult of Mithras, see p. 515*) have been identified.

GALLERIA DORIA PAMPHILJ
& GALLERIA COLONNA

These two collections represent the most important private collections in Rome open to the public. They are housed in the families' sumptuous palaces, which are still their residences and are beautifully kept. The power of both the Doria Pamphilj and Colonna families was enhanced when two of their members became pope (respectively Innocent X and Martin V). In the 18th century Olimpia Pamphilj married Filippo II Colonna.

GALLERIA DORIA PAMPHILJ
Map p. 622, 2C

Open 10–5; closed Thur. T: 06 679 7323.

The huge Palazzo Doria Pamphilj on the Corso has been the residence since the 17th century of the Doria Pamphilj, a famous Roman noble family. The palace contains the Galleria Doria Pamphilj, the most important of the patrician art collections to have survived in the city. The period rooms, richly decorated in white, red and gold, and beautifully maintained, provide a sumptuous setting for the fine paintings.

The palace, which was first built in 1435, has a façade on the Corso by Gabriele Valvassori (1731–34), who is known exclusively for the work he carried out for the Doria Pamphilj family, both here (also inside the palace) and in the church of Sant'Agnese in Agone. Built at a time when Roman architecture tended towards a Classical style, it shows the influence of European art and is usually considered the finest and most balanced Rococo work in the city.

The north façade, which faces onto Piazza del Collegio Romano (now the visitors' entrance) and has two handsome wings, is earlier (by Antonio del Grande, 1663).

There is a delightful little tea room with a fountain on the ground floor. There is no heating in winter so it can be extremely cold. The beautifully kept rooms, with sumptuous decorations and creaky parquet floors, retain an unforgettable old-world atmosphere of grand living and elegance, maintained by the exceptionally courteous uniformed staff.

The Doria Pamphilj Collection

The collection was initiated in 1651 by the Pamphilj pope Innocent X, who decreed that the pictures and furnishings in Palazzo Pamphilj in Piazza Navona were to be inherited by his nephew Camillo, son of the pope's acquisitive sister-in-law Olimpia Maidalchini. Important additions were made to these works of art when Camillo married Olimpia Aldobrandini, widow of Paolo Borghese. In 1760 Prince Andrea (IV) Doria added his family bequests, and the present arrangement follows that of his time. The collection has been protected by the state since 1816.

Detail of the portrait of the Pamphilj pope Innocent X, by Velázquez (1650).

Sala del Poussin: The walls are covered with 17th-century landscapes by Gaspard Dughet, brother-in-law of Nicolas Poussin (*see p. 167*) and often known as 'Il Poussin'.

Sala dei Velluti: Named after its late 18th-century red velvet wall-hangings, the room contains two fine **busts by Alessandro Algardi** of Innocent X and Benedetto Pamphilj.

Sala da Ballo: With the adjacent smaller ballroom, this was decorated at the end of the 19th century with silk hangings. The smaller room has an 18th-century ceiling fresco of *Venus and Aeneas*, and a Gobelins tapestry woven for Louis XIV from a 16th-century Flemish design, representing the month of May. The **family chapel**, the dimensions of which give it the appearance of a small church, was designed by Carlo Fontana (1691) and the altar of rare marbles and the ivory crucifix by Ercole Ferrata date from the same century. Alterations were made to Fontana's work in the 18th and 19th centuries.

The Galleria: Hung with paintings arranged around four sides of a courtyard, it was redesigned by Valvassori in 1731–34. This was where the family would stroll with their guests to show off their most precious possessions.

First Gallery: On the left wall are a number of works by Annibale Carracci, a famous member of the Bolognese school of painters who came to work in Rome in 1595. His very fine *Flight into Egypt* (i5) shows a new Classical concept of landscape painting. His work

was to have a great influence on **Claude Lorrain**, born in France but who worked all his life in Rome, where he was considered one of the finest painters of his time, and worked with Poussin and Dughet, before his death in the city in 1682. He too is represented here with several landscapes, including *Mercury stealing the Oxen of Apollo* (i21), one of the most lyrical of his typical idealized scenes. There are a number of works also by 16th-century painters (Garofalo, Lodovico Cigoli, Paris Bordone, and Carlo Saraceni). On the window wall is a work by the Netherlandish painter **Quinten Massys**, born in 1465. Entitled *The Userers* (i47), this is one of several satirical genre scenes by this artist who, influenced by Erasmus, was intent on laying bare the negative qualities of his avaricious and acquisitive contemporaries. The *Portrait of Agatha van Schoonhoven* (i63) by another Netherlander, Jan van Scorel, shows how the artist combined the qualities of his native school of painting with those of the great Venetian masters. It was painted in 1529 and van Scorel is known to have been in Rome earlier in the same decade.

Second Gallery (Galleria degli Specchi): This is the loveliest part of Valvassori's design, resplendent with gilded mirrors. In the Cabinet is the superb *Portrait of Innocent X*—the gem of the collection—commissioned by that pope in 1650 from the great Spanish painter Velázquez. It was painted during Velázquez' second stay in Rome, and is among his most powerful portraits. Displayed beside it is a sculpted bust of the same pope by **Bernini**. The gallery is lined with Roman statues on a small scale chosen to fit their setting. The portrait of Joan of Aragon, who was a Colonna princess, is a copy of a painting by Raphael.

GALLERIA DORIA PAMPHILJ

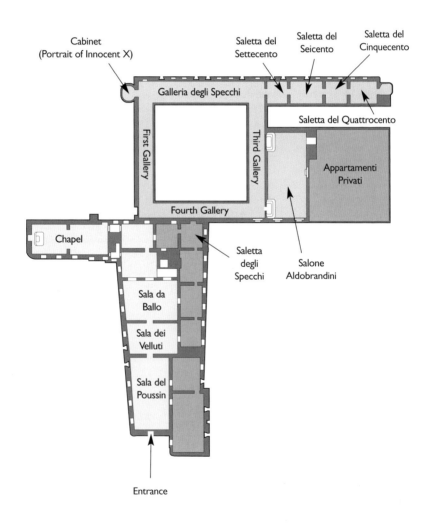

At the end of the Galleria degli Specchi is a series of four rooms overlooking the Corso with prettily decorated ceilings. Works grouped according to period (but in reverse chronological order) are exhibited here.

Saletta del Settecento: Displayed here are Italian views by Netherlandish painters of the early 18th century.

Saletta del Seicento: The room contains two early **masterpieces by Caravaggio**. *The Rest on the Flight into Egypt* is a tender work with charming naturalistic details, the scene dominated by the incredibly graceful figure of a young angel playing the Child to sleep, providing a totally innovative element in the iconography for this famous biblical scene which was much favoured by painters. The *Penitent Magdalene* (*illustrated overleaf*) shows the desolate figure of the saint (for which Caravaggio used the same model as for the Madonna in the other painting) abandoned in a bare 'room'. The iconography for this painting is also entirely new, and indeed it is only the exquisitely-painted flask of oil on the floor (her customary attribute) which suggests this is intended to portray the Magdalene.

Saletta del Cinquecento: Here are two very fine paintings: a double portrait by **Raphael** and *Salome with the head of St John the Baptist* by **Titian**, and other works by masters of the Veneto school.

Saletta del Quattrocento: The room contains 15th-century works by the Ferrarese painter Lodovico Mazzolino (including his *Massacre of the Innocents*) and by Antoniazzo Romano, Garofalo, Gian Battista Benvenuti Ortolano, and Bernardino Parentino. There is also another satirical genre work by Massys, entitled *The Hypocrites*, and a *Deposition*, one of the best works painted at the height of his career, by the famous Flemish painter **Hans Memling**. At the end is a little cabinet with three busts—portraits of Filippo Andrea V Doria, his wife Mary Talbot, and her sister.

Third gallery: On the left wall, *The Triumph of Virtue* (q2), an unfinished sketch for the painting now in the Louvre, is a good work by Correggio. There are more works by Claude Lorrain and Garofalo, both painters well represented in the gallery; a *Madonna* (q19) by Guido Reni; and two works (*The Return of the Prodigal Son*; q13 and *St John the Baptist in the Desert*; q23) by Guercino, who succeeded Reni as the most important painter of the Bolognese school in the mid-17th century. The scene of a battle in the Port of Naples (q21) was painted by **Pieter Brueghel the Elder** the year before he visited Rome in 1553. Also here are two paintings by Sassoferrato. On the window wall are *Madonna and Child with St John the Baptist* (q46) by Giovanni Bellini and his *bottega*; landscapes by Paul Bril; scenes from the Old Testament by the Bassano family; and works by Garofalo, Guercino, Boccaccio Boccaccino, Jan Frans van Bloemen, and Federico Barocci (*Study of a Head*; q66).

Fourth gallery: The bust of Olimpia Aldobrandini Pamphilj is by Algardi. Here are three works by **Jan Brueghel**

of the portly cardinal Girolamo I Colonna, and three works by Guercino, which the cardinal purchased for the collection.

Throne Room: The pope of the day would be received by the family in this room. As in other princely houses the chair is turned to the wall so that no one else can sit in it. Here are the three Colonna portraits: *Martin V, Oddone Colonna* (144), a copy from a work by Pisanello; *Marcantonio II Colonna* by Scipione Pulzone (149); and *Felice Colonna Orsini* (150), thought to be a copy of a work by Pulzone. The nautical chart was presented by the Roman people to Marcantonio II and the parchment diploma given him by the Roman senate after the Battle of Lepanto.

Room of Maria Mancini or **Room of the Primitives:** On the entrance wall is a *Resurrection of Christ* by **Pietro da Cortona** (143), with no fewer than five members of the Colonna family being helped out of their tombs by angels in order to follow the Saviour to heaven. Opposite the window is the *Madonna and Child Enthroned with Angels* (179), a very elegant work in the International Gothic style by **Stefano da Zevio** (one of the most delightful paintings in the collection). The fine portrait of a young man in profile, traditionally identified as Guidobaldo della Rovere, Duke of Urbino, is attributed to Rocco Zoppo (who worked closely with the more famous Umbrian painter Perugino). There are also Madonnas by Giuliano Bugiardini (35), Bernardino Luini (107)

and Bartolomeo Vivarini (198), and a *Crucifixion* (10), the only signed work known by Jacopo Avanzi, a Bolognese painter of the early 15th century.

Appartamento della Principessa Isabelle (*for admission, see p. 143 above*): The suite consists of 11 more sumptuously decorated and furnished rooms on the ground floor of Palazzo Colonna, named after Isabelle Sursock, wife of Marcantonio Colonna, who restored the apartment in the early 20th century. It contains paintings by Gaspar van Wittel, the Dutch painter known as Vanvitelli, who carried out 107 works, including numerous views of Rome, for the Colonna between 1681 and 1732. In the Sala Rosa are small paintings by Jan Brueghel the Elder dating from the 1590s, and a self-portrait by Sofonisba Anguissola. The vault of the Sala della Fontana is painted by Pinturicchio (c. 1485–92). The red granite crocodile dates from the 3rd century AD, and the superb painting of *Two Saints with Abbot Niccolò Roverella* (part of a polyptych) is by **Cosmè Tura**. The Sala del Tempesta is named after the artist who painted the seascapes on the walls in the 17th century. The adjoining room was decorated by **Gaspard Dughet** with delightful landscapes. The Dining Room, formerly used as a library, has a vault decorated in the late 16th century by a group of artists including Pomarancio, Giovanni Baglione, Jacopo Zucchi and Ferraù Fenzoni. The Sala del Mascherone has a Roman pavement (4th century AD) and various ancient marble fragments.

SANTI APOSTOLI
Map p. 622, 2C

Open 7–12 & 4–7.

The basilica may have been founded by Pelagius I and the Byzantine viceroy Narses around 560, to commemorate the defeat and final expulsion of the Goths from the peninsula by Narses. At this time Rome was under the control of the Eastern Empire, ruled from Ravenna, and the joint dedication to the Apostles Philip and James was borrowed from Constantinople, where these two apostles had always been highly venerated. The church was restored and enlarged from the 15th century and given its Baroque appearance when it was almost completely rebuilt by Carlo Fontana in 1702–14.

The unusual façade, which has the appearance of a palace rather than a church, is in a mixture of styles. The stately Renaissance double loggia of nine arches, attributed to Baccio Pontelli, was built at the expense of Cardinal Giuliano della Rovere, afterwards Pope Julius II (who lived next to the church in Palazzo dei Santi Apostoli, and whose father is buried in the church). Baroque windows were installed in the upper storey by Carlo Rainaldi, c. 1665. Rainaldi also provided the balustrade above with statues of the Apostles. Behind this and above it the Neoclassical upper façade of the church, added by Valadier in 1827, can be seen.

In the portico, on the left, is the tomb of the engraver Giovanni Volpato, by his much more famous pupil Antonio Canova (1807). On the right is an exquisite bas-relief found in Trajan's Forum dating from the 2nd century AD, representing an eagle holding an oak-wreath in its talons. Also here is a lion, signed by Pietro Vassalletto, member of a family of sculptors active in Rome in the 12th century (*see p. 479*). The two red marble lions flanking the entrance portal date from the same period.

The Interior

The Baroque interior is on a vast scale, with an exceptionally broad nave. The effect of immensity is enhanced by the manner in which the lines of the vaulting continue those of the massive pillars, and the lines of the apse those of the nave.

From the end near the entrance the surprising effect of relief achieved by the little-known painter Giovanni Odazzi in his contorted group of *Fallen Angels*, on the vault above the high altar, can be seen. On the ceiling of the nave is the *Triumph of the Order of St Francis*, a late work (1707) by Baciccia (the Angels and Evangelists were added in the late 19th century by Luigi Fontana). Baciccia, born in Genoa, spent most of his life in Rome (where he died in 1709) and—as a friend of Bernini—was given numerous commissions for altarpieces and portraits, though is best remembered for his vault decorations. The most successful are in the Gesù (*see p. 292*).

South aisle: The first chapel contains a beautiful *Madonna and Child* by **Antoniazzo Romano**, the most important Roman artist of his time, who con-tinued to paint Madonnas in an archaic Byzantine style against a gold ground in the late 15th century. It was commissioned for this chapel by the illustrious

Greek scholar Cardinal Bessarion (1389–1472; *see p. 337*), who is recorded in an epitaph of 1682 (and a delightful relief portrait in a medallion) on the second pillar in the north aisle. In the second cloister (*see below*) there is a Latin and Greek inscription which was dictated by the cardinal for his own tomb.

Against the second south pillar is a **monument to Clementina Sobieska**, wife of James Stuart, the Old Pretender (*see opposite*), by Filippo della Valle. The chapel at the end of the aisle preserves eight columns from the 6th-century church.

High altar: The *Martyrdom of St Philip and St James* is by Domenico Muratori, who produced very few paintings after this one—thought to be the largest in Rome (14m by over 6.5m).

Sanctuary: Here are the tombs of several members of the Riario family, which supplied numerous cardinals over the centuries: that of Cardinal Pietro, on the left, is a particularly beautiful work by the school of Andrea Bregno, with a *Madonna* by Mino da Fiesole. Fragments of famous frescoes, exquisite works by Melozzo da Forlì, which formerly covered the 15th-century apse, are preserved in the Quirinal and in the Vatican picture gallery.

Steps in front of the sanctuary lead down to the confessio. The **relics of the Apostles Philip and James** are preserved here, and, in the chapel to the left, the beautiful **tomb of Raffaele della Rovere** (d. 1477), brother of Sixtus IV and father of Julius II, with a serene effigy by Andrea Bregno. The other chapels here were decorated in 1876–77 in the

style of the catacombs, and foundations of the earlier church can be seen.

North aisle: At the east end of the aisle, around the door into the sacristy, is the first important work in Rome by Canova, the **mausoleum of Clement XIV**, a masterpiece of Neoclassical art (1783–87). When it was completed it won Canova renown throughout Europe. Something of the state of Italian art at the time can be guessed from the French writer Stendhal's comment that Canova 'had emerged quite by chance out of the sheer inertia which this warm climate imposed ... nobody else in Italy is the least like him'.

In the second chapel is a surprising altarpiece since it shows St Joseph of Copertino 'flying' as he celebrates Mass. This St Joseph (from Copertino near Lecce in southern Italy) became a Franciscan and was widely known for his powers of levitation, but the official Church was sceptical and he was only canonized some hundred years after his death in 1663 (when this painting by Giuseppe Cades celebrated the event). The two columns flanking the altar are reputedly the largest known works in *verde antico*, a marble only found in Thessaly in Greece.

Cloisters (*entered at no. 51*): The two Renaissance cloisters contain a bas-relief of the *Nativity* by the school of Arnolfo di Cambio; an early Christian sarcophagus; and, in the second cloister, a **memorial to Michelangelo**, whose body was temporarily placed here after his death in Rome in 1564 before it was transported to Florence for his funeral service and burial in Santa Croce.

On the opposite side of Piazza dei Santi Apostoli is Palazzo Odescalchi, which extends to the Corso. The façade on the piazza is by Bernini, with additions by Niccolò Salvi and Luigi Vanvitelli (1750). The orange-coloured Baroque Palazzo Balestra (formerly Muti) was once owned by the Stuarts of Scotland and England (*see box*).

THE JACOBITES IN ROME

The exiled house of Stuart was descended from James I of England (and VI of Scotland), whose grandson James II was forced to abdicate from the English throne in 1688 because of his Roman Catholic sympathies. Members of this royal line and their supporters became known as Jacobites. James II's son, James Stuart (1688–1766), nicknamed the 'Old Pretender', first lived in France and then came to Rome, where Clement XI presented him with Palazzo Balestra on the occasion of his marriage in 1719 to Clementina Sobieska. Although his wife died in 1735 he continued to live here until his own death, when he was given a grand funeral in St Peter's with no fewer than 22 cardinals present. A portrait of him survives in the Galleria Doria Pamphilj.

His son, Charles Edward (1720–88; the 'Young Pretender' or 'Bonnie Prince Charlie'), who was born in Palazzo Balestra, led the last Jacobite rebellion in Scotland in 1745–46. It ended in his decisive defeat at Culloden, after which he was forced to escape to France, from where he returned to Rome. Here he married Louise de Stolberg and they moved to Florence, where the Prince led a dissolute, drunken life and his wife escaped to a convent with the help of the poet Count Vittorio Alfieri. Years later, when Alfieri was giving a private performance of one of his plays in the Spanish embassy in Piazza di Spagna, he met Louise again and they lived together for the rest of their lives. Bonnie Prince Charlie died in Palazzo Balestra in 1788.

The Young Pretender's younger brother was Henry, Duke of York (also born in Palazzo Balestra, in 1725), who was made a cardinal, and as 'Henry IX' was the last of the Stuarts. Known as Cardinal York he was given the bishopric of Frascati, just outside Rome in the Alban hills, where he died in 1807. When the Young Pretender died, his brother saw that his body was buried in the Duomo of Frascati (where his cenotaph remains) before it was moved to the Vatican Grottoes. The Cardinal built a convent on Monte Cavo near Frascati, and restored a chapel in Santa Maria in Trastevere. The three last Stuarts are commemorated in St Peter's with a monument by Antonio Canova (*see p. 415*), paid for in part by King George IV.

'talking' statues (*see p. 281*); with his flat beret, he was once thought to be a caricature portrait of Martin Luther, but the figure more probably represents Abbondio Rizio, a heavy drinker. In 1751, Vanvitelli attributed the sculpture to Michelangelo.

The next palace on the left, Palazzo Simonetti (no. 307), was for many years in the 18th century a centre of the political and cultural life of the city as the residence of Cardinal de Bernis, ambassador of Louis XV at the papal court. In 1833 it was purchased by the important Roman Boncompagni-Ludovisi family.

Opposite is the church of **San Marcello** (*open 7–12 & 4–7*), of ancient foundation, dedicated to the very early pope Marcellus, who reigned for a year or so in the first decade of the 4th century. A popular legend survives which suggests that the emperor Maxentius ordered him to work as a stable-boy in stables on this site and that he died in the job. The very fine concave façade (1683) is perhaps the best work in the city by Carlo Fontana, who succeeded Bernini as papal architect. After a fire in 1519 the interior was rebuilt to a design by the Tuscan sculptor and architect Jacopo Sansovino, who also carved the tombs on the west wall of Cardinal Giovanni Michiel (d. 1503) and his nephew Bishop Antonio Orso (d. 1511). The cardinal's tomb (on the right as you look back at the door) is supported by a pile of books since he was specially remembered for his donation of a large collection of manuscript volumes to the library of the convent. Sansovino left the city for Venice in 1527, where he spent the rest of his life designing Classical buildings for the Doge derived from the ancient monuments he had seen in Rome. Most of the frescoes in the main body of the church date from the 17th century.

On the ceiling of the fourth south chapel are frescoes of the *Creation of Eve*, *St Mark* and *St John the Evangelist*, begun by Perino del Vaga and completed after the 1527 Sack of Rome (*see p. 23*) by Daniele da Volterra and Pellegrino Tibaldi. Beneath the altar, which has a fine 14th-century Crucifix (said to be miraculous; there is a book where you can inscribe a petition for yourself or others), is an ancient Roman cippus. The chapel opposite has frescoes by Taddeo Zuccari and on the right wall busts of three members of the Frangipani family by Alessandro Algardi.

The piazza and church of Sant'Ignazio

Just off the left side of the Corso (reached by Via del Caravita) is the delightful Rococo **Piazza di Sant'Ignazio** (*map p. 622, 2C*) a theatrical masterpiece by Filippo Raguzzini (1728). The buildings have curving façades which fit into a careful decorative scheme in relation to the streets between them. The effect is that of a stage-set rather than a piazza. The central building is now used by the Cultural Ministry and the special *carabinieri* police force in charge of safeguarding Italy's cultural heritage

The Jesuit **church of Sant'Ignazio** (*open 7.30–12.30 & 4–7.15*) rivals the Gesù in magnificence. It was begun in 1626 by Cardinal Ludovico Ludovisi as the church of the Collegio Romano (*see p. 545*) to celebrate the canonization of St Ignatius Loyola, founder of the Jesuits, by the cardinal's uncle Gregory XV.

The church was designed by Carlo Maderno and others, and was executed by Orazio Grassi, a Jesuit mathematician from the college, who is also responsible for the fine façade (his only architectural work).

The spacious aisled interior is sumptuously decorated. In the **vaulting of the nave and apse** are remarkable paintings, the masterpiece of Andrea Pozzo. Pozzo, himself a Jesuit, was the greatest exponent of the *quadratura* technique, which used painted architectural elements to provide illusionistic decorations on walls and ceilings, and which became extremely popular in the Baroque period. These works, his most brilliant achievement, represent the missionary activity of the Jesuits and the triumph of St Ignatius. The amazing *trompe l'oeil* perspective projects the walls of the church beyond their architectural limits, and Pozzo even provided a cupola, never built because of lack of funds, in a canvas 17m in diameter. The vaulting and 'dome' are best seen from a small yellow disc set in the pavement about the middle of the nave. On the west wall are two allegorical figures by Alessandro Algardi. The second chapel on the south side, lavishly decorated with rare marbles, has an altarpiece of the *Death of St Joseph*, one of numerous altarpieces carried out by Francesco Trevisani for churches in Rome in the early 18th century.

In the sumptuous transept chapels, both also designed by Andrea Pozzo, with marble barley-sugar columns, are large marble high-reliefs: on the south side, the *Glory of St Aloysius Gonzaga*, a member of the Jesuit Order, by Pierre Legros (a French sculptor who worked in Rome for the Jesuits), with a lapis lazuli urn containing the remains of the saint; on the north side, the *Annunciation* by Filippo della Valle (one of the best works by this early 18th-century sculptor), and a lapis lazuli urn with the

The Annunciation, by Filippo della Valle.

relics of St John Berchmans (d. 1621, another Jesuit), and two 18th-century angels by Pietro Bracci (who worked with Filippo della Valle on the Trevi fountain). In the chapel to the right of the high altar is the elaborate funerary monument to Gregory XV and his nephew Cardinal Ludovisi, the founders of the church, also by Legros.

In Piazza di Pietra (reached by Via di Burro and Via di Pietra, in front of Sant'Ignazio) are the splendid remains of the huge **Temple of Hadrian**, built by Antoninus Pius in 145 and dedicated to his father. Now incorporated in the façade of the Chamber of Commerce building, the high wall of the cella survives, along with the peristyle of the right side with 11 disengaged fluted Corinthian columns (15m high). The houses in front follow the line of the portico which used to surround the temple. The square is filled with cafés and bars.

Piazza Colonna and Piazza Montecitorio

Piazza Colonnna (*map p. 622, 1C*) was for centuries considered the centre of the city, and is important in Italy today since it is the official residence of the Prime Minister. Beside a graceful fountain with a particularly attractive veined pink-and-grey marble basin designed by Giacomo della Porta (the dolphins are a 19th-century addition by Achille Stocchi), rises the monument from which the piazza derives its name, the majestic **Column of Marcus Aurelius**, or *Colonna Antonina*. It is made entirely of Italian marble from Luni, and is formed of 27 blocks. The ancient level of the ground was nearly 4m lower than at present. The shaft measures 100 Roman feet (29.6m), and the total height of the column, including the base and the statue, is nearly 42m. In the interior (*no admission*) are 203 steps lit by 56 tiny windows.

The column was erected between AD 180 and 196 in honour of Marcus Aurelius' victories over the Germans (169–73) and Sarmatians (174–76), and dedicated to him and his wife, Faustina. The philosopher-emperor Marcus Aurelius led his troops in all these important battles, which delayed the barbarian invasions of Italy for several centuries. The column was inspired by that of Trajan (*see p. 114*), but instead of being the focal point of a forum, it was in the centre of an important group of monuments of the Antonine period. The ancient base was decorated with Victories, festoons and reliefs. The summit was originally crowned with figures of Marcus Aurelius and Faustina, but in 1589 Domenico Fontana replaced the imperial statues with one of St Paul.

Around the shaft a bas-relief ascends in a spiral of 20 turns, interrupted halfway by a Victory; the lower part of the relief commemorates the war against the Germanic tribes, the upper that against the Sarmatians. On the third spiral (east side) the Roman soldiers are represented as being saved by a rainstorm, which in the 4th century was regarded as a miracle brought about by the prayers of the Christians in their ranks.

The Prime Minister's residence is the huge **Palazzo Chigi**, dating from the 16th century, and enlarged (and given a fine courtyard) in the following century, when it was acquired by the Sienese Chigi family. The family moved to Rome and became celebrated at this time when Fabio Chigi became Pope Alexander VII. The splendid library founded by this pope remained here until the palace and its contents were sold by the Chigi to the state in 1917 (and in 1923 the library was donated by the state to the

Vatican). After a period of use by various ministries it was restored in 1961 as the official seat of the Prime Minister of Italy.

On the west side of the piazza the façade of Palazzo Wedekind (1838), incorporates on the ground floor a handsome portico with 12 Ionic marble columns, brought from a Roman building at Veio. The little church on the south side is San Bartolomeo dei Bergamaschi (1561). Across the Corso is a huge covered shopping arcade in the form of a Y built in 1914. Formerly called the Galleria Colonna it was restored and renamed in 2003, the year of his death, after the great film star Alberto Sordi, much beloved by Romans. His incredibly long and successful career began when Fellini chose him for his film *Lo Sceicco Bianco* in 1951.

Piazza di Montecitorio, behind (west of) Piazza Colonna, is named after the huge **Palazzo di Montecitorio** (*open for guided tours on the first Sun of the month, 10–5.30*) which, since 1871, has been the seat of the Camera dei Deputati. This, together with the Senato della Repubblica (*see p. 271*), represents the parliament of Italy: both houses have identical legislative duties and exercise political control over the government. The 630 deputies, who have to be at least 25 years old, are elected every five years by Italians over the age of 18. The two houses sit together to elect the president of the Republic.

The original palace was begun for the Ludovisi family in 1650 by Bernini, who was responsible for the general plan of the building and for the idea of enhancing the effect of the façade by giving it a convex, slightly polygonal form. In 1918 it was enlarged and given its new façade by Ernesto Basile, with a red-brick Art Nouveau front on Piazza del Parlamento. In the interior the chamber, also of this period, is panelled in oak and brightly illuminated from above by a row of windows in the cornice, below which is an encaustic frieze by Aristide Sartorio, begun in 1908, representing the development of Italian civilization. The fine bas-relief in bronze in honour of the royal House of Savoy is by Davide Calandra.

The **obelisk** (22m high) in the centre of Piazza di Montecitorio, was originally erected at Heliopolis by Psammetichus II (c. 590 BC). It was brought to Rome by Augustus to celebrate his victory over Cleopatra, and set up in the Campus Martius, where it served as the gnomon of an immense sundial. In 1748 it was discovered underground in the Largo dell'Impresa (an open space north of Palazzo di Montecitorio) and in 1792 it was erected on its present site.

Back on the Corso, on the right in a wide piazza is the church of **San Silvestro in Capite** (*open 7–12.30*). The *capite* refers to a relic of the head of St John the Baptist which is preserved here. The church was founded by Pope Stephen III (752–57) on the site of a Roman building, possibly Aurelian's Temple of the Sun. It was bestowed on the English Roman Catholics by Leo XIII in 1890, and is now administered by the Irish order of the Pallottini, which also holds services in English. The 12th-century campanile is still surmounted by a bronze cockerel of the same date (it recalls the cock which crowed three times when St Peter betrayed Christ). The interior is interesting for its 17th-century works: the nave vault by Giacinto Brandi; the second south chapel with an altarpiece of *St Francis* by Orazio Gentileschi, and a cupola painted by Pomarancio; and the first north chapel with a *Crucifixion* by Francesco Trevisani.

The northern Corso

After Via Convertite the Corso narrows. Via Frattina, on the right, is the first of several long, straight pedestrian streets, lined with fashionable shops, between the Corso and Piazza di Spagna (*see p. 172*). In this area a Roman arch (probably dating from the 2nd century AD, once spanned the road: it was demolished in 1662 by Alexander VII in order to straighten the line of the Corso here.

The basilica of **San Lorenzo in Lucina**, in a pretty piazza opposite, probably dates from the time of Sixtus III (432–40) or even earlier, but was rebuilt in the 12th century, and again in 1650. The restored campanile (which has several rows of small *logge* with colonnettes), the portico with six Ionic columns, and the doorway remain from the 12th-century church. In the first chapel on the south side a reliquary contains part of the gridiron on which the titular saint, Lawrence, was supposedly martyred. In the second chapel on the left pillar is the tomb of Nicolas Poussin, who lived in Rome for many years (*see p. 167*): the monument was commissioned in 1830 by the great French writer of the Romantic movement Chateaubriand, when he came to Rome as a minister in the French government. The **fourth chapel designed by Bernini** for Gabriele Fonseca, Innocent X's doctor, is decorated with pretty stuccoes and has a fine portrait bust (left of the altar), one of numerous such expressive works in which the great sculptor faithfully portrayed his famous and less famous contemporaries. The *Crucifixion* on the high altar is by the prolific Bolognese artist Guido Reni, who was at work in Rome at the turn of the 16th century. On the north side, the decorative fifth chapel was designed by Simon Vouet, a French painter who was in Rome at the beginning of the 17th century and was greatly influenced by the work of Reni: his two paintings here of St Francis are considered amongst his best works.

Excavations have revealed remains of the early Christian basilica built above Roman edifices, including a private house and a market building of brick-faced concrete, thought to date from the time of Hadrian (*usually open at 4.30 on the last Sat of the month.*)

The Corso widens at **Santi Ambrogio e Carlo al Corso** (*open 9.30–12 & 4 or 5–7*), dedicated to two great bishops of Milan, St Ambrose and St Charles Borromeo, who lived in the 4th and the 16th centuries respectively, and were both the most influential prelates of their day. It is the only work in Rome by Onorio Longhi (1612), and was completed by his son Martino (the Longhi were an important family of architects, and Onorio's father, also called Martino, carried out numerous works in the city). The cupola is a fine late work (1668) by Pietro da Cortona, which recalls Michelangelo's dome of St Peter's, and is also an important feature of the skyline of the city. The heavily restored façade was completed at the end of the 17th century. In the grand Baroque interior, the poorly lit high altarpiece, *The Madonna Presenting St Charles Borromeo and Ambrose to Christ*, is a particularly good 17th-century work by Carlo Maratta, and on an altar behind it is a rich urn containing the heart of St Charles Borromeo.

The Baroque interior of Santi Ambrogio e Carlo with Carlo Maratta's high altarpiece.

Mausoleum of Augustus and the Ara Pacis

In the centre of the ugly Piazza Augusto Imperatore (*map p. 266, B1*), laid out in 1936–38, are the remains of the tomb of Augustus, one of the most sacred monuments of ancient Rome (*see p. 550*). Towards the Tiber is the **Ara Pacis**, in a new museum designed by Richard Meier. This monumental altar was reconstructed in 1937–38 from scattered remains and from reproductions of dispersed fragments. The carved decoration is a splendid example of Roman sculpture, influenced by Classical Greek and Hellenistic art, and represents the supreme achievement of Augustan art.

The *Ara Pacis Augustae* was consecrated in the Campus Martius in 13 BC, and dedicated four years later, in celebration of the peace that Augustus had established within the Empire. This much is known from the document (*Res gestae Divi Augusti*) which the emperor had had engraved on bronze tablets a year before his death in AD 14.

In 1568, during excavations for the foundations of Palazzo Fiano on the Corso, nine blocks belonging to the frieze of the altar were found and bought by Cardinal Ricci da Montepulciano for the Grand Duke of Tuscany. To facilitate transport to Florence (they are now in the Uffizi), each block was sawn into three pieces. The cardinal overlooked two other blocks unearthed at the same time. One of these passed to the Louvre, the other to the Vatican Museum. Three hundred years later, during a reconstruction of the palace, other parts of the altar were found, and acquired in 1898 by the Italian government for the Museo Nazionale Romano. In 1903 and 1937 excavations brought to light the basement of the altar and further fragments. The pieces from the Museo Nazionale Romano and the Uffizi were recovered; those in the Louvre, the Vatican and the Villa Medici were copied, and in 1938 the altar was reconstructed, as far as possible, in its original form, though its original position was further south, close to the Via Lata, between the present Piazza del Parlamento and Piazza di San Lorenzo in Lucina.

Built throughout of Luni marble, it has a simple base with two horizontal bands, which supports an almost square walled enclosure, with two open and two closed sides. The external decoration of this is in two zones divided by a horizontal Greek key-pattern border. The lower zone is covered with an intricate and beautiful composition of acanthus leaves on which are swans with outstretched wings. In the upper zone is a frieze of reliefs with a decorated cornice above it. Between the jambs of the main or north entrance are scenes illustrating the origins of Rome. The left panel, which is almost entirely lost, represented the Lupercalia; the right panel shows *Aeneas Sacrificing the White Sow*. The panels of the south entrance depict Tellus, the Earth Goddess, possibly an allegory of Peace, on the left, and a much-damaged Roma on the right. The side panels illustrate the ceremony that took place during the consecration of the altar itself: the procession includes Augustus, members of his family, state officials and priests.

The interior of the enclosure is also in two zones; because sacrifices took place here, the lower part has no decoration other than simple fluting. The upper zone, however, is decorated with beautifully carved bucrania. On the altar wall are reliefs of the *Suovetaurilia*, or sacrifice of a boar, a ram and a bull.

For the Corso further north and Piazza del Popolo, see following chapter.

PIAZZA DEL POPOLO

Piazza del Popolo (*map p. 620, 2A–B*) was designed to provide a scenic entrance to the city from Via Flaminia and the north, and numerous travellers in past centuries recorded their first arrival in Rome through the monumental and historic **Porta del Popolo**, which occupies almost the same site as the ancient *Porta Flaminia*. The outer face (1561) is by Nanni di Baccio Bigio, born in Florence, who had a stormy relationship with Michelangelo, but who here apparently followed a design by the great architect (the two side arches were only opened in 1879). It was here in 1655 that Queen Christina of Sweden made a triumphant entry into Rome on horseback and dressed as an Amazon: the inner face of the gate had been redesigned in her honour by her great admirer and close friend Gian Lorenzo Bernini.

QUEEN CHRISTINA OF SWEDEN

Queen Christina of Sweden (1626–89) was the daughter of the 'Champion of Protestantism' King Gustavus Adolphus, whom she succeeded in 1632 at the age of six. She was not crowned until 1650 but during her brief reign Stockholm became a centre of European culture and among numerous foreign visitors to her court was the philosopher Descartes. A very clever woman who never wished to marry (rumours abounded of her sapphic inclinations), Christina abdicated in 1654 and converted to Roman Catholicism (a religion prohibited in Sweden). Pope Alexander VII received her warmly into the Church and even allowed her to stay inside the Vatican on her arrival in Rome. She then moved into Palazzo Riario alla Lungara, where she was visited by the leading artists and writers of the city, and she founded an academy in 1680 for literary and political discussions (*see p 386*). However she soon became critical of the Counter-Reformation movement, and took up with a faction of cardinals who were opposed to certain aspects of the Roman Church. Despite this she left her library to the Vatican and is buried in the grottoes of St Peter's.

The piazza was created in 1538 for Paul III in strict relationship to the three long straight streets, which penetrate the city here as a trident. The two twin-domed churches were added in the 17th century, and the piazza was given its present symmetry by Giuseppe Valadier after the return of Pius VII (*see p. 421*) from France following the fall of Napoleon in 1815.

An **obelisk**, 24m high, rises between four charming fountains with lions, which spout water (they had probably been projected by Domenico Fontana in the 16th century but were only installed here by Valadier in 1823). The obelisk's hieroglyphs celebrate the glories of the pharaohs Rameses II and Merenptah (13th–12th centuries BC). After the conquest of Egypt Augustus had the obelisk transported to Rome from Heliopolis, and it was dedicated to the Sun in the Circus Maximus. Domenico Fontana (whose nephew Carlo and son Francesco were also important architects in Rome; *see p. 236*) moved it here in 1589, as part of the urban plan of Sixtus V: he had already succeeded in erecting the huge obelisk in Piazza San Pietro for the same pope.

Between the Corso and the two other long streets which lead from here into the centre of Rome are a pair of decorative Baroque churches (*not always open*), **Santa Maria dei Miracoli** and **Santa Maria in Montesanto**. The façades, which had been designed by Carlo Rainaldi, were modified by Bernini and Carlo Fontana (1671–78). In the centre of each hemicycle is a fountain with marble groups dating from 1824, on the left, *Neptune with two Tritons*, on the right, *Rome between the Tiber and the Anio*, both by Giovanni Ceccarini, and at the ends are more Neoclassical statues of the Four Seasons. A winding road, also designed by Valadier, ascends the Pincian Hill past the abundant monumental fountain (known as a *mostra*) at the termination of the Acqua Vergine Nuova. It is one of numerous such fountains built to display the pressure of the water on its arrival in the city from one of Rome's aqueducts (and behind it a series of pipes and conduits distribute the water to various parts of town). An incongruous green gate is usually wide open here so you can go right inside the building where the sound of water envelops you as it comes cascading down the walls from a hidden source (one of the most refreshing spots in the city on a hot day).

SANTA MARIA DEL POPOLO
Map p. 620, 2A–B

Open 7–12 & 4–7.
This church, dedicated to the Virgin, was apparently built at the expense of the city (the *popolo Romano*), hence its name. The peaceful interior is a wonderful place to see works of art of all periods, including masterpieces by Bernini and Caravaggio. There are push-button lights in some chapels and in the apse.

Legend relates that this area had been the burial ground of the Domitia family, a member of which was the evil emperor Nero, and so it was believed to be the haunt of demons. In 1099 Pope Paschal II ceremoniously cut down a walnut tree here since it was thought to be giving shelter to these demons in the form of a group of black crows. He then founded a chapel on the site. The church was rebuilt in 1227 and again under Sixtus IV (1472–77).

The simple early-Renaissance façade is attributed to the architect and sculptor Andrea Bregno, who also carved a number of tombs in the church. The interior was renovated by Bernini.

Pinturicchio: *Adoration of the Child* (c. 1490).

DOMINICVS·RVVERE·CARD·S·CLEMEN
TIS·CAPELLAM·MARIAE·VIRG·GENE

Caravaggio: *The Crucifixion of St Peter* (1600–01).

High altar and apse: The triumphal arch is decorated with fine 17th-century gilded stuccoed reliefs. Over the high altar is the venerated *Madonna del Popolo*, a 14th-century painting. The apse, with its shell design, is one of the earliest works in Rome by **Bramante**, and was commissioned by Julius II (*there is a light on the left*). Here are the two splendid tombs of Cardinal Girolamo Basso della Rovere (1507) and Cardinal Ascanio Sforza (1505), signed by the Tuscan artist Andrea Sansovino. The frescoes high up in the vault—illustrating the *Coronation of the Virgin*, as well as the Evangelists, Sibyls, and Four Fathers of the Church—are the best works in the church by **Pinturicchio** (1508–09), an Umbrian artist of chiefly decorative instinct, who did some of his best work in Rome, notably in Santa Maria in Aracoeli (*see p. 56*) and in the Borgia Rooms in the Vatican (*see p. 438*). The stained glass, also commissioned by Julius II, is by Guillaume de Marcillat.

North transept: The first chapel to the left of the choir has two dramatic paintings by **Caravaggio**, the *Crucifixion of St Peter* and *Conversion of St Paul*. These famous masterpieces were executed in 1600–01. In the first (*pictured opposite*) St Peter is shown already nailed to the heavy cross, but our interest is taken up more with the mechanics of just how the three executioners (only one of whose faces is partly visible) were able to elevate it, as well as the pathos involved in seeing three hale and hearty executioners inflict such cruel torture on a frail old man. Again, in the *Conversion of St Paul* (*pictured overleaf*), it is not the saint we are drawn to but the lovely old cart horse as he steps carefully over the prostrate figure of Saul who has 'seen the light'. After the strong naturalism of these two works, it is perhaps difficult to appreciate the altarpiece here of the *Assumption*, which was commissioned at the same time but

is painted in such a different style—nevertheless it is a very fine work by **Annibale Carracci**, who also designed the frescoes in the barrel-vault above, with attractive stuccoes.

North aisle: The third chapel has fine monuments to the Mellini family. The earliest ones are low down on the right wall: to the right of the altar is the exquisite small tomb of Cardinal Pietro Mellini (1483). To the left of the altar is a bust of Urbano Mellini by **Alessandro Algardi**, who also designed the beautiful tomb of Giovanni Garzia Mellini on the left wall, with a half-figure portrait of the cardinal.

The second chapel is the well-lit, octagonal Chigi Chapel, founded by the great banker Agostino Chigi (1465–1520). It is a fusion of architecture, sculpture, mosaic, and painting designed by **Raphael** in 1513–16. The lovely mosaics in the dome were executed by a Venetian artist from cartoons by Raphael: God the Father, the Creator of the Firmament, is surrounded by symbols of the seven known planets, each of which is guided by an angel, as in Dante's conception. Work on the chapel was interrupted in 1520 by the deaths of both Chigi and Raphael, and it was only completed after 1652 for Cardinal Fabio Chigi (Alexander VII) by Bernini. The frescoes depicting the *Creation* and the *Fall*, between the windows, and the medallions of the Seasons, are by Francesco Salviati (1552–54). The altarpiece of the *Nativity of the Virgin* is by **Sebastiano del Piombo** (1530–34; *see p. 387*); the bronze bas-relief in front, *Christ and the Woman of Samaria*, by Lorenzetto, was

intended for the base of the tomb of Agostino Chigi, but was moved here by Bernini. By the altar are statues of the prophets Jonah (left), a particularly successful work designed by Raphael and executed by Lorenzetto, and the famous *Habakkuk* (right) by **Bernini**. By the entrance to the chapel are the prophets Daniel with the lion, also by Bernini, and Elijah, by Lorenzetto. The remarkable pyramidal form of the tombs of Agostino Chigi and of his brother Sigismondo (who died six years after Agostino in 1526), executed by Lorenzetto, was dictated by Raphael's architectural scheme and derived from ancient Roman models. They were altered in the 17th century, again by Bernini. The unfinished burial crypt below the chapel, with another pyramid would, in Raphael's original design, have been visible and illuminated from the chapel above. The lunettes above the tombs were painted by Raffaele Vanni in 1653. The marble intarsia figure of Death, with the Chigi *stemma*, in the centre of the pavement was added by Bernini.

South aisle: Here there are more frescoes by **Pinturicchio** in the first chapel, including a delightful *Adoration of the Child* over the altar (*pictured on p. 161, above*). Also here are the tombs of three cardinals by Tuscan artists (that on the right is perhaps by Antonio da Sangallo the Younger) and that on the left by Mino da Fiesole and Andrea Bregno. The second chapel was well designed, by Carlo Fontana, using a great variety of precious marbles, to house the tombs of the Cybo family. The huge altarpiece of the *Assumption and Doctors of the Church* is by Carlo Maratta. The third chapel has a lovely Pinturicchio altarpiece: the *Madonna and Saints*. In the fourth south chapel the beautiful bronze effigy of Cardinal Pietro Foscari, is sometimes attributed to Vecchietta (c. 1485).

The former Augustinian convent adjoining the church was the **residence of Martin Luther** during his mission as a priest here in 1511. It was only nine years later that Leo X issued a bull against his writings which Luther burnt publicly in the square of Wittenberg: his subsequent excommunication marked the beginning of the German Reformation.

Caravaggio: detail of *The Conversion of St Paul* (1600–01).

built the other English church in Rome, now the American Episcopal church of St Paul's). The red-brick façade is typical of Street's Victorian works, and in the interior are mosaics (in the apse) designed by Burne-Jones, and ceramic tiles inspired by William Morris.

The church of **Sant'Atanasio dei Greci**, further up on the same side, was designed by Giacomo della Porta, who built numerous palaces, churches and fountains in the city in the late 16th century, but is best remembered for the work he carried out on St Peter's. It has elegant twin bell-towers, which are also a characteristic feature of the earlier church of the Trinità dei Monti at the top of the Spanish steps nearby (*see p. 176*), also probably designed by della Porta. Erected for the Greek community in Rome, it is still officiated by the Pontifical Greek College with Byzantine rites in Greek.

The delightful little edifice next door was built as an artist's studio, and is now open to the public (*open 8.30–8.30; closed Sun*): this belonged to Adamo Tadolini, a pupil of Canova, who worked here in the first part of the 19th century producing numerous statues and funerary monuments in the style of his master (who also apparently used the studio in 1816–18). The studio and its contents remained in the Tadolini family—three more of whom (Scipione, Giulio and Enrico), in later generations, were also sculptors—until 1967. Now privately owned, visitors are welcome to explore the labyrinth of nooks and crannies filled to the brim with models and casts by the Tadolini, and a tiny space still arranged as a studio. There is also a bar and restaurant (*open only at*

lunchtime). Books are available for consultation, and the unusual atmosphere—when this used to be the meeting place of protagonists of the political, literary and artistic life of the city—has to some extent been retained.

Against the wall outside the studio is a very worn Roman **statue of a reclining Silenus**, which once decorated a fountain set up after 1571 by local residents by order of Pius V, in return for the pope's concession of water from the newly restored Acqua Vergine for the numerous gardens and orchards that used to exist in this district. It was one of the first fountains in the city erected by private citizens for the use of the public. It was recomposed in the street in 1957 above a small antique marble fountain basin, and until a very few years ago it was still the custom to write slogans against the present governors of Rome and Italy on the wall behind. It came to be known as *Babuino*, from the word for baboon, signifying 'dolt' or 'fool', and gave its name to the street. It was one of Rome's 'talking' statues (*see p. 281*).

At no. 149 is the Collegio Greco, founded in 1576 for Greek clerics after the fall of Constantinople in the hope of healing the Eastern schism, and moved here when the Greek church was built (the plaque to Clement XIII records its reconstruction in 1769).

No. 79 on the right is where Wagner stayed in 1876. Next door but one (no. 89) was the family residence of Giuseppe Valadier, well known as the architect of nearby Piazza del Popolo. His father Luigi, a famous silversmith, had his workshop here. Both were greatly admired by their contemporaries, and it is known that the pope himself, Pius VI, called on them here.

Turn left up Via Alibert, named after a theatre built here in 1718 by the French family of Alibert, which was the most famous theatre in Rome in the 18th century. On the corner of Via Margutta, it was destroyed by fire in 1863 and on the site a hotel was built, where Franz Liszt (Wagner's father-in-law and already a celebrated composer and pianist) stayed, receiving the title of Abbé from the church in Rome in 1865.

In the peaceful **Via Margutta** many of the houses have creepers or wisteria on their façades. Dating from the 16th century, this street was famous as the residence of numerous Dutch and Flemish painters in the 17th century. Paul Bril is recorded here in 1594–95, and a census of 1634 revealed that there were 104 foreign painters (mainly French, Dutch, and Flemish) in this area out of a total of 244 artists at work in the city that year. The area was favoured by foreigners since the pope had declared that all those who 'came from afar' to live in this area would be exempt from taxes. It is still a street of artists, with art galleries and studios with interesting courtyards and gardens facing towards the Pincio. In spring and autumn a street fair is held where paintings are for sale. There are also now a number of antique shops. At no. 56 a small luxury-class hotel was opened in 2002 aptly named Hotel Art. The fountain a little further along, decorated with artists' tools, was set up in 1927. Beyond is a large building (no. 53; mostly reconstructed in the 19th century) of artists studios, set back from the road, with a garden. Here Sir Thomas Lawrence founded the British Academy of Arts in 1821.

At the end of the street on the left, beside the doorway to an apartment building at no. 110, the names of Federico Fellini and Giulietta Masina are recorded simply as 'Marguttiane' or 'inhabitants of the street': the great film director Fellini, born in 1920, lived on the fourth floor for many years until his death in 1993. He is remembered for his numerous films, including *La Dolce Vita* (1960) and *Roma* (1972), which document life in the city in those periods. The little square of shops here, designed in 1998, doesn't appear to have anything to do with the Roman townscape.

We know that the English sculptor John Flaxman, who lived and worked in Rome from 1787 to 1794 (and ran an office of the Wedgwood ceramic manufactory which had been opened in the city), had his studio in this area, and that in 1797 it was taken over by another Neoclassical sculptor, Bertel Thorvaldsen (1770–1844), from Denmark, who remained in Rome for the next 40 years as Canova's main rival, and was nominated president of the prestigious Accademia di San Luca (*see p. 211*). He restored a number of ancient Roman statues now in the Vatican museums, and received the commission for the tomb of Pius VII in St Peter's on the pope's death in 1823. His famous bust of Lord Byron was used for the monument to the English Romantic poet in the Borghese Gardens, near which a piazza is named after Thorvaldsen, and where his statue of Jason now stands (donated to Rome by the city of Copenhagen).

PIAZZA DI SPAGNA
& THE PINCIO

Piazza di Spagna was for centuries the focus of the artistic and literary life of the city. Foreign travellers usually chose their lodgings in the *pensioni* and hotels in the vicinity, and the English colony congregated here. John Evelyn, on his first visit to Rome in 1644, stayed near the piazza; Keats died in a house on the square; and the British Consul formerly had his office here. The Brownings' Roman residence was nearby (on the corner of Via Bocca di Leone and Vicolo del Lupo). A delightful English 'tea-room' is still open in the square, and the English church is in the neighbouring Via del Babuino.

The piazza is the place which perhaps best characterizes the opulent air of Rome, since it is in the pedestrian streets which lead from it down to the Corso—Via Condotti, Via Frattina and Via Borgognona—that the most elegant shops are to be found, and some of the grandest old-established Roman hotels are nearby. The famous Spanish Steps provide a theatrical background to the piazza, always busy with tourists and Romans. In addition to Keats' House, the elegant apartment of the painter Giorgio de Chirico almost next door can also be visited. Both give a remarkable insight into Roman residences of their day. Close to the top of the Spanish Steps is the Villa Medici, which retains its splendid 16th-century garden (*limited access; see below*), the most important one to have survived in the middle of Rome. The public gardens of the Pincio, a famous promenade in the 19th century, offer splendid views.

PIAZZA DI SPAGNA
Map p. 620, 3B

In the centre of the long and irregular Piazza di Spagna is the Fontana della Barcaccia, a delightful fountain, once thought to be the masterpiece of Pietro Bernini, but now usually considered to be the work of his famous son Gian Lorenzo. The design of a leaking boat is well adapted to the low water-pressure of the fountain. It is one of the most 'accessible' fountains in the city, and there are almost always people sitting on its rim to refresh themselves.

The theatrical Scalinata della Trinità dei Monti or **Spanish Steps** were built in 1723–26 to connect the piazza with the church of the Trinità dei Monti and the Pincio. They are a masterpiece of 18th-century town planning and the most famous (and almost the only) work of Francesco de Sanctis. The monumental flight of 137 steps, which rises between picturesque houses, some with garden terraces, has always been a well-loved haunt of Romans and foreigners. The steps are covered with tubs of magnificent azaleas at the beginning of May.

In an elegant pink 18th-century house marked with a plaque (at the foot of the steps on the right), is the apartment with a little vine-covered terrace where the poet

John Keats spent the last three months of his life. This is now the **Keats-Shelley Memorial House** (*open Mon–Fri 9–1 & 3–6; Sat 11–2 & 3–6; closed Sun; T: 06 678 4235*) and retains the atmosphere of that time. The entrance is at no. 26 in the piazza; the museum is on the second floor. The house was a small *pensione* in 1820, when Keats booked rooms for himself and his friend Joseph Severn, having been advised by his doctor to spend the winter in Rome. Keats led what he himself described as a 'posthumous life' here until his death from tuberculosis on 23 February 1821, aged 25. He was buried in the Protestant Cemetery (*see p. 470*). Severn came back to Rome as British Consul (1860–72), and when he died in 1879 at the age of 85 he chose to be buried next to Keats.

The house was purchased in 1906 by the Keats-Shelley Memorial Association and first opened to the public in 1909 as a delightful little museum and library dedicated to the English writers Keats, Shelley, Byron and Leigh Hunt, all of whom spent much time in Italy. The library contains more than 7,000 volumes and numerous autograph letters and manuscripts. Material relating to Shelley and Byron, including a painting of Shelley at the Baths of Caracalla by Severn, is displayed in the *Salone*. The reliquary of Pius V was later used as a locket for the hair of John Milton and Elizabeth Barrett Browning and was owned by Leigh Hunt (see Keats' poem *Lines on Seeing a Lock of Milton's Hair*). The kitchen was in the small room opening onto a terrace on the Spanish Steps, and Severn's room now contains mementoes of Severn, Leigh Hunt, Coleridge and Wordsworth. The death mask of Keats and a sketch by Severn of the poet on his deathbed, are preserved in the little room where he died. The Landmark Trust in the UK has the use of the apartment above the museum, and it is available for short rents (*for information, T: 44 1628 825925*).

The house opposite, on the left foot of the Spanish Steps, which retains its fine deep russet

Detail of the Fontana della Barcaccia, thought to be by Bernini.

colour, was built by de Sanctis to form a pair with Keats's house. Here **Babington's English Tea Rooms** (*open daily 9–8.30*), a charming old-fashioned café (which also serves lunch), survive. You pay extra for your memorable surroundings.

At no. 31 Piazza di Spagna, a few doors along from the Keats Museum, is the **Casa Museo di Giorgio de Chirico** (*open 1st Sun of the month except in Aug; otherwise by appointment Tues–Sat 10–1; T: 06 679 6546*). Opened to the public in 1998, the apartment on the fifth floor was the home and studio of Giorgio de Chirico (1888–1978), one of the most important European painters of the early 20th century, famous as the inventor of the Metaphysical style of painting before the First World War. This was characterized by a magic, enigmatic atmosphere sometimes created by the presence of mannequins, and strange objects unusually juxtaposed in his still lifes, and a sense of unreal space and perspective in his deserted townscapes. De Chirico lived here from 1947 until his death and is buried in the church of San Francesco a Ripa (*see p. 384*). His Polish wife Isabella Far, who died in 1990, established a foundation dedicated to the artist in 1986. The house gives a fascinating glimpse of a delightful Roman residence, as well as providing a very clear idea of the artistic achievements of de Chirico, since the 50 works here were chosen and hung by the painter himself. His home and studio remain as they were furnished at his death. Most of the works date from the 1960s and 1970s: his earliest period is less well documented. The house has three floors, with the bedrooms and studio—containing objects and terracotta models as he left them—on the upper floor with a terrace above. On the main floor the living-room has some important self-portraits dating from the 1940s (and one painted in 1959), as well as portraits of his wife. The dining-room has numerous lovely still lifes, and the last room has some Metaphysical works, including, strangely enough, copies made by the artist of his earliest paintings.

In the fashionable Via Condotti, named after the conduits of the Acqua Vergine, is the renowned **Caffè Greco**, founded in 1760 and a national monument since 1953. It retains its delightful interior, with numerous little sitting-rooms with small round marble-topped tables. It is decorated with personal mementoes and self-portraits of some of its most famous patrons, who included Goethe (*see p. 170*), Gogol, Berlioz, Stendhal, Baudelaire, Bertel Thorvaldsen and Wagner.

The northern end of Piazza di Spagna is particularly attractive, with its row of 18th-century houses, and four tall palm trees, and a flower stall (the entrance to the subway station, the only one in the very heart of the city, is discreetly hidden along a side street). The opposite end of the piazza runs into Piazza Mignanelli, where the Column of the Immaculate Conception (1857) commemorates the establishment by Pius IX in 1854 of the dogma of the Immaculate Conception of the Virgin Mary in the womb of her mother St Anne. Here is Palazzo di Spagna, the residence since 1622 of the Spanish ambassador to the Vatican, which gave the main piazza its name. It is a good building with a fine courtyard by Antonio del Grande (1647).

The Collegio di Propaganda Fide (which belongs to the Vatican State so it has the privilege of extraterritoriality) has a façade, with detailed friezes, by the great Baroque architect Francesco Borromini, built for the Congregazione di Propaganda Fide founded by Gregory XV in 1622: the college was instituted by his successor Urban VIII for the training of missionaries (including young foreigners).

The church of **Sant'Andrea delle Fratte** (*open 6.30–12.40 & 4–7*) belonged to the Scots before the Reformation. The composer Alessandro Scarlatti was married here in 1678. The unfinished tower and refined, delightful campanile, both by Borromini, were designed to make their greatest impression when seen from Via Capo le Case.

In the second chapel on the right is the tomb of Judith Falconnet (1856), interesting because the recumbent figure is by the American artist Harriet Hosmer, who was a great friend of Elizabeth Barrett and Robert Browning. To the left of the north side door is the epitaph of an earlier female artist, Angelica Kauffmann (1741–1807). This Swiss painter, who came to live in Rome in 1781, soon became the centre of the foreign artistic community in the city, where she was greatly admired by Goethe. She was extremely wealthy and one of the most successful Neoclassical painters of her time, well known for her portraits. Earlier in her career she had lived in London where she had been a founding member of the Royal Academy and a close friend of Sir Joshua Reynolds. Works by her can still be seen nearby at the Accademia di San Luca and the Galleria Nazionale in Palazzo Barberini.

Back room of the Caffè Greco.

The cupola and apse were decorated in the 17th century by Pasquale Marini, when the three huge paintings depicting the Crucifixion, Death and Burial of St Andrew were hung here: they are by Giovanni Battista Lenardi, Lazzaro Baldi and Francesco Trevisani. By the high altar are two beautiful marble angels by Bernini, sculpted for Ponte Sant'Angelo but replaced on the bridge by copies. The cloister has a pretty little garden with cypresses and orange trees.

AT THE TOP OF THE SPANISH STEPS

On the terrace at the top of the Spanish Steps is Piazza della Trinità dei Monti with its church. From the balustrade there is a fine view of Rome with the dome of St Peter's in the distance, beyond the dome of Santi Ambrogio e Carlo al Corso, and to the left the top of the Column of Marcus Aurelius. On the near right the Villa Medici (*described below*) can be seen. The obelisk here, probably brought to Rome in the 2nd or 3rd century AD, when the hieroglyphs were copied from those on the obelisk in Piazza del Popolo, formerly stood in the Gardens of Sallust (*see p. 550*). Pius VI decided to have it erected on this spot in 1788.

The church of the **Trinità dei Monti** (*usually open 10–1 & 4–6.30; when closed, ring at the door of the small side staircase on the left*) attached to the French Convent of the Minims, was begun in 1493 by Louis XII. It was restored at the expense of Louis XVIII after damage caused by Napoleon's occupation in 1816.

The unusual 16th-century façade has a double staircase by Domenico Fontana, and characteristic twin bell-towers probably designed by Giacomo della Porta. The interior is divided into two parts by a grille, only one part of which may ordinarily be visited. The third chapel on the south side and the second chapel on the north side contain superb works by the Tuscan artist Daniele da Volterra, who was a close friend and follower of Michelangelo (whom he recorded in a famous bronze portrait bust; *see p. 42*). These are probably the best works Daniele ever painted: the beautiful *Assumption*, with a remarkable design, includes a portrait of Michelangelo (the last figure on the right): he also designed the chapel (although it was executed by his pupils). The *Descent from the Cross* is thought to have been executed from a design by Michelangelo: it is an especially fine work and was returned here in 2005 after its restoration (it had been damaged when it was transferred to canvas in 1811).

The first chapel on the south side has an altarpiece and frescoes by Giovanni Battista Naldini. The other part of the church contains lovely frescoes by Perino del Vaga, Giulio Romano and others, in finely decorated chapels. In the north transept the fourth chapel on the left has the *Assumption and Death of the Virgin* by Taddeo Zuccari, finished by his brother Federico. Excavations by the French Academy beneath the convent have revealed traces of a Roman building which seems to have had a terrace on the hillside similar in form to the Spanish Steps.

From the piazza there is a good view of the long, straight **Via Sistina** which descends to Piazza Barberini (*see p. 225*) and then ascends the Quirinal Hill as Via delle Quattro

Fontane. This handsome thoroughfare was laid out by Sixtus V as the Strada Felice, which ran up and down four hills of the city for some 3km via Santa Maria Maggiore all the way to Santa Croce in Gerusalemme, decorated at certain points by obelisks. Most of the illustrious visitors to Rome between the days of Napoleon and 1870 (when the French garrison withdrew from the city and papal rule ended with the entry of the Italian army into Rome) seem to have lodged in this street. Gogol (1809–52) lived at no. 126; no. 48 housed in succession Giovanni Battista Piranesi (1720–78), Thorvaldsen and the architect and archaeologist Luigi Canina (1795–1856). At the top end the street still has some old-established luxury hotels and elegant shops.

In the triangle formed between Via Sistina and Via Gregoriana is the charming and bizarre **Palazzo Zuccari**, built by the artist Federico Zuccari as his residence and studio. Sir Joshua Reynolds lived here in 1752–53 and the German archaeologist and antiquarian Winckelmann in 1755–68. In 1900 it was bought by Enrichetta Hertz, who left her library, with the palace, to the German government. The Biblioteca Hertziana is now one of the most famous art history libraries in the country (*recently reopened after restoration*). The entrance on Via Gregoriana has an amusing portal and two windows in the form of gaping monsters.

VILLA MEDICI
Map p. 620, 3B

Open with guided tours of the gardens Feb–May on Sat and Sun at 10.30 and 11.30. These times are subject to change: to check, T: 06 6761210. The interior is only open for exhibitions, but these are normally of the highest interest.

The Villa Medici, on the edge of the Pincian Hill, has been the seat of the French Academy since 1803. It is still one of the most important cultural institutes in Europe, and the most beautiful villa to have preserved its garden in the centre of Rome. The garden front, which can only be seen on a guided tour, is particularly handsome and interesting for its Classical sculptures. Its two towers make it one of the most conspicuous buildings on the skyline of Rome, almost always visible from a distance.

History of the Villa Medici
The villa, built by Nanni di Baccio Bigio and Annibale Lippi for Cardinal Ricci da Montepulciano in 1564–74, was bought by Cardinal Ferdinando de' Medici in 1576. He enlarged it with the help of Bartolomeo Ammannati and the villa was soon considered to be one of the grandest residences in the city. Cardinal Ferdinando's famous collection of ancient Roman sculpture was kept here: he had the garden façade decorated with Classical sculpture and the garden itself decorated with ancient busts and statues. In 1775 the masterpieces of the collection (including the so-called *Medici Venus*, the *Wrestlers* and the Niobe group) were transferred to the Uffizi gallery in Florence, while the less important pieces were used to decorate the Boboli Gardens in the same city.

The Pincio was laid out as a Romantic park by Giuseppe Valadier in 1809–14 on the Pincian Hill (46m). Adjoining the Villa Borghese, it forms the largest public garden in the centre of Rome and it is especially crowded on holidays. The wonderful view from the terrace of the Piazzale Napoleone is dominated by the dome of St Peter's.

On a terrace is the Casina Valadier (1813–17), now an open-air café, though often closed. Among the habitués of its most sumptuous period as a fashionable restaurant in the early 20th century were Richard Strauss, Mussolini, King Farouk, Mahatma Gandhi and Chiang Kai-shek. The view from its terrace is even better than that from Piazzale Napoleone. The monumental entrance to the garden of Villa Medici with the colossal Roman statue of *Dea Roma* can be seen nearby.

The park is intersected by broad avenues passing between magnificent trees, many of them remarkable specimens of their kind. One of these avenues, Viale dell'Obelisco, runs east to join Viale delle Magnolie in the park of the Villa Borghese (*see p. 189*). The obelisk which gives the avenue its name was placed here in 1822: it was found in the 16th century outside the Porta Maggiore, where it may have decorated the *Circus Varianus* (*see p. 368*). The hieroglyphs suggest that it was originally erected by Hadrian on the tomb of his lover Antinous, who drowned in the Nile in 130. It may have been transported from Egypt by Elagabalus in the 3rd century. Throughout the park are busts of celebrated Italians from the days of ancient Rome to the 20th century. Of the fountains, the most notable are the Water Clock, in Viale dell'Orologio, and the Fountain of Moses.

The Pincio is bounded on the north and east by massive walls, part of which is the Muro Torto, or *Murus Ruptus*, the only stretch of the Aurelian Walls that was not fortified by Belisarius against the Goths: he was prevented from doing so by the Romans who told him it would be defended by St Peter. The wall has indeed survived, even though it has seemed for centuries to be on the point of collapsing.

VILLA BORGHESE

The magnificent Villa Borghese (*map p. 620*) is Rome's most famous public park, and the most extensive in the centre of the city, with a circumference of 6km and an area of 688 hectares. It is connected with the Pincio and the Villa Giulia, so that the three form one huge green area, intersected in every direction by avenues and paths, with fine oaks, giant ilexes, umbrella pines and other trees, as well as statues, fountains and terraces. It also contains the suburban villa that houses the famous Museo and Galleria Borghese.

The Villa owes its origin, in the 17th century, to Cardinal Scipione Borghese, Paul V's nephew. In the 18th century Prince Marcantonio Borghese, the father of Prince Camillo Borghese (who married Pauline Bonaparte), employed Jacob More from Edinburgh to design the gardens. Early in the 19th century the property was enlarged by the addition of the Giustiniani Gardens. In 1902 it was bought by the state, then handed over to the city of Rome, and opened to the public.

Approaches

On foot the Villa Borghese is best approached from Porta Pinciana (*map p. 620, 3C*), or from the bridge over Viale del Muro Torto, which is reached through the gardens on the Pincian Hill. The park can also be reached from the north by the scenic flight of steps in front of the Galleria Nazionale d'Arte Moderna. A monumental entrance to the park was erected from Piazzale Flaminio, just outside Porta del Popolo. Traffic is excluded from the main area of the park, which is traversed by the electric bus no. 116.

MUSEO & GALLERIA BORGHESE

NB: This is the only museum in Rome where it is obligatory to book your visit in advance. (T: 06 328101; you are given a booking number and the time of your visit; you should go to the entrance at least 15mins beforehand to pick up and pay for your ticket). Open 9–7.30; closed Mon. Entrance allowed only every two hours, at 9, 11, 1, 3 and 5. Ticket valid for two hours; during that time you can visit the rooms on your own at will. The ticket office, information desk, bookshop, bar and toilets are on the lower ground floor (often unpleasantly crowded). The collection of sculptures is mostly on the ground floor, and the gallery of paintings on the upper floor. Unless it is raining, the entrance to the ground floor is up the outside steps through the doors under the central portico (with fragments of a triumphal frieze showing the Emperor Trajan); otherwise it is from the lower ground floor up a spiral staircase. Handsheets are in each room.

History of the Museo and Galleria Borghese

The Casino Borghese was begun for the Borghese family in 1608 by Flaminio Ponzio, Paul V's architect, and continued after his death in 1613 by Jan van Santen (Giovanni Vasanzio). It was altered for Marcantonio IV Borghese by Antonio Asprucci and time for his historical canvases and for his skilled use of colour, and Vincenzo Gemito, also from Naples and very successful, and who produced fine sculptures including portraits and genre figures, are also represented in this section. The chronological display starts in the large central room (*see plan*).

(1) Sala dell'Ercole: The room is named after the colossal statue, three and a half metres high, of *Hercules and Lichas*, made in 1815 by **Canova**. Hercules is shown seizing the foot and hair of his friend Lichas in fury (after the latter has brought him some unwelcome news), and he seems about to hurl him through the air. Canova told the story of some admirers of his who saw the statue in his studio and at once took it to represent the strength of the French nation in the act of overcoming the Monarchy. The sculptor ironically pointed out to them that it could just as well be taken as an allegory of the strength of the great nation in overthrowing 'licentious liberty'. Also displayed here is a collection of Neoclassical statues from the Torlonia collection. The historical paintings, many dating from the 1870s include works by the northern Italian painter Tranquillo Cremona (his *Marco Polo* is an early work) and Stefano Ussi (*Prayer in the Desert*). But the most famous painting of this period is the *Sicilian Vespers*, the most important work of **Francesco Hayez** (several versions of this masterpiece exist), the Venetian painter who spent most of his brilliant career in Rome. It records a famous incident in 1282 (which took place in Palermo outside a church at the hour of Vespers) which provoked a rebellion against the French and which came to symbolize the pride of the Sicilians and their struggle for independence against foreign rule—a courageous stand particularly admired

many centuries later during the Italian Risorgimento. Hayez, who was President of the Brera Academy in Rome and produced classical 'Academic' paintings, is also remembered as a Romanticist.

(2) Sala della Psiche: The room is named after a Neoclassical statue by **Pietro Tenerani**, displayed here with other works by this very fine sculptor. There is a typical portrait by Andrea Appiani, who worked for Napoleon in Milan. Some of **Ippolito Caffi**'s numerous views of Rome are exhibited here (he is also known for his Venetian scenes and landscapes of the East).

(3) Sala del Sappho: Here are exhibited works by the important Tuscan sculptor **Giovanni Dupré** (including his *Sappho*). Also here are two busts by the American sculptor Hiram Powers (of his wife and daughter), who lived in Florence for some 36 years in the mid-19th century. The **Macchiaioli School** of painters, active in Tuscany before 1864, took their inspiration directly from nature, and their works are characterized by *macchie* or spots of colour. They came to be known as the Tuscan Impressionists. Giovanni Fattori, the most famous exponent of the school, is here represented by a portrait of his first wife, and Silvestro Lega's *The Visit* (1868) is particularly beautiful. Other painters of this group include Antonio Puccinelli (note his very fine portrait of Nerina Badioli), Stefano Ussi and Vincenzo Cabianca.

GALLERIA NAZIONALE D'ARTE MODERNA

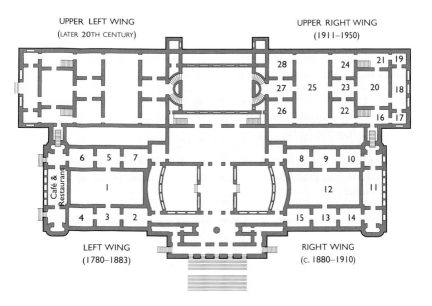

(4) **Sala dello Jenner:** Giulio Monteverde belonged to the school of Verism, and his statue here of Edward Jenner, the English physician who discovered vaccination in 1796, is one of his most important early works. The little painting hung here entitled *The Bather* is another work by Hayez. The painting by Tranquillo Cremona of two children (*The Two Cousins*), is a well-known Romantic work, and another skilled artist who worked in the same Romantic vein, Antonio Fontanesi, is also represented here.

(5) **Sala Morelli:** This room is dedicated to **Domenico Morelli**, who was the most important Neapolitan painter of his time. Here are exhibited some of his fine Historical works (including *Tasso and Eleonora d'Este*), as well as his beautiful religious paintings and portraits (note in particular *Virginia Villari*).

(6) **Sala della Cleopatra:** The *Cleopatra* in question is a marble sculpture by the little-known Alfonso Balzico. Also here are works by artists from Naples, including a terracotta statuette of Brutus and a bust of a Philosopher, both by the very skilled **Vincenzo Gemito**, showing how much he was influenced by late Classical works. Gioacchino Toma's touching works are characterized by their Verism.

Ground floor, right wing

Room 31. More material from *Falerii*, including a 4th-century temple.

Room 32: The coffin made out of the trunk of an oak-tree is from *Gabii*, an important Latin town in the 7th–6th centuries BC on the Via Praenestina, half-way between Rome and Palestrina. An antefix with a maenad's head comes from Lanuvio in the Alban hills.

Room 33: This room is dedicated to finds from *Satricum*, near present-day Latina in southern Lazio, which was famous for its temple of Mater Matuta in the 6th century BC. Later, when the city was included in the territory of the Volsci, it was burnt by the Latins and then destroyed by the Romans.

Room 34: At the end of the corridor are works from Palestrina, about 40km east of Rome, which was the ancient *Praeneste*, a flourishing centre of Latin and Volscian civilization from the 7th century BC up until the Roman era. Since the trade and industry of Etruria and Latium were derived from the same sources, the culture here naturally had much in common with the Etruscans. The most interesting finds are those from the **Barberini and Bernardini tombs**, two important examples of the Oriental period (7th century BC), in which objects in gold and silver, as well as bronzes and ivories, show the influence of Egyptian, Assyrian and Greek art. Digs in 1855 and 1866 unearthed the contents of tombs in the locality of Colombella, just south of the town of Palestrina, and these constitute the Barberini collection.

The earliest pieces were in a large tomb covered with marble slabs of the 7th century BC, the bronzes from the 4th to the 2nd centuries BC were found in deep-laid tombs. The so-called 'Bernardini Tomb', discovered in 1876, was a trench-tomb lined with tufa and covered by a tumulus, and the contents correspond exactly with the style of objects found in the Barberini tombs and those from the Regolini-Galassi tomb in the Vatican.

Notable among the goldsmith's work are two pectorals, or large buckles, of gold granulated work, decorated with cats' heads, chimaeras and sphinxes; a libation cup in silver-gilt with a pharaoh in triumph, horses and an Assyrian royal hunt; and a cauldron, for heating or cooling water, in silver-gilt, with six serpents on the brim, and decorated with horsemen, foot-soldiers, farmers and sheep being attacked by lions. The ivories include cups; a lion with a dead man on his back; fragments in the shape of human arms, which may have served as mirror-handles. Among the bronzes are a conical vase-stand with fantastic animals in repoussé; and a throne in sheet-bronze, with ornamental bands and figures of men and animals; and a splendid collection of bronze mirrors.

Room 35: The last room contains works from centres inhabited by the Umbri, north of Lazio, in present-day Umbria. Finds include goldsmith's work and a bronze helmet inlaid with silver from Todi, and a beautiful Attic bowl with the maker's signature (Pampheios), showing Odysseus evading Polyphemus.

THE TREVI FOUNTAIN
& QUIRINAL HILL

THE TREVI FOUNTAIN
Map p. 622, 1C

The huge Trevi Fountain (*Fontana di Trevi*) is one of the most famous sights of Rome, and its most magnificent fountain. It is also perhaps the city's most exuberant and successful 18th-century monument, made all the more extraordinary by its confined setting in such a small square. The abundant water, which forms an essential part of the design, fills the little piazza with its sound.

The name Trevi may come from *tre vie*, referring to the three roads which converged here. Its waters are those of the Acqua Vergine Antica, an aqueduct which runs almost entirely underground, and was built by Agrippa from a spring some 20km east of the city to supply his public baths near the Pantheon in 19 BC. It also feeds the fountains of Piazza di Spagna, Piazza Navona and Piazza Farnese.

The original 15th-century fountain was a simple and beautiful basin by Leon Battista Alberti, and it was restored by Urban VIII, who is said to have obtained the necessary funds from a tax on wine. Many famous architects, including Bernini, Ferdinando Fuga and Gaspare Vanvitelli presented projects for a new fountain. In 1732 Clement XII held a competition and the little-known Roman architect and poet Niccolò Salvi was given the commission. His theatrical design incorporated, as a background, the entire Neoclassical façade of Palazzo Poli, which had been completed in 1730.

The fountain was completed in 1762, after Salvi's death, by others including Pietro Bracci, who carved the tritons. It was restored for the first time in 1989–91.

Decoration of the fountain
The palace façade has niches containing a figure of Neptune in the centre, flanked by statues symbolizing Health (right) and Abundance (left). The bas-reliefs above represent the legendary virgin from which the aqueduct took its name pointing out the spring to the Roman soldiers, and Agrippa approving the plans for the aqueduct. The four statues above these represent the Seasons with their gifts. At the summit are the arms of the Corsini family, with two allegorical figures. On the enormous artificial rock, built out of tufa, two giant tritons, one blowing a conch, conduct the winged chariot of Neptune pulled by marine horses (known as *hippocampi*) which appear to splash and gallop through the water.

The fountain as symbol
There is still a rooted tradition—which seems to have grown up only at the end of the 19th century—that if you throw a coin over your shoulder into the fountain before

St Andrew the fisherman (holding a net, and with other marine motifs) below the cupola in Bernini's Sant'Andrea al Quirinale.

tour of the façade is one of the most important guiding motifs in Bernini's work, appearing again in his drawings for the eastern elevation of the Louvre and in the church of the Assumption in Ariccia. The forecourt, in the form of a half ellipse, anticipates the elliptical nave, and balances the repeated aedicule and half ellipse of the altar recess. Bernini chose this form because of its symbolic meaning: by arranging the side-chapels radially he placed the emphasis not on the horizontal–vertical axis but on the oblique axiality of the St Andrew's Cross.

The interior is very fine, with columns, pilasters and frames in pink and grey marble, and gilded and stuccoed decorations. Bernini's Classical architecture is combined with his original lighting effects: each chapel is lit by windows high up behind the altars. A fisherman—another allusion to the titular saint Andrew—and numerous cherubim look down from the lantern and surmount the high altarpiece: these were executed by Bernini's assistant Antonio Raggi, who was particularly skilled in stuccowork.

The fine 17th-century altarpieces include works by Baciccia, Giacinto Brandi and Maratta, and the high altarpiece, with the *Crucifixion of St Andrew*, is by Borgognone. The sacristy (*unlocked on request*), where the pretty frescoed ceiling is part of Bernini's design, has a lavabo probably by the master himself.

BERNINI & THE DECORATION OF ROME

Gian Lorenzo Bernini (1598–1680), one of the most famous architects and sculptors of all time, was born in Naples but came to Rome as a boy and remained here almost all his life, except for a short stay in France in 1665 at the invitation of Louis XIV. He began work with his father Pietro, himself an able sculptor. The boy Gian Lorenzo was considered a prodigy: in 1617 the Borghese pope Paul V ordered him to carve his bust, and the pope's nephew, Cardinal Scipione Borghese, commissioned Bernini's first important sculptures, which are still in the Galleria Borghese. He was at once recognized as the greatest artist working in Rome.

Subsequently the Barberini pope Urban VIII became his most important patron as well as a close friend, and called on Bernini to work on St Peter's. Many artists came to Rome to benefit from his guidance, and his workshop was busy carrying out the numerous commissions he received as the most celebrated sculptor and architect in Europe. After the death of Urban VIII, however, Bernini fell temporarily out of favour with the papal court, even though in the end Urban's successor Innocent X did give him the commission for his great fountain in Piazza Navona. Bernini also carried out a great deal of work for Alexander VII: besides the church of Sant'Andrea, for this Chigi pope he designed Piazza San Pietro, a wing of the Palazzo Quirinale, and the Chigi Chapel in Santa Maria del Popolo, as well as more work in St Peter's and the Vatican. Today his remarkable buildings, fountains, sculptures and funerary monuments can be seen all over the city, and his great urban interventions on the approach to St Peter's remain as testimony to his brilliant skills in planning spaces within the fabric of the city.

SAN CARLO ALLE QUATTRO FONTANE
Map p. 623, 1D

This small oval church, lovingly called *San Carlino* by the Romans (*usually open Mon–Fri 10–1 & 3–6; Sat 10–1; Sun 12–1 & 3–6*), is a masterpiece by Francesco Borromini, and it was his first important commission in Rome, often considered his most innovative work. It is difficult to describe the structural richness of the façade; still more difficult to appreciate it, as the church stands right on the street in a cramped corner site, with traffic roaring mercilessly past it and the fountains at each corner of the busy crossroads (the *quattro fontane* after which it is named). Borromini created a two-storey tripartite front with a concave-convex-concave rhythm behind the pilasters at ground level, a rhythm echoed—but not quite replicated—in the three concave bays on the upper façade. Borromini subtly combines geometrical archetypes with poetic citations of nature. Thus the angels' wings over the niche above the portal form a peaked arch which is mirrored in the peak above the gable medallion.

Entrance façade of San Carlo alle Quattro Fontane, showing the undulating sweep of its design, and the repeated peaks of the angels' wings and pointed gable end.

Borromini spent his early apprenticeship on the construction site of Milan's cathedral, and he uses his experience of the medieval design techniques of *quadratura* and *triangulatura* to create the swinging line of the inner wall. The structural affinity of the façade with the interior is wholly intentional.

The interior, begun in 1638 (some 30 years before the façade), has convex and concave surfaces in a complex geometric design using triangles in a unifying scheme: the symbolism throughout is of the Holy Trinity. The small cloister, which is entered from the church, also designed by Borromini, is one of the most original architectural spaces in Rome, based on the architect's delicate sense of curved lines and ingenious designs (even every other pillar of the balustrades on the upper floor is turned upside down). Instead of reinforcing the corners of the cloister arcades with pillars or other supporting structures, Borromini left them open at ground level, raising over each a convex wall structure which anticipates the prestressed concrete of later centuries.

A charming little spiral staircase (again with a unique design, around a twisted central pillar) leads down to the crypt, with another fantastical play of curves linked by a continuous cornice, and unusual side chapels. It is thought that Borromini intended this as the place of his own burial.

THE ARCHITECTURE OF FRANCESCO BORROMINI

Borromini (1599–1667) was born in northern Italy, and when he first came to Rome worked as a collaborator of Carlo Maderno. He designed numerous churches as well as palaces in the city, including the Collegio di Propaganda Fide, Palazzo della Sapienza, Palazzo Barberini, and Palazzo Falconieri on Via Giulia. His best-known churches, apart from San Carlo, are Sant'Agnese in Agone and the Chiesa Nuova. His work is distinguished by its geometrical complexities, the continual use of curves, and its extraordinary imaginativeness. One of his most important commissions was from Innocent X (the only pope who preferred Borromini to Bernini), when he was put in charge of major restoration work at San Giovanni in Laterano, and skilfully managed to retain much of the earlier building in his grand new design. He was known to have had an irascible nature, which made his relationship with his patrons difficult. His introverted temperament was in strong contrast to the ebullient nature of Bernini, and this inevitably led to antagonisms between the two—but this was later exaggerated in popular legend, and in fact they both found themselves working side by side at certain times (for instance at Palazzo Barberini and at St Peter's). Borromini also left some exquisite small, delicate works which still distinguish the appearance of the city—the spiral tower of Sant'Ivo which was later copied many times, especially in German architecture; and the fantastical campanile of Sant'Andrea delle Fratte. The fascinating perspective device he designed for Cardinal Spada in the garden of his palace demonstrates his remarkable imagination. After contributing so much to the wonderful appearance of the city it is sad to think that his life ended in suicide.

PALAZZO BARBERINI
Map p. 623, 1D

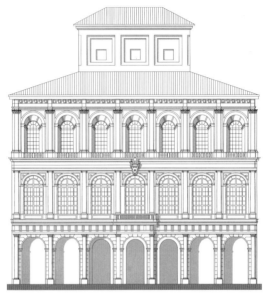

PALAZZO BARBERINI: CENTRAL SECTION OF THE FAÇADE

Open 9–7; closed Mon. T: 06 4824184. Entrance changes periodically, but at present it is on Via delle Quattro Fontane (where the huge stone pilasters and iron grille were added in the 19th century by Francesco Azzurri) through a garden of palm trees.

Palazzo Barberini, one of the grandest palaces in Rome, was begun by Carlo Maderno for the Barberini pope Urban VIII in 1624. Work was continued on the central block by Bernini, and Borromini designed the windows of the top storey, the stairs and some doorways. Pietro da Cortona was also involved as architect, and painted the famous ceiling fresco in the huge main hall.

One wing of the palace now houses part of the Galleria Nazionale d'Arte Antica. This important collection was opened to the public in 1895 in Palazzo Corsini (*see p. 375*), where part of it is still housed. It is pre-eminent in Italian Baroque painting, although there are also some good examples from the 15th and 16th centuries, and a large selection of foreign works. The gallery has been partially closed for rearrangement for many years and has a neglected feel which makes it difficult to appreciate the quality of the paintings, which are at present crowded together in just two rooms.

Raphael: *'La Fornarina'* (1518–19).

The right wing of the palace has been occupied for years by offices and club rooms of the armed forces: these have been scheduled to be moved out to another building for many years to create space for the collection.

Galleria Nazionale d'Arte Antica

Three busts by Bernini are displayed in the entrance. The monumental flight of stairs was probably also designed by Bernini. On the first floor, on the left is the *Salone*, with Pietro Cortona's magnificent ceiling fresco (*see box on previous page*). Some of the masterpieces of the collection have been temporarily hung here. These include two important works by Caravaggio: *Narcissus*, and *Judith with the Head of Holofernes*. The *St Francis in Meditation* is also attributed to him. The *Portrait of a Lady* (or of a Sibyl) by Guido Reni was traditionally thought to be a portrait of Beatrice Cenci, a young girl of 22 who was executed in 1599 for having, a year earlier, hired assassins, together with her step-mother Lucrezia and brother Jacopo, to kill her father. Although Beatrice never confessed to parricide even under torture, she was beheaded. Her father was known to have been a very violent man and was also accused of incest. Her story caught the imagination of the Romantics and in 1819 Shelley, while staying in Livorno, wrote his famous verse drama *The Cenci*. He had seen this portrait in Palazzo Colonna when he came to Rome the previous year, and Stendhal, Charles Dickens and Nathaniel Hawthorne all mention the painting, which did much to augment the aura of tragedy which surrounded the figure of Beatrice. It is interesting that her story

still held so much significance that as recently as 1999 the municipality of Rome saw fit to erect a plaque to her memory on Via di Monserrato on the site of the prison of Corte Savella where on 11th September 1599 she set out for the gallows ('an exemplary victim of unjust justice').

In the so-called Sala dei Marmi is another temporary exhibition of some of the best-known works in the collection. The *Portrait of a Lady* by Raphael (*pictured on p. 221*; also attributed to his pupil Giulio Romano) became known as '*La Fornarina*' when the Romantics identified the sitter

Guido Reni's *Portrait of a Lady,* thought to be a portrait of Beatrice Cenci.

with Margherita, daughter of the Sienese baker (or *fornaio*) Francesco Luti, and supposedly Raphael's mistress. The portrait has many similarities (in the sense that it appears to be the same sitter) with another superb portrait by Raphael known as *La Velata*, now in the Palatine Gallery in Palazzo Pitti in Florence. Raphael was engaged to be married to Cardinal Bibbiena's niece, Maria, who predeceased him. Also displayed here is a painted bust of *Ceres* by Baldassare Peruzzi and *Mary Magdalene* by Piero di Cosimo.

A spiral staircase leads up to nine rooms with well preserved Rococo decorations (1750–70), where the Barberini family lived up until 1960. The rooms are also interesting for their period furniture. The dining-room is particularly charming. The paintings are by Paolo Monaldi (1763–70).

VIA VENETO & THE LUDOVISI DISTRICT

Map p. 623, 1D & p. 620, 3C

Piazza Barberini was transformed between the wars into one of the busiest traffic hubs in the city. Isolated in the centre of the square in this unpleasant setting is Bernini's masterpiece, the **Fontana del Tritone** (1642–43), with four dolphins supporting a scallop shell on which is seated a triton (or merman) who blows a single jet of water through a conch shell held up in his hands. Surviving drawings by Bernini show that he made a careful study of where the water would fall, but since the water pressure is now lower the full effect can no longer be appreciated: the spray was meant to have reached the scallop shell, and from there the water would brim over into the lowest basin. Commissioned by the Barberini pope Urban VIII, it is decorated with the beautifully-carved Barberini coat of arms with the emblem of the bee.

On the north side of the square, at the beginning of Via Veneto, is the small, reconstructed Fontana delle Api, designed by Bernini a year later, also decorated with the Barberini bee and with an inscription on the scallop shell stating that the water is for the use of the public and their animals. The small marble basin below was designed at the beginning of the 20th century when the fountain was moved from its original site on the corner of Via Sistina, and recomposed here.

Via Veneto

The broad and tree-lined Via Veneto, correctly Via Vittorio Veneto (named after a conclusive victory by the Italian army over the Austrians in 1918), opened in 1886, is lined with luxury hotels, great mansions and famous cafés: it was especially fashionable for its ambience of *la dolce vita* in the 1960s (after the success of Federico Fellini's film of that name). It runs through part of the huge site of the beautiful park, now obliterated, of the **Villa Ludovisi**, which was acquired from 1621 onwards by Cardinal Ludovico Ludovisi, nephew of Pope Gregory XV. He had bought some 19 hectares of land by the time of his death and designed a garden which was much admired by John Evelyn. Later travellers who mentioned it include Goethe (1787), Stendhal (1828), Hippolyte Taine (1864) and Henry James (1883). The last descendant of the family, Ippolita Ludovisi (princess of Piombino) married Gregorio Boncompagni, Duke of Sora (a descendant of Pope Gregory XIII) and in their nuptial agreement it was decided that the two surnames should be used perpetually by their heirs and descendants. By now the property included an area of some 30 hectares from the stretch of walls between Porta Pinciana to Porta Salaria, down to the present Via Boncompagni and all the area to the southwest now occupied by Via Vittorio Veneto as far as Via di Porta Pinciana.

In 1883 the Boncompagni-Ludovisi were forced (by a retroactive law introduced by the Italian government) to divide their immense wealth between all their relatives and so they decided to destroy the gardens and sell off the huge property as building land. Despite an international outcry, work began on felling the trees and laying out new roads in 1885 and most of the buildings had been constructed by 1889. The only survival of the original villa and gardens is the **Villa Aurora** (*entered at no. 46 Via Lombardia, map p. 620, 3C; usually open Fri morning but only by previous appointment; T: 06 483942*). The first Roman scene in Henry James's novel *Roderick Hudson* takes place in the gardens here. The garden-house contains a fine ceiling-painting of *Aurora and Fame* by Guercino (1621). Some one hundred pieces of the famous Ludovisi collection of Classical sculpture, founded by Cardinal Ludovico, were bought by the state in 1901: now part of the Museo Nazionale Romano, they are exhibited in Palazzo Altemps (*see p. 272*). The name Ludovisi is perpetuated in the name of this aristocratic district of the city.

The **church of the Cappuccini**, or Santa Maria della Concezione, is architecturally simple and unpretentious in accordance with Franciscan ideals and in strong contrast to the Baroque works of its time (1626). Its founder was Cardinal Antonio Barberini, whose burial place in the church is marked by an inscription on the pavement in front of the high altar, which reads *hic jacet pulvis, cinis et nihil* ('here lies nothing but dust and ashes'). In the interior are paintings by important artists, all of whom produced many works for Roman churches and were born in the 1580s or 1590s: Honthorst, Domenichino, Andrea Sacchi, and Pietro da Cortona. The delightful painting of *St Michael* in the first chapel on the south side is by Guido Reni, born in 1575. A painting of *St Francis* (which is sadly kept locked away in the convent) is considered by some scholars to be by Caravaggio (and by others to be a contemporary copy): the simple Franciscan life of poverty was a favourite subject for this great painter, who was out of sympathy with the pomp and excesses of the contemporary Church.

A cemetery (*entered down the stairs to the right of the church; open 9–12 & 3–6; closed Thur*) has five subterranean chapels decorated from the 17th century onwards with the bones and skeletons of over 4,000 Capuchins, arranged in patterns. It has for centuries been one of the 'sights' of Rome, and this macabre place is still much visited.

At the top of Via Veneto is **Porta Pinciana**, a handsome fortified gateway erected by Honorius around 403 and since enlarged. On either side can be seen a long stretch of the Aurelian Walls (272–79) with 18 turrets. Outside the gate is the park of Villa Borghese (*see p. 189*).

THE BATHS OF DIOCLETIAN & DISTRICT

The vast **Piazza dei Cinquecento** (*map p. 623, 1F*) is by far the largest square in Rome, though it is really no more than a network of roads and the terminus or junction of many bus services, and is always busy with traffic. In winter hundreds of thousands of starlings come to roost here at dusk. At one end stands Stazione Termini, one of the largest railway stations in Europe. Rome's two underground lines intersect here. The reconstruction of the station began in 1938, was delayed by the Second World War, and it was not opened until 1950; it was modernized in 2000. A gigantic quasi-cantilever construction, sweeping upwards and outwards, serves as a portico. The station was named after the Baths (Termini) of Diocletian which are close by.

In front of the station, on the left, is the best-preserved fragment of the Servian Wall, formed of massive blocks of tufa. This wall, some 11km long, was traditionally attributed to Servius Tullius, sixth king of Rome; it is now thought that the wall dates from about 378 BC, although sections of an earlier earthen bank (*agger*), which may be the work of Servius have been identified. There were 12 gates in the wall. Further fragments of the wall were unearthed during the reconstruction of the station. Beneath the station remains of a private house and of baths were found, with good mosaics, dating from the 2nd century AD (*not at present open to the public*).

Adjoining Piazza dei Cinquecento is the large circular **Piazza della Repubblica**, the best known work by the neo-Renaissance architect Gaetano Koch (1896–1902), where the semicircular porticoed fronts of the *palazzi* follow the line of the exedra of the Baths of Diocletian. The abundant waters of the Fountain of the Naiads (1870) are supplied by the Acqua Marcia, which terminates here. This aqueduct, built from Tivoli to Rome in 144 BC, was one of the most important and longest of the Roman aqueducts. The same springs were tapped for a new aqueduct, built in part of cast-iron by a private Anglo-Italian company for the Papal States, called the Pia Marcia and inaugurated in 1870 by Pius X. The four groups of faintly erotic reclining nymphs, symbolizing the spirits of rivers and springs, and the central Glaucus, are by Mario Rutelli (1901–11).

Santa Maria degli Angeli

Santa Maria degli Angeli (*open 7.30–12.30 & 4–6.30*) occupies the great central hall of the Baths of Diocletian, converted into the church of the Carthusian convent. It is used for state funerals. The work of adaptation was carried out in 1563–66 for Pius IV to a design by Michelangelo. He placed the entrance of the church at the short southeast side of the rectangle and thus had at his disposal a nave of vast proportions. The effect was spoiled by Vanvitelli who, instructed by the Carthusian fathers in 1749, altered the orientation. He made the entrance in the long southwest side and so converted the nave into a transept. To compensate for the loss of length, he built out on the northeast side an apsidal choir, which broke into the monumental southwest wall of the frigidarium. The façade on Piazza della Repubblica, with Vanvitelli's doorway, incorporates an apsidal wall, all that is left of the calidarium.

In the disappointing interior, the circular vestibule stands on the site of the tepidarium. Here, on the right, is the tomb of Carlo Maratta (d. 1713; *see box*), and on the left that of Salvator Rosa (d. 1673), the Neapolitan painter, many of whose romantic landscapes were painted in the city. By the entrance into the transept, on the right, stands a fine colossal statue of St Bruno, the founder of the Carthusian Order, by the celebrated French sculptor Jean-Antoine Houdon, made when he was studying at the French Academy in Rome from 1764–68.

The vast transept is nearly 100m long, 27m wide and 28m high. The eight monolithic columns of red granite, nearly 14m high and 1.5m in diameter, are original; the others (almost indistinguishable), in brick, were added when the building was remodelled. To the right, in the pavement, are a meridian dating from 1703; and the tomb, by Antonio Muñoz, of Marshal Armando Diaz (d. 1928), Italian commander-in-chief in the First World War. The huge paintings include works by Pompeo Batoni, Domenichino, Pomarancio, and Carlo Maratta. In the choir (reserved for prayer so difficult to see) is a monument to Pius IV, based on a design by Michelangelo. The door to the sacristy in the left transept leads to a room with remains of the frigidarium of the Baths of Diocletian, and a display explaining the history of the building.

Andrea Sacchi (1599–1661) and *Carlo Maratta* (1625–1713)

Andrea Sacchi was born near Rome. As a pupil of Cavaliere d'Arpino he worked in the Classical style and was a highly skilled draughtsman and frescoist. He carried out altarpieces for several churches in the city, and one of his best works is the *Death of St Anne* in San Carlo ai Catinari (*see p. 304*). He also received commissions from the Vatican, notably for the decoration of the drum of the cupola of the Baptistery of San Giovanni in Laterano (now replaced by late 19th-century copies). Because of this he was allowed burial in the Lateran basilica next door. Several mosaics in St Peter's reproduce his paintings, and he worked in the Chapter House of that great church. Today perhaps the best of his works to be seen in Rome is the *Vision of St Romuald* in the Vatican Picture Gallery.

Carlo Maratta is known to have been his pupil, and he soon took over as the most important painter at work in Rome in the late 17th century. An extremely prolific artist, his altarpieces can be seen in numerous churches in the city (amongst his works are those in the basilica of San Marco and in the church of Santi Ambrogio e Carlo). He interpreted the spirit of the Counter- Reformation on a grand scale and had the assistance of many pupils who came to work in his studio. Like his master Sacchi, his paintings are reproduced in a number of mosaics in St Peter's. He received commissions from Alexander VII both here and in Siena, and his portrait of Alexander's successor Clement IX (now in the Vatican Picture Gallery) is one of his most successful works.

The Dogali monument

In the gardens on Viale Einaudi there is monument by Francesco Azzurri, erected in memory of 548 Italian soldiers ambushed at Dogali, Eritrea, in 1887. It incorporates an Egyptian obelisk found in the Isaeum Campense (*see p. 263*), inscribed with hiero-glyphs recording the glories of Rameses the Great or Sesostris, the pharaoh of the time of Moses. Its companion is in Florence. The monument, first erected in front of the old railway station, was moved here in 1924; in 1936–44 it was decorated with the Lion of Judah, plundered from Addis Ababa.

THE BATHS OF DIOCLETIAN
Map p. 623, 1E–F

Open 9–7.45; closed Mon; T: 06 3996 7700. The entrance to the Baths of Diocletian is at present through the garden in front of the railway station.

The splendid vaulted rooms of the Baths of Diocletian (*Terme di Diocleziano*) once pro-vided a superb setting for the collections of the Museo Nazionale Romano, founded here in 1889. Most of the museum has been moved to Palazzo Massimo alle Terme (*see p. 237 below*), and the massive Roman buildings are closed indefinitely for restoration, with the exception of the Octagonal Hall (*see p. 234 below*). However, in 2001 the huge col-lection of epigraphs belonging to the museum was beautifully rearranged here in mod-ern halls on the site of a Carthusian monastery built into the ruins in the 16th century, and a proto-historic section opened on the first floor of the large cloister.

Construction of the baths

Begun in 299, the baths were completed in less than eight years by Diocletian and Maximian. They were the largest of all the ancient Roman baths, and could accommo-date over 3,000 people at once. They covered a rectangular area, c. 380m by 370m, cor-responding to that now bounded on the southeast by Piazza dei Cinquecento, on the southwest by Via Torino, on the northwest by Via Venti Settembre, and on the north-east by Via Volturno. The main buildings included a calidarium, tepidarium and frigi-darium. The calidarium, which survived into the late 17th century, occupied part of Piazza della Repubblica. The tepidarium and the huge central hall of the baths are now occupied by the church of Santa Maria degli Angeli (*see below*). The frigidarium was an open-air bath behind this hall. Numerous large and small halls, nymphaea and exedrae were located within the precincts. The baths were plundered for their building materi-als in the 16th–19th centuries.

The only entrance to the baths was on the northeast side, near the present Via Volturno. On the southwest side the closed exedra was flanked by two circular halls: one of these is now the church of San Bernardo alle Terme, the other was at the corner of Via Viminale and Via delle Terme. A third, octagonal hall, on the corner of Via Parigi at the northwest angle of the main complex, is open to the public (*described on p. 234*).

Round Hall: Here is a display of Archaic finds (8th–5th centuries BC). In the central case is the oldest testimony of the Greek alphabet so far found in Italy: it is on a simple vase found in *Gabii* in Lazio, traditionally dated around 770 BC, but now thought to be even older (late 9th century). Next to it the *aryballos*, a vessel with a globular body and narrow neck in black terracotta (*bucchero*), bears a votive inscription in Etruscan. Found near Veio, it is dated to the late 7th century BC. Exhibited in a wall case on the left is a reproduction of the golden brooch known as the '*fibula praenestina*', famous in the late 20th century when most scholars decided it was a fake: if it is, instead, original it would provide the earliest known example of a Latin inscription (early 7th century BC). Also on this wall is a display of ceramics, with inscriptions, found in a votive deposit beneath the Lapis Niger (*see p. 69*) in the Roman Forum (a cast of which is exhibited here). A fragment of a cup in *bucchero* ware found in the Regia in the Forum bears the owner's name, Rex, thought to refer to one of the last kings of Rome. Architectural fragments of the late 7th and early 6th centuries BC from the Regia are also exhibited here. Displayed on its own is an inscription in tufa from Tivoli, which may refer to Publius Valerius, the first Republican consul of Rome (509 BC).

Other cases in the centre display finds from recent excavations on the slopes of the Palatine, some of which bear the letter V, which seems to refer to the cult of Juno Sospita (Juno the Saviour), which flourished in the 6th–5th centuries BC.

In the wall cases on the right are finds from a sanctuary in *Lavinium* in Lazio (*see below*), including a bronze inscription of the late 6th century BC, with a dedication to the twin heroes Castor and Pollux, the earliest reference so far found in Lazio to the Greek cult of the Dioscuri, taken to be the sons of Zeus and brothers of Helen of Troy. There are other stone inscriptions to divinities dating from the 6th century BC, including one in tufa from Tivoli.

Main Hall: The main hall displays works from the early Republican period (4th–3rd centuries BC). In the first case on the right are black varnish ceramics with inscriptions dating from the 3rd century BC found in the Tiber in Rome. Some of these, including ex-votos, belonged to the sanctuary of Aesculapius erected in 289 BC on the Isola Tiberina (*see p. 315*). A large marble basin with a dedication to Hercules from a sacred font dating from the 3rd century BC is the oldest known example of an inscription with metal lettering. Other finds come from sanctuaries in Roman cities in Lazio, including *Lanuvium* (Lanuvio), an ancient city famous for its sanctuary of Juno Sospita, the site of which has been found in the Alban hills near Genzano. Against the wall are four large *cippi* (late 4th and early 3rd centuries BC) from Lavinium excavated at Pratica di Mare near the sea, which, according to an ancient legend, was the town founded by Aeneas, after his escape from Troy, and named after his wife. Numerous ancient Roman historians, as well as Virgil, upheld this myth, and as early as 300 BC a tradition existed at Lavinium itself which attributed its foundation to the

Trojan hero. A tomb sanctuary dedicated to him, in the form of a tumulus burial chamber, restored in the 4th century BC, was found nearby, and the *cippi* come from here.

Displayed on their own at the end of the room are seven remarkable sculptures from a sanctuary dating from the late 4th or early 3rd century BC found at Ariccia: these include busts of Demeter (or Ceres), and her daughter Kore (or Persephone), and three seated female statues in terracotta.

On the left side of the room are ceramics bearing the names of members of the Rabirii family whose tomb was unearthed at *Tusculum*, near Frascati, another important Roman centre. A bronze inscription and finds from a temple at *Norba* (present day Norma), dating from the late 3rd century BC, are also displayed here. In the last case are objects from *Praeneste* (Palestrina), one of the oldest towns of Lazio, which was thriving as early as the 7th century BC, and which for long remained independent of Rome. It was famous for its cult of Fortuna Primigenia, especially after about 130 BC when a huge Temple of Fortune was built in the town, the most grandiose Hellensitic edifice in Italy. The very unusual 'crown' exhibited here is decorated with acanthus leaves and bears an inscription to Fortuna Primigenia, and next to it is a little cippus in the form of a pine cone, with the name of a dead man.

In the room to the left are displayed inscriptions dating from the late Republican period (2nd–1st century BC). These include several with names of slaves, and one found recently near the Meta Sudans (*see p. 103*) relating to a company of singers and actors which gave performances of Greek plays. There are also inscribed statue bases, and inscribed stone panels announcing public works. The funerary inscriptions set up by artisans in the city include that of Atistia, the wife of the baker whose grand travertine tomb still stands beside the Porta Maggiore (*see p. 368*). A fragment of an inscription in handsome lettering records the funerary oration of a husband to his wife, pronounced between 8 and 2 BC. A group of terracotta pots, found in Via di Porta Sebastiano bear inscriptions with a name and date, probably referring to the cremated person to whom the small piece of bone found inside belonged.

At the end of the main hall there is a dedication in bronze originally set up by a group of players of wind instruments, beneath a bronze statue of Tiberius, dating from 7 BC which was found on the slopes of the Palatine in 1992–93. On the same site a large statue base in marble was unearthed with handsome inscriptions, ordered by the same group of musicians, relating to four statues of Augustus, Nero, Claudius, and Agrippina, mother of Nero. Three fragments of Luni marble were part of a calendar with a list of magistrates who held office in Rome between 43 BC and 3 AD.

Second floor

A circular stair leads to the second floor where a very fine display of epigraphs illustrates the social structure of the Roman empire, and other aspects of Roman life. On the left balcony are exhibited numerous epigraphs from a dynastic monument belonging to the

Room VIII: The ornamental wall-fountain decorated with mosaics and shells was found in Nero's villa at Anzio. Also here are paintings from a building near a port on the Tiber, with scenes of boats and fishing, including numerous delightful fish, and stucco decoration from the hypogeum of Aguzzano.

Room IX: Mosaics here are from the villa of Septimius Severus at Baccano, including four quadrangles showing four charioteers holding their horses.

Room X: The wall paintings date from the 3rd–4th centuries AD, including one

of Venus, known as the *Dea Barberini*, found near the baptistery of San Giovanni in Laterano in the 17th century, when it was restored as the *Dea Roma*.

Room XI: This last room has superb polychrome marble intarsia panels in *opus sectile*. The two panels from the basilica of Junius Bassus on the Esquiline (early 4th century AD) show a mythological scene with Hylas, and the start of a chariot race. The head of the sun god Helios-Sol was found in the Mithraeum beneath Santa Prisca on the Aventine.

Basement

The vaults in the basement house the treasury, with valuable jewellery and coins. There is also an important study collection open to scholars. The first room has a display illustrating Diocletian's edict of AD 301, which attempted to combat inflation. It is known from some 132 marble fragments found all over the Empire from 1709 onwards and is of fundamental importance to scholars for the understanding of the Roman economy. Another room has a fine exhibit of gold jewellery, two alabaster cinerary urns, and a sarcophagus found on the Via Cassia with the well-preserved mummy of an eight-year-old girl.

The large main hall (entered through armoured doors) houses the most important numismatic collection in Italy, covering all periods of its history. The exhibits come from the Gnecchi collection of Roman and Byzantine coins, the Kircher collections acquired by the state in 1913, and the collection of King Vittorio Emanuele III. The superb display, divided into eleven sections, includes some 1,800 pieces.

The first section is dedicated to the goddess Juno Moneta and the mint on the Capitoline Hill, the Santa Marinella hoard of bronze ingots, and the earliest coined metal (4th–3rd centuries BC). The second section illustrates coins in the Republican era, and the third and fourth sections the Imperial period. Sections five to eight cover the Goths, Byzantines, Lombards, Franks and Normans. A circular area is dedicated to pontifical coinage. Sections nine and ten display late medieval and Renaissance coins, and the last section has 19th century coins up to the Unification of Italy, and those minted during the reign of Vittorio Emanuele III.

SANTA MARIA MAGGIORE & THE ESQUILINE HILL

Piazza dell'Esquilino is overlooked by the imposing apse of Santa Maria Maggiore, approached by steps. The obelisk here, nearly 15m high, was set up by Sixtus V in 1587 as part of the design to fit the vistas in his long, straight Strada Felice (*see p. 177*). Like its twin in Piazza del Quirinale, it once stood outside the entrance to the Mausoleum of Augustus (*see p. 550*). The façade of the huge church faces Piazza Santa Maria Maggiore, which occupies the highest point of the Cispian summit of the Esquiline Hill. In this square rises a fluted *cipollino* column (just half a metre shorter than the obelisk) from the Basilica of Maxentius in the Forum. It was set up here in 1613 for Paul V by Carlo Maderno and crowned with a statue of the Virgin. Maderno also designed the fountain at its base, decorated with dragons and masks in travertine.

SANTA MARIA MAGGIORE
Map p. 623, 2E

Open 7–6 or 7. The museum is open 9.30–6.30. The Loggia delle Benedizioni, with its 13th-century mosaics, is open twice a day (at 9.30 & 1). The church tends to be very crowded with tour groups; it is best to visit early.

The basilica of Santa Maria Maggiore manages to retain the original magnificence of its interior more completely than the other three great patriarchal basilicas (San Giovanni in Laterano, St Peter's and San Paolo fuori le Mura). It still has its 5th-century plan and contains important mosaics, elaborate tombs and sumptuous chapels erected by the popes in the 16th and 17th centuries. The basilica has extraterritorial status.

History of the basilica

According to a 13th-century legend, the Virgin Mary appeared on the night of 4th–5th August c. 358 to Pope Liberius (352–66) and to John, a patrician of Rome, telling them to build a church on the Esquiline. She told them that in the morning they would find a patch of snow covering the exact area to be built over. The prediction fulfilled, Liberius drew up the plans and John built the church at his own expense. The original title was therefore *Santa Maria della Neve* (of the Snow) and a pontifical mass is still held here annually on 5th August to commemorate the miraculous snowfall. The church was afterwards called *Santa Maria del Presepe*, after a precious relic of the crib of the Infant Jesus, which is displayed on the high altar every year on Christmas morning, when there is a procession in its honour.

A basilica was indeed built here by Pope Liberius on the site of a Roman edifice, and was called the *Basilica Liberiana*. In 366 supporters of the antipope Ursinus barricaded themselves in the church and surrendered only when the partisans of Pope Damasus I

(?Valentine); on the left, St Praxedes, St Pudentiana and St Agnes, and four half-length female figures including Paschal's mother Theodora (with the square nimbus). The altar-niche has a charming *Madonna and Child* (with His arms held out to us) between the sister saints Praxedes and Pudentiana. Here you can closely examine the mosaic technique; it is also permanently lit, whereas there is a coin-operated light for the rest of the chapel. The pavement is perhaps the oldest known example of *opus sectile*. The bases of the four supporting columns also date from Paschal's time, except for the one on the right of the altar—a fine 5th-century Roman work—which he carefully reused. In a niche on the right are fragments of a column brought from Jerusalem after the Sixth Crusade (1228), and said to be that at which Christ was scourged. There are not many other relics in Rome of such doubtful authenticity still so boldly exhibited (note the charming little old-fashioned display case).

In the main church, on the **choir arch**, are depicted the *New Jerusalem*, with the elect preceded by angels and received into Heaven by St Peter and St Paul, with Christ in the centre between Elijah and Moses, and the Apostles. On the inner face are *Christ and Saints*. The **apse arch** shows the *Lamb of God* with the seven golden candlesticks, the symbols of the Evangelists, and 24 Elders raising their crowns as a sign of glory. The **semi-dome** has Christ between St Peter, St Pudentiana and St Zeno on the right and St Paul, St Praxedes and St Paschal on the left (the latter's square nimbus indicates he was still alive when the mosaic was executed); below them are shown the Lamb, the flock of the Faithful and a dedicatory inscription; above, the monogram of Paschal I. The apse mosaics are evidently derived from those in Santi Cosma e Damiano (*see p. 125*).

Other works of art in the church

The nave has 16 granite columns and six piers supporting an architrave made up of ancient Roman fragments. On the left and right of the sanctuary are six beautiful Roman columns of very unusual design incorporating the form of acanthus and laurel leaves. The effective 16th-century *trompe l'oeil* frescoes are by Paris Nogari, Baldassare Croce, and Agostino Ciampelli. In the nave pavement a large porphyry disc with an inscription indicates the well where St Praxedes supposedly hid the bones of Christian martyrs.

The choir is reached by steps of *rosso antico*. The fine Baroque baldacchino is by Francesco Ferrari (1730). In the crypt beneath are four early Christian sarcophagi, including one with the remains of the sisters St Praxedes and St Pudentiana, and a 13th-century Cosmatesque altar with a very damaged fresco above depicting the Madonna between the two saints.

Tombs in the church include two of cardinals—Alain Coëtivy (1474) by Andrea Bregno, and Pantaleon of Troyes (d. 1286), with Cosmatesque fragments attributed to Arnolfo di Cambio. On a nave pillar the monument to Giovanni Battista Santoni (d. 1592), is one of the earliest works of Gian Lorenzo Bernini.

The third chapel in the north aisle has good late 16th-century frescoes by Cavaliere d'Arpino and an altarpiece of the same date by Federico Zuccari. In the second chapel in the south aisle are 17th-century paintings and frescoes by Ciro Ferri and Borgognone. A chair and table used by St Charles Borromeo are preserved in the church.

Santa Pudenziana

Santa Pudenziana (*open 8–12 & 4–6; map p. 623, 2E*) is one of the oldest churches in Rome, thought to have been built c. 390 above a Roman thermal hall of the 2nd century. It was rebuilt several times later, notably in 1589. The church is dedicated to Pudentiana, sister of Praxedes (*see p. 250 above*), and daughter of the Roman senator Pudens, a legendary figure who is supposed to have given hospitality to St Peter in his house on this site when the Apostle first arrived in Rome. The church is now well below the level of the modern street. It is little visited by tourists, and after the crowds of Santa Maria Maggiore is a soothing relief. The façade was rebuilt and decorated in the 19th century; the fine campanile probably dates from the late 12th century. The good doorway preserves a medieval frieze in relief.

The interior

The church contains an extremely interesting **apse mosaic**, the earliest of its kind in Rome, dating from 390. It was damaged by a 16th-century restoration, which removed the two outermost Apostles at each end and cut the others in half. It shows *Christ Enthroned*, holding an open book (with the inscription *Dominus conservator ecclesiae pudentianae*), between St Peter and St Paul and the Apostles and two female figures representing the converted Jews and the converted pagans (or Gentiles), who are presenting wreaths. The Roman character of the figures is marked; the magisterial air of Christ recalls representations of Jupiter, and the Apostles, in their togas, resemble senators. Above is a mountain crowned by a jewelled Cross and four symbolic heavenly creatures, usually interpreted as symbols of the Evangelists.

The iconography of this remarkable work has been closely studied by scholars for its significance in the early development of Christianity in Rome: it dates from the time of Theodosius, who declared Christianity as the state religion. Here the bearded Christ is depicted enthroned in divine majesty seated on a purple cushion in a posture which recalls statues of Roman emperors. He is shown being acclaimed by the Apostles, again using gestures which seem to be derived from acclamation scenes of late Roman emperors. It would appear that Imperial motifs were deliberately used in early Christian iconography to strengthen the position of the church in Rome. Paul is included to bring the number of Apostles to twelve and this is one of the earliest instances in which we see him take pride of place with Peter beside Christ. He was in many ways the most important figure in early Christian Rome, and his letters were used to justify the authority the emperor might exercise over the Church. The arrangement of Christ seated in the centre of a semicircle may well reflect the way services were taken in the apsidal east ends of early Christian basilicas. The unusual arcaded portico which surrounds the scene has not been satisfactorily explained, but above it the buildings (which include houses, *thermae* and a basilica) are thought to represent Jerusalem and the Holy Sepulchre in the 4th century.

Sadly the Roman columns of the church have been partially covered by piers. The dome was painted by Pomarancio. In the chapel at the end of the north aisle an altar, presented in the 19th century by Cardinal Wiseman (who was appointed by the pope as Roman Catholic archbishop of Westminster), encloses part of the legendary Communion-table of St Peter; the rest of it is in San Giovanni in Laterano. The Baroque Cappella Caetani, by Francesco da Volterra, was finished by Carlo Maderno.

THE ESQUILINE HILL

The Esquiline (65m), the highest and most extensive of the Seven Hills of Rome, has four summits. Most of the Oppius or Oppian Hill is covered by a park (the Parco Oppio), on the site of the Baths of Titus and of Trajan and of Nero's Domus Aurea (*see p. 107*). The Cispius, extending to the northeast, is crowned by the basilica of Santa Maria Maggiore (*see above*). The other two summits are the Subura, above the low-lying district of that name, and the Fagutalis, named from a beech grove (from *fagus*, a beech).

HISTORY OF THE ESQUILINE HILL

The four summits of the Esquiline, together with the three of the Palatine, formed the early city of the *Septimontium*. According to the erudite Varro, the name Esquiline was derived from the word *excultus*, which referred to the ornamental groves planted on the hill by Servius Tullius, including the *Querquetulanus* (oak grove) and *Fagutalis* (beech grove).

Formerly a place of vineyards and gardens, most of the hill was considered an unhealthy place to live, but the area between the modern Via Cavour and the slopes of the Oppian Hill, called the *Carinoe*, was a fashionable residential district. Pompey lived here, in a small but famous house that was occupied after his death by Antony. The fabulously rich Maecenas (c. 70–8 BC) also had a villa here (a garden building of which survives, which he left to his close friend Augustus. The remarkable Roman statues unearthed here are exhibited in the Centrale Montemartini (*see p. 474*). The fame of Maecenas as a generous patron of the arts (he was particularly praised for this quality by Horace, who may also have had a house here) survives to this day—his name is still used in modern parlance to describe a great patron. The poets Virgil and Propertius, who were admired by Maecenas, also lived on the hill. The villa of Maecenas was eventually acquired by Nero, who incorporated it in his famous Domus Aurea, and the site was afterwards occupied by the Baths of Titus.

Via Cavour

Via Cavour, now an important traffic artery of the city, was opened in 1890 when many old houses were destroyed: its construction has been seen by many urban architects as one of the most damaging interventions ever made to the townscape of Rome (but the project to extend it all the way to the Tiber was mercifully halted).

A flight of steps called Via San Francesco di Paola is on the site of the ancient *Via Scelerata*, which apparently received its name—the 'Wicked Way'—from the impious act of Tullia, who here drove her chariot over the dead body of her royal father Servius Tullius in 535 BC. According to legend she was responsible for ordering her brother-in-law Tarquinius Superbus to murder both her husband and her father, so that he would become king and she could marry him. Tarquinius, indeed, became the last of the the the six Etruscan kings who ruled Rome after Romulus.

The steps pass beneath an archway above which is an attractive Doric loggia, once part of the house of Vannozza Catanei (1442–1518), the beautiful mistress of Pope Alexander VI, and mother of four of his children, including Lucrezia and Cesare Borgia. Near the base of a medieval tower, with bands of black and white stone, is the large 17th-century palace which houses the administrative offices of the Istituto Centrale del Restauro (a state restoration centre), which now has its main laboratories in the former Istituto di San Michele (*see p. 383*).

SAN PIETRO IN VINCOLI
Map p. 623, 3E

Open 7.30–12.30 & 3.30–6. Entrance up the covered steps from Via Cavour.
The church was restored in 1475 under Sixtus IV by Meo del Caprina, who was responsible for the façade, with its beautiful colonnaded portico. The splendid simplicity of the façade is echoed in the basilican interior. Though much affected by restoration, it preserves its 20 ancient fluted columns with Doric capitals (the Ionic bases were added in the 17th century). The nave, almost four times as wide as the aisles, has a ceiling painting representing the cure of a person possessed by an evil spirit through the touch of the holy chains.

THE CHAINS OF ST PETER

The two chains with which St Peter was supposedly fettered in the *Tullianum* (*see p. 122*) are said to have been taken to Constantinople. In 439 Juvenal, Bishop of Jerusalem, gave them to the Empress Eudoxia, wife of Theodosius the Younger. She placed one of them in the basilica of the Apostles at Constantinople, and sent the other to Rome for her daughter Eudoxia, wife of Valentinian III, who was Emperor of the Western Empire 425–455. In 442 the younger Eudoxia gave the chain to St Leo I (pope 440–61) and built this church (called the *Basilica Eudoxiana* or St Peter *ad Vincula*: 'St Peter in bonds') to house it. Later the second chain was sent to Rome. On being brought together, the two chains are said to have miraculously united. They have ever since been amongst the most revered relics in any church in Rome.

The Tomb of Julius II

The famous unfinished masterpiece of Michelangelo, who was so harassed while working on the monument that he called it the 'tragedy of a sepulchre', is at the end of the south aisle. Hindered by his quarrels with Julius II and by the jealousy of that pope's successors, Michelangelo finally abandoned work on the tomb, and the great pontiff, who had contemplated for himself the most splendid monument in the world, lies uncommemorated in St Peter's. Some 40 statues were to have decorated the tomb, including the two *Slaves* now in the Louvre, and the four unfinished *Slaves* in the Accademia Gallery in Florence, but no idea of the original design of the monument can be gained from this unsatisfactory grouping of statues and niches. Only a few magnificent fragments remain here, notably the powerful figure of *Moses*, Michelangelo's most strongly individualized work, in whose majestic glance is seen the prophet who spoke with God. The satyr-like horns represent beams of light, a traditional attribute of the prophet in medieval iconography, based on a mistranslation of the Hebrew word for the radiance that emanated from Moses' head after his interview with the Almighty (it was confused with the Hebrew word for horns). The beautiful figures of *Leah* and *Rachel* on either side—symbols of the active and contemplative life—are also by Michelangelo. The rest is his pupils' work, although the effigy of the pope, for long thought to be by Maso del Bosco, was attributed by some scholars to Michelangelo during restoration work in 1999. The pose is based on the reclining figures on Etruscan tombs. The *Madonna* is by Alessandro Scherano; the *Prophet* and *Sibyl* by Raffaello da Montelupo.

Moses, Rachel (left) and *Leah* (right) carved by Michelangelo for the Tomb of Julius II.

THE TOMB OF POPE JULIUS II

The project for the tomb of Pope Julius II stretched over 40 years of Michelangelo's career (between 1505 and 1545), and was in constant transformation during that period. The changes it underwent are documented in six surviving contracts, each of which successively reduced the scale of the original—highly ambitious— scheme. At its inception, the plan was to create one of the grandest Christian tombs ever built, to be placed above the sepulchre of St Peter at the centre of the basilica in Rome: and the new St Peter's which Julius conceived and began was to become thereby an everlasting mausoleum to himself, as Peter's greatest apostolic successor. What we see now is a deflated and ill-proportioned shadow of that project: the artist himself would acknowledge it to be a fundamentally unsatisfactory assemblage of disparate relics and ideas from earlier versions. The exact dimensions and design of the original plan are not clear: but we know that it was to have been a massive, free-standing structure with three tiers in pyramidal arrangement, surrounding an internal chamber. At the summit was to have been either the pope's sarcophagus supported by angels, or a seated effigy of the pope. Below this, on the middle level, were the dominating figures of Moses and St Paul (emblems of the two Testaments), paired with a Sybil and a Prophet: of these, the *Moses* (1515) alone remains, unusually portrayed in the seated position. On the lowest level was an allegorical arrangement, which played magnificently on the way Classical and Antique architecture uses human figures as architectural elements: here, in Michelangelo's conception, the figures were not just supporting the cornice, but were miraculously coming to life and breaking free of their bonds. Sometimes called 'slaves', 'prisoners' or 'captives', sometimes referred to as 'dying' and at other times as 'awakening', these powerfully suggestive figures of male nudes are seen by some as representing the provinces subjugated by Julius, and by others as personifying the Liberal Arts, awakened during his enlightened reign. For the artist, they were expressions of the soul's struggle against mortal flesh, and they were to be alternated with figures of Victory (one was partially realized and is now in the Palazzo Vecchio in Florence). The programme of the whole structure could be seen therefore as an allegory of the ascent of the soul, from its inchoate battles against the bonds of the flesh, up through the purification afforded by the teachings of the Church, to its final emancipation in death.

After Julius died in 1513, the project lost momentum, and was eventually reduced to no more than a small façade on a wall, in which assistants contributed major elements, on the suggestions and drawings of the master. Only the *Moses*, on the insistence of the trustees of the will, was included from the original project. Massive, craggy and incandescent as *Moses* is, he fits ill with the often lifeless figures which surround him. His unforgettable, oblique glance takes its power from Michelangelo's passionate engagement with the project at the outset.   N.McG.

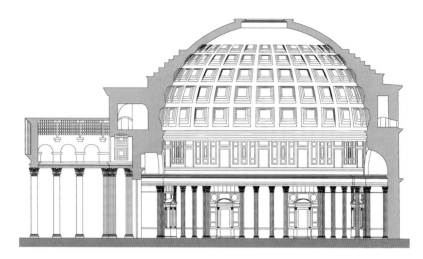

PANTHEON: SECTION

retained the name of Pantheon. Hadrian characteristically set up the dedicatory inscription on the pediment of the pronaos—M. AGRIPPA, L.F. COS. TERTIUM FECIT ('Marcus Agrippa, son of Lucius, consul for the third time, had [this building] made')—in honour of its original builder.

The Pantheon was restored by Septimius Severus and Caracalla. Closed and abandoned under the first Christian emperors and pillaged by the Goths, it was given to Boniface IV by the Byzantine emperor Phocas, whose column is in the Roman Forum (*see p. 76*). Boniface consecrated it as a Christian church in 609. It was dedicated to *Santa Maria ad Martyres*—there was a legend that some 28 wagonloads of martyrs' bones had been transferred here from the catacombs. On a 12-day visit to Rome in 667, Constans II, Emperor of Byzantium, robbed the temple of what the Goths had left, and in particular stripped off the gilded roof-tiles, which were probably of bronze. Benedict II restored it (684), Gregory III roofed it with lead (735), and Anastasius IV built a palace beside it (1153).

When the popes took up residence in Avignon (*see p. 265*) the Pantheon served as a fortress in the struggles between the rival Roman aristocratic families of the Colonna and the Orsini. In 1435 Eugenius IV isolated the building, and from then on it was the object of such veneration that a Roman senator on taking office swore to preserve 'Maria Rotonda' intact for the pontiff, together with the relics and sacred treasures of the city.

The monument was greatly admired during the Renaissance; Pius IV repaired the bronze door, and had it practically recast (1563). The Barberini pope Urban VIII, however, employed Bernini to add two clumsy turrets in front, which became popularly known as the 'ass-ears of Bernini' until they were finally removed in 1883. Urban also melted down the bronze ceiling of the portico to make the baldacchino for St Peter's and 80 cannon for Castel Sant'Angelo, an act of vandalism that prompted the 'talking' statue Pasquino's stinging gibe, '*Quod non fecerunt barbari fecerunt Barberini*' ('What the barbarians did not do, the Barberini did').

Alexander VII had the portico restored in 1662, and the level of the piazza lowered to provide a better view of the façade; Clement IX surrounded the portico with an iron railing (1668); Benedict XIV restored the interior and the atrium. The first two kings and the first queen of Italy are buried here.

The Exterior

A pedimented pronaos precedes a gigantic domed rotunda, with a rectangular feature as wide as the pronaos and as high as the cylindrical wall inserted between the two. This combination of a pronaos and rotunda gives the building a special place in the history of architecture. Originally the pronaos was raised by several steps and preceded by a large rectangular paved forecourt much larger than the present piazza, although the huge dome was only ever visible from the interior.

The portico is nearly 34m wide and 15.5m deep, and has 16 monolithic Corinthian columns of red or grey granite, without flutings, each 12.5m high and 4.5m in circumference. The superb capitals and the bases are of white marble. The three columns on the east side are replacements, one by Urban VIII (1625), the others by Alexander VII (1655–67); the arms of these popes can be seen in the decoration of the capitals. Eight of the columns stand in front, and the others are disposed in four rows, so as to form three aisles, the central one leading to the bronze door, which dates from the time of Pius IV, and the others to the two great niches which may formerly have contained colossal statues of Augustus and Agrippa.

The Interior

The visual impact of the domed interior is unforgettable. The use of light from the opening in the roof displays the genius of the architect. The great dome has five rows of coffers diminishing in size towards the circular opening in the centre, which measures almost 9m across. The intricate design of the coffers is mainly responsible for the effect of space and light (and this is even more noticeable now that they are in the process of being cleaned). They were probably ornamented with gilded bronze rosettes. The height and diameter of the interior are the same—43.3m. The diameter of the dome, the largest masonry vault ever built, exceeds by more than one metre that of the dome of St Peter's. Its span, which contains no brick arches or vaults, begins at the level of the highest cornice seen on the outside of the building, rather than, as it appears in the interior, at the top of the attic stage.

The cylindrical wall is 6m thick. It contains seven great niches, or recesses; except for the central apse, each is preceded by two Corinthian columns of *giallo antico* and flanked by pilasters. The apse instead has two free-standing columns. Between the recesses, which originally contained statues, are eight shrines (*aediculae*), those flanking the apse and entrance with triangular pediments, and the others with segmented

South side

The baptistery has a *Noli me Tangere* by Marcello Venusti and the bust of Ladislao di Aquino (d. 1621) by Francesco Mochi. The fourth chapel was designed by Carlo Maderno. The altarpiece of the *Annunciation* is by Antoniazzo Romano (1500): the painting shows Cardinal Juan de Torquemada (uncle of Tomás de Torquemada, the Inquisitor) presenting three poor girls to the Virgin, and commemorates the Confraternity of the Annunziata, founded in 1460 to provide dowries for penniless girls. The fifth chapel has an altarpiece of the *Institution of the Eucharist* by Federico Barocci. At the sides are the tombs of the parents of Clement VIII, by Giacomo della Porta, and in a niche to the left a statue of Clement.

In the south transept is the **Cappella Carafa**, entered under a fine marble arch, attributed to Giuliano da Maiano, with a beautiful balustrade. The chapel contains celebrated frescoes by Filippino Lippi, who had to interrupt his work (temporarily) on his other great fresco cycle in the church of Santa Maria Novella in Florence (for Filippo Strozzi) when he received this commission from Cardinal Olivieri Carafa in 1489. On the right wall, below, is *St Thomas Confounding the Heretics*, the central figures being Arius and Sabellius. Sabellius' heresy tried to confute the idea of the Trinity, maintaining that God was not 'one in three' but a single 'unity'. Arius denied the divine nature of Christ, which caused one of the most serious crises in early Christianity. The two youths in the right-hand group are probably portraits of the future Medici popes Leo X and Clement VII, both buried in this church. In the lunette above is *St Thomas Aquinas in Prayer*. On the altar wall is the *Assumption*, with a splendid group of angels, and an altarpiece of the *Annunciation*, with St Thomas Aquinas presenting Cardinal Carafa to the Virgin, also by Filippino. On the left wall is the monument of Paul IV (d. 1559).

To the left of this chapel is the tomb of Guillaume Durand (d. 1296), bishop of Mende, by Giovanni di Cosma, with a beautiful 13th-century mosaic of the *Madonna and Child*. The third chapel has Carlo Maratta's *Madonna and Saints*. The fourth chapel has a frescoed ceiling by Marcello Venusti.

Choir and high altar

In the choir, at the foot of the steps on the left, is a **statue of *The Risen Christ*** by Michelangelo (1514–21), for which the great artist was paid 200 ducats (a princely sum). Standing in marked *contrapposto*, Christ carries the instruments of the Passion (the rod and vinegar sponge, and Cross); the tiny size of the latter gives it a purely symbolic value. Michelangelo's original figure was nude; the bronze drapery is a later addition. Under the 19th-century high altar lies the body of **St Catherine of Siena**. It was St Catherine who persuaded Gregory XI to return from Avignon to Rome, and her remarkable letters are preserved. She was proclaimed a patron saint of Italy in 1939 and became a patron saint of Europe in 1999. In the apse behind are the **tombs of the Medici popes** Leo X (left) and Clement VII, designed by Antonio Sangallo the Younger, with statues by Raffaello da Montelupo and Nanni di Baccio Bigio respectively. In the pavement is the slab-tomb of Cardinal Pietro Bembo (1547), secretary to Pope Leo X from 1512 to 1520, and friend of Michelangelo, Raphael and Ariosto.

THE POPES IN AVIGNON & THE GREAT WESTERN SCHISM

For 70 years in the 14th century the popes abandoned Rome for the south of France, causing a scandal in the rest of Christendom. This 'Avignon period' began when the archbishop of Bordeaux, who had been elected pope *in absentia* in 1305, was persuaded by the French king Philip the Fair to set up his court in Avignon. Political disturbances in Italy made this seem a good idea to Clement V (as the archbishop now was), and he and his seven successors ruled from the comfortable Palais des Papes. Shocked contemporaries—such as the poet Petrarch and St Catherine of Siena—begged these French popes to return to Rome, but it was not until 1377 that Gregory XI re-established papal government in the eternal city, by then in a pitiful state of abandon and neglect. (Since this Gregory, there has never been another French pope.)

The Avignon interlude contributed to an even worse disaster: the Great Schism, which lasted from 1378 to 1417. This rupture of ecclesiastical unity produced a situation whereby there were two or even three popes at once, each claiming to be the true successor to St Peter and denouncing his rival or rivals. The Church has since decided which were the true popes (Urban VI, Boniface IX, Innocent VII, Gregory XII) and which were the so-called antipopes; but it was by no means clear at the time, and indeed it was not until 1958 that the status of Baldassarre Cossa, 'John XXIII', was finally determined: in that year Angelo Roncalli took the same name and regnal number, thus indicating that his 15th-century predecessor had never been true Bishop of Rome.   M.R.

North side

To the left of the choir in the north transept, in a passageway which serves as an exit, are several large monuments, including those of Cardinal Michele Bonelli (Alexandrinus) by Giacomo della Porta, and of Cardinal Domenico Pimentel designed by Bernini. You can see the pavement **tomb of Fra' Angelico** here, with an effigy taken from his death mask, attributed to Isaia da Pisa. The Florentine painter died in the convent of the church in 1455, and the charming epitaph (in the chapel behind the tomb, to the right of the altar) was composed by Pope Nicholas V, whose chapel in the Vatican the friar had frescoed. The chapel has a 15th-century altarpiece (a processional standard painted in tempera on silk) of the *Madonna and Child*. The tomb of Giovanni Arberini (d. c. 1470) is by a Tuscan sculptor (Agostino di Duccio?), who incorporated a splendid bas-relief of *Hercules and the Lion*, probably a Roman copy of an original Greek work of the 5th century BC. To the left is the entrance to the 17th-century sacristy, behind which is the **room in which St Catherine of Siena died** in 1380 (it was brought here from Via di Santa Chiara by Cardinal Barberini). The poorly-preserved frescoes are by Antoniazzo Romano and his school (1482). At the end of this transept is the Cappella di San Domenico, containing the monument of Benedict

XIII (d. 1730), with sculptures by Pietro Bracci. At the corner of the nave and transept is the charming small tomb of Andrea Bregno (1421–1506), with his bust. On the second nave pillar is the tomb of the nun Maria Raggi, a colourful early work by Bernini.

Between the fourth and third chapels of the north aisle is the tomb of Giovanni Vigevano (d. 1630), with a bust by Bernini (c. 1617). The third chapel has a tiny altarpiece of the *Redeemer*, attributed to Perugino or Pinturicchio. In the second chapel (*under restoration*) the tomb of Gregorio Naro, showing the cardinal kneeling at a priedieu, has recently been attributed to Bernini. Near the door is the tomb of Francesco Tornabuoni (1480) by Mino da Fiesole, and above is that of Cardinal Tebaldi (1466) by Bregno and Giovanni Dalmata.

The Baths of Agrippa

The monastery, once the headquarters of the Dominicans, was the scene of Galileo's trial in 1633 when he was condemned by the Inquisition for his contention that the Earth was not at the centre of the Universe (he was rehabilitated in 1992 by John Paul II). The Dominicans were left a library by Cardinal Girolamo Casanate which they opened in the convent in 1701. The Biblioteca Casanatense (*entrance at 52 Via Sant' Ignazio*) specializes in theological texts and works on the history of Rome. Off Via dei Cestari—where shops sell liturgical articles for the numerous clergy who come to visit the Vatican—in Via dell'Arco della Ciambella, part of the circular wall of the central hall of the **Baths of Agrippa** is charmingly incorporated into the street architecture. These were the first public baths in the city, begun by Agrippa in 29 BC, and restored by Hadrian. The brick-faced concrete dates from the 3rd century. Agrippa was a close friend of Augustus and supported the emperor by financing numerous ambitious building projects in Rome, including the Pantheon, these baths, three aqueducts and hundreds of fountains. He married Augustus' only child Julia (they feature, with one of their sons, as figures on the Ara Pacis; *see p. 158*). Wanton and wayward though she was, Julia enjoyed the prospect of becoming empress (Agrippa was considered Augustus' obvious successor); but Agrippa and his two children all predeceased Augustus, and Julia and her mother ended their lives in exile.

PIAZZA NAVONA
& ITS DISTRICT

This chapter covers one of the loveliest parts of the city, centering on the delightful Piazza Navona, one of the places which best illustrates the spirit of Rome: the entirely successful adaptation of a Classical building (in this case a Roman circus) to the urban structure of succeeding centuries; the triumph of Bernini's Baroque style with his splendid fountain of the Four Rivers, which also provides a setting for an Egyptian obelisk brought to the city by a Roman emperor; and the relaxed festive atmosphere typical of the Romans, who come here to enjoy the scene.

The highly distinctive Baroque architectural style of Francesco Borromini (*see p. 219*) can be seen both in the façade of Sant'Agnese in the piazza, and in the courtyard of the Sapienza and church of Sant'Ivo nearby. Also in the district is Palazzo Altemps, now part of the Museo Nazionale Romano, with the beautifully displayed Ludovisi collection.

PIAZZA NAVONA
Map p. 622, 2B

The form of this piazza, preserving the dimensions of the Stadium of Domitian, a building which could probably hold some 30,000 spectators, represents a remarkable survival within the modern city. Its appearance, surrounded by stately palaces and churches and with fountains in its centre, has remained almost totally unchanged since at least the beginning of the 18th century, as numerous paintings and prints of old Rome attest. It is the most animated square in Rome, beloved of the Romans as well as visitors, and the cafés and restaurants have tables outside for most of the year. It is usually very crowded and many street artists, buskers and performers of all kinds are always at work here.

Its name is derived from the athletic games, the *Agones Capitolini*, held here after the stadium was inaugurated in AD 86. In the Middle Ages the piazza was called the Campus Agonis; hence *agone, n'agona* and *navona*. Festivals, jousts and open-air sports took place here, and it was also used as a market place from 1477 until 1869. From the 17th to the late 19th centuries the piazza was flooded every weekend in August for the entertainment of the Romans; the nobles enjoyed the spectacle from their carriages. Nowadays, at Christmas, statuettes for the Christmas crib are sold here, and the fair and toy-market of the *Befana* (Epiphany) is held here.

The fountains
Three splendid fountains decorate the piazza. The **Fontana del Moro** at the south end was designed by Giacomo della Porta in 1576, with sculptures by Taddeo Landini, and others. In 1874 these were replaced by copies made by Luigi Amici, and in 1909 the

originals were moved to the Giardino del Lago in Villa Borghese (*see p. 190*). The fountain was altered by Bernini in 1653 when he designed the central figure, known as *Il Moro* (the Moor), executed by Antonio Mari.

The central **Fontana dei Quattro Fiumi** (Fountain of the Four Rivers) is one of Bernini's most famous works. It was Innocent X who had the idea of decorating Piazza Navona with a fountain to provide a support for the tall obelisk which he decided to move here after it had lain in five pieces in the Circus of Maxentius on the Via Appia for centuries. But he deliberately excluded Bernini from the list of leading sculptors of the day when he asked for designs. Bernini decided to produce a model anyway, and a nephew of the pope managed to show it to Innocent, who was unable to resist giving Bernini the commission in 1648. Four colossal allegorical figures are seated on a triangular base of travertine rock. They represent the Danube, Ganges, Nile and Rio della Plata: the four most famous rivers of the four continents then known, and were carved by Bernini's assistants, Antonio Raggi, Giacomo Antonio Fancelli, Claude Poussin and Francesco Baratta. A horse and a lion with long flowing tails inhabit the caves in the hollow rock below, seen from both front and back, and near a scaly sea monster with a snout there is a sea serpent in the water. The rock is overgrown with various carved plants and a palm tree. The popular story told to illustrate the rivalry between Bernini and Borromini—that the Nile is holding up an arm to block out the sight of Sant'Agnese—is apocryphal, since the fountain was finished in 1651, before Borromini started work on the church.

The obelisk, which was cut in Egypt, was brought to Rome by order of Domitian, where the Emperor had Roman stonemasons carve hieroglyphics referring to himself as 'eternal pharaoh' and Vespasian and Titus as gods. It is crowned with the dove, the Pamphilj (Pope Innocent X's) emblem.

The fountain at the north end of the square, the **Fontana di Nettuno**, showing Neptune struggling with a marine monster or giant octopus, surrounded by nereids and sea-horses, is by Antonio della Bitta and Gregorio Zappalà (1878).

Sant'Agnese

The church of Sant'Agnese in Agone (*open 9–12 & 4–7 except Mon morning*) is an ancient church built on the ruins of the stadium which Christian tradition marks as the spot where St Agnes was exposed (*see p. 480*). It was reconstructed for Innocent X by Girolamo Rainaldi and his son Carlo in 1652, who were still at work on the Pamphilj pope's palace next door; the following year they were substituted by Francesco Borromini, who provided the splendid concave façade, which adds emphasis to the dome. On the death of Innocent X in 1655 Borromini was out of favour with his successor, and by 1657 he had abandoned work on the church. His collaborator Giovanni Maria Baratta completed the façade and the twin bell-towers.

The small Baroque interior has an intricate Greek-cross plan in which a remarkable effect of spaciousness is provided by the cupola. Innocent X's family crest, the

Figure representing the River Ganges, from Bernini's *Fontana dei Quattro Fiumi*.

Palazzo della Sapienza has a fine Renaissance façade by Giacomo della Porta. Until 1935 it was the seat of the University of Rome, founded by Boniface VIII in 1303, and the university is still known as *La Sapienza* after the palace. It now houses the Archivio di Stato, and exhibitions are held in a library designed by Borromini. The beautiful court, also designed by Borromini, has porticoes on three sides, and the church of **Sant'Ivo** (*open 8.30–5; Sat and Sun 9–12*) at the far end. Begun for the Barberini pope, Urban VIII, both the courtyard and the church incorporate his device (the bee) into their design, as well as Alexander VII's Chigi device of mounds. The dome is crowned by an ingenious spiral tower, a unique feature of the city skyline, but later copied many times, especially in German architecture. The church is a masterpiece of the Baroque, with a remarkable light interior painted in white and enitrely devoid of decoration.

PALAZZO ALTEMPS
Map p. 622, 1B

Open 9–7.45; closed Mon; T: 06 3996 7700. For the Archaeological Card, see p. 568.
Palazzo Altemps houses the Ludovisi collection of ancient Roman sculptures from the Museo Nazionale Romano. The remains of Cardinal Altemps' collection, part of the Mattei collection, and the pieces of Egyptian sculpture which belong to the Museo Nazionale Romano are also displayed here. The arrangement of the works has, as far as possible, attempted to illustrate 17th-century antiquarian taste. There are plans to exhibit other former private collections in the building.

The collection is beautifully displayed and very well labelled, with excellent diagrams (also in English) in each room showing where the antique statues have been restored.

History of Palazzo Altemps and the Ludovisi Collection
The palace was begun before 1477 by Girolamo Riario. Building was continued by Cardinal Francesco Soderini of Volterra (1511–23) and completed after 1568 by Cardinal Marco Sittico Altemps and his descendants, for whom Martino Longhi the Elder worked. Longhi was responsible for the charming turret-shaped belvedere, an innovative architectural feature and later much copied.

In the 16th century Cardinal Altemps started his collection of antique sculptures here. The 16 statues that survive from Altemps' collection (all the rest have been dispersed, and some of the finest are now in the Vatican, British Museum and Louvre) are preserved here. The Ludovisi collection was begun in 1621 by Cardinal Ludovico Ludovisi, nephew of Pope Gregory XV, to decorate his villa and garden near Porta Pinciana (*see p. 226*). He acquired part of the Altemps collection, and other pieces from the Cesi and Mattei families. The collection was further enriched by finds from excavations, some of which were carried out in his own garden. He employed Bernini and Algardi to restore and integrate the statues. The first pieces were dispersed in 1665 but the collection and villa (which became the property of Gregorio Boncompagni) became famous as a place to visit among travellers to Rome. A fashion grew up for copying the statues and making casts of them: Goethe was able to obtain a cast of the colossal head of Juno when he visited the city (*see p. 171*). His friend Johann Winckelmann, the distinguished German scholar who was considered the greatest expert on Classical works in Rome during the 18th century, made a detailed study of the statues, and the collection continued to grow in the 19th century. In 1883, however, the Villa Ludovisi and its garden were destroyed for building land. In 1901 the state bought 104 pieces of the collection, which include some very fine Greek and Roman works, although the provenance is mostly unknown. The collection is particularly interesting as a reflection of 17th-century taste for the antique, and shows the skill with which so many of the pieces were restored at that time.

Alessandro Algardi (1598–1654)
Algardi would be Rome's most important sculptor of the 17th century were it not for the dominating presence of Bernini. His studio was large and, under Innocent X, when Bernini was out of favour, Algardi received numerous official commissions. His art is an interesting counterbalance to that of his great contemporary: introspective rather than grand and extrovert; static, more than dynamic; timeless, rather than ephemeral. His innate seriousness and quiet solemnity (particularly in his fine portraits) also distinguishes him from two other great contemporaries, Francesco Mochi and François Duquesnoy. He was called to Rome in 1625 by the Bolognese Cardinal Ludovico Ludovisi and spent the next six years restoring his collection of antique sculpture, and imbibing thereby a Classicism that instinctively appealed to his sober nature. Many of these statues can be seen in Palazzo Altemps, as well as the *Dadoforo* (*see p. 279 below*), which was created by Algardi from an antique Greek marble torso. Although Pope Urban VIII favoured Bernini as a sculptor, Algardi designed the tomb of Leo XI in St Peter's and that of Giovanni Garzia Mellini in the church of Santa Maria del Popolo, and executed the statues of St Philip Neri in the sacristy of Chiesa Nuova and of Innocent X in Palazzo dei Conservatori on the Campidoglio. Less adventurous than his contemporaries in varying the surfaces of the marble and in evoking a plasticity from the stone, his pieces can have a glassy frigidity to them—a characteristic he capitalized on magnificently in his portrait bust of the terrifying Donna Olimpia Maidalchini in the Doria Pamphilj collection. In his greatest work, however, the high-relief of the *Meeting of Pope Leo the Great and Attila* (1646) in St Peter's, Algardi overcomes this tendency, and, in a vibrant and dramatic surface, pulls the viewer into this determining moment in Rome's history.

The handsome courtyard was begun by Antonio da Sangallo the Elder in 1513–17, continued by Baldassare Peruzzi and completed by Martino Longhi at the end of that century. Some statues which were part of the original Altemps collection, and some very damaged statues which formed part of the Mattei collection, removed from the Villa Celimontana in 1996, are displayed here.

PALAZZO ALTEMPS
(FIRST FLOOR)

Room 18: This small room contains a kneeling statue of Venus made in the Hadrianic era, but derived from a 4th-century BC work.

Room 19: Here a bust of a satyr in grey *bigio* marble, thought to have been restored by Bernini, is displayed on top of a funerary urn and altar from the 1st century AD. The beautiful figure of Hermes, dating from the late 1st or early 2nd century AD, was carefully restored by Algardi, whose workshop probably also restored the statue of Aesculapius (late 2nd century AD) in 1627.

Room 35 (entered from Room 19): Here you'll see two statues of Bacchus: the one with a panther was made up from antique pieces in the 17th century, and the other dates entirely from the

17th century and was made as a fake Classical work. The Satyr dates from the 2nd century AD but the arms are modern.

Room 36: The splendid bull (the god Apis) in serpentine porphyry is an Egyptian work (2nd century BC) brought to Rome during the Empire and discovered in 1886 on the Esquiline Hill.

Room 20: Delightful 15th-century frescoes attributed to the circle of Melozzo da Forlì show a tapestry covered with wild flowers, behind a sideboard on which are displayed plates, ewers and candlesticks which were wedding presents given to Girolamo Riario and Caterina Sforza when they were married in 1477. Three important statue groups are displayed here. A **Roman statue of**

a seated male, formerly thought to represent Ares, is now displayed beside a female statue (2nd century BC) which has recently been identified as Thetis, the mother of Achilles. Scholars now believe this was the statuary group representing Achilles with his mother which was described by Pliny as adorning the Temple of Neptune in the Campus Martius. The statue of Achilles was found in the early 17th century and restored by Bernini. The standing group of *Orestes and Electra* is signed by the Greek artist Menelaus, pupil of Stephanos. Pliny mentions Stephanos as being the assistant of Pasiteles (early 1st century AD). Winckelmann was the first to identify the figures as Orestes with his sister Electra at the tomb of their father Agamemnon. The head of the *Seated Warrior* (2nd century AD) is not original, although it, too, is an antique work.

Room 21: The famous **Ludovisi Throne** (*see box*), found at the end of the 19th century in the Villa Ludovisi, is displayed here.

THE LUDOVISI THRONE

The central subject of the *Ludovisi Throne* is apparently the birth of Aphrodite, who rises from the sea supported by two figures representing the Seasons. It is thought to have been intended for the statue of a divinity, and is usually considered to be a Greek original of the 5th century BC. On the right side is the figure of a young woman sitting clothed on a folded cushion; she is taking grains from a box and burning them in a brazier. On the left side is a naked flute girl, also sitting on a folded cushion, playing a double pipe.

The Throne is, nevertheless, the subject of fascinating debate. Only one other such 'throne' is known: the *Boston Throne*, now widely held to be a fake. The *Ludovisi Throne* has not been so stamped, but its provenance, purpose and iconography continue to bewilder scholars. In form and size it is most like a sarcophagus, yet its iconography is not matched on other funerary monuments. What is more puzzling are a number of apparent illogicalities: the figures are not as naturalistic as one would expect from late Archaic sculpture. Aphrodite's ear is in the wrong place, for example; the anterior arms of the two Seasons are longer than the near arms, and the folds of their garments descend from the near flank and fall on the inside of the anterior ankle. The feet are akin to what we know from vase painting, but not otherwise from sculptural relief. All in all, the mood of the design is impressionistic. It is, indeed, more design than representation, and this, some scholars argue, suggest that it might well be a forgery.

And yet the 5th-century BC bas-reliefs found at the Greek city of Locri in southern Italy bear many stylistic resemblances to the Throne. Locri was a known cult centre of Aphrodite, and there is even a claim that its temple has a 'gap' in it, where the Throne could once have been.

WALK TWO

THE OLD STREETS CLOSE TO PIAZZA NAVONA

This walk explores narrow streets typical of old Rome, passing interesting palaces, as well as two important churches in the peaceful district around Piazza Navona.

Piazza Pasquino, a few steps out of the southwest end of Piazza Navona, is in fact just a busy little open space where several narrow roads converge and cars are always parked, so the worn, mutilated statue on one corner is easy to miss. But ever since it was placed here in 1501 this has been one of the best-loved statues of the Romans, always known as **Pasquino**. Apparently named after a tailor who lived in the vicinity, it is a fragment of a marble group thought to represent Menelaus with the body of

Patroclus, a copy of a Hellenistic work of the Pergamene school which may once have decorated the Stadium of Domitian. When it was in a much better state, Bernini admired it as the finest Classical work he had seen. It is the most famous of Rome's 'talking' statues (*see opposite*), and slogans ridiculing contemporary Italian politicians are still often attached to it, although they are now sometimes rather too long and complicated and have lost a little of their sense of fun and irony.

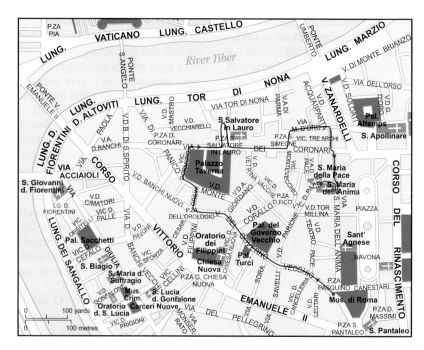

ROME'S 'TALKING' STATUES

The tailor Pasquino is thought to have originated the custom of attaching witty or caustic comments on topical subjects to the pedestal of this statue, a means of public satire which thus came to be known as *pasquinade*. This effective (and anonymous) way of getting at the city governors, and in particular of criticizing the papacy, was much in vogue in the 17th century before the days of the free press. Many printing houses and bookshops opened in the vicinity of the piazza.

Pasquino was the most famous of the 'talking' statues in the city, but labels were attached to various others so that they could carry on witty 'conversations'. *Madama Lucrezia*, a colossal antique bust now in Piazza San Marco, conversed with the statue of a river god called 'Marforio', which is now in the courtyard of Palazzo Nuovo on the Capitoline Hill. Other statues included *Abbot Luigi*, a statue of a Roman in a toga, which is still outside the church of Sant'Andrea della Valle, and the Facchino, the bust of a 16th-century water vendor in Via Lata. The only other 'talking' statue which survived as such up until a few years ago was Babuino, a very damaged Roman figure of a reclining Silenus, in Via del Babuino. Stendhal noted in 1816: 'What the people of Rome desire above all else is a chance to show their strong contempt for the powers that control their destiny, and to laugh at their expense: hence the dialogues between "Pasquino" and "Marforio".'

With your back to Pasquino, the narrow **Via del Governo Vecchio**, an ancient winding papal thoroughfare with many traces of the early Renaissance, leads straight ahead. It now has a bustling atmosphere with numerous small cafés and restaurants, and a miscellany of shops selling all kinds of merchandise from wine to old clothes. Note the old palace at no. 104, with *trompe l'oeil* windows on the top storey, the old Confraternity of the Stigmata of St Francis.

The street is named after **Palazzo del Governo Vecchio**, the palace at no. 39 built in 1473 by Cardinal Stefano Nardini, who was made Governor of Rome by Paul II. When the residence of the Governor of Rome was moved in the 18th century to Palazzo Madama, this palace was referred to as the 'old' palace of the Governor. It has a splendid Renaissance portal, but is at present covered for restoration. Opposite is the beautiful little Palazzo Turci (no. 123), which has been carefully restored. Its perfect proportions and lovely architectural details make it clear to see why it was once attributed to Bramante. It stands on its own between two narrow streets and has arched doorways and five storeys of round-arched windows with carved stone frames. It has lovely brickwork and a handsome inscription recording its first owner, Pietro Turci, and the date 1500.

Beyond, on the left corner of Via della Chiesa Nuova, is a grand 18th-century tabernacle with a modern request by a local inhabitant not to throw rubbish

Descent from the Cross by Francesco Salviati, amongst the last works (c. 1560) by this very able Florentine painter who also worked extensively in Rome.

In the peaceful little piazza behind Santa Maria dell'Anima is the beautiful church of **Santa Maria della Pace** (*unfortunately often closed even though it is officially meant to be opened by a custodian Tues–Fri 10–12.45*). It was rebuilt by Sixtus IV (1480–84) to celebrate victory over the Turks. There was also a popular legend that a miraculous image of the Virgin in the portico of the old church bled on being struck by a stone. The architect is believed to have been Baccio Pontelli. The church was partly rebuilt in 1611 and again later in the century by order of Alexander VII, under whose auspices the façade and beautiful semicircular porch with Tuscan columns were erected by Pietro da Cortona (*see p. 223*); his design for the delightful little piazza and the surrounding area was never completed, even though this, and the aedicule façade of the church with its concave portico, clearly inspired Bernini's design for Sant'Andrea al Quirinale (*see p. 215*). The aedicule itself, with a segmented pediment enclosed within a triangular pediment, seems to borrow from Michelangelo's Medici Chapel. The design is deliberately theatrical, even to the 'stage-wings' which accommodate the split in the street which passes to both sides of the church itself. A model of elegance and ingenuity, the plan also has remarkable practicality: the enlarging of the area in front of the entrance allowed carriages just enough space to turn and drop their passengers—an important consideration in a densely-packed mediaeval quarter, for a church which had suddenly become a fashionable venue due to the patronage of the Alexander VII, who made the church particularly his own.

The interior consists of a domed octagon preceded by a simple rectangular nave. The first chapel on the south side was founded by Agostino Chigi. Around 1511 he commissioned Raphael to paint the splendid frescoes above the arch, showing the Cumaean, Persian, Phrygian and Tiburtine Sibyls, to whom the future is being revealed by angels. Their varying reactions of awe and wonder are beautifully conveyed in look and gesture. Although probably the least known works by this great painter in the city, they are amongst his most remarkable, and they were splendidly restored in 2003. Above them are four Prophets (Daniel, David, Jonah and Hosea), by Raphael's pupil Timoteo Viti. On the altar is a fine bronze of the *Deposition* by Cosimo Fancelli.

The second chapel (Cesi) was designed by Antonio da Sangallo the Younger, and has very fine marble decoration by Simone Mosca (1540–42). The ruined frescoes in the window lunette are by Rosso Fiorentino. The Cesi tombs and sculptures are by Vincenzo de' Rossi.

In the niche in the first chapel on the north side is a beautiful fresco of the Virgin, St Bridget and St Catherine, with the donor Ferdinando Ponzetti, by Baldassare Peruzzi, who also painted the small frescoes of Old Testament subjects on the vaulting of the niche (and the *Presentation in the Temple* in the sanctuary). At the sides of the chapel

SANTA MARIA DELLA PACE

are the exquisite little tombs of the Ponzetti family (1505 and 1509), with delicately carved decoration and four busts. The second chapel has a much-darkened altarpiece of the *Madonna and Saints* by Marcello Venusti, perhaps from a design by Michelangelo.

In the octagon, above the high altar by Carlo Maderno, is the highly venerated 15th-century image of the *Madonna della Pace*. The beautiful marble tabernacle in the Chapel of the Crucifix (left) is attributed to Pasquale da Caravaggio.

The cloisters, where exhibitions are now held, commissioned in 1504 by Cardinal Oliviero Carafa, are among Donato Bramante's finest works in Rome. They have two rows of arcades one above the other—columns of the upper row rise from the centres of the arches in the lower row.

CARAVAGGIO IN ROME

Although paintings by Caravaggio are to be found all over the city, those in the two churches described below, just a few steps from each other close to Piazza Navona, are among his finest.

Caravaggio (1571–1610)

Michelangelo Merisi da Caravaggio was always known simply as Caravaggio, since it was thought he had been born in the town of the same name near Bergamo in Lombardy, although he may in fact have been born in Milan. He was the most important painter in Italy in the 17th century and made Rome the most influential centre of art in the country during his lifetime. He also had a profound influence on a large school of painters who came to be known as the *Caravaggeschi*, and the great number of copies of his works which exist demonstrate how much he was appreciated for his novel ideas. His works are characterized by a striking use of light and shadow, and for their dramatic realism and intensity of imagery. He was able to reduce images to the essentials making use of brightly illuminated colours. He produced superb still-lifes and genre scenes, and (mostly after 1601) numerous paintings of religious subjects.

Caravaggio came to Rome around 1592, and established himself rapidly as an artist of note. He had a violent temperament and, in 1606, after a quarrel with his opponent in a ball game, murdered him. He was condemned to death and forced to flee Rome. He went in disguise to Naples before setting sail for Malta, where he became a Knight of Malta but was caught and imprisoned for a time. He escaped to Sicily in 1608. He still managed to paint, however, and several of his masterpieces of this period are preserved on both islands. Believing he would be able to obtain the pope's pardon he decided to return to Rome, but died on the way back, not yet 40 years old, of malaria contracted on the beach near Porto Ercole.

He was a famous painter in his lifetime and among his patrons were Vincenzo Giustiniani (*see p. 288 below*) and Cardinal Scipione Borghese (a number of masterpieces painted for him are still hung in the Galleria Borghese). As well as his paintings in the two churches described below, and in Santa Maria del Popolo, his other masterpieces in Rome are now preserved in the Galleria Doria Pamphilj, the Pinacoteca Capitolina, and the Galleria Corsini. Apart from his numerous Italian followers, the influence of his style of painting can be seen in other great painters such as Velázquez and Rembrandt.

Caravaggio's works were largely ignored in the 18th century when the French school was in vogue as he was considered too realistic and 'modern'. Nineteenth-century travellers to the city rarely mention him, but he was 'rediscovered' in the 1950s, after an exhibition in Milan and the publication of numerous studies of his paintings. His works are now considered amongst the great 'sights' of the city.

SAN LUIGI DEI FRANCESI
Map p. 622, 2B

Open 7.30–12.30 & 3.30–7; closed Thur afternoon.

This is the French national church in Rome (1518–89). The façade, attributed to Giacomo della Porta, has two superimposed orders of equal height. The interior was heavily encrusted with marble and decorated with white and gilded stucco to a design by Antonio Dérizet (1756–64). The **Contarelli Chapel** (the fifth in the north aisle; *coin light*) contains three famous and very well-preserved paintings of scenes from the life of St Matthew by Caravaggio, painted for this chapel in 1597–1603. This was Caravaggio's first ever public commission, executed for the heirs of Cardinal Matthieu Cointrel. The Apostle Matthew was chosen as subject matter clearly because he was Cointrel's titular saint. The *Calling of St Matthew* is a beautifully balanced Classical composition. It was painted to face the canvas showing *St Matthew's Martyrdom*. The altarpiece of *St Matthew and the Angel* shows the angel seeming to fall right out of the sky (which was to be a recurrent theme in Caravaggio's later works). The colour red, always greatly favoured by Caravaggio, is much in evidence in these works, and would have had an even stronger impact on Caravaggio's contemporaries since all the participants are dressed in contemporary clothes. These paintings are considered by many scholars to be his masterpiece, dating from his early Classical and luminous period, devoid of the intense, sometimes overpowering, drama of his later works. They were painted at a time when Caravaggio was beginning to be sought after as an artist: at the same time as this he worked on paintings of St Peter and St Paul for a chapel in Santa Maria del Popolo (*see p. 160*). The vault of this Contarelli Chapel has late-Mannerist frescoes by Cavaliere d'Arpino, who was Caravaggio's master.

On the first pillar is a monument to the famous French 17th-century painter Claude Lorrain who worked in Rome (*see p. 139*), by another, but less well-known French painter François Lemoyne, who was in Rome in 1723. Against the first pillar in the south aisle is the monument to the French who fell in the Siege of Rome in 1849 (*see p. 389*). The second south chapel was frescoed around 1614 with scenes from the life of St Cecilia (damaged by restoration), by the Bolognese painter Domenichino, who spent most of his life in Rome where he was much influenced by Annibale Carracci—these are among his best-known early works. The altarpiece is a copy by Guido Reni of Raphael's famous *Ecstasy of St Cecilia* now in the Pinacoteca in Bologna.

The decorations in the fourth south chapel celebrate the conversion to Catholicism of Clovis, King of the Franks, who was baptized at Rheims by St Remigius in 496. They date from the 16th century and are Mannerist works by Jacopino del Conte, Pellegrino Tibaldi, and Girolamo Sermoneta. The high altarpiece is an *Assumption of the Virgin* by Francesco Bassano.

Palazzo Giustiniani

Nearly opposite the church is the orange-coloured Palazzo Giustiniani, designed by Girolamo Fontana; the main doorway is by Borromini. The palace was built in 1590 by the wealthy banker Vincenzo Giustiniani, Caravaggio's famous patron who owned no fewer than 13 of his works, including the first version of *St Matthew and the Angel* painted for the Contarelli Chapel in San Luigi dei Francesi, which was rejected (Giustiniani's painting was taken subsequently to Berlin where it was destroyed in the Second World War). Giustiniani also kept his important collection of antique sculpture here, but it was sadly dispersed in the early 19th century.

SANT'AGOSTINO
Map p. 622, 1B

Open 7.45–12 & 4.30–7.30.
The church of Sant'Agostino was built for Cardinal d'Estouteville by Giacomo da Pietrasanta (1479–83). The severely plain façade is one of the earliest of the Renaissance. The church is dedicated to St Augustine, author of the *Confessions*, whose mother, St Monica, is buried here.

The interior was renovated by Luigi Vanvitelli (1750). In the first chapel on the north side is the **Madonna di Loreto**, or *Madonna dei Pellegrini*, commissioned from Caravaggio in 1604 for this altar by Ermete Cavalletti (*there is a light on the left*). This is one of the most beautiful but least-known paintings by Caravaggio in the city: the graceful figure of the Madonna appears at the door of her house to show the blessing Child to two kneeling peasants who have come on a pilgrimage. According to legend, in 1294 the *Santa Casa* or House of the Virgin was miraculously transported by angels from Nazareth to near Rijeka, in Croatia, and from there across the Adriatic to a laurel wood in the Marche. This place became known as Loreto (from the word for a laurel grove) and is still one of the great pilgrimage shrines in the Catholic world. As in many of Caravaggio's works, the iconography is extremely unusual; in most other paintings of this subject the house itself is shown being transported through the sky. Caravaggio's detractors were very critical of the peasant's dirty feet when the painting was first exhibited on this altar, but today it appeals to us perhaps above all because of its extraordinary sense of humanity, and for the powerful sense it gives of the burden Mary bore and the sorrows she was to endure. The Child by His size seems about four years old, and must be heavy for her to carry. This literal burden suggests the metaphorical one.

The church contains good frescoes on the vault and nave by Pietro Gagliardi (1855), including five prophets on the nave pilasters which accompany the splendid *Prophet Isaiah* frescoed on the third pillar on the north side by Raphael. This was commissioned by the Humanist scholar Giovanni Goritz in 1512 for his funerary monument, and shows how much the painter was influenced by Michelangelo's frescoes in the Sistine Chapel. It was restored by Daniele da Volterra. Beneath it is a lovely *Madonna and Child with St Anne*, sculpted from a single block of marble by Andrea Sansovino. At the west end is the so-called *Madonna del Parto* by Jacopo Sansovino (1521), a greatly venerated statue and the object of innumerable votive offerings from expectant mothers. The two 17th-century angels holding stoups at the west end are by Antonio Raggi.

In the south aisle, the first chapel contains paintings by Marcello Venusti, a 16th-century painter whose altarpieces can be seen in many Roman churches, as well as in the Galleria Doria Pamphilj. Some of these are copies from Michelangelo, whose inspiration is clear in his entire production. The second chapel has the *Madonna della Rosa*, a copy by Avanzino Nucci of the original painting by Raphael, which was stolen from Loreto and never recovered. The third south chapel has a 17th-century altarpiece by Giacinto Brandi (who also painted the one in the fifth chapel in the north aisle). In the south transept is the Chapel of Sant'Agostino, with an altarpiece of the saint between St John the Baptist and St Paul the Hermit by Guercino and side panels by his school. The chapel is decorated with 18th-century stuccoes and contains the Baroque tomb of Cardinal Renato Imperiali by Paolo Posi. On the high altar (1628), below two angels designed by Bernini, is a Byzantine *Madonna* brought from Constantinople.

In the chapel to the left of the choir is the **tomb of St Monica**, mother of St Augustine. Monica was born in Carthage, where she lived as the unhappy wife of a drunken, debauched husband. He was also a pagan: his wife's Christian piety both irritated him and made him slightly in awe of her, which very likely made him more brutal than ever. After her husband's death she followed Augustine to Italy, and it was through her that he was baptized (in Milan). She died suddenly in 387 in a hostel at Ostia, from where she was about to set sail to return to Africa with Augustine (a fragment of her tombstone is preserved in the church of Santa Aurea at Ostia Antica; *see p. 517*). Her relics were bought to this church from Ostia in 1430 and in 1455 the Humanist Maffeo Vegio commissioned the tomb (attributed to Isaia da Pisa), but most of it was dismantled in an 18th-century restoration. Only the beautiful effigy remains here, above a Roman sarcophagus held to be the saint's original tomb (but four Doctors of the Church which belonged to the monument are now in the little vestibule at the north door).

The next little chapel—seen through a gate—was decorated by Giovanni Lanfranco (1616–19). The chapel in the north transept has a marble group on the altar of St Thomas distributing alms, finished in the 17th century by Ercole Ferrata. The second north chapel was designed by Bernini (the 16th-century Crucifix is by Ventura Salimbeni).

SUMPTUOUS CHURCHES OF THE COUNTER-REFORMATION

The three churches of the Gesù, Sant'Andrea della Valle and the Chiesa Nuova, all close together on the Corso Vittorio Emanuele, were built in the 16th century for the most important new religious orders founded in the Counter-Reformation, and it is interesting to compare their gorgeous decorations, funded by wealthy clerics.

ROME & THE COUNTER-REFORMATION

In 1527, when Pope Clement VII took sides with Francis I of France against the Holy Roman Emperor Charles V, Charles allowed troops of mercenaries to sack Rome. For eight days the drunken soldiery ravaged a defenceless city, while the pope cowered inside Castel Sant'Angelo. The cruelty and blasphemy of the rabble exceeded all bounds, yet the full horror of the Sack of Rome was interpreted by contemporaries in religious terms: it was God's vengeance on the evils of the age, and it made a mockery of the optimism of the High Renaissance. Rome lost its prestige as a centre of humanism, and its population fell to around 30,000. This humiliation for Clement VII as well as the attacks on the papacy by Martin Luther—who had visited Rome in 1511—preluded the period of the Counter-Reformation. The Farnese pope Paul III recognized the urgency of reforming the Church and the new cardinals he created were often scholars. He upheld the symbolic significance of Rome as the 'Holy City' in an attempt to counteract the diffusion of Protestant churches in Europe, and the prestige of the pope was re-established when Paul made peace with Charles V, and he made a triumphal entry into Rome in 1536. During Paul's reign the Council of Trent was convoked (in 1545), which undertook to reform the church and deal with the Protestant threat. Further sessions were held under his successor Paul IV, also a rigid defender of the Catholic Church (the powers of the Inquisition were increased under his pontificate). Gregory XIII's reign saw the restoration of numerous churches in the city, and the opening of new ones, notably the Gesù. Sixtus V did more than any of his predecessors to improve and adorn the city in celebration of the Catholic Church.

The Jesuit Order was founded by Ignatius Loyola in 1534 and, after 1540 when Paul III approved the Order, it became an extremely important part of the Counter-Reformation movement, when the Catholic Church placed renewed emphasis on learning. In 1585 the Jesuit Collegio Romano was founded by another Spaniard, St Francis Borgia, third in succession after Ignatius Loyola as General of the Jesuits. Its pupils were to include eight popes in later centuries: Urban VIII, Innocent X, Clement IX, Clement X, Innocent XII, Clement XI, Innocent XIII and Clement XII.

THE GESÙ
Map p. 622, 2C

THE GESÙ

Open 6–12.30 & 4–7.15.

The Gesù, or the Church of the Most Sacred Name of Jesus (*Santissimo Nome di Gesù*), is the principal Jesuit church in Rome and the prototype of the sumptuous style to which the order has given its name. Both the façade by Giacomo della Porta and the interior by Vignola were important to the subsequent development of Baroque church design in Rome. It was built between 1568 and 1575 at the expense of Cardinal Alessandro Farnese. The cupola, planned by Vignola, was completed by della Porta.

The Interior

The heavily decorated interior has a longitudinal plan, with an aisleless nave and lateral chapels: this design provided a huge space for the faithful to attend sermons, and gave the high altar for the celebration of the Eucharist even greater prominence. Here the architecture perfectly serves the ideas of the Counter-Reformation: while Protestant Europe was destroying images and stripping churches, Rome was responding with ceremony as theatre, with emphasis on the high altar, where the mystery of the Mass was celebrated. The idea of inserting a row of *coretti* (little niches like opera-boxes, from which spectators could enjoy the services) above the side chapels was thereafter frequently reused.

On the vault is a superb fresco of the *Triumph of the Name of Jesus*, a remarkably original work with marvellous effects of foreshortening, the **masterpiece of Baciccia**. Carried out in 1672–83, it marks one of the high points of Roman Baroque painting. Baciccia's career centred on Rome, where he was a favourite painter in ecclesiastical circles (he painted many portraits of cardinals, some of which can now be seen in Palazzo Corsini and the Museo di Roma) and patrician families. He was befriended by Bernini, whose portrait he painted (now in the Galleria Nazionale d'Arte Antica in Palazzo Barberini) and he provided the altarpiece above Bernini's famous statue in San Francesco a Ripa. Other altarpieces by him are to be found in several churches of Rome, but he is best remembered for this superb painted ceiling, the details and design of which can also be studied at close range in his exquisite little sketch for it which survives in the Galleria Spada (*see p. 303*). The frescoes of the cupola and the tribune are also by Baciccia, and he designed the stucco decoration, although this was executed by Antonio Raggi and Leonardo Retti. The marble decoration of the nave dates from 1858–61.

The six side chapels were decorated by some of the most important artists working in Rome from the time the church was consecrated in 1584. These include Agostino Ciampelli, Federico Zuccari, Ventura Salimbeni, Francesco Bassano, and Pomarancio (who frescoed two of the chapels on the north side).

In the north transept is one of the most elaborate Baroque altars in Rome. The **altar-tomb of St Ignatius**, founder of the Jesuit Order, is by the Jesuit lay brother Andrea Pozzo (*see p. 153*) with the help of many assistants (1695–1700) and is resplendent with marble and gilded bronze; the columns are encrusted with lapis lazuli and bronze decorations. Above is a group of the Trinity with a terrestrial globe covered with lapis lazuli. In front of the altar is a magnificent balustrade, and at the sides are marble groups: *Religion Triumphing over Heresy* by Legros (right), and *Barbarians Adoring the Faith* by Jean-Baptiste Théodon (left).

The chapel in the opposite transept commemorates the great Spanish missionary St Francis Xavier, who was a companion of St Ignatius Loyola. It was designed by Pietro da Cortona and Carlo Fontana, and the altarpiece showing the saint's death by Carlo Maratta is based on a sketch by Pietro da Cortona. An arm of the saint is preserved in a silver gilt reliquary. It was removed from his body, which is preserved in Goa, which he evangelized, and brought to Rome in 1614.

The presbytery and high altar, sumptuously decorated with coloured marbles, were redesigned in 1840 by Antonio Sarti when the huge altarpiece of the *Circumcision* by Alessandro Capalti was installed. At this time the tomb of Cardinal Roberto Bellarmine was destroyed, but his bust by Gian Lorenzo Bernini was preserved and given a Neoclassical setting (on the left of the altar). Bellarmine was a devout Jesuit with firm ideas about the powers of rulers. He antagonized James I of England by refusing to recognize the Divine Right of Kings. In Rome he clung staunchly to the view that the pope had only 'indirect' temporal authority. In matters of dogma he was a pragmatist rather than a zealot. Knowing that the Church's position was immovable, he advised Galileo not to be too vocal in his support for Copernican theory.

The two pretty little circular domed chapels on either side of the main apse were decorated by the Jesuit artist Giuseppe Valeriani just after the dedication of the church, and the elegant sacristy by Girolamo Rainaldi also dates from this time.

Each year, the *Te Deum* is sung in this church on 31st December and is a magnificent traditional ceremony.

To the right of the Gesù's façade, at no. 45 Piazza del Gesù, is the entrance to the rooms (*open Mon Sat 4–6; holidays 10–12*) where St Ignatius lived from 1544 to his death in 1556. They contain mementoes, paintings and documents. An adjoining corridor was decorated by Andrea Pozzo c. 1680.

SANT'ANDREA DELLA VALLE
Map p. 622, 2B

Open 7.30–12 & 4.30–7.30.
The church was begun in 1591 and financed by Cardinal Alfonso Gesualdo, for the Order of the Theatines, which had been founded in 1524 by Giampietro Carafa (afterwards Paul IV). Architects involved included Giacomo della Porta and Pier Paolo Olivieri. It was continued by Carlo Maderno, who crowned it with a fine dome, the highest in Rome after that of St Peter's. The façade was added in the following century (1665) by Carlo Rainaldi.

The Interior

The aisleless interior has a high barrel-vault and spacious apse. Inspired by the Gesù, it gives the impression of a sumptuous reception hall rather than a house of prayer. On the south side, the first chapel, by Carlo Fontana, has green marble columns and fine 17th-century sculptures by Antonio Raggi. The design of the second, the Strozzi Chapel, shows the influence of Michelangelo and contains reproductions in bronze of his *Pietà* and also of the *Leah* and the *Rachel* from the projected tomb of Julius II (*see p. 257*). High up on the walls before the crossing are similar monuments to two popes of the Piccolomini family—Pius II (d. 1464) and Pius III (d. 1503).

In the dome, high up above the crossing, is the *Glory of Paradise*, considered one of the best works (1621–27) of Giovanni Lanfranco, a painter from Parma who produced a number of early Baroque works in Rome. His more famous contemporary, Domenichino, added the Evangelists in the pendentives, as well as the six Virtues and scenes from the life of St Andrew in the vault of the apse, but these are perhaps less inspired works. Domenichino, a leader of the Bolognese school of painters, came to

Rome in 1602 where he watched Carracci paint his great ceiling fresco in Palazzo Farnese (and was allowed to carry out some minor decorative details there). He went on to produce numerous frescoes in Roman churches, often on the vaults. Although he was a most prolific painter who also supplied altarpieces for other Roman churches, and produced some fine idealized Classical landscapes, after his work in Sant'Andrea della Valle he realized that he was unable to establish himself as the pre-eminent fresco painter in the city and he left for Naples where he spent the last ten years of his life. The gigantic frescoes above and on either side of the high altar, showing the *Martyrdom of St Andrew*, were executed by the decorative artist Mattia Preti several decades later.

The first chapel on the north side, frescoed by Passignano, has four good late 16th–early 17th-century sculptures: on the left, *Mary Magdalene* by Cristoforo Stati, and *St John the Baptist* by Pietro Bernini (Gian Lorenzo's father); and on the right, *St John the Evangelist* by Ambrogio Bonvicino and *Santa Marta* by Francesco Mochi.

Opposite the church façade is a fountain by Carlo Maderno decorated with an eagle and a dragon, and against the side wall of the church in the little Piazza Vidoni, there is a Roman statue called 'Abbot Luigi', one of Rome's 'talking statues' (*see p. 281*).

CHIESA NUOVA
Map p. 622, 2A

Open 9–12 & 3–6.
The Chiesa Nuova or Santa Maria in Vallicella was built under the inspiration of St Philip Neri. Born in Florence in 1515, Neri came to Rome c. 1530, where he became known for his kindness and good works, and for his skill at attracting followers to help him in his mission of caring for pilgrims and for the sick, convalescent and mentally unwell. He was later ordained, and founded the Oratorian Order, so named because its members met in a small oratory. Neri was an outstanding figure of the Counter-Reformation, known affectionately as the 'Apostle of Rome', and in recognition of his contribution, in 1575, Gregory XIII gave him Santa Maria in Vallicella, which he proceeded to rebuild as the Chiesa Nuova, the 'new church', with the patronage of Cardinal Pier Donato Cesi and his brother Angelo. Among the architects were Martino Longhi the Elder (1575–1605) and the façade shows the influence of that of the Gesù.

The Interior
The handles of the entrance doors are decorated with flaming hearts: the *cor flammigerum*, St Philip Neri's emblem. The vault, apse and dome were decorated by Pietro da Cortona (1664), and the whole church is brilliantly gilded. In the sanctuary are

Scene from the tripartite *Martyrdom of St Andrew* by Mattia Preti in Sant'Andrea della Valle, typical of many such huge religious scenes commissioned for Roman churches in the 17th and 18th centuries.

three very fine paintings by Rubens, commissioned by the Oratorians before the artist left Rome in 1608 (*see p. 167*).

A **Nave:** The ceiling fresco by Pietro da Cortona shows *St Philip's Vision of the Virgin*. It tells how in a dream St Philip saw the church roof about to fall; on waking he found it miraculously hanging in mid-air. The fresco shows the Virgin holding the splintered beams aloft.

B **Dome and apse:** The frescoes, again by Pietro da Cortona, show *The Glorification of the Trinity* (in the apse) and *The Assumption* (in the dome).

C **High altar:** The paintings here are the only works by Rubens still in a church in the city. Resplendent with colour, they are Saints Domitilla, Nereus and Achilleus (to the right); and Saints Gregory, Maurus and Papianus (to the left). Over the altar itself is the *Madonna and Angels*. The central panel, painted on slate, can be moved aside to reveal the icon of *Santa Maria in Vallicella*, a miraculous image once seen to shed blood, which was placed in the church by order of St Philip Neri.

D **Cappella Spada:** This chapel, under a fine 18th-century cantoria, was designed by Carlo Rainaldi, with an altarpiece of the *Madonna between St Charles Borromeo and St Ignatius* by Carlo Maratta. St Charles Borromeo was a particular admirer of the work of the Oratorians.

E **Chapel of the Coronation:** Above the altar is the *Coronation of the Virgin*,

by Cavaliere d'Arpino, the master of Caravaggio.

F **Chapel of St Philip:** St Philip Neri is buried beneath the altar of this sumptuous chapel (1600–04), whose walls are adorned with gorgeous panels in *pietre dure*. The saint's portrait in mosaic is copied from a painting by Reni. The paintings around the walls, depicting scenes from his life, are by Pomarancio. Pomarancio (Cristoforo Roncalli) inherited his soubriquet from his master Niccolò Circignani. They worked together at the Vatican, and Cristoforo went on to produce rhetorical Mannerist frescoes for a number of churches in Rome, amongst the most successful of which are these in the Chiesa Nuova. A good example of Niccolò's work can be seen in San Giovanni dei Fiorentini (*see p. 312*).

G **Chapel of the Presentation:** The beautiful painting of the *Presentation of the Virgin in the Temple* is by Federico Barocci.

H **Sacristy:** In the fine 17th-century sacristy, with a fresco by Pietro da Cortona, is a statue of *St Philip Neri and an Angel* by Alessandro Algardi. From here there is access to another chapel and the rooms of St Philip Neri with works by Guercino, Pietro da Cortona, Reni and Garofalo, and memorabilia of the saint.

CHIESA NUOVA & ITS CONVENT

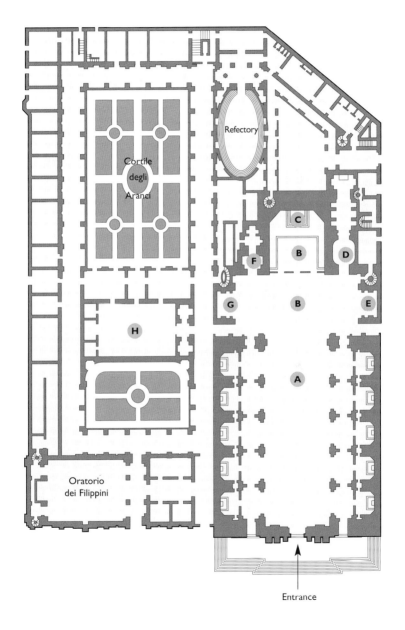

Entrance

The Oratorio and piazza

In the adjoining **Oratorio dei Filippini** (*marked on the plan on previous page*), rebuilt largely by Francesco Borromini (1637–52), St Philip instituted the musical gatherings which became known as oratorios, and which have given their name to a form of musical composition. The façade, between that of a church and a palace, has a remarkably subtle design, with all the hallmarks of Borromini's authorship. Its dynamic, curvilinear frontage sounds an unexpected note among a run of flat, static façades. The shallow concavity of the outer wall has an extraordinary tense energy, as if it were bent under pressure. Elements of the idiosyncratic window designs and of the curves of the pediments are carried through into the interior too—even to the design of the fireplaces—giving a satisfying unity to the whole. The extensive convent buildings, also by Borromini, are now occupied by the Biblioteca Vallicelliana (specializing in books on the history of Rome), the Municipal Archives and various learned societies.

In the piazza in front of the Chiesa Nuova there is a charming fountain in the shape of a soup tureen.

AROUND CAMPO DEI FIORI

This is one of the most delightful parts of the city, bustling with Romans going about their daily business, with numerous artisans' workshops and shops selling old furniture. The narrow old streets, which retain their typical *sanpietrini* cobbled surface without pavements, surround Campo dei Fiori, a market place where many of the local inhabitants come to buy fruit and vegetables. Just out of the square are two of the most important Renaissance palaces in Rome: Palazzo della Cancelleria and Palazzo Farnese, both built by wealthy cardinals and graced with splendid courtyards. Nearby is Palazzo Spada, dating from the following century and with beautiful exterior stucco decorations, which can be visited to see its important gallery of 17th- and 18th-century paintings and a *trompe l'oeil* perspective by Francesco Borromini in the garden.

CAMPO DEI FIORI

Map p. 622, 2B

Campo dei Fiori was once a meadow (as the name—'the field of flowers'—suggests), but it became one of the most important *piazze* in Rome in the 15th century. Since 1869 it has been a market place, with stalls selling fruit and vegetables, fish, and groceries as well as household goods and clothing. However in the last year or so the typical canvas

Ettore Ferrari's monument to Giordano Bruno.

shades and lovely old baskets from which the merchandise was sold have been replaced by more anonymous stalls similar to those seen all over Italy in outdoor markets. The piazza is now surrounded by a charming miscellany of narrow houses, with some simple cafés. The fountain in the form of a soup tureen, in pink porphyry and granite, has been here since 1898. From it you can see, in the distance, the top of the Baroque spiralling campanile of Sant'Ivo. The beautiful old Via dei Cappellari, which leads out of the piazza is worth exploring for its artisans' shops and pretty houses.

Executions occasionally took place here, and in 1600 the Neoplatonist thinker and philosopher **Giordano Bruno** was burned alive as a heretic, on the spot now marked by a dramatic monument to him by Ettore Ferrari (1889). Bruno's death at the hands of the Inquisition made him a hero to anti-clerical 19th-century liberals, but his ramblings philosophical and theological writings are unlikely to have appealed to them in detail, for he was by no means a proto-liberal. Born in 1545 in Nola near Naples (as 'the Nolan' he makes an appearance in James Joyce's *Finnegan's Wake*), Bruno joined the Dominicans in 1562 and was ordained priest, but his restless spirit and speculative intellect soon brought him into conflict with authority. For 17 years he wandered around Europe, teaching the 'Art of Memory' as well as his own hermetic and esoteric doctrines. He visited Paris, Wittenberg and Prague, and spent the years 1583–85 in England, where he worked as a spy for the government, may have met Shakespeare, and was accused at Oxford of plagiarism. While staying with the Mocenigo in Venice he was betrayed by his hosts to the Inquisition. Sent under escort to Rome, he arrived there on 17th January 1593. Seven years later to the day, after a lengthy trial, Bruno was put to death.

At the end of the square behind the statue, where there is a hodge-podge of buildings, terraces, half-destroyed houses, advertisements, and an old cinema, the white corner of the late 16th-century façade of the only grand palace here can be seen on the left. This is Palazzo Pio (Righetti), which faces the little Piazza del Biscione (note the carved lions climbing out of the first floor windows), which was built over the ruins of the **Theatre of Pompey**, the impressive remains of which can be seen on request at the restaurant (Pancrazio) which has been in part of the ground floor of the palace since

1922. Dating from 55 BC, this was Rome's first stone-built theatre and it was surmounted, on the highest part of the cavea, by a Temple of Venus. Until then theatres in Rome had been erected in wood since they were considered places where the public could get out of hand; to avoid such a danger it was felt best to make them temporary structures so they could easily be demolished if circumstances made it necessary. By erecting a temple to dominate his theatre, Pompey hoped to avoid trouble. It is known that the great rectangular Porticus of Pompey stood to the east of the theatre, off which opened the Curia (the remains of which have been identified in Largo Torre Argentina; *see p. 549*). It was on this spot that Julius Caesar was murdered on 15th March 44 BC at the foot of a statue of Pompey—perhaps the very one now in Palazzo Spada (*see overleaf*).

An archway leads into a dark passageway, which emerges by the old (deconsecrated) chapel of Santa Maria di Grottapinta: the semicircular shape of the auditorium of the Theatre of Pompey can still be seen in the later buildings (which still incorporate a theatre): this is one of the most remarkable continuations of urban layout to have survived in Rome.

PALAZZO FARNESE
Map p. 622, 2A

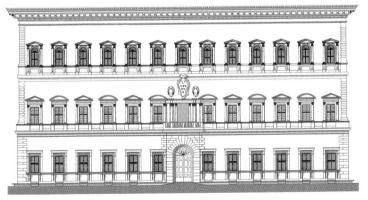

PALAZZO FARNESE

A few metres west of Campo dei Fiori the bustling atmosphere abruptly changes, in the elegant and peaceful Piazza Farnese, created by the Farnese in front of their splendid palace. Here are two huge baths of Egyptian granite, brought from the Baths of Caracalla in the 16th century and used by members of the Farnese family as a type of 'royal box' for the spectacles which were held in the square. They were adapted as fountains (using the Farnese lilies) in 1626 and the sound of water still pervades the square which is surrounded by a group of distinguished town houses. **Palazzo**

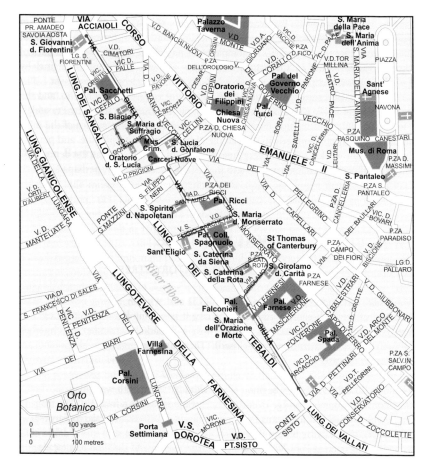

Fuga. Skulls flank the entrance. The right-hand alms box, dating from 1694, shows Death claiming a victim, and asking passers-by for alms for sufferers from malaria contracted in the Roman Campagna. Malaria remained a serious threat up until the end of the 19th century: as late as 1883 Augustus Hare in his *Walks in Rome* was warning visitors about this mysterious and dangerous illness when from June to November certain areas of the city, including the gardens of the Villa Borghese, the Caelian and Aventine, were 'a constant prey to fever'.

Palazzo Falconieri next to the church, enlarged by Borromini (who also designed the Falconieri family crypt; *see p. 312 below*), is distinguished by its side pilasters: terms of female breasts topped by giant falcons' heads. It has been the seat of the Hungarian Academy since 1928. Several rooms inside have fine ceilings decorated in stucco by Borromini. Cardinal Fesch, Napoleon I's uncle, lived here in the early 19th century and amassed a splendid collection of paintings which was, however, dispersed after his death. The little courtyard can be seen, with its two palm trees and a fountain.

A narrow road leads right to Piazza Santa Caterina della Rota, where there are three churches. **Santa Caterina della Rota** (*usually closed*) has a fine ceiling from a demolished church and 18th-century works. Just off the square, on Via di Monserrato, is the exterior in Romanesque style, including an elaborate portal by Luigi Poletti.

On Via di Monserrato is the church of **St Thomas of Canterbury** (*entrance at no. 45*), attached to the Venerabile Collegio Inglese. The ground on which they stand has been the property of English Catholics since 1362, when a pilgrim hospice was built here. Thomas Cromwell (Henry VIII of England's future minister and adviser) came here as a young man in 1514. Ironically it was on Cromwell's advice that St Thomas Becket's shrine in Canterbury was destroyed in 1538. The Collegio was founded in 1579 by the Jesuits, as a seminary for the training of priests as missionaries to England. The record of visitors shows the names of Thomas Hobbes (1635), William Harvey (1636), John Milton (1638), John Evelyn (1644) and Cardinal Manning (in the late 19th century). The church was rebuilt to Virginio Vespignani's design in 1866–88, a free adaptation of a Romanesque basilica, with elaborate gilded decorations. The frescoes of English martyrs in the matroneum are based on an earlier cycle, lost when the old church was destroyed, which were painted by Niccolò Circignani and included scenes of the death of Edward Campion in 1581. The beautiful tomb effigy of Cardinal Christopher Bainbridge, Bishop of York (d. 1514), borne on two Romanesque lions, is attributed to Nicola Marini. The monument to Thomas Dereham (d. 1739) is by Ferdinando Fuga, with sculptures by Filippo della Valle.

Also in the piazza is the church of **San Girolamo della Carità** (*if closed, ring at no. 63 Via San Girolamo*), rebuilt in the 17th century with a façade by Carlo Rainaldi. The Cappella Spada (first on the right), formerly attributed to Borromini, is now thought to be the work of a sculptor and architect who worked mostly in Naples, Cosimo Fanzago. To the left of the high altar is a decorative chapel (1710) dedicated to St Philip Neri, by Filippo Juvarra.

In Via Giulia there follow a series of palaces interesting for their courtyards. The church of **Santa Caterina da Siena** (*open on holidays at 10.30*) was rebuilt by Paolo Posi in 1766. The **Palazzo del Collegio Spagnuolo** next door (19th century) has a large coat of arms high up on the façade. In the courtyard are several fine tombs, notably that of Cardinal Giovanni de Mella, attributed to Andrea Bregno. In a room off the courtyard is the monument to Pedro de Foix Montoya; this incorporates a remarkable portrait bust, an early work (c. 1621) by Bernini.

A street on the left leads past a tailor's workshop to **Sant'Eligio degli Orefici** (*closed for restoration*). In 1509 Julius II gave the confraternity of Roman goldsmiths permission to erect a church contains some fine works. In the south aisle, the third chapel contains a beautiful altarpiece of *St Jerome* by Santi di Tito, with on the right wall another painting of the saint in his studio by Lodovico Cigoli, and on the left wall the *Construction of the Church with St Jerome* by Domenico Cresti (usually known as Passignano). The altarpiece in the south transept of *St Cosmas and St Damian at the Stake*, by Salvator Rosa, was one of his last works, with a superb nude figure fleeing the flames, which shows the influence of Michelangelo. The funerary busts are by Algardi (on the left) and Ercole Ferrata (on the right). The chapel to the right of the sanctuary, the Cappella della Madonna preserves a fresco (much restored) of the *Madonna and Child* by **Filippino Lippi**, held to be miraculous. Until 1640 this was in a street tabernacle in the nearby Vicolo delle Palle, where it commemorated a miracle which occurred when a man who lost at a game of bowls had in fury hit the image of the Madonna with his ball and as a result remained paralyzed for 40 days. The chapel to the left of the sanctuary was decorated by Giovanni Lanfranco (before his work in Sant'Andrea della Valle; *see p. 293*), with vault frescoes, two paintings, and lovely stuccoes.

The fifth chapel on the north side has frescoes by Niccolò Circignani (also known as Pomarancio; his signature was found during recent restoration work), and an altarpiece of *St Francis* by Santi di Tito. The fourth chapel has putti on the wall-tombs of the Bacelli, carved by François Duquesnoy, a Flemish sculptor who came to Rome in 1618. He is above all remembered for his delightful chubby putti, of which these are good examples.

Behind the high altar is a crypt sepulchre of the Falconieri family, a fine late work by **Borromini**, who is also buried in this church.

A little **museum** (*entered from the church or from 2 Via Acciaioli; open Mon–Fri 10–5; Sat 10–2*) preserves treasures from the church. These include a Tuscan statuette of St John the Baptist dating from around 1495; a bust of Antonio Coppola by Pietro Bernini (the head may be the work of his son Gian Lorenzo when he was aged around twelve or fourteen); and a bust of Antonio Cepparelli (a documented work by Gian Lorenzo, 1622). The bell is one of the oldest in Rome (1253). The church silver and reliquaries include a foot of Mary Magdalene (an unusual relic dating from the 15th or 16th century). A painting shows reliquaries of St Philip Neri, who lived here before moving to the Chiesa Nuova (*see p. 294*). The balcony above the high altar of the church provides a splendid view of the interior (one of the very few churches in Rome where such a view is possible).

WALK FOUR

THE DISTRICT NEAR THE GHETTO & ISOLA TIBERINA

This area immediately west of the Capitoline Hill, although in the very centre of the city, includes some unexpectedly peaceful narrow streets which preserve much of the character of old Rome. The small *piazze* are decorated with fountains, palaces and churches, and the characteristic *sanpietrini* paving and a few old-fashioned shops survive. In the interesting area of the Ghetto are some Roman remains, including the Theatre of Marcellus. The Isola Tiberina is the only island in the Tiber.

In the 16th century a palace was constructed in part of the huge cavea of the ancient Roman **Theatre of Marcellus** (*open 9–6*). The façade remains—and it now shows what many ancient buildings in the city must have looked like when they were converted over the centuries

for new uses. The theatre, planned by Julius Caesar, was dedicated in 13 or 11 BC by Augustus to the memory of his nephew (Octavia's son) and son-in-law, Marcellus, who had died in 23 BC at the age of 19. It was restored by Vespasian and Alexander Severus. The building

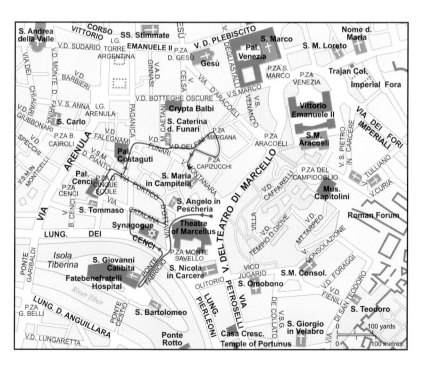

was pillaged in the 4th century for the restoration of Ponte Cestio (*see p. 317 below*). It was fortified in the early Middle Ages and made into a stronghold by the Savelli and Orsini families. Renaissance architects frequently studied the theatre. In the 16th century it was converted into a palace for the Savelli by Baldassare Peruzzi, who built the façade into the curved exterior. The theatre was restored in 1932, when numerous houses and shops on the site were demolished, but the palace façade remains—a fine example of a Roman building which still contains a later building.

The cavea originally had at least two tiers of 41 arches, the first with Doric and the second with Ionic engaged columns probably crowned by an attic of the Corinthian order. Only 12 arches in each of the first two tiers survive; the upper stage has disappeared. The theatre could probably have held some 15,000 spectators. Beside the theatre are three tall columns which belonged to the Temple of Apollo Medico, built in 433 BC and restored by the consul Caius Sosius in 33 BC. Beyond are the ruins of the Temple of Bellona, built in 296 BC.

Emerging from the archaeological area, you see on your right the **Portico of Octavia**, once a huge rectangular portico (c. 119m by 132m) with about 300 columns, which enclosed two temples dedicated to Jupiter and Juno. Erected by Quintus Caecilius Metellus in 146 BC, it was reconstructed by Augustus in honour of his sister Octavia c. 23 BC, and restored by Septimius Severus in AD 203. The southern extremities of the area of the portico have been exposed, and remains of columns to the west and the stylobate to the east can also be seen. In the wide Via del Portico d'Ottavia, right by the Portico, no. 25 has two ancient Roman architraves framing the doorway.

The entrances consisted of two propylaea with eight columns and four piers; the one on the southwest survives and now serves as a monumental entrance to the church of Sant'Angelo in Pescheria (*closed for restoration*), founded in 755 (and rebuilt in the 16th century). It contains a fresco of the *Madonna Enthroned with Angels* attributed to Benozzo Gozzoli or his school, and an early 12th-century *Madonna and Child*. The portico was used from the 12th century as a fish market (hence the name of the church, *in Pescheria*) up until the destruction of the Ghetto in 1888. An arch was added, and the pediment repaired in the Middle Ages. From this church Cola di Rienzo (*see p. 36*) and his followers set out to seize the Capitoline on the night of Pentecost, 1347. Here also, from 1584 until the 19th-century papacy of Pius IX, Jews were forced to listen to a Christian sermon every Saturday. On the wall of the little 'medieval' house here (now the headquarters of the antique monuments and archaeological excavations office of the Comune di Roma) a plaque commemorates the 2,091 Roman Jews who died in concentration camps in the Second World War (along with 6,000 other Italian Jews). The date when they were deported (16th October 1943) is also recorded here.

The area roughly occupied by the **old Ghetto** (and now also recognized as the site of the Circus of Flaminius; 221 BC) stretched from the area of the Theatre of Marcellus to Via Arenula, and between Via del Portico d'Ottavia and the Tiber. From 1556 onwards, under Pope Paul

IV, the Jews of Rome were segregated and lived here subject to various restrictions on their personal freedom (although to a lesser degree than in other European countries). Pope Paul forced them to wear distinctive yellow hats and to sell their property to Christians. The walls of the Ghetto were torn down only in 1848, and the houses demolished in 1888 before the area south of Via del Portico d'Ottavia was reconstructed around the new synagogue. At this time many of the inhabitants were forced to find new accommodation and some moved across the river to Trastevere, although many Jewish people still live in the area. Further atrocious suffering was caused to the Roman Jews when the anti-semitic laws were enforced in 1938, and many were deported to concentration camps the year before the liberation of the city by the Americans in 1944.

From here, turn towards the Tiber. Lungotevere dei Cenci faces the **Isola Tiberina**, a pretty little island in the river, reached by Ponte Fabricio, the oldest Roman bridge to have survived in the city and still in use for pedestrians. The inscription over the fine arches records the name of the builder, Lucius Fabricius, and the date, 62 BC. The bridge is also known as the *Ponte dei Quattro Capi* from the two double herms of the double-headed Janus on the parapet. Remains of the 'Ponte Rotto' can be seen in the bed of the river, downstream (though the view is better from Ponte Palatino). This is a single arch of the *Pons Aemilius*, the first stone bridge over the Tiber, the piers of which were built in 179 BC, and were connected by arches in 142 BC. From the 13th century onwards it was repaired numerous times,

but finally collapsed in 1598 and since then has been known as the 'broken bridge'.

The island, which provides an easy crossing-place on the Tiber, is thought to have been settled early in the history of Rome. During a plague in the city in 293 BC the Sibylline Books were consulted and ambassadors were sent to the famous sanctuary of Asclepios, the god of healing, at Epidaurus in Greece. They returned with his symbol, the sacred serpent, which escaped from its basket and was found on this island, so it was decided that here a temple to the god, called by the Romans Aesculapius, should be erected: the building was dedicated in 289 BC. Ever since, the island has been associated with the work of healing. It is now largely occupied by the hospital of the Fatebenefratelli, founded in 1548 and modernized by Cesare Bazzani in 1930–34, when the lovely palms and pine trees were planted. The island is surrounded with a wide pavement of travertine (reached by steps beside the hospital on the south side). From here it is possible to walk under the Roman bridge, and at the end nearest the Ponte Rotto you can see remains of the travertine facing which decorated the island in Roman times: the stone is sculpted in the form of a ship with a (now defaced) human head carrying the serpent of Aesculapius.

The church of **San Giovanni Calibita**, on your right as you cross the bridge, was founded in the 11th century and reconstructed in 1640. In the 18th-century interior is a ceiling painting by Corrado Giaquinto. Opposite is a tall medieval tower, formerly part of an 11th-century fortress, and beyond it

Piazza San Bartolomeo, where the church of **San Bartolomeo**, on the site of the Temple of Aesculapius, was built in the 10th century in honour of St Adalbert, Bishop of Prague, and several times restored, notably by Orazio Torriani in 1624. The tower is Romanesque, and the interior contains 14 antique columns, and an ancient sculptured well-head on the chancel steps, probably from the original church. There is a hall crypt beneath the transept. In the former convent there is a Jewish hospital, founded in 1882.

The south side of the island is joined to Trastevere (*see p. 369*) by the Ponte Cestio, probably built by Lucius Cestius in 46 BC, restored in AD 370, and rebuilt in 1892, the central arch to its original design and measurements.

Return to the mainland now, and turn left along the Lungotevere. The monumental **Synagogue** on the right was built by Vincenzo Costa and Osvaldo Armanni in 1899–1904. It contains a **Museum of Jewish Art** (*open Mon–Thur 9–4.30; Fri 9–1.30; Sun 9–12; closed Sat; T: 06 6840 0661*) illustrating the history of the community in the city. A Holy Ark in marble dating from 1523, but incorporating some Roman fragments, which was demolished in 1908–10, has been reconstructed and exhibited in the vaults. Walking round the Synagogue brings you back to Via del Portico d'Ottavia. At nos 2–1 is the **Casa di Lorenzo Manilio**, with a handsome long inscription in fine marble lettering dating the house in the ancient Roman manner, to 2,221 years after the foundation of

Rome (i.e. 1468), and decorated with ancient Roman sculptural fragments, including a sarcophagus with the portrait busts of the dead. An excellent little Jewish bakery called 'Il Boccione' survives on the corner here (at no. 1): it retains a remarkable atmosphere of old Rome. On the façade facing Piazza Costaguti, the patriotic invocation *Have Roma* ('Hail Rome!') can be seen above three of the first-floor windows, which also date from the time of Manilio. Also here is a pretty little 18th-century chapel, in a wide passageway.

The unattractive Piazza delle Cinque Scole was laid out in the 19th century when the Ghetto was demolished, with a fountain from Piazza Giudea by Giacomo della Porta. The name of the piazza recalls the five synagogues which once occupied a building here. **Palazzo Cenci** at the far end belonged to the family of Beatrice Cenci who was beheaded for parricide in 1599 (*see p. 224*). Going round it to the right is Monte dei Cenci, an artificial mound—probably on Roman remains—with a pretty little piazza between Palazzo Cenci and the church of San Tommaso dei Cenci (*sometimes open on Sun at 10.30*). An ancient Roman altar has been set into the façade. It contains a chapel frescoed by Sermoneta (1575) and two carved Roman brackets supporting a side altar. The restaurant Piperno (*see p. 566*) serves Jewish specialities.

Retrace your steps to Via del Portico d'Ottavia. Via della Reginella, a survival from the old Ghetto, leads to the little Piazza Mattei, with the charming

Ponte Fabricio and the Isola Tiberina, with a medieval tower on the left and the bell-tower of San Giovanni Calibita opposite.

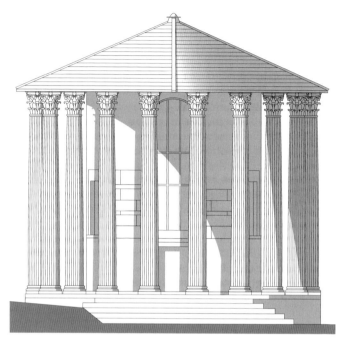

TEMPLE OF HERCULES VICTOR

The little round **Temple of Hercules Victor** was for long thought to be dedicated to Vesta, but an inscription from the base of a cult statue found here confirmed its dedication to Hercules Victor. It also dates from the end of the 2nd century BC and is the oldest marble edifice to survive in Rome. A charming little building, it consists of a circular cella of solid marble, surrounded by 20 fluted columns, with exquisite capitals. After severe damage in the 1st century AD the temple was restored under Tiberius and some of the columns and capitals replaced, using the (easily distinguishable) white Luni marble. One of the columns is missing on the north side but its base remains. The original roof and ancient entablature have not survived. In the Middle Ages the temple became the church of Santo Stefano delle Carrozze and later Santa Maria del Sole.

The fountain is by Carlo Bizzaccheri (1717)—a good work for its period but lacking in true style: the two tritons don't have the strength Bernini would have given them. The entrance to a side conduit of the Cloaca Maxima (*see below*) can be seen here under a square travertine lid.

Near ugly municipal public offices set up by the Fascist regime in 1936–37 is the eccentric **Casa dei Crescenzi**, a unique example of a mansion built by a wealthy Roman in the Middle Ages. Formerly a tower guarding the river, it dates from c. 1100 and the inscription over the door states that it was erected by one Nicolaus, son or descendant of Crescentius and Theodora, probably members of the Alberic family, the most powerful clan in Rome at the end of the 10th century. It is constructed mainly from fragments of Classical buildings or medieval copies of Roman works. The bricks of the lower storey are formed into half-columns, with rudimentary capitals. A fragment of the upper storey and its arcaded loggia survives. It is now used by the Centro Studi per la Storia dell'Architettura, and concerts are occasionally held here, but it is otherwise closed to the public.

SANTA MARIA IN COSMEDIN
Map p. 622, 4C

Open 10–1 & 3–5 or 2.30–6.30; sung Mass on Sunday at 10.30.

Santa Maria in Cosmedin is a fine example of a Roman medieval church, preceded by a little gabled porch and arcaded narthex. It has lost much of its atmosphere in recent years, however, and is often hurriedly visited by tour groups since their buses can park directly outside.

The building incorporates two earlier structures, the arcaded colonnade of the Imperial Roman *Statio Annonae* (market inspector's office), and the side walls of a porticoed hall, part of an early Christian welfare centre, or *diaconia* (c. 600). The oratory was enlarged into a basilican church, with a matroneum and three apses, by Hadrian I (772–95); assigned to Greek refugees driven from Constantinople by the iconoclastic persecutions, it became known as the Schola Graeca. Its other name, 'in Cosmedin', probably comes from the Greek verb to adorn, referring to the work of embellishment carried out by Pope Hadrian. Cardinal Alfano, chamberlain of Calixtus II, rebuilt the church around 1123, closed the galleries, and added the schola cantorum. The church was over-restored and the pretty 18th-century façade torn down in 1894–99; it has again been restored recently.

The fine tall campanile of seven storeys dates from the 12th century. Beneath the portico, to the left, is the so-called **Bocca della Verità**, a large cracked marble disc representing a human face, the open mouth of which was believed to close on the hand of any perjurer who faced the ordeal of placing it there. It is in fact a slab that once closed an ancient drain, and was put here in 1632. It is much visited by tourists, who like to have their photographs taken with their hand in the mouth. Also here is the tomb of Cardinal Alfano (*see above*). The principal doorway is the work of a certain 'Johannes' from the Veneto (11th century).

The Interior

The fine interior, with a nave and two aisles each ending in an apse, closely follows the layout of the 8th-century basilica, with some 12th-century additions. The arcades are supported on antique columns with good capitals grouped in threes between piers. In the first part of the nave remains of the arcaded colonnade and side walls of the *Statio*

The Vico Jugario is on the site of the Roman road that connected the *Forum Holitorium*—the vegetable and oil market which extended from the Capitoline Hill to the Tiber— with the Roman Forum. It skirts the foot of the Capitoline Hill (reached from here by a path and steps called Via di Monte Caprino) near the arcades of a portico built of *peperino* in the Republican era, and a medieval fortified mansion which has been over-restored.

The church of **Sant'Omobono** (*open only on the first Sun of the month at 11*) has a 16th-century façade. It contains a 17th-century lunette showing God as divine tailor putting a fur coat on Adam. Excavations around the church, which began in 1937, continued in the 1960s and are still not completed, have revealed traces of habitation as early as the 9th century BC. Known as the Area Sacra di Sant'Omobono, this is closed but partly visible through the railings: remains have been unearthed on seven different levels, the oldest dating from c. 1500 BC. Traces of hut dwellings of the 9th–8th centuries BC, similar to those on the Palatine, have also been found. The archaeological evidence has thrown new light on the origins of Rome and the presence of the Etruscans here in the 7th and 6th centuries BC.

Two Archaic temples (mid-6th century BC), dedicated to Fortuna and Mater Matuta, and traditionally thought to have been founded by Servius Tullius (ruler of Rome in 578–535 BC), rest on an artificial mound in which were found Bronze Age and Iron Age shards and imported Greek pottery of the 8th century BC. In front of the temples are two Archaic altars, possibly dedicated to Carmenta, a water-goddess. The most conspicuous remains mostly date from after 213 BC when the temples were reconstructed. The material found on the site, including a terracotta group of Hercules and Minerva from one of the temples, is kept in the Antiquarium Comunale (*see p. 341*).

San Nicola in Carcere

San Nicola in Carcere (*open 7.30–12 & 4.30–7; holidays 10.30–1; map p. 622, 3C*) is an 11th-century church, probably on the site of an older sanctuary, which was reconstructed and consecrated in 1128. It was remodelled in 1599 by Giacomo della Porta, who designed the façade using three columns from a Roman temple, and detached from the surrounding buildings in 1932, and major excavations were carried out on either side of the church at the end of the 20th century.

The church occupies the site of three Republican temples in the *Forum Holitorium*, which are thought to have been dedicated to Janus, Juno Sospita and Spes. The first, to the right of the church, was Ionic hexastyle, with columns on three sides only. Its remains can be seen incorporated in the south wall of the church. Remains of the second are also incorporated in the church. The third was on the left of the church.

The interior has fine antique columns from the temples with diverse capitals, and a beautiful ancient urn in green porphyry beneath the high altar and baldacchino. At the end of the left aisle is an altarpiece of the *Ascension* by Lorenzo Costa, one of the very few works in Rome by this important artist, who was born in Ferrara and worked mostly in Emilia and Mantua. The apse frescoes date from 1865. The Roman remains beneath the church can sometimes be visited.

THE CIRCUS MAXIMUS, AVENTINE HILL & BATHS OF CARACALLA

Only the shape of the Circus Maximus, the largest circus in ancient Rome, survives, but it is impressive for all that, and can be enjoyed as a public park from which there is a very fine view of the monumental ruined Roman buildings at the southern end of the Palatine. The Aventine Hill rises on the southwest side of the Circus Maximus. It has two summits: the Aventine of ancient Rome (40m), which is close to the Tiber, and the Piccolo Aventino, to the south. These are now divided by the busy Viale Aventino. The Baths of Caracalla are among the most imposing Roman remains in the city.

NB: Though bus 628 runs from Largo Torre Argentina to the Circus Maximus and Baths of Caracalla, public transport in this area is unreliable and subject to change, so it is sometimes best to walk from the Circus to the Baths.

CIRCUS MAXIMUS
Map pp. 622–23 4C–D

The Circus Maximus (*Circo Massimo*) lies in the Valle Murcia, between the Palatine and the Aventine hills. Now planted with grass and unenclosed, it is used as a public park (and sometimes also for political demonstrations).

The circus was the first and largest in Rome. According to Livy, it dates from the time of Tarquinius Priscus (c. 600 BC), who is said to have inaugurated a display of races and boxing matches here after a victory over the Latins; but the first factual reference to it is in 329 BC. The circus was altered and enlarged on several occasions.

In the time of Julius Caesar its length was three *stadia* (1,875 Roman feet) and its width one *stadium*. The resultant oblong was rounded at one end and straight at the other. Tiers of seats were provided all round except at the short straight end; here were the *carceres*, or stalls for horses and chariots. In the centre, running lengthwise, was the *spina*, a low wall terminating at either end in a *meta*, or conical pillar, denoting the turnings of the course. The length of a race was seven circuits of the spina. Though primarily adapted for chariot races, the circus was also used for athletic contests, wild-beast fights, and (by flooding the arena) for mock sea-battles. It could accommodate from 150,000 to 385,000 spectators; its capacity varied from one reconstruction to the next.

The circus was destroyed by fire under Nero (AD 64) and again in the time of Domitian. A new circus was built by Trajan; Caracalla enlarged it and Constantine restored it after a partial collapse. The last games were held under the Ostrogothic king Totila in AD 549.

WALK FIVE

ALONG VIA DI PORTA SAN SEBASTIANO

This charming old cobbled road envelops you unexpectedly in a rural atmosphere with shady gardens and woods on either side, above high walls, typical of old Rome at its most picturesque. However, when the traffic light at its entrance changes, the cars race along it totally destroying its tranquillity. It leads directly to the Via Appia Antica (*described on p. 484ff*).

A short way down on the right, beyond a walled garden, is the ancient church of **San Cesareo** (*usually open on Sun; T: 06 700 9016*) rebuilt at the end of the 16th century, with a façade attributed to Giacomo della Porta. Inside is some very fine Cosmati work (very similar to that in Santi Nereo ed Achilleo; *see p. 335 above*), including the high altar, the bishop's throne, the transennae, the candelabrum, the ambo and the fronts of the side-altars. The two angels beneath the high altar are probably from a 15th-century tomb by Paolo Romano. The beautiful wooden ceiling, gilded on a blue ground, bears the arms of the Aldobrandini pope Clement VIII (1592–1605), who restored the church in 1600. The apse mosaic of the *Eternal Father* was designed by Cavaliere d'Arpino, who also painted the frescoes. The baldacchino dates from the time of

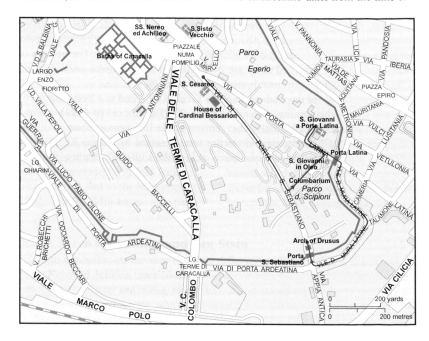

Clement VIII. Below the church (*but closed indefinitely*) is a large black-and-white mosaic of the 2nd century AD. The fantastic sea-monsters, animals and figures may have decorated the floor of Roman baths.

Beyond the church, at no. 8 on the right, you can see the garden of the 15th-century **House of Cardinal Bessarion** (*not at present open to the public*). A native of Trebizond and Bishop of Nicaea, he accompanied the Greek Emperor John Palaeologus to Italy in 1439 in an attempt to bring about a union between the Greek and Roman churches, but soon afterwards joined the Roman church and was made a cardinal. A famous Humanist scholar, he bequeathed his remarkable collection of Greek and Latin manuscripts to the Biblioteca Marciana in Venice in 1468. The delightful house and garden are a good example of a 15th-century summer home. The house, owned by the Comune of Rome, contains 15th-century frescoes and wall-paintings of garlands and ribbons which cast painted shadows, and overall patterns of acanthus leaves and pomegranates.

About 500m further along the road, at no. 9 on the left, beside two old columns and a little fountain, can be seen the neglected entrance to the **Tomb of the Scipios**. This has sadly been closed for many years. The tomb, one of the first to be built on the Via Appia, was discovered in 1780. It was built for Lucius Cornelius Scipio Barbatus, consul in 298 BC, and great-grandfather of Scipio Africanus. Many other members of the *gens* Cornelia were buried here, up to the middle of the 2nd century BC (the sarcophagus of Scipio Barbatus and

the funerary inscriptions found here were removed to the Vatican; *see p. 455*).

Beside the tomb an open gate leads into a peaceful little public park called the **Parco degli Scipioni**. A gate at the far end leads into the rural Via di Porta Latina where, in a quiet cul-de-sac (go left and then right), with a large cedar and ancient well, is the picturesque church of **San Giovanni a Porta Latina** (*open 6.30–1 & 3.30–7, undergoing restoration*). It has a narthex of four Roman columns, and a beautiful 12th-century campanile. Founded in the 5th century, it was rebuilt by Hadrian I in 772, and restored several times, but the interior retains its beautiful 11th-century basilican form. It contains 12th-century frescoes restored in 1940. The apse has three lovely windows of selenite, and a fine marble pavement in *opus sectile*.

In the other direction Via di Porta Latina leads to the gate in the walls, past the little octagonal chapel of **San Giovanni in Oleo**, traditionally marking the spot where St John the Evangelist stepped unharmed from a cauldron of boiling oil. Rebuilt in the early 16th century during the reign of Julius II, it has an interesting design, formerly attributed to Donato Bramante, but now usually thought to be by Antonio da Sangallo the Younger or Baldassare Peruzzi. It was restored in 1658 by Francesco Borromini, who added the frieze. The interior (*usually locked*) contains stuccoes and paintings by Lazzaro Baldi. Beside it a gate into the garden has a very worn plaque announcing the **Columbarium of Pomponius Hylas**, one of the best-preserved burial places of its kind in existence. It is an underground chamber with niches that con-

SAN GREGORIO MAGNO

Map p. 623, 4D

Open 9–12.30 & 3.30–6; closed Sat; the three oratories (of greater interest than the church) are open Tues, Thur, Sat and Sun 9.30–12.30.

The church of San Gregorio Magno is a medieval church altered and restored in the 17th and 18th centuries. It is dedicated to St Gregory the Great, one of the greatest popes in the history of the church. From a wealthy patrician family, he founded a monastery here on the site of his father's house, and dedicated it to St Andrew. He himself was a monk here before (unwillingly) becoming pope in 590, the first monk ever to reach that position. The city was suffering from a long period in which its possession had been contested between Goths and Byzantines, but Gregory succeeded in establishing control and effectively asserted the temporal power of the papacy (which was to last right up until the 19th century). From his time onwards the history of Rome became intricately connected with that of the Roman church. He did much to help the inhabitants of Rome during terrible plagues, and rescued them from starvation. He revised the Roman liturgy (his letters and sermons became famous) and he had a special interest in music. St Augustine was prior in this monastery and it was here in 596 that he received Gregory's blessing before setting out with 40 other monks on his famous mission to convert the English to Christianity. The church and adjoining chapels have many connections with St Gregory.

The church

The staircase, façade and lovely atrium (1633) are by Giovanni Battista Soria (a Roman architect clearly influenced by both Carlo Maderno and Pietro da Cortona), and are considered his masterpiece. In the atrium are several fine tombs, including (near the entrance) that of Sir Robert Peckham (d. 1569), a self-exiled English Catholic. There is a memorial to Sir Edward Carne (d. 1561), another English Catholic and an envoy of Henry VIII and Mary I. Beside the convent door is a tomb (of two brothers called Bonsi) by Luigi Capponi, a little-known sculptor who carved a number of tombs in Roman churches in the last two decades of the 15th century.

The church (*for admission ring at the door of the convent on the right in the atrium*) was rebuilt in 1725–34 by Francesco Ferrari. It preserves 16 antique columns and a restored mosaic pavement. At the end of the south aisle is the Chapel of St Gregory, with a fine altar-frontal, also sculptured by Luigi Capponi, and a good painting of the saint by an Emilian painter called Sisto Badalocchio, one of very few works by him in Rome (though several are concentrated in this area; *see opposite and overleaf*). The marble chair dating from the 1st century BC is known as the 'Throne of St Gregory'.

The Salviati Chapel (*at present locked*), by Francesco da Volterra and Carlo Maderno, has an ancient fresco of the *Madonna* (repainted), which supposedly spoke to St Gregory, and a fine tabernacle by the school of Andrea Bregno (1469). The altarpieces in the nave date from the 18th century.

The oratories

On the left of the church are the three oratories (*open Tue, Thur, Sat, Sun 9.30–12.30*) surrounded by ancient cypresses. These were part of a monastery founded by St Gregory, the rest of which was demolished in 1573 and the two chapels were restored in 1602. In the centre is the **chapel of Sant'Andrea**, preceded by a portico with four antique *cipollino* columns. Inside on the right is a very fine painting of the *Flagellation of St Andrew* by Domenichino, and on the left *St Andrew on the way to his Martyrdom* by Guido Reni. On the entrance wall are depictions of St Sylvia and St Gregory by Giovanni Lanfranco. The altarpiece of the *Madonna in Glory between St Andrew and St Gregory* is by Pomarancio. Above the altar, in the space between the original roof and the lower Renaissance wooden ceiling, there is an 11th-century mural (not at present visible).

The chapel on the left, **Santa Barbara**, contains a statue of St Gregory by Nicolas Cordier. The 3rd-century table is believed to be the one at which St Gregory served twelve paupers daily with his own hands, among whom an angel once appeared as a thirteenth; this legend gave the alternative name to the chapel, the *Triclinium Pauperum*. A fresco on the left, by Antonio Viviani (1602), commemorates the famous incident which culminated in St Augustine's mission: apparently Gregory saw some fair-haired children at a slave market in Rome, and upon hearing that they were English, declared '*non Angli sed Angeli*' ('not Angles but angels'—irreverently but wittily transposed in *1066 and All That* as 'not angels but Anglicans'.

The chapel on the right, **Santa Silvia**, was built in 1603 and dedicated to St Sylvia, mother of Gregory. It contains her statue by Nicolas Cordier, and a lovely fresco of an angel choir by Guido Reni (with the help of Sisto Badalocchio).

Antiquarium Comunale

Viale del Parco del Celio (beware of trams) leads up to the Casina dei Salvi, where part of the **Antiquarium Comunale**, also known as the Antiquarium del Celio, is housed (*though closed for restoration; T: 06 700 1569; map p. 623, 4D*). The antiquarium was founded in 1885 for objects unearthed during excavations in Rome, and illustrates the everyday life of the city from earliest times to the end of the Empire. This extremely important archaeological collection, with some 60,000 works, was first exhibited here in 1894, but much of it, housed in Palazzo Caffarelli on the Capitoline Hill, has remained inaccessible to the public for decades. It includes material dating from the 9th–6th centuries BC from the Esquiline necropolis, finds from excavations near Sant'Omobono and on the Capitoline.

In the garden are architectural fragments, tombs, reliefs and inscriptions. The small collection arranged here a few years ago has finds dating from the Imperial period, including frescoes from Roman houses, bronze waterspouts and valves dating from the late Empire and an interesting model of a water pump. The mosaic with the scene of a port was found in the gardens of Palazzo Rospigliosi in 1878 during the construction of Via Nazionale. There are also household items, jewellery, cooking and eating utensils, iron hand-tools for working wood and marble, instruments for measuring liquids, solids and distances, and heavy farming tools.

SANTI GIOVANNI E PAOLO
Map p. 623, 4E

The picturesque Clivo di Scauro ascends gently. On the right are remains of a 6th-century basilican hall of the library erected to contain Christian texts by Pope St Agapitus I, on the site of his family mansion on this hill. Through a window you can see the Roman masonry in the foundations of the chapels. The 17th-century portal (which provided access from the Clivo di Scauro) bears a fresco of the *Ecce Homo* by Badalocchio, the Borghese dragons and the name of Cardinal Scipione Borghese (*see p. 182*). In the little garden here are walls dating from the Republican period. The road continues uphill beneath the medieval buttresses (which span the road) of the church of Santi Giovanni e Paolo past its fine apse, a rare example of Lombard work in Rome, dating from 1216. The tall façade of a Roman house is incorporated in the left wall of the church and here is the entrance to the **Roman Houses** (*Case Romane*) beneath the church of Santi Giovanni e Paolo (*open 10–1 & 3–6; closed Tues and Wed; T: 06 7045 4544*). These were restored in 2000 when a small antiquarium was also redisplayed in a circular room adjoining the archaeological area. The Roman remains are particularly interesting for their wall paintings.

According to tradition this was the site of the house where John (Giovanni) and Paul (Paolo), two court dignitaries under Constantine II, lived in the mid-4th century. They were martyred by Julian the Apostate and were buried here. Excavations began at the end of the 19th century and at least four phases of habitation have been found from the 1st–5th centuries AD including two Roman apartment houses with shops (2nd–3rd centuries AD), a Roman *domus*, and a Christian house and an oratory founded before 410 by the senator Byzantius and his son Pammachius, a friend of St Jerome.

In the first room are explanatory panels, and straight ahead is a room with delightful wall paintings of youths bearing garlands and a great variety of birds beneath putti amongst vines. The rooms to the right have architectural frescoes with painted imitation marble, and figures of philosophers, goats and masques. In the little medieval oratory (near the road) are 9th-century frescoes including a rare representation of the *Crucifixion* in which the figure of Christ is robed. In another area there is a nymphaeum with a striking fresco of Persephone and a nereid, and boats manned by cupids. An iron staircase leads up to the confessio, decorated with 4th-century frescoes the significance of which is not entirely clear: on the end wall is a praying figure, perhaps one of the martyrs, between drawn curtains, at whose feet are two other figures. On the right are St Priscus, St Priscillian and St Benedicta (who tried to find the remains of the martyrs and were themselves killed), awaiting execution with eyes bound; this is thought to be the oldest existing painting of a martyrdom.

The antiquarium exhibits Roman and medieval finds, including sculptural fragments, ceramics dating from the 3rd–4th centuries AD, terracotta and glass (1st century BC–1st century AD), 12th-century Islamic ceramic plates removed from the campanile in 1951, a 12th-century fresco detached in 1955 from the oratory perhaps covering an 8th-century work, roof tiles, architectural fragments, *opus sectile* decorations, and amphorae.

The church

The church of Santi Giovanni e Paolo (*open 8.30–12 & 3.30–6; closed Fri and Sun morning*) stands beside the 12th-century convent built above remains of the Temple of Claudius (*see p. 346*). The church was built above Roman houses and an early Christian oratory (*described above*). This was demolished by Robert Guiscard in 1084, and rebuilding was begun by Paschal II (1099–1118) and continued by Hadrian IV (Nicholas Breakspear, the only English pope; *see p. 419*), who was responsible for the apse and the campanile. Excavations carried out in 1949 revealed the early Christian façade and some of the ancient constructions beneath the convent.

The travertine blocks of the temple are clearly visible in the base of the beautiful tall campanile (45m), the first two storeys of which were begun in 1099–1118, and the five upper storeys completed by the middle of the 12th century. The Islamic ceramic plates inserted into the masonry are copies of the originals now displayed in the antiquarium (*see previous page*).

The 12th-century Ionic portico has eight antique columns and is closed by an iron grille (1704). Above it is a 13th-century gallery and the early Christian façade with five arches. The 13th-century Cosmatesque doorway is flanked by two lions and surmounted by an eagle with a rabbit in its talons. The interior (frequently used for weddings), hung with chandeliers, with granite piers and columns, was restored in 1718 by Antonio Canevari. The ceiling dates from 1598 and the floor, in *opus alexandrinum*, was restored in 1911. A tomb-slab in the nave, protected by a railing, commemorates the burial place of the two martyrs to whom the church is dedicated. Their relics are preserved in a porphyry urn under the high altar. In the third south chapel, designed by Filippo Martinucci (1857–80), is the altar-tomb of St Paul of the Cross (1694–1775), founder of the Passionists, whose convent adjoins the church. The apse has

The graceful campanile of Santi Giovanni e Paolo.

frescoes by Pomarancio. In a storeroom (*unlocked by the sacristan*) on the left of the high altar can be seen a remarkable fresco of *Christ and the Apostles*, dated 1255, by a painter of the Roman school showing the influence of Byzantine art.

Outside the church, beyond a door beside the Campanile, are remains of the *Claudianum*, two storeys of a huge Roman portico connected with the Temple of Claudius (*see overleaf*). In the piazza are some arches of Roman shops dating from the 3rd century AD. Here a rusticated gate leads to the delightful public park of the **Villa Celimontana** (*see overleaf*).

THE EASTERN CAELIAN
Map p. 623, 4E

At the other end of the picturesque Via di San Paolo della Croce, which runs between two garden walls above which can be seen orange trees, is the **Arch of Dolabella and Silanus** (AD 10), a single archway that Nero afterwards used for his aqueduct to the Palatine.

The entrance to the former hospice of the Trinitarian church of **San Tommaso in Formis** (*open only on Sun at 10.30*) is on the right. St John of Matha died here in 1213: he founded the order of Trinitarians for the redemption of slaves, and above the doorway is a mosaic (c. 1218) of *Christ between two Christian Slaves*, one white, the other black.

Further on, also on the right, is the church of **Santa Maria in Domnica** (*open 9–12.30 & 4.30–7.30*) or *della Navicella*, of ancient foundation. Its title is a corruption of *Dominica* (Chief). The alternative name is derived from the Roman stone boat that Leo X had made into a fountain (with a pretty pebble-mosaic pool) in front of the church. The boat was probably a votive offering from the *Castra Peregrina*, a camp for non-Italian soldiers, which was on this hill.

The present church was restored by St Paschal I (pope 817–24), who is commemorated in the apse mosaic. It was practically rebuilt in the 16th century by Cardinal Giovanni de' Medici (later Leo X) from the designs of Andrea Sansovino, and has a graceful portico. In the lovely interior the nave contains 18 granite columns; over the windows is a frieze by Perino del Vaga from designs by Giulio Romano. On the triumphal arch, flanked by two porphyry columns, is a beautifully coloured 9th-century mosaic of Christ with two angels and the Apostles, and the larger figures of Moses and Elijah below; in the semi-dome, St Paschal kisses the foot of the Madonna and Child surrounded by a throng of angels. The crypt contains interesting Roman sarcophagi, fragments of 9th-century plutei, and a 17th-century altar.

The *opus alexandrinum* pavement of Santi Giovanni e Paolo glimmers in the light of the chandeliers. (The urns are placed here in preparation for wedding flowers.)

Detail of the *Annunciation* by Masolino, above the entrance to the Chapel of St Catherine.

the thirst of the faithful (represented by stags) and watering the pastures of the Christian flock. Below are the Lamb of God and 12 companions.

On the apse wall below are impressive large 14th-century frescoed figures of Christ, the Virgin and the Apostles. To the right is a lovely wall-tabernacle, probably by Arnolfo di Cambio.

c Chapel of St Catherine:
The chapel is entirely covered with beautiful frescoes by Masolino da Panicale, commissioned by Cardinal Branda Castiglione, who was bishop of the Hungarian city of Veszprém from 1412–24, as well as the titular cardinal of this church in the same period. He had already called Masolino to his home in northern Italy, Castiglione Olona, to carry out frescoes there.

triumphal arch are Christ and the Symbols of the Evangelists, and below (on the right), St Peter and St Clement, with boat and oars, Jeremiah and Jerusalem, and on the left, St Paul and St Lawrence, Isaiah and Bethlehem. In the apse-vault (*illustrated on p. 351*) is the Dome of Heaven with the Hand of God above Christ on the Cross. The 12 doves on the Cross represent the Apostles. Beside the Cross are the Madonna and St John. From the foot of the Cross springs a vine with acanthus leaves, encircling figures of St John the Baptist, the Doctors of the Church and other saints, while the rivers of Paradise flow down from the Cross, quenching

Masolino collaborated with the younger artist Masaccio, and some art historians still debate whether the two masters did not work together on this fresco cycle (as they had done in the Brancacci Chapel in Florence); Vasari's statement that this chapel was totally the work of Masaccio has not been accepted. It is certainly known that both Masaccio and Masolino were in Rome in 1428, and the chapel is undoubtedly one of the most important early Renaissance works in Rome.

Above the entrance arch is the *Annunciation* in an open loggia (between a roundel with God the Father), and on the main wall, the *Crucifixion*. On the

SAN CLEMENTE
(UPPER CHURCH)

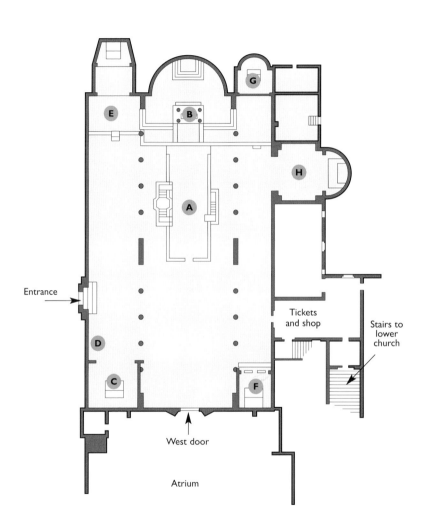

Entrance

Tickets
and shop

Stairs to
lower
church

West door

Atrium

left wall, scenes from the life of St Catherine of Alexandria: at the top left the saint is shown, dressed in blue, in a circular temple before an idol, discussing the merits of Christianity with the Emperor Maxentius. The scene next to this shows her being visited in prison by the emperor's wife, whom she converts and whom Maxentius therefore sentences to death (the empress is also shown being beheaded). The three scenes below illustrate St Catherine converting a group of Roman orators to Christianity in the magisterial presence of the emperor, who in anger has them burnt (this scene is also shown, taking place outside a window). In the centre Catherine is about to be pulled apart by two wheels (hence her attribute of the wheel and the derivation of 'Catherine wheels') but is saved by the intervention of an angel which destroys these instruments of torture. The last scene shows her final martyrdom as she is beheaded.

On the opposite wall are scenes from the life of St Ambrose; in the archivolt, the Apostles; and in the vault, the Evangelists and Fathers of the Church.

On the left entrance pier is St Christopher.

D **Masolino sinopie:** Outside the chapel are two *sinopie* found during restoration: one for the *Beheading of St Catherine*, and one for the *Crucifixion*.

The sculpture and paintings in the rest of the church, described below, date from later centuries. The walls of the nave were decorated with a cycle of paintings in 1713–19 under the direction of Giuseppe Chiari, who also executed the *Triumph of St Clement* on the ceiling.

E **Chapel of the Rosary:** Sebastiano Conca painted *Our Lady of the Rosary* in this chapel in the north aisle (where the tomb of Cardinal Antonio Venier, who died in 1479, incorporates columns from a 6th-century tabernacle).

F **Chapel of St Dominic:** Here are three paintings of scenes from the *Life of St Dominic*, also attributed to Sebastiano Conca.

G **Chapel of St John the Baptist:** Just inside the gate are two late 15th-century tombs of prelates: that of Archbishop Giovanni Francesco Brusati is by Luigi Capponi, and that of Cardinal Bartolomeo Roverella is a beautiful work by Andrea Bregno and Giovanni Dalmata. This chapel contains late 16th-century works: frescoes attributed to Jacopo Zucchi and a statue of St John the Baptist.

H **Chapel of St Cyril:** The *Madonna* on the altar is attributed to Sassoferrato (one of several versions of this painting).

Detail of the mosaic of the Crucifixion in the vault of the apse of San Clemente, with 12 doves representing the Apostles. The Cross is flanked by the Virgin and St John.

The lower church

Off the south aisle is the entrance to the lower church (*for admission, see above*), the apse of which was built above a Mithraeum (3rd century). This formed part of a late-1st-century apartment house. Below this again are foundations of the Republican period. The staircase, which has miscellaneous fragments of sculpture, descends to the frescoed narthex. Most of the precious early frescoes in the lower church are in the process of restoration.

Narthex: At the foot of the steps a catacomb can be seen through a grate in the floor. On the right wall is a remarkable fresco dating from the late 11th century of the *Legend of St Clement*, who was banished to the Crimea and there executed by drowning in the Black Sea. The scenes include the miracle of a child found alive in a church at the bottom of a sea full of fish. Below are St Clement and the donor of the fresco.

On the other side of the nave entrance is the *Translation of St Cyril's Body* from the Vatican to San Clemente (also 11th century).

Nave: The wide nave is obstructed by the foundation piers of the upper church, and unequally divided by a supporting wall. Immediately to the left is a 9th-century fresco of the *Ascension*, with the Virgin in the centre surrounded by the Apostles, St Vitus and St Leo IV (with a square nimbus). In the corner are very worn frescoes of the *Crucifixion*, the *Marys at the Tomb*, the *Descent into Hell* and the *Marriage at Cana*.

Further along, past an embedded column with spiral fluting, on the left wall of the nave is the *Story of St Alexis* (11th century): the saint (*see p. 329*) returns home unrecognized and lives for 17 years beneath a staircase; before dying he sends the story of his life to the

pope, and is thus recognized by his wife and father. Above this is the lower part of a fresco of *Christ amid Angels and Saints*. Further on is the *Story of Sisinius*: the heathen Sisinius follows his Christian wife in secret, in that way hoping to capture the pope, but he is inflicted with a sudden blindness; below, Sisinius orders his servants to seize the pope, but they, also struck blind, carry off a column instead. Painted inscriptions, which are among the oldest examples of Italian writing, suggest these scenes also refer to the building of the church. Above is the surviving lower part of a fresco of St Clement enthroned by St Peter, St Linus and St Anacletus, his predecessors on the pontifical throne.

Right aisle: Here (the second 'corridor' beyond the nave) in a niche is a 5th- or 6th-century Byzantine *Madonna*, which may have been originally a portrait of the Empress Theodora; female saints with the crown of martyrdom; and a beardless Christ. The frescoes, much damaged, probably depict the Council of Zosimus, the Story of Tobias, and the Martyrdom of St Catherine. At the end are a sarcophagus of the 1st century AD with the story of Phaedra and Hippolytus, and a Byzantine figure of Christ (7th or 8th century), almost totally obliterated.

Left aisle: Above the entrance from the narthex are some extremely faded frescoes of uncertain subjects. In the floor is a circular recess, once thought to be an early baptismal piscina, but which some scholars now think could be the remains of a bell foundry. At the end of the left aisle, beyond the remains of a tomb, venerated as that of St Cyril, the apostle of the Slavs (869), excavations are in progress of an area where a font has been found.

The first-century church

A 4th-century staircase descends to the 1st-century level with a 'palazzo', and a Mithraic temple of the late 2nd or early 3rd century. Around the corner at the bottom, to the right, is the pronaos of the temple, with very damaged stucco ceiling ornaments; opposite is the triclinium with benches on either side and an altar in the centre showing Mithras, in his Phrygian cap, sacrificing a bull to Apollo, and in the niche behind is a statue of Mithras; the vault imitates the roof of a cavern, as Mithras is said to have been born in a cave. (*For more on the cult of Mithras, see p. 515.*) At the far end of the corridor, to the right and seen through a gate, is the presumed Mithraic school with a mosaic floor and stuccoed vault, where catechumens were instructed.

From the pronaos, a door on the left leads to the 1st-century 'palazzo', probably belonging to the family of Flavius Clemens, which lies beneath the lower basilica. A long narrow passage divides the temple area from the thick tufa wall of the building constructed, after Nero's fire, on Republican foundations. Only two sides of this building have been excavated. Immediately to the right at the bottom of a short flight of steps is a series of rooms which preserve their herring-bone paving; the last two are the best-preserved rooms of the palace, showing the original brickwork, and a spring: the sound of its gushing waters pervades the whole lower building.

The second side of the building is reached by returning to the opening from the corridor; beyond a room where the spring water has been channelled away by tunnels are seven more vaulted rooms. From the last room a short flight of steps leads up to a gate beyond which can be seen a small catacomb, which was probably used in the 5th or 6th century, as it was within the city walls. A staircase on the right leads up to the lower church and exit.

SANTI QUATTRO CORONATI
Map p. 623, 4E

Church usually open 6.15–8; on holidays closed 12.30–3. Chapel of St Sylvester, cloister and crypt usually open 9.30–12 & 4.30–6; holidays 9.30–10.45 & 4–5.45, although—since it belongs to a convent—the opening hours are subject to change.

Via dei Querceti skirts the foot of the high wall of the fortified 12th-century monastery and church of Santi Quattro Coronati. The steep Via dei Santi Quattro on the left, an

AROUND SAN GIOVANNI IN LATERANO

Around the busy Piazza di San Giovanni in Laterano (*map p. 617, 3A*) are assembled some of the most important monuments in Christian history, including the first church of Rome. For centuries the popes exhibited masterpieces of Classical sculpture here, symbolizing the power of ancient Rome, including the equestrian statue of Marcus Aurelius, the She-wolf, and the *Spinario* (all of them now in the Capitoline museums). Here in 1588, on a line with Via di San Giovanni and Via Merulana, Domenico Fontana set up the red granite obelisk, the oldest in the city. It had been erected by Thothmes IV in front of the Temple of Ammon at Thebes (15th century BC), and was brought to Rome by Constantius II (357) to decorate the Circus Maximus, where it was discovered in three pieces in 1587. It is the tallest obelisk in existence (31m high, 47m with the pedestal), even though one metre had to be sawn off during its reconstruction.

Approaches

On foot, the most pleasant approaches to San Giovanni in Laterano are by Via di San Giovanni in Laterano from the Colosseum, or by Via di Santo Stefano Rotondo from the Caelian Hill. Otherwise the monuments are best reached by public transport, since the district is not particularly attractive.

SAN GIOVANNI IN LATERANO
Map p. 617, 3A

Open 7–6; 7–7 in summer.

History of San Giovanni in Laterano

The church of San Giovanni in Laterano is the cathedral of Rome and of the world (*Omnium urbis et orbis Ecclesiarum Mater et Caput*). The basilica derives its name from the rich patrician family of Plautius Lateranus, who, having been implicated in the conspiracy of the Pisoni against the emperor Nero in 65 AD, was deprived of his property and put to death. Excavations in the 20th century in the neighbouring Via Aradam revealed a large Roman building thought to be the house of the Pisoni and Laterani expropriated by Nero. The property afterwards passed to Constantine as the dowry of his wife Fausta. In this *Domus Faustae*, church meetings were probably held as early as 313. The emperor presented it, together with the land occupied by barracks (excavated in 1934–38 beneath the nave of the present basilica) built in the 2nd century for his private horseguards, the *Equites Singulares*, to St Melchiades (pope 311–14), for the purpose of building a church for the see of Rome.

EGYPTIAN OBELISKS

There are 13 obelisks in Rome but only five are left in Egypt itself. These monolithic tapered shafts were constructed by the Egyptians to symbolize the sun. They were often set up in pairs to decorate the entrance to temples, and incised with inscriptions in hieroglyphs. After Egypt was annexed as a Roman province in 30 BC, Egyptian art exerted an important influence on the Romans, and an Egyptian Temple of Isis was erected in the city (*see p. 263*). There was a vogue for Egyptian works of art, many of which were transported to Rome, including obelisks which were often dedicated to Apollo or the sun. The obelisks were reused in the 16th century in papal urban planning schemes to decorate *piazze* and gar-

dens, and to create vistas at the end of new streets. Others were discovered either abandoned or buried in the 17th and 18th centuries and were re-erected in the city. Bernini set up one as the crowning point of his splendid fountain in Piazza Navona, and obelisks also decorate the fountains in Piazza della Rotonda and Piazza del Popolo. Bernini placed another, from the Temple of Isis, squarely on the back of a delightful elephant outside the church of Santa Maria sopra Minerva. In the 18th century the obelisks in Piazza Trinità dei Monti and Piazza del Quirinale were set up. The latter used to form a pair with that in Piazza dell'Esquilino, and they were originally used by Augustus to flank the entrance to his mausoleum. The obelisk in Piazza di Montecitorio, formerly the gnomon of a huge sundial in Campus Martius, was only rediscovered in the 18th century, when it was erected outside the Italian parliament. There are also two obelisks in the Pincio gardens and the park of Villa Celimontana (this one used to form a pair with the obelisk in Piazza della Rotonda). They all bear Egyptian hieroglyphs, with the exception of the one in Piazza San Pietro outside St Peter's, which has no inscription; the two in Piazza Trinità dei Monti and Piazza Navona had their hieroglyphs recut by the Romans. There is yet another Egyptian obelisk in Piazza dei Cinquecento, this time incorporated into a monument commemorating the Battle of Dogali in 1887.

Giovanni Baglione and Bernardo Cesari, illustrate the conversion of Constantine, his gift of the land to Pope Melchiades and the building of the first basilica.

In the **south transept** are the great organ by Luca Blasi (1598), supported by two columns of *giallo antico*, and the tomb **(11)** of Innocent III (d. 1216) by Giuseppe Lucchetti (1891), erected when Leo XIII brought the ashes of his great predecessor from Perugia. Beside it is the entrance to the **museum**, arranged in two corridors. It consists of church silver, reliquaries and vestments, as well as two fine statues of St Peter and St Paul by Deodato di Cosma. In the corner in the little Cappella del Crocifisso **(12)** is a Cosmatesque kneeling statue of Boniface IX (late 14th century).

In the **north transept** is the tomb of Leo XIII **(13)**, by Giulio Tadolini (1907). At the end is the Altar of the Holy Sacrament **(14)**, by Pier Paolo Olivieri, dating from the time of Clement VIII, flanked by four antique bronze columns.

On the right is the Cappella del Coro **(15)**, with fine stalls of c. 1625.

J **The apse:** Rebuilt by Virginio and Francesco Vespignani in 1885 when the fine apse mosaics were destroyed and replaced by new ones. The original mosaics were designed by Iacopo Torriti and Iacopo da Camerino (1288–94) from an antique model. Beneath the *Head of Christ* (the copy of a mosaic fabled to have appeared miraculously at the consecration of the church) the Dove descends on the bejewelled Cross. From the hill on which it stands four rivers flow to quench the thirst of the Faithful. On the left are the Virgin with Nicholas IV and St Peter and St Paul, and on the right St John the Baptist, St John the Evangelist and St Andrew; the figures of St Francis of Assisi (left) and St Anthony of Padua (right) were added by Nicholas IV. Kneeling at the feet of the Apostles in the frieze below are the tiny figures of the artists Torriti and Camerino.

The cloister

(*Entrance fee.*) Undoubtedly the masterpiece of Iacopo and Pietro Vassalletto (c. 1222–32), it is a magnificent example of Cosmatesque (*see p. 57*) art. The columns, some plain and some twisted, are adorned with mosaics and have fine capitals. The frieze is exquisite. In the centre is a well-head dating from the 9th century. Many interesting fragments from the ancient basilica are displayed around the cloister walls.

The most interesting sculpture here is in the south walk: the tomb of Cardinal Riccardo Annibaldi, the first important work of Arnolfo di Cambio in Rome (c. 1276), reconstructed from fragments, which include reliefs and the recumbent statue. Inscriptions include one in marble dating from 1072 recording the restoration of the basilica by Pope Alexander II, and one in bronze dating from 1196. An antique marble chair, with Cosmati decorations from the time of Pope Nicholas IV, was used as a papal throne, and there are various other pieces of Cosmati work. Roman fragments include sarcophaghi and a cippus. The little museum displays the beautiful cope of Boniface VIII, of 13th-century English workmanship. Also here are two Florentine tapestries (1595–1608), numerous gifts, including a French cope given to Pius IX, and a model of the Column of the Immaculate Conception (1854) in Piazza di Spagna.

Giacomo della Porta (1539–1602)

Giacomo della Porta was the dominant architect in Rome during the last decades of the 16th century. His artistic personality is difficult to detect, however, for the majority of his work was either a continuation of projects begun by others, or else work of his own destined to be finished or transformed by others (for example Carlo Maderno's completion of Sant'Andrea della Valle). Although born on Lake Lugano into a well-known family of stonemasons and sculptors, Giacomo's formation was predominantly Roman, in the circles of Michelangelo and Vignola. His limpid, elegant, thoroughbred style, which generally eschewed pomp and theatricality, can be nicely appreciated in two works right in the centre of the city: first, in the pair of sculptural and powerfully geometric fountain basins in Piazza Navona, which contrast markedly with Bernini's later showpiece in the centre; and then at the Palazzo della Sapienza nearby, where his clear, arcaded courtyard is in sharp contrast to the façade of Borromini's chapel of Sant'Ivo, added some 70 years later. In his continuation of the work of others, della Porta was always respectful of the spirit of the projects he inherited, yet he often made a number of crucial changes. He notably adapted Michelangelo's design for the cupola of St. Peter's, giving it a more pointed profile, accentuating the external ribs, and simplifying the lantern, leaving thereby his stamp on the city's most famous silhouette. The dominating central window in the façade of Michelangelo's Palazzo dei Conservatori is another important and beautiful modification. He was one of many architects to work on San Giovanni in Laterano, for which he built the transepts. His most influential work was the façade for Vignola's church of the Gesù, where his emphasis on a more centralized and vertical design, enhanced by the doubling of the pediment over the central door, was to inspire many of the city's later Baroque façades. When della Porta died in 1602 he was working on the hilltop villa for the Aldobrandini family at Frascati. Here, at last, his fantasy is given full rein, and he creates grandeur with the minimum of physical construction, ingeniously adapting his Classical vocabulary to enhance the villa's splendid, solitary setting. N.McG.

The Baptistery of San Giovanni

The baptistery (*open 7–12.30 & 4–7.30*) was built by Constantine c. 315–24, but was not, as legend states, the scene of his baptism as the first Christian emperor (337). It is octagonal in design, although the original baptistery, designed for total immersion and derived from Classical models, may have been circular. It was remodelled by Sixtus III (432–40), and its design was copied in many subsequent baptisteries.

In the interior are eight columns of porphyry erected by Sixtus III; they support an architrave which bears eight smaller white marble columns. In the centre is the green basalt font. The 17th-century decorations were added by Urban VIII, and the harsh frescoes of scenes from the life of St John the Baptist on the drum of the cupola are modern copies of works by Andrea Sacchi.

The interesting chapels are kept unlocked but you have to push the doors open. The **Chapel of St John the Baptist (16)** was founded by the martyred pope St Hilarius (461–68). It preserves its original doors (once thought to come from the Baths of Caracalla), which resound musically when opened. The **Chapel of St Cyprian and St Justina** (or St Secunda and St Rufina) **(17)** occupied the narthex of Sixtus III, altered to its present form in 1154. Over the door is a relief of the *Crucifixion* after Andrea Bregno (1492). High up on the wall can be seen a fragment of the original marble intarsia decoration of the baptistery. In the north apse is a beautiful 5th-century mosaic with vine tendrils on a brilliant blue ground. A door leads out into a courtyard, from where the outer face of the narthex with two splendid, huge antique columns supporting a fine Roman architrave can be seen.

The **Chapel of St Venantius (18)**, added by Pope John IV in 640, contains mosaics commissioned by Pope Theodore I (642–49): in the apse, the *Head of Christ* flanked by angels and the *Madonna with Saints and Pope Theodore*, and on the triumphal arch, the martyrs whose relics Pope John brought from Dalmatia and (high up) views of Jerusalem and Bethlehem. Remains of 2nd-century Roman baths built above a 1st-century villa, with a mosaic pavement, can also be seen here. The structure of the original baptistery is visible in the walls and beneath the apse.

The **Chapel of St John the Evangelist (19)**, dedicated by St Hilarius, with bronze doors of 1196, is decorated with another lovely 5th-century vault mosaic of the Lamb surrounded by symbolic birds and flowers. The altar has alabaster columns. On the left is a late 15th-century painting of *St Leo Praying to St John* by Luigi Capponi.

PALAZZO LATERANENSE
Map p. 617, 3A

Adjoining the basilica, and facing Piazza di Porta San Giovanni, is Palazzo Lateranense, the Lateran Palace, used by the popes before the move to Avignon in 1309. The old palace, which dated from the time of Constantine, was almost destroyed in the fire of 1308 which devastated San Giovanni in Laterano. On the return from Avignon in 1377 the Holy See was transferred to the Vatican. In 1586 Sixtus V demolished or displaced what the fire had left and ordered Domenico Fontana to carry out a complete reconstruction. The new Lateran was intended to be a summer palace for the popes, but they used the Quirinal instead. The interior was restored in 1838. Under the Lateran Treaty of 1929 the palace was recognized as an integral part of the Vatican City. It is now the seat of the Rome Vicariate and offices of the Rome diocese, and home to the Vatican history museum (*see below*).

Museo Storico del Vaticano
Open for guided tours at 9, 10, 11, and 12 except Sun; combined ticket with the Vatican museums. Entrance from the portico at the main (east) façade of the basilica of San Giovanni in Laterano.

The Papal Apartments, with late Mannerist frescoes by Giovanni Guerra and others and some good ceilings, contain interesting 17th- and 18th-century tapestries, Gobelins and Roman works made in the San Michele workshops. The well-labelled historical museum is displayed on three sides of a loggia. It illustrates the history of the papacy from the 16th century to the present day; papal ceremonies of the past; and the Papal Guards, disbanded by Paul VI in 1970.

Scala Santa

On the east side of Piazza di San Giovanni are three survivals from the old Lateran palace: the Scala Santa, the Sancta Sanctorum and the Tribune. The building that houses the **Scala Santa** and chapel of the Sancta Sanctorum (*open 6.15–12.15 & 3–6.30*) was designed by Domenico Fontana, architect of the new Lateran Palace, in 1589. In the 15th century the staircase from the old palace was declared to be that

from Pilate's house which Christ descended after his condemnation: a legend related how it had been brought from Jerusalem to Rome by St Helen, mother of Constantine. The 28 Tyrian marble steps are protected by boards, and worshippers are only allowed to ascend them on their knees. In the vestibule are 19th-century sculptures by Ignazio Jacometti. The vault and walls of the Scala Santa and the side staircases were decorated at the end of the 16th century under the direction of Giovanni Guerra and Cesare Nebbia.

At the top is the chapel of the **Sancta Sanctorum**, or chapel of St Lawrence, the private chapel of the

Scala Santa, the 'Holy Steps', said to be the stairs from Pilate's house, trodden by Christ.

pope, which preserved the most sacred relics removed from the old Lateran Palace. Mentioned in the *Liber Pontificalis* in the 8th century, it was rebuilt in 1278 and is never open, though partly visible through the grating It contains frescoes and mosaics carried out for Pope Nicholas III (1277–80), restored for the first time in 1995. Protected by a silver tabernacle presented by Innocent III is the relic which gives the chapel its particular sanctity. This is an ancient painting on wood of Christ, which could date from as early as the 5th century, although it has been many times repainted and restored. It is said to have been begun by St Luke and an angel: hence its name *Acheiropoieton* ('made without hands'). The precious relics and their reliquaries are now exhibited in the Vatican Museums. The chapel has a beautiful Cosmatesque pavement. The other rooms in the building have been occupied by a Passionist convent since 1953.

To the east of the Scala Santa is the **Tribune**, erected by Ferdinando Fuga for Benedict XIV in 1743 and decorated with good copies of the mosaics from the 'Triclinium of Leo III', the banqueting hall of the old Lateran Palace. In the centre is *Christ Sending the Apostles to Preach the Gospel*; on the left, Christ is seen giving the keys to St Sylvester and the *labarum*, or standard of the Cross, to Constantine; on the right, St Peter gives the papal stole to Leo III and the banner of Christianity to Charlemagne. A fragment of the original mosaic is in the Museum of Christian Art in the Vatican (*see p. 446*).

Piazza di Porta San Giovanni

This huge space is often used for political demonstrations or music concerts, and here the festival of San Giovanni (St John the Baptist) is celebrated with a traditional fair on the night of 23rd–24th June. **Porta San Giovanni**, built in 1574 by Giacomo del Duca, superseded the ancient *Porta Asinaria*, on the site of the *Porta Coelimontana* of the Servian Wall. The old gate (being restored), with its vantage-court, can be seen between two fine towers to the west of the modern gateway.

Outside the gate the busy Via Appia Nuova leads out of the city through the extensive southern suburbs towards the Alban hills.

On Viale Carlo Felice, a busy traffic artery, parallel to a stretch of the Aurelian Walls, the public gardens were restored in 2000. These were laid out in 1926 by Raffaello de Vico on the site of a park created by the Cistercian monks of Santa Croce, who planted avenues of over 500 mulberry trees and elms here in 1744.

SANTA CROCE IN GERUSALEMME
Map p. 617, 3B–C

Open 8–12 & 4.30–7.

The church of Santa Croce in Gerusalemme, perhaps the least well known of the 'Seven Churches' of Rome (*see p. 407*), has been occupied by Cistercians since 1561. According to tradition, it was founded by Constantine's mother, St Helen, finder of the True Cross, hence the church's dedication, to the Holy Cross in Jerusalem. It was in fact probably built some time after 326 within part of the large Imperial palace erected for St Helen in the early 3rd century on the southwest extremity of the city. The principal edifice was known as the *Sessorium*, and the church took the name of *Basilica Sessoriana*. Here was enshrined a relic of the True Cross, saved in Jerusalem by St Helen. It was rebuilt in 1144 by Lucius II, who added the campanile. The present building dates from its reconstruction by Benedict XIV in 1743–44.

The impressive theatrical façade and oval vestibule were built to a very original design by Domenico Gregorini and Pietro Passalacqua in 1744. The interior dates from the same period, with vault paintings of *St Helen in Glory* and the *Apparition of the Cross* towards the east end by Corrado Giaquinto, and a graceful baldacchino above the high altar where the basalt tomb encloses the remains of St Caesarius and St Anastasius.

Works from earlier centuries include (near the west door, to the right) the long epitaph of Benedict VII (d. 983), who is buried here, and the tomb on the east wall of Cardinal Quiñones (d. 1540), by Jacopo Sansovino. The second south altarpiece, *St Bernard introducing Vittore IV to Innocent II*, is by Carlo Maratta. In the apse is a large fresco cycle of the *Invention of the Cross*, attributed to Antoniazzo Romano, pupil of Benozzo Gozzoli and the leading Roman artist of the early Renaissance, whose art never quite loses its medieval quality. The Cosmatesque (*see p. 57*) pavement was restored in 1933.

A stairway at the end of the south aisle leads down to the **Chapel of St Helen**. It contains a statue of the saint, adapted from an ancient Roman figure of Juno found at Ostia (which was copied from the Barberini statue now in the Vatican; *see p. 458*). The altar is reserved for the pope and the titular cardinal of the basilica. The beautiful mosaic in the vault, the original design of which was probably by Melozzo da Forlì (c. 1480), was restored by Baldassare Peruzzi and later by Francesco Zucchi. It represents Christ and the Evangelists, with St Peter and St Paul, St Sylvester (who died here at Mass), St Helen and Cardinal Carvajal. The Gregorian Chapel, built by Cardinal Carvajal in 1523, has an early 17th-century Roman bas-relief of the *Pietà*.

At the end of the north aisle in the **Chapel of the Relics**, by Florestano di Fausto (1930), pieces of the True Cross are preserved, together with other greatly venerated relics. In the convent are kept some of the church's works of art including fragments of 12th-century frescoes detached from the roof of the nave, a 14th-century fresco of the *Crucifixion*, and French 14th-century statues of St Peter and St Paul.

Museo Nazionale di Strumenti Musicali

On the right of the basilica are remains of the **Amphitheatrum Castrense** (*no admission*), a graceful edifice built of brick by Elagabalus or Alexander Severus for amusements of the Imperial court, incorporated with the Aurelian Walls by Honorius. To the left of the basilica, in the gardens of the former Caserma dei Granatieri, rises a large ruined apsidal hall known since the Renaissance as the Temple of Venus and Cupid. It was built in the early 4th century by Maxentius or Constantine.

In the barracks here are two military museums, and the fine **Museo Nazionale di Strumenti Musicali** (*open 8.30–7.30; closed Mon; T: 06 701 4796; map p. 617, 3C*), with a remarkably representative display dating from Roman times to the 19th century, most of it collected by the tenor Evangelista Gorga (1865–1957).

The attractive building of c. 1903, in the Art Nouveau style, looks north to a section of the Aurelian Walls. On the other side of the building, near the basilica, are more Roman ruins. The collection is beautifully displayed in rooms on the first floor (some of which can be closed because of lack of custodians). Displays range from archaeological material, including Roman works in terracotta and bronze, to exotic instruments from the Far East, America, Africa and Oceania. One of the highlights is the pianoforte built by Bartolomeo Cristofori in 1722. Cristofori had invented an instrument which he called an *arpicembalo*, '*che fa il piano e il forte*' (which produces loud and soft notes) at the beginning of the century. Only three of his pianos survive (the other two are in New York and Leipzig), and this one used to be part of the collection of Benedetto Marcello, the famous Venetian composer who lived in the early 18th century. There are curiosities such as 19th-century walking-sticks which convert into violins and flutes, a glass harmonica, and the famous Barberini Harp, a unique instrument commissioned by the Barberini family of Rome in the first years of the 17th century and decorated with splendid gilded carvings. Its triple row of strings enables chromatic notes to be played on it, even though it is without pedals.

To the east of the barracks, across Viale Castrense and outside the Aurelian Walls, are the well-preserved remains of the extensive *Circus Varianus*, dating from the reign of Elagabalus (218–22).

Porta Maggiore

This gate in the Aurelian Walls (*map p. 617, 3B*) was built by Claudius in AD 52, and was formed by the archways carrying the Acqua Claudia and the Anio Novus over the Via Praenestina and the Via Casilina. It was restored by Honorius in 405, when he added a guardhouse, the foundations of which can still be seen. The ancient *Via Praenestina* and *Via Labicana* which pass under the arches can still be seen. On the outside of the gate is the unusual tomb of the baker Marcus Virgilius Eurysaces, a public contractor, and his wife Atistia. This pretentious monument, built entirely of travertine, dates from c. 30 BC. The circular openings represent the mouths of a baker's oven; above is a frieze illustrating the stages of bread-making. Unfortunately Porta Maggiore is now seriously disturbed by traffic on all sides. At no. 17 Via Prenestina a remarkable and very well preserved building of the 1st century AD was unearthed in 1916. This, the **Basilica di Porta Maggiore**, is approached by a modern staircase beneath the railway. It has the rudimentary form of a cult building, with a central porch, an apse at the east end, a nave and two arched aisles with no clerestory. This became the basic plan of the Christian church. The ceiling and walls are covered with exquisite stuccoes representing landscapes, mythological subjects, and scenes of early childhood; the principal design of the apse is thought to depict the death of Sappho. The purpose for which it was built is still under discussion: it may have been a type of funerary hall, or have been used by a mystical sect, perhaps the Pythagoreans.

TRASTEVERE

Trastevere (*map p. 622, A3–B4*), the area 'across the Tiber' (*trans Tiberim*) on its right bank, is enclosed between the Janiculum Hill and the Vatican. Since the Middle Ages it was always essentially the popular district of Rome, and its inhabitants seemed to retain the characteristics of the ancient Romans, who are said to have been proud and independent. Since Roman times this area of the city was for long distinguished by its numerous artisans' houses and workshops. In the last decade or so it has become one of the most fashionable places to live in Rome, and now has a cosmopolitan atmosphere, with numerous well-known restaurants and *trattorie*.

Highlights of the area are the basilica of San Crisogono, Santa Maria in Trastevere, Villa Farnesina, and, in the south of the district, the church of Santa Cecilia and San Francesco a Ripa, with a statue by Bernini.

NB: Tram line no. 8 connects Largo Torre Argentina (map p. 622, 2B) with Trastevere.

HISTORY OF TRASTEVERE

This was the 'Etruscan side' of the river, and only after the destruction of *Veii* by Rome in 396 BC did it come under Roman rule. In earliest Republican days, this bank of the Tiber was occupied by Lars Porsenna in his attempt to replace the Tarquins on the Roman throne. On the higher ground at the foot of the Janiculum, and along the waterfront, suburban villas were built by the aristocracy. The magnificent wall paintings from a villa next to the Villa Farnesina, dating from the Augustan age and then destroyed, were excavated in the late 19th century and are now preserved in the Museo Nazionale Romano at Palazzo Massimo. Under the Empire the district became densely populated by artisans and dock-workers. It was probably not entirely enclosed by walls before the time of Aurelian (270–275). Trastevere was home to a great number of Jews, who are recorded here as early as the 2nd century BC, before they were confined to the Ghetto on the other side of the river (*see p. 314*). It was a republican stronghold during the Risorgimento; here Mazzini found support in 1849, and here in 1867 Giuditta Tavani Arquati, with her family, made an attempt to incite the city on Garibaldi's behalf. In July, the lively festival of *Noantri* ('We others') takes place here.

At the foot of Ponte Garibaldi is the busy Piazza Gioacchino Belli, named after the poet (1791–1863) who wrote popular verses and satirical sonnets in the Roman dialect. The monument here, which shows him in a frock coat and top hat, is by Michele Tripisciano (1913). Old Trastevere stretches on either side of the busy Viale.

is a worn fresco of three saints, showing St Chrysogonus in the centre, and at the sides the two companions supposedly martyred with him, St Anastasia and a certain St Rufo. The church was orientated towards the west: looking at the apse, to the left (or south) behind a closed gate is a small room which was a baptistery, in which numerous Roman fragments found during the excavations are kept. A few marble steps lead up beside the south wall of the church, with traces of frescoes dating from the 6th–8th centuries (including a roundel with a pope, thought to be Sixtus II). Halfway along the wall you will notice a change in the masonry which distinguishes the earliest building (in brick) from the later basilica. There are two pagan sarcophagi here: the one beautifully carved with the Muses, found in the baptistery, might have been used as a font. On the other side of the apse is another small room, known as the Secretarium, traditionally thought to have been used for the storage of vestments. It has interesting traces of its original 6th–7th-century pavement in white marble tesserae and green serpentine marble discs. The pagan sarcophagus (3rd century) with marine scenes with tritons and nereids was found here; it was reused in the Middle Ages. More traces of frescoes dating from the 8th and 10th centuries can be seen on the north wall of the church: the best-preserved are those from a 10th-century cycle showing the life of St Benedict, with a scene of the saint in a hood healing a leper covered with spots.

To Santa Maria in Trastevere

The old Via della Lungaretta, on the line of the last stretch of the ancient Roman *Via Aurelia*, leads past the façade of Sant'Agata and on the left, in Via San Gallicano, the huge hospital of San Gallicano, a remarkable utilitarian building by Filippo Raguzzini (1724). The handsome long, low façade, with the two floors divided by a balcony, incorporates a church in the centre.

The street continues past numerous restaurants and *trattorie* straight on to the delightful **Piazza di Santa Maria in Trastevere**, filled with the sound of water from its fountain, of Roman origin, said to be on the site of a fountain of pure oil. As the inscriptions record, it was restored over the centuries by some of the most important architects at work in the city: Donato Bramante, Giacomo della Porta, Bernini and (most recently, in 1692) by Carlo Fontana. Palazzo di San Calisto, the grandest palace in the square, was rebuilt in the 17th century.

SANTA MARIA IN TRASTEVERE
Map p. 622, 3A

Open 7–7.30.
The large basilica of Santa Maria in Trastevere dates mainly from the 12th century and preserves some beautiful mosaics from that period, as well as a number of other important works of art. The church was constructed by Julius I (337–52), and was probably the first church in Rome dedicated to the Virgin. According to legend a hostel for veteran soldiers existed near the site, and some sort of Christian foundation is

known to have existed here under St Calixtus (217–22). The great basilica of Julius I was rebuilt by Innocent II in 1140, and slightly modified later.

The Exterior

The unusual exterior consists of a façade with a long mosaic panel beneath the tympanum dating from the 12th–13th centuries showing the Madonna surrounded by ten female figures with lamps (two of which are extinguished), of uncertain significance. Above rises the typical Romanesque campanile while below is a portico crowned by four statues, added by Carlo Fontana in 1702. Its walls are covered with an interesting lapidary collection, including Roman and medieval fragments, many of them with Christian symbols, such as the dove. The three doorways incorporate Roman friezes.

The Interior

In the splendid 12th-century interior are 21 vast ancient columns from various Roman buildings, some with fine bases and (damaged) capitals. The gilded wooden ceiling was designed by Domenichino (1617), who painted the central *Assumption*. There is also a fine ceiling in the crossing with a high-relief of the same scene (16th century). The Cosmatesque pavement (made up from old material) and the decoration on the walls of the nave and triumphal arch were executed when the church was remodelled by Pius IX in the 19th century. The charming 15th-century tabernacle at the beginning of the south aisle is by Mino del Reame. In the north aisle is the tomb of Innocent II, who died in 1143, only erected by Pius IX in 1869, and the **Avila Chapel**, designed by Antonio Gherardi (1680–86), with a remarkable Baroque dome supported by angels and a very unusual altar with an odd perspective device.

The choir is preceded by a marble screen made up of transennae and plutei, many of them remade in the 19th century. Near a Paschal candlestick is the spot on which a miraculous fountain of oil is supposed to have flowed throughout a whole day in the year of Christ's Nativity in the Roman building. The baldacchino over the high altar is by Virginio Vespignani. The wonderful **mosaics of the triumphal arch and apse** (1140) are particularly fine, with exquisite details including fruit and flowers on the soffit of the arch: on the arch, the Cross with the symbolic Alpha and Omega between the seven candlesticks and the Evangelical emblems; at the sides, Isaiah and Jeremiah, beside two palm trees, and above them the rare and touching symbol of the caged bird, representing Christ imprisoned because of the sins of man ('*Christus Dominus captus est in peccatis nostris*': *Lamentations of Jeremiah, IV:20*). In the semidome, Christ and the Virgin are shown enthroned beneath the hand of God bearing a wreath and the monogram of Constantine. On the right are St Peter, St Cornelius, St Julius and St Calepodius; on the left St Calixtus and St Lawrence, and Pope Innocent II with a model of the church. Lower down in the apse and on the triumphal arch are six rectangles with more exquisite mosaic scenes from the life of Mary by Pietro Cavallini (c. 1291). Cavallini, a painter and mosaicist, was active almost entirely in Rome, though little of secure attribution now survives. The best examples of his work are in Trastevere, here and in the church of St Cecilia (*see p. 380*). Beneath until the end of the 19th. Here their library and art collection was formed and is still preserved as part of the Galleria Nazionale d'Arte Antica, which is divided between this palace and Palazzo Barberini (*see p. 220*). It is particularly rich in 17th- and 18th-century paintings of the Roman, Neapolitan and Bolognese schools, but also has important works by Fra' Angelico, Rubens, van Dyck, Murillo and Caravaggio.

History of Palazzo Corsini and its collection

The palace was built by Cardinal Domenico Riario in the 15th century, and rebuilt by Ferdinando Fuga for Cardinal Neri Maria Corsini, nephew of Clement XII (Lorenzo Corsini) in 1732–36, when the family moved from Florence to Rome. The palace had been the residence of Queen Christina of Sweden, who died here in 1689 (*see p. 159*). In 1797 General Duphot was killed near here in a skirmish between the French democratic party and the papal dragoons just a year before the French entered Rome and proclaimed a republic, and Pius VI was taken as a prisoner to France. In 1800 Madame Letitia Bonaparte, Napoleon I's mother, came to live in the palace.

The Corsini collection of paintings was founded in the 17th century by the uncle of Clement XII, and works were added by Clement himself while he was still cardinal, and then by his nephew Cardinal Neri. In 1827 their descendant Tommaso rearranged the collection and opened it to the public, but after his death the family moved back to Florence. In 1883 the palace was sold, and the collection of paintings donated to the state; together with numerous other works of art it became part of the Galleria Nazionale d'Arte Antica. The original Corsini collection can be identified since it carries the inventory numbers 1–606.

First floor

Vestibule: Here are displayed Neoclassical sculptures including works by John Gibson and Pietro Tenerani.

Room I: Corsini portraits are hung here, including a bust of Clement XII Corsini by Pietro Bracci; and 18th-century paintings by Pompeo Batoni, Sebastiano Conca and Francesco Trevisani.

Room II: The *Madonna and Child* and *Scenes from the Life of Christ* are by **Giovanni da Milano**, the only work in Rome by this very skilled Lombard painter, and his first known work (c. 1355). The *Madonna and Child* by the

17th-century Spanish painter **Bartolomé Murillo** is one of his finest versions of a subject for which Murillo was famous up until the 19th century, when his works fell somewhat from favour due to their over-sweet tones. The *Madonna and Child* by **van Dyck** was probably painted during the artist's stay in Italy—the *St Sebastian Tended by Angels* was also once attributed to van Dyck, but is now considered the work of his master **Rubens**, here clearly influenced by Michelangelo's Sistine ceiling, which Rubens saw when he first came to Rome. Other Flemish painters represented with fine portraits include Pourbus the Younger and Joos van Cleve (Bernardo Clesio). The portrait of Cardinal Alessandro Farnese is by Perino del Vaga, and there is a self-portrait by Federico Barocci. Also hung here is one of a number of portraits painted by **Titian** of Philip II of Spain. Florentine works include paintings by Franciabigio and Fra' Bartolomeo, as well as a triptych by **Fra' Angelico**, with the *Last Judgement*, flanked by the *Ascension* and *Pentecost*, thought to have been painted by this famous artist on one of his two visits to Rome (the first in around 1445 and the second around 1450–55). The Last Judgement was a subject Fra' Angelico often painted. Francesco Francia is represented by *St George* and there is a small bronze of the *Baptism of Christ* by **Algardi**.

Room III: The lovely *Madonna and Child* by **Orazio Gentileschi** was attributed to his friend (and master) Caravaggio in the Corsini inventories. The *St John the Baptist* is definitely by the more famous master, however, and is a subject **Caravaggio** often painted.

Room IV: This room is home to works by Jacques Callot (better known as an engraver), Jan Frans van Bloemen and Luca Carlevaris, and landscapes by Gaspard Dughet.

Room V: The room is decorated by a follower of the Zuccari brothers, and survives from the old Palazzo Riario. Queen Christina of Sweden (*see p. 159*) is believed to have died in this room in 1689: her portrait as Diana is by Justus van Egmont (c. 1656). A terracotta bust of the Chigi pope Alexander VII, attributed to Bernini, is also exhibited here.

Room VI: In the centre is the marble *Corsini Throne*, dating from the 2nd or 1st century BC and carved with scenes of hunting and sacrifice. It is possibly a Roman copy of an Etruscan piece: another of Rome's mysterious 'thrones' (*see Ludovisi Throne, p. 277*). It has been in the palace since 1700. The paintings include *Andromeda* by Francesco Furini, and a Corsini portrait by Baciccia.

Room VII: With a splendid view of the palm trees in the Orto Botanico (*see p. 378*) and of the Garibaldi monument on the Janiculum, the room has paintings by the 17th-century Emilian artists Guido Reni, Giovanni Lanfranco, Guercino and Sassoferrato.

Room VIII: Works here are by Salvator Rosa, Mattia Preti and Luca Giordano.

The palace also houses the **Accademia Nazionale dei Lincei**, founded by Prince Federico Cesi in 1603 for the promotion of learning, and said to be the oldest surviving institution of its kind. Galileo was a Lincean. With it are incorporated the Biblioteca dell'Accademia (1848), with 100,000 volumes and other publications; the Biblioteca Corsiniana, founded in this palace by the Corsini in 1754 and at the time the most important library in Rome, together with that in the Vatican (it has been preserved intact and has a valuable collection of incunabula, manuscripts and autographs); and the Fondazione Caetani, whose object is to promote scientific knowledge of the Muslim world.

beautiful painted pergola with festoons of fruit and flowers. The innovative decorative programme was provided by Raphael—who probably also made the preparatory cartoons, since drawings of some of the scenes survive by him—but the paintings were executed by his pupils, Giulio Romano, Francesco Penni, Giovanni da Udine and Raffaellino del Colle, in 1517. The loggia was well restored in 1693, and again in 1997. The story is taken from Apuleius' *The Golden Ass*, written in the 2nd century AD and the only Latin novel to have survived in its entirety. The young girl Psyche incites the jealousy of Venus because of her beauty: Venus therefore throws almost impossible obstacles in her way before she can finally drink the cup of immortality in order to marry Cupid.

On the short wall towards the Loggia of Galatea the first pendentive shows *Venus and Cupid*; on the long wall, opposite the garden, is the beautiful group of the *Three Graces with Cupid*; *Venus with Juno and Ceres*; *Venus on her Way to Visit Jove* (in a chariot); *Venus Talking to Jove* (identified by an eagle). On the end wall is *Mercury*. On the garden wall, Psyche (always dressed in green) is shown giving a phial to Venus; also here is the *Kiss between Cupid and Jove*; and finally *Mercury Accompanying Psyche to Olympus*. In between these pendentives are playful cupids, with birds and symbols of the gods. In the centre of the vault are two painted cloths, shown as if draped from the pergola, on which the happy end to the legend is portrayed in two scenes: the *Council of the Gods*, and the *Nuptial Banquet*.

On the upper floor is the **Sala delle Prospettive**, the drawing-room, with charming *trompe l'oeil* imaginary views of Rome and mythological subjects by Peruzzi. The bedroom, known as the **Sala delle Nozze di Alessandro e Rossana**, contains the *Marriage of Alexander the Great and Roxana* frescoes by another Sienese painter, Sodoma. The bedroom scene opposite the windows is particularly fine, with the nude figure of Alexander, and no fewer than 22 playful cupids.

SANTA CECILIA IN TRASTEVERE & ITS DISTRICT
Map p. 622, 4B

Open 9.30–1 & 4–6.15. Roman remains beneath the church open same hours; the frescoes by Pietro Cavallini in the Benedictine convent can be seen 10.15–12.15; Sun 11.15–12.30.
Santa Cecilia in Trastevere is a lovely church in a quiet district of the city. It was built on the site of the house of St Cecilia and her husband St Valerian, whom she converted to Christianity. St Cecilia, a patrician lady of the Cecilia family, was martyred in 230, during the reign of Alexander Severus. She was shut up in the calidarium of her own baths (*see below*) to be scalded to death. Emerging unscathed, she was beheaded in another room of her house, but the executioner did such a bad job that she lived for three days afterwards. She was buried in the Catacombs of St Calixtus.

This building was adapted to Christian use probably in the 5th century, and in 820 the body of St Cecilia was transferred here and a basilica erected by Paschal I

(817–24). Her relics were rediscovered in 1599 and she was ceremonially re-interred in the church by Pope Clement VIII, after which she became a particularly revered Roman saint. As the reputed inventor of the organ, she is the patron saint of music: on her feast day on 22nd November churches hold musical services in her honour.

The church, radically altered from the 16th century onwards, was partly restored to its original form in 1899–1901. The elaborate façade was provided by Ferdinando Fuga in the early 18th century as an entrance to the atrium preceding the church where there is a delightful fountain designed in 1929 around a large ancient Roman marble vase for ceremonial ablutions (which has been outside the basilica since the Middle Ages). The buildings on either side house convents. The slightly leaning campanile, and the church portico, with four antique Ionic columns bearing a frieze of 12th-century mosaic medallions, both date from around 1120.

The Interior

The interior was transformed in the early 18th century into an aisled hall, when grilles were provided in the upper gallery for the nuns to attend services, and a fresco by Sebastiano Conca of the *Coronation of St Cecilia* was installed in the centre of the ceiling. In 1823 the original columns were enclosed in piers. On the west wall, to the left of the door, is a monument of Cardinal Niccolò Forteguerri (d. 1473), who assisted Pius II and Paul II in their suppression of the great feudal clans—a beautiful work attributed to Mino da Fiesole (restored in 1891). Mino, a skilled Renaissance sculptor who worked mostly in Florence, carved a number of other tombs in Roman churches. On the other side of the door is the tomb of Cardinal Adam Easton (d. 1398), a distinguished English churchman who was appointed cardinal in 1381, deposed by Urban VI c. 1386, and reappointed by Boniface IX in 1389. It bears the arms of England.

In the south aisle, the first chapel under the organ loft contains a fresco of the *Crucifixion* (?14th century). A corridor (*closed for restoration*), with landscapes by Paul Bril, the Flemish painter who painted many other similar works in palaces and churches in Rome in the late 16th century, and a marble figure of *St Sebastian* attributed to Lorenzetto, leads to the ancient calidarium, where St Cecilia was to be scalded to death. The steam conduits are still visible. On the altar is the *Beheading of St Cecilia*, an early work by Guido Reni, who also painted the tondo of the *Mystical Marriage of St Cecilia and St Valerian* opposite. These are amongst a number of works this famous Bolognese artist painted in Rome in the first decade of the 17th century.

The second chapel is the Cappella dei Ponziani, with ceiling frescoes and, on the walls, saints, all by a 15th-century painter from Viterbo called Pastura, who produced mostly frescoes close to the style of Perugino and Pinturicchio. The 18th-century Cappella delle Reliquie has a ceiling fresco and painting of St Cecilia, the only painted works by the architect Luigi Vanvitelli. The last chapel contains the elaborate tomb (1929) of Cardinal Rampolla, who was responsible for the excavations beneath the church. In the chapel at the end of the aisle is a very damaged 13th-century fresco detached from the portico showing the discovery of the body of St Cecilia, and the apparition of the saint to Paschal I.

along Lungotevere Testaccio. In 193–174 BC a market was constructed there, backed by the *Porticus Aemilia*, a wharf with extensive storehouses some 500m in length.

To the right, on this side of the Tiber, the Porta Portese, built by Innocent X (1644–55) replaces the former *Porta Portuensis*, the southern gate in the 3rd-century Aurelian Walls which protected Trastevere. (The famous Sunday-morning Porta Portese flea market, the largest second-hand market in Rome, is much further south, near Stazione Trastevere.)

In Piazza San Francesco d'Assisi stands the church of **San Francesco a Ripa** (*open 7–12 & 4–7*), built in 1231 to replace the old hospice of San Biagio, where St Francis stayed in 1219. The last chapel on the left has the famous statue of the *Blessed Lodovica Albertoni*, showing her in a state of mystical ecstasy. It is a late work by Bernini, displayed effectively by concealed lighting. Above is an altarpiece by Baciccia. The other chapels on the north side have been well restored: adjoining the first is the burial chapel of Giorgio de Chirico (*see p. 174*), and in the second chapel is an early *Annunciation* by Francesco Salviati. Above the sacristy, lined with 17th-century wood cupboards, is the cell of St Francis (usually shown on request), which contains relics displayed in an ingenious reliquary, and a 13th-century painting of the saint.

Towards the Tiber

Santa Maria dell'Orto has an unusual façade crowned with obelisks, attributed to Vignola, and an ornate interior containing 17th- and 18th-century works. The church of **San Giovanni Battista dei Genovesi** (*open only for services; the cloister is open Tues and Thurs 3–6; if closed, ring at the door*), although restored, dates from 1481. The remarkable 15th-century cloister has an arcaded lower gallery and a trabeated upper storey, which surrounds a beautiful garden of orange trees. Here can be seen the east end of the church of Santa Cecilia.

In Piazza in Piscinula is the small church of **San Benedetto** (*if closed, ring at the door to the right of the façade*) with a charming miniature 11th-century roofed campanile, the smallest in Rome; the bell is dated 1069. Inside, on the left of the vestibule, a fine doorway leads into an ancient cross-vaulted cell in which St Benedict is said to have lived. To the left of the entrance door is a detached and restored 13th-century fresco of the saint. Eight antique columns with diverse capitals divide the nave from the aisles. The old pavement is Cosmatesque. Above the altar is a painting of *St Benedict*, and a damaged fresco of the *Madonna and Child*, both dating from the 15th century. On the opposite side of the piazza is the restored medieval *Casa dei Mattei*, with a 15th-century loggia and 14th-century cross-mullioned windows.

The remains of a **Roman firestation** or guardroom (*open only by appointment, T: 06 6710 3819; entrance at 9 Via della VII Coorte*) can be seen in Via di Monte Fiore. At the time of Augustus the fire brigade in Rome was organized into seven detachments to protect the city. This station was discovered during excavations in 1865–66: interesting graffiti referring to reigning emperors, from Severus to Gordian III, and a bath or nymphaeum survive (the station was built on the site of a 2nd-century private house).

THE JANICULUM

The Janiculum or *Gianicolo* (*map p. 619*), though not counted as one of the Seven Hills of Rome, is a ridge rising steeply from the Tiber and running approximately parallel to its course for the whole of its length. The hill's highest point, to the south, is Porta San Pancrazio (82m); to the north it reaches almost as far as Piazza San Pietro. It is now mostly covered with parks and gardens, and offers wonderful views from the ridge. It has two important churches: at its southern end, San Pietro in Montorio, with a superb fresco by Sebastiano del Piombo and the celebrated Tempietto by Bramante in its courtyard; and to the north, Sant'Onofrio. Some way further west, outside Porta San Pancrazio, is the huge public park of Villa Doria Pamphilj.

Approaches

The Janiculum is served by bus no. 115 which runs every 10mins except on Sunday. On foot the prettiest approach is from Trastevere, taking Via Garibaldi or Vicolo del Cedro behind Piazza Sant'Egidio.

HISTORY OF THE JANICULUM HILL

The hill's ancient name was *Mons Aureus*, which referred to the yellow sand which covers its surface. The name of *Mons Janiculus* is derived from the old Italian deity Janus, who, according to legend, founded a city on the hill; his temple was in the Roman Forum. Numa Pompilius, the Sabine successor of Romulus, was buried on the Janiculum, and Ancus Marcius, the fourth king, is said to have built the *Pons Sublicius* over the Tiber to connect the Janiculum with the city of Rome. The hill provided a natural defence against the Etruscans, but it does not appear to have been fortified until after 87 BC, during a period of civil strife between Marius and Sulla, when a wall was built from *Pons Aemilius* to the *Porta Aurelia* (Porta San Pancrazio). Part of the Janiculum was included within the Aurelian Walls, and it was completely surrounded by Urban VIII when he built his wall in 1642.

The attractive **Via Garibaldi**, with two raised pavements on either side, leads uphill from Trastevere towards the Janiculum (on the skyline the huge Acqua Paola fountain, described below, is prominent). At the end of the first straight section of the road, before a sharp turn to the left, is the entrance gate at no. 27 to **Santa Maria dei Sette Dolori** (*open only for a service from 7–8am*), an Augustinian convent (now mostly used as a hotel as there are only five nuns left here). The unfinished façade (1646) of the church, begun by Francesco Borromini in 1643, is visible from the gate. The intricate curved design is clear in the brickwork, even though its stone facing is lacking. Borromini typically gave the church an unusual plan: it is oblong with rounded ends, with two apses in the middle of the long sides, and a continuous series of pillars connected by a heavy cornice. Unfortunately, inappropriate decorations were added later in the 17th century.

Above on the right is the former entrance gate to the **Bosco Parrasio**, where in 1725 the academy of Arcadia was established. It was founded in 1690 to carry on the work of the academy inaugurated by Queen Christina of Sweden ten years before for the discussion of literary and political topics. The object of Arcadia was to eliminate bad literary taste and to purify the Italian language, and it exercised a profound influence on Italian literature during the 18th century. In 1786 Goethe was admitted as a 'distinguished shepherd'. Later its importance waned and in 1926 it was absorbed into the Accademia Letteraria Italiana. The paintings which belong to the academy are at present kept at the Museo di Roma (*see p. 543*). The gardens (now privately owned) include a small wood or 'Arcadian' *bosco*. In Via di Porta San Pancrazio is a huge building, restored in 1993, which since 1964 has housed the Spanish Liceo Cervantes. At the corner an old marble sarcophagus serves as a fountain, with a worn lion's head put up here in 1627 by Urban VIII (restored in 1937).

Via Garibaldi continues to mount in sweeping curves, but a short cut leads via steps lined with a *Via Crucis* sculpted by a pupil of the Spanish Academy in 1957 beyond a gate on the right of the road up to a terrace with a group of palm trees. Here is the Royal Academy of Spain, founded in 1873 in a former Franciscan convent. The view includes the high dome of Sant'Andrea della Valle, and, on the right, the hill of the Aventine with many of its churches visible on the skyline.

SAN PIETRO IN MONTORIO
Map p. 619, 2D

Open 7.30–12 & 4–6.30.
The church of San Pietro in Montorio was built on a site wrongly presumed to have been the scene of St Peter's crucifixion. Mentioned in the 9th century, a papal bull of Sixtus IV granted the Franciscan convent here to his Spanish confessor, the Blessed Amadeo de Silva, in 1472. The church was rebuilt in 1481, to a design by Baccio Pontelli, at the expense of King Ferdinand of Aragon and his wife Isabella, Queen of Castile. Philip III of Spain carried out work to shore up the hill and create the terrace in front of the church. The apse and campanile, damaged in the siege of 1849 (*see p. 28*), were restored in 1851. Raphael's *Transfiguration* (now in the Vatican Pinacoteca) adorned the apse from 1523 to 1809. The church is traditionally taken to be the burial place of Beatrice Cenci, beheaded as a parricide at Ponte Sant' Angelo in 1599 (*see p. 224*). The fine simple travertine façade is attributed to the school of Andrea Bregno.

The Interior
In the interior on the south side, the first chapel contains a *Flagellation*, a superb work by Sebastiano del Piombo from designs by Michelangelo. Commissioned by the

Florentine banker Pierfrancesco Borgherini in 1521, its composition skilfully fits the curved wall of the chapel and the painted columns accentuate the motion of the tortur-ers grouped around the central column, against which the twisted figure of Christ is superbly portrayed. The semi-nude figures are rendered with extraordinary power. St Peter and St Francis are depicted on either side of the scene, and above is a *Transfiguration*, also by Sebastiano, though it lacks the force and drama of the *Flagellation* scene. The lunette of the second chapel has a charming *Coronation of the Virgin* with dec-orative angels, of uncertain attribution. The fifth chapel has two tombs, both with effi-gies and two statues above, good works by Bartolomeo Ammannati who also designed the heavy balustrade supported by groups of over-large putti. The altarpiece of the *Conversion of St Paul* by Giorgio Vasari includes his self-portrait. The apse is decorated with a copy of Guido Reni's *Crucifixion of St Peter*, now in the Vatican.

> ### *Sebastiano del Piombo* (c. 1485–1547)
>
> Sebastiano Luciani, called 'del Piombo' because of his appointment as keeper of the papal seals, which were made of lead (*piombo*), is an unusual figure in the history of Italian painting in that he was an artist of Venetian training and style, who worked in the very different milieu of Rome and in the circles of Raphael and Michelangelo. His paintings are characterized by an innate, almost patrician, refinement and by a deeply shadowed and sensitive modelling which imparts to his figures a sculptural monumentality. His images are thoughtful, and often so static that they can possess an eerie stillness. He is unquestionably a painter of great talent—talent which Vasari, perhaps exaggerating his laziness, considered to have been unfulfilled.
>
> Sebastiano trained in Venice with Giovanni Bellini and worked with Giorgione, the latter being his greatest influence. A Venetian love of tonal harmony and an instinct for evoking mood through landscape, which he picked up from Giorgione, remained with him all his life: but his contact with Michelangelo's work, once he had moved to Rome in 1511, soon brought out a grander and more sculptural quality. His figures (in particular his nudes) become much more monumental, but still retain a softness and sensuality, giving them a quality which lies somewhere between flesh and statuary. Sebastiano's *Flagellation* in the church of San Pietro in Montorio shows how well he is able to balance these two elements. In his painting technique, and as a portraitist of considerable psychological insight, he equals Raphael—who effectively blocked his progress to the most important commissions: Michelangelo befriended him and made him to all intents and purposes his deputy in Rome. In the wider context of High Renaissance art, Sebastiano treads a solitary path: his textured light and crepuscular mood was alien to the bold, classicizing taste of Rome. Yet few artists have ever succeeded so well in giving a human and sensual dimension to that Classicism.   N.McG.

On the north side, the fifth chapel was designed by Daniele da Volterra. This is the burial place of two Irish noblemen exiled to Rome: Hugh O'Neill, Earl of Tyrone, having been a leader in the Irish revolt supported by Spain against Elizabeth I and then James I, was forced to flee and died in Rome in 1616. Rory O'Donnell, Earl of Tyrconnel, also involved in this Irish rebellion, died in Rome the year after he plotted to seize Dublin Castle in 1607. The fourth chapel, designed by Carlo Maderno, is entirely covered with pretty stuccowork attributed to Giulio Mazzoni: the three paintings are by a Flemish artist, probably Dirk Baburen (1617), a pupil of Caravaggio. The altar in the **Raimondi Chapel** is an early work (1640–47) by Bernini, showing his typical skill in dramatizing the effect by hidden lighting, and the unusual relief of the *Ecstasy of St Francis* was executed by his pupils Francesco Baratta and Andrea Bolgi. Near the west door is the tomb of Giuliano da Volterra (d. 1510), by a follower of Andrea Bregno.

The Tempietto

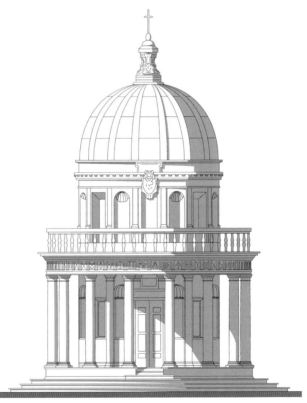

THE TEMPIETTO

The door on the right of the church gives access to a peaceful little courtyard with the famous little Tempietto (*open 9.30–12.30 & 2–4; 4–6 in summer; closed Mon*), an extremely important Renaissance work by Donato Bramante, though its date is still uncertain—either 1499–1502 or 1508–12. Erected on what was thought to be the exact site of St Peter's martyrdom, it is a miniature circular building with 16 Doric columns of granite, and combines all the grace of the 15th century with the full splendour of the 16th. Perfectly proportioned and raised on three circular steps, it includes numerous Classical elements—columns, a frieze with triglyphs, scallop shell niches, and pilasters—but has a Mannerist balcony around the top. It is particularly pleasing because of its tiny scale, which allows you to establish an intimate relationship with it. Bramante's original project envisaged a circular single-storeyed cloister, which would have made the effect even more remarkable. The upper chapel has a Cosmatesque pavement and a rather stiff statue of St Peter attributed to Lorenzo Marrina. Stairs designed by Bernini lead down to a crypt with pretty stuccoes by Giovanni Francesco Rossi.

ROME & THE RISORGIMENTO

The city took an active part in the agitated period of the Risorgimento, the political renaissance of Italy in the 19th century, and shared with the rest of Europe the revolutionary ideals of liberty and independence. A republic was proclaimed by an elected assembly in Rome under the guidance of Giuseppe Mazzini, and the pope fled to Gaeta. When the French sent an army commanded by Nicolas Oudinot in support of the pope in 1849, the defence of the city was entrusted to the able hands of Giuseppe Garibaldi, who made a famous stand for the Roman Republic on this hill declaring '*Roma o Morte*'. The stand was unsuccessful, and Rome—for a time at least—remained under papal control

In 1867 Garibaldi made another attempt to rouse the Romans against the papal government with the help of the Cairoli brothers, who were killed in the same year. In 1870 the French garrison, which had occupied Castel Sant'Angelo since 1849, finally withdrew from the city, and a month later the Italian army, under Raffaello Cadorna, entered Rome through a breach in the walls beside the Porta Pia. This brought an end to the papal rule of the city, and Rome was proclaimed the capital of united Italy in 1871.

The Janiculum in the Risorgimento

Via Garibaldi continues uphill past the exterior of the church where a cannon ball fired by the French in 1849 is preserved on a plaque set up in 1895 as a memorial to the struggle to secure Rome's independence, also recorded across the road by a huge monument (1941) by Giovanni Jacobucci (*open Tues–Sun 9–1*), which commemorates those who fought for the Italian Republic in 1849–70. It has patriotic inscriptions, and a crypt with a golden mosaic ceiling in which the names of all those who died fighting for the Republic are recorded around the tomb of Garibaldi's aide Goffredo Mameli (1827–49), the republican, poet and author of *Fratelli d'Italia*, the Italian national anthem. An inscription records the message to the Romans of 2nd July 1849, signed by the triumvirate of Giuseppe Mazzini, Carlo Armellini, and Aurelio Saffi. There are numerous memorials to this period of Roman history all over the Janiculum Hill, where most of the fighting took place. The recent renewed interest in the Risorgimento movement has meant that this monument is now open to the public.

AROUND THE ACQUA PAOLA
Map p. 619, 2D

The huge fountain of the **Acqua Paola** was constructed—as its handsome inscription states—for Paul V, by Giovanni Fontana and Flaminio Ponzio (1612), using marble from the Forum of Nerva. The water, which flows abundantly from the subterranean Aqueduct of Trajan, itself fed by springs near Lake Bracciano about 48km northwest of Rome, falls into a large granite basin added by Carlo Fontana in 1690, beneath six columns, four of which are from the façade of Old St Peter's. The building now unexpectedly houses a small theatre with some 100 seats, run by a theatre club—but only open in summer. The fountain is turned off during performances. When the club is open you can ask to go up to the roof above the fountain, from where there is a splendid view. A plaque set up in 1726 records the owners of each of the conduits served by the aqueduct. The charming little garden with bougainvillea and vines has some Classical fragments.

To the Villa Doria Pamphilj
At the top of the hill is the **Porta San Pancrazio**, built by Urban VIII, and rebuilt by Virginio Vespignani in 1857 after the decisive battle here between the French forces and Garibaldi in 1849. This gate, once known as the *Porta Aurelia*, was the starting-point of the Via Aurelia.

To the right of the gate is the **Villa Aurelia** (also rebuilt after 1849), surrounded by a lovely garden, acquired by the American Academy in Rome in 1911 (the main seat of the Academy, with the library, is now on the other side of the road, entered from Via Masina). Viale delle Mura Gianicolensi, skirting a magnificent stretch of walls, leads south to the **Villa Sciarra**, with a beautiful garden laid out in 1902–30 by George Wurts (*open daily 7–dusk*). It has particularly fine wisteria which flowers in early spring. Beyond is the residential district of Monteverde.

In front of Porta San Pancrazio, Via di San Pancrazio, a road full of fast traffic, almost impossible to cross on foot, leads down past a residential district in Via Giacinto Carini, in which a plaque set up in 2000 marks the house (no. 45) where the writer Pier Paolo Pasolini lived from 1959 to 1963. In Via di San Pancrazio are the ruins of the Vascello, a Baroque villa where Goffredo Mameli and Luciano Manara were killed in a last sally in 1849. Just beyond (on a straight line from the San Pancrazio gate, and between two very busy roads) is the entrance to the **Villa Doria Pamphilj** or Belrespiro (*open daily sunrise–sunset*), by far the largest park in Rome (9km in circumference). It was laid out in 1644–52 for Prince Camillo Pamphilj, nephew of Innocent X. It is now owned partly by the state and partly by the Comune of Rome. Beyond a huge orange gate erected in 1859 the noise of the city is left behind, as the grounds slope downhill with meadows and numerous fine trees in which the Casino del Bel Respiro is conspicuous. The historic gardens within the park were restored in 2000. The views beyond take in the environs of Rome (including stretches of the open countryside of the Roman Campagna) as well as the city, and the splendid umbrella pines are a special feature of the park, which also has numerous palms and deciduous and ilex trees. The grounds were cut in two in 1960 by the Via Olimpica.

The **Casino del Bel Respiro**, a splendid Baroque building dating from 1644–52, is the most important architectural work of Alessandro Algardi. He was assisted by Giovanni Francesco Grimaldi, and possibly also Bernini. Algardi was responsible for the stuccoes (1646). Surrounded by a formal garden it is sometimes used for receptions by the Italian state (*not normally open to the public*). On the northern edge of the park, approached from Via Aurelia Antica, is the **Villa Vecchia** at no. 183, decorated with exquisite stuccoes by Francesco Nicoletti in 1749–51.

PASSEGGIATA DI GIANICOLO
Map p. 619, 2D–p. 618, 3C

Beside Porta San Pancrazio is the beginning of the Passeggiata di Gianicolo, a wide avenue with fine pine trees laid out in 1884 across the former grounds of the Villa Corsini, above the fortifications of Urban VIII. At Piazzale del Gianicolo, where there is a panoramic terrace, the road is joined by that from the Acqua Paola, and numerous busts of heroes of the Risorgimento (*see p. 389 above*) decorate the gardens. Here stands the huge equestrian statue of Garibaldi, 7m high, by Emilio Gallori, erected in 1895 on the site of the hero's exploits of 1849. Around the base are four bronze groups: in front, *Charge of Manara's Bersaglieri* (Rome, 1849); behind, *Battle of Calatafimi* (Sicily, 1860); at the sides, *Europe* and *America*. Every day you can see a cannon wheeled out of the storeroom below the terrace by a small group of soldiers who fire a blank shot at 12 noon, which can be heard all over the centre of the city.

The Passeggiata now goes downhill. On the right is the Villa Lante, built by Giulio Romano in 1518–27, and owned by Finland since 1950. On the left is the bronze equestrian statue of Anita Garibaldi, Garibaldi's wife, by Mario Rutelli, presented by the Brazilian Government in 1935 to honour her Brazilian origin, and incorporating her tomb. Further on is a memorial tower by Manfredo Manfredi, presented to Rome in 1911 by Italian residents in Argentina.

From this point there is an especially fine view of Rome, even better (because it is clear of trees) than that from Piazzale del Gianicolo above. The avenue continues

Hall of the Library, with ceiling frescoes by Luzio Luzi and stuccoes by Sermoneta (16th century). The marble chimneypiece is by Raffaello da Montelupo. The furniture includes four dower chests and a 15th-century wardrobe.

A small vestibule leads out of the Hall of the Library into the central **Room of the Secret Archives**, or of the Treasury. The walnut cupboards in this room were used for the archives inaugurated by Paul III. In the middle are some large chests in which Julius II, Leo X and Sixtus V kept the Vatican treasury. A Roman staircase ascends to the **Round Hall** (*kept locked*), situated beneath the statue of the Angel and above the last room. Formerly used as a political prison, it now contains the iron core of the Angel, a cast of the head, and the original sword.

The staircase continues up to the terrace at the top of the castle, scene of the last act of Puccini's opera *Tosca*. Above—on a small, higher terrace—can be seen the huge bronze **Angel** (4m high, by Peter Anton Verschaffelt; 1752), shown in the act of sheathing his sword. This commemorates the vision of Gregory the Great after which the castle is named (*see p. 395 above*). The bell known as the *Campana della Misericordia* used to announce the execution of capital sentences. The view from the terrace is superb.

The ramparts

The ramparts are traversed by open walkways which encircle the Roman structure and connect the four bastions of the square inner ward: these are signposted to the right from the drawbridge near the entrance. The first part of the walkway passes above a terrace with four 15th-century cannon and piles of marble and stone cannon balls, once part of the castle's ammunition store. Beyond the Bastion of St Matthew are the mills used from the time of Pius IV to grind flour for the castle. At the Bastion of St Mark is the beginning of the covered way that connects the castle with the Vatican, the Corridoio or Passetto (*no admission; see p. 401*). Just before the Bastion of St Luke is the **Chapel of the Crucifix**, or of Clement XII, in which condemned criminals attended Mass before execution. The circuit continues above the reconstructed gate of 1556, the present entrance to the castle, to the Bastion of St John, beyond which steps lead down to ground level.

WALK SIX

THE BORGO

The Borgo, a district on the right bank of the Tiber, has always been associated with the Catholic Church, since it was here that St Peter was buried and the first church of St Peter's built on the site of his tomb. It was the stronghold of the papacy from 850 until 1586, when it was formally incorporated in the city of Rome. Five streets in the district still have the prefix 'Borgo'.

HISTORY OF THE BORGO

The Borgo was known in ancient Rome as *Ager Vaticanus*. It was chosen by Caligula for his circus, which was enlarged by Nero. The site of the Circus of Nero, just south of the basilica of St Peter's, has been identified in excavations. In the adjoining gardens many Christians were martyred under Nero in AD 65, including St Peter, who was buried in a pagan cemetery nearby. Over his grave the first church of St Peter's was built (c. AD 90) to commemorate his martyrdom. Also within the Ager Vaticanus, Hadrian built his mausoleum (now Castel Sant'Angelo; *see p. 396*) in 135.

Inscriptions found on the temples of Cybele and Mithras suggest that paganism retained its hold with great tenacity until the late 4th century. Despite this, churches, chapels and convents were built round the first church of St Peter, and the district attracted Saxon, Frankish and Lombard pilgrims. Around this time it came to be called the *borgo* (borough), a name of Germanic origin from *borgus*, meaning a small fortified settlement. In 850 Leo IV (847–55) surrounded the Borgo with walls 12m high, fortified with circular towers, to protect it from the incursions of the Saracens: hence the name *Civitas Leonina* or Città Leonina. Remnants of the wall survive to the west of St Peter's. The Leonine City became the papal citadel: within its walls John VIII was besieged in 878 by the Duke of Spoleto; in 896 Arnulph of Carinthia attacked it and Formosus crowned him emperor. Gregory VII took refuge in the Castel Sant'Angelo from the Emperor Henry IV.

During the 'Babylonian captivity' (1309–78), when the papacy was in Avignon (*see p. 265*), the Borgo fell into ruin, but when the popes returned they chose the Vatican as their residence in place of the Lateran. Eugenius IV and Sixtus IV in the 15th century, and Julius II and Leo X in the early 16th, were active in developing and embellishing the Borgo. The original area was enlarged to the north of Borgo Angelico. After the Sack of Rome in 1527, however, the Borgo became one of the poorest and least populated districts of Rome, and in 1586 Sixtus V relinquished the papal claim to the area, so that it was united to the city.

From Castel Sant'Angelo the broad, austere **Via della Conciliazione** leads towards St Peter's. The approach to the great basilica was transformed by this broad straight thoroughfare, typical of Fascist urban planning, which was completed in 1937 to celebrate the accord reached between Mussolini's government and the papacy (*see p. 30*). Its construction involved the destruction of two ancient streets of the Leonine City to reveal St Peter's and Bernini's colonnades in a way which their architect had never intended.

The avenue passes on the right the Carmelite church of Santa Maria in Traspontina (1566–87). Beyond is **Palazzo Torlonia** (formerly Giraud), a delightful reproduction of the Palazzo della Cancelleria (*see p. 305*), built by Andrea Bregno in 1495–1504 for Cardinal Adriano Castellesi. The cardinal gave the palace to the English king Henry VII, and Henry VIII then donated it to his papal legate, Cardinal Campeggio. The Torlonia themselves were a self-made family of merchants and bankers, staunchly loyal to the papal state. In 1870 the head of the clan is said to have altered the colours of his livery because it bore too much resemblance to that of the king.

On the corner of Via dell'Erba is **Palazzo dei Convertendi**, built in the second half of the 17th century and re-erected in its present position in 1937 when Via della Conciliazione was constructed. It occupies the site of a house built by Bramante for Raphael, who died in it in 1520.

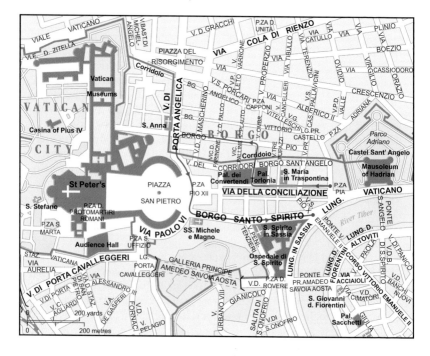

Turn up Via dell'Erba. Parallel to Via della Conciliazione is **Borgo Sant'Angelo**, which is skirted by the wall that supports the Corridoio or *Passetto*, the covered way, pierced by gates, connecting Castel Sant'Angelo with the Vatican. It was built in 1277–80 by Nicholas III above Leo IV's 9th-century defensive wall. It was reconstructed by the Borgia pope Alexander VI, who used it as an escape route from the Vatican in 1494. It was again used in 1527 when Clement VII took refuge in the castle from the troops of Charles V.

Go through the gate and up to **Borgo Pio**, the prettiest street to have survived in the Borgo. Partly closed to traffic, it is a local shopping street and has several *pizzerie*. It leads you up to an eagle-guarded gateway on Via di Porta Angelica. Here turn left. Suddenly you are in **Piazza di San Pietro**, where the crowds, the hubbub, the queues and the litter are possibly much the same as in the days of the medieval pilgrims.

Cross the square towards Borgo Santo Spirito. Here a flight of steps leads up to the little church of **San Michele e Magno** (*open Sun mornings*), founded in the 8th century and retaining a 13th-century campanile. Inside is the tomb of the painter Raphael Mengs (d. 1779).

Go up **Borgo Santo Spirito**. Devoid of shops and restaurants, it is by far the most tranquil of the streets here. On the corner of Via dei Penitenzieri (named after the Penitentiaries, who hear confessions in St Peter's) is **Santo Spirito in Sassia** (*open 7–12 & 3–7.30*), a church founded in 726 for Saxon pilgrims by Ine, king of Wessex, who died in Rome in the same year. It is known

that this was the place where English clerics and visitors stayed when they came to Rome in the Middle ages. The church was rebuilt in 1540 by Antonio da Sangallo the Younger: the design of the façade was probably his, but the work itself was done in 1585 by Ottavio Mascherino. The campanile, entirely Tuscan in character, and attributed to Baccio Pontelli, is one of the most graceful in Rome.

In the interior the wooden ceiling dates from 1534–49. On the west wall are two interesting paintings in elaborate frames: the *Visitation* by Francesco Salviati, and the *Conversion of Saul*, attributed to Marco da Siena. On the south side, the first chapel contains the *Pentecost* by Jacopo Zucchi; and the second chapel, the *Assumption* by Livio Agresti. The interesting little porch in front of a side door with two columns has 16th-century frescoes and a pretty ceiling. It supports the organ of 1546–52. The huge apse was covered with frescoes by Jacopo and Francesco Zucchi in 1583. On the north side, the third chapel has a 16th-century crucifix and frescoed decorations in Roman style imitating precious marbles with figures in grisaille. On the second altar, the *Coronation of the Virgin* is by Cesare Nebbia.

It was from the ramparts of the Leonine City near here that Benvenuto Cellini, according to his own statement, shot the Constable de Bourbon in 1527; a plaque on the outer wall of the church, however, attributes the deed to Bernardo Passeri, another goldsmith.

Adjoining the church are the buildings of the huge **Ospedale di Santo Spirito**, founded by Innocent III c.

when the second fountain was begun. Between the obelisk and each fountain is a round porphyry slab from which you have the illusion that each of the colonnades has only a single row of columns.

Covered galleries, also decorated with statues, unite the colonnades with the portico of St Peter's. The gallery on the right, known as the Corridore del Bernini and leading to the Scala Regia, is closed by the Portone di Bronzo. A great staircase of three flights leads up to the portico of the basilica. At the foot are colossal statues of St Peter (by Giuseppe de Fabris) and St Paul (by Adamo Tadolini), set up by Pius IX. In this piazza on 13th May 1981 a Turk, Mehmet Ali Agca, made an attempt on the life of Pope John Paul II.

ST PETER'S

St Peter's or the *Basilica di San Pietro in Vaticano*, on a vast scale, is perhaps the world's most imposing church. It is built on the site of a basilica begun by Constantine, the first Christian Emperor, and also where the Apostle St Peter was buried after his martyrdom close by. This splendid church was famous throughout Europe, but in the mid-15th century it was decided to rebuild it on an even grander scale: this herculean task, carried out by the leading architects of the time, was only completed in the early 17th century.

Opening times
The basilica is open 7–7; Oct–Mar 7–6. The entrance (and security check) is now on the right of the piazza (and the exit on the left). There can be queues except early in the morning and late in the evening. The treasury is open 9–6.15; Oct–Mar 9–5.15. The dome can be ascended 8–5.45; Oct–Mar 8–4.45, although it is closed when the pope is in the basilica (often Wed morning). The Vatican Grottoes (Tombe dei Papi) are open 7–6; Oct–Mar 7–5, except when the pope is in the basilica. Group tours of the necropolis and tomb of St Peter (described on p. 418) are conducted most days 9–12 & 2–5; the visit takes about 1hr and groups are limited to 15 people. Apply in writing or in person to the Ufficio Scavi (beneath the Arco della Campana, left of St Peter's) Mon–Fri 9–5; T: 06 6988 5318.

Dress
You are not allowed inside St Peter's or the Vatican City wearing shorts or mini-skirts, or with bare shoulders.

Services
Mass is held on Sun at 7, 8, 9 and 10, with Sung Mass at 10.30, and frequently during the week. Holy Communion can be taken in the Cappella del Santissimo Sacramento throughout the day on Sun. There are often special services being held for groups in side chapels and in the Grottoes. For information on services, T: 06 6988 5318.

Papal audiences

General audiences usually take place at 10 or 10.30 on Wed mornings in the New Audience Hall, or in the piazza (when the pope is transported by jeep). The New Audience Hall is reached under the colonnade to the left of the façade of St Peter's. A special section is set aside for newly married couples. Audiences are now also sometimes held in St Peter's. Application to attend an audience can be made in writing to the Prefetto della Casa Pontificia, Città del Vaticano, 00120 Rome; T: 06 6988 3017; 06 6988 5863. Otherwise you can apply in person at the Portone di Bronzo, in the colonnade to the right of St Peter's, 9–1. At the far end of the Corridore del Bernini is the Scala Regia, the staircase leading to the Sala Regia. At a table at the entrance you are asked to fill in a form and take it to the office of the Prefettura on the first floor, reached by the Scala Pia.

Information office

In Piazza San Pietro, to the left of the façade of the basilica. Open Mon–Sat 8.30–7 (closed Wed, when papal audiences are being held in the piazza); T: 06 6988 2019; www.vatican.va

THE OLD ST PETER'S

According to the *Liber Pontificalis*, around AD 90 Pope St Anacletus built an oratory over the tomb of St Peter, close to the Circus of Nero, near which he had been martyred. It is now thought that there may have been a confusion of names, and that St Anicetus (155–66) was probably responsible for the oratory. At the request of Pope St Sylvester I the Emperor Constantine began a basilica on the site of this oratory c. 319–22. It was consecrated on 18th November 326. This basilica was 120m long and 65m wide, about half the size of the present edifice. In front is a great quadrangular colonnaded portico. The nave and double aisles were divided by 86 marble columns, some of which were said to have been taken from the Septizodium on the Palatine (if so, this was long before the demolition of that building by Sixtus V). It contained numerous monuments to popes and emperors, was decorated with frescoes and mosaics, and was visited by pilgrims from all over Europe. Charlemagne was crowned here by Leo III in 800. Some of its relics are preserved (*see p. 416*). Its façade is shown in Raphael's fresco of the *Incendio di Borgo* in the Raphael Rooms in the Vatican.

THE NEW ST PETER'S

In the middle of the 15th century the old basilica showed signs of collapse, and Nicholas V, recognizing its importance to the prestige of the Roman Catholic faith, decided to rebuild it. He entrusted the work to Bernardo Rossellino, Leon Battista Alberti and Giuliano da Sangallo, but on Nicholas's death in 1455, building work was virtually suspended for half a century. Julius II decided on a complete reconstruction and employed for the purpose Donato Bramante, who started work in 1506. Most of the old church was dismantled, and much was destroyed which could have been preserved: Bramante was nicknamed 'Bramante Ruinante'. The new basilica was on a dentives are huge mosaics of the Evangelists: the pen held by St Mark is 1.5m long. On the frieze below the drum is inscribed in letters nearly 2m high: *Tu es petrus et super hanc petram aedificabo ecclesiam meam et tibi dabo claves regni caelorum* ('Thou art Peter, and upon this rock I will build my church; and I will give unto thee the keys of the kingdom of heaven'). The dome is divided into 16 compartments, corresponding to the windows of the drum, by ribs ornamented with stucco; in these compartments are six bands of mosaic by Cavaliere d'Arpino, representing saints, angels and the company of Heaven; in the lantern above is the Redeemer.

Under a canopy against the pier of St Longinus is the famous **bronze statue of St Peter E**, seated on a marble throne. It was once believed to date from the 5th or 6th century, but since its restoration in 1990, is considered to be the work of Arnolfo di Cambio (c. 1296). The extended foot of the statue has been worn away by the touch of worshippers. The statue is robed on high festivals.

High altar

Over the high altar rises the great **baldacchino F**, designed by Bernini and unveiled on 28th June 1633 by Urban VIII. This colossal Baroque structure, a combination of architecture and decorative sculpture, is cast from bronze taken from the Pantheon. Four gilt-bronze Solomonic columns rise from their marble plinths, which are decorated with the Barberini bees (Urban VIII was a Barberini). The columns resemble in design the *Colonna Santa* (*see p. 416*) but are decorated with figures of genii and laurel branches. They support a canopy from which hang festoons and tassels and on which angels by Duquesnoy alternate with children. From the four corners of the canopy ascend ornamental scrolls, which support the globe and cross. Inside the top of the canopy the Holy Spirit is represented as a dove in an aureole.

The **high altar**, at which only the pope may celebrate, is formed of a block of Greek marble found in the Forum of Nerva and consecrated by Clement VIII on 26th June 1594. It covers the altar of Calixtus II (d. 1123), which in turn encloses an altar of Gregory the Great (d. 604). It stands over the space that is recognized as the tomb of St Peter.

In front is the **confessio G**, built by Maderno and encircled by perpetually burning lamps. It is directly above the ancient Roman necropolis where the Tropaion of Gaius (*see p. 422*) was found, below the Vatican Grottoes. The mosaic niches and urn mark the burial place of St Peter.

East end

At the east end of the church two porphyry steps from the old basilica lead to the tribune, the most conspicuous object in which is the **Cathedra of St Peter H**, an ambitious and theatrical composition by Bernini (1665). This enormous gilt-bronze throne is supported by statues of four Fathers of the Church: St Augustine and St Ambrose of the Latin Church (in mitres), and St Athanasius and St John Chrysostom of the Greek Church (bare-headed). It encloses an ancient wooden chair inlaid with ivory, said to have been the episcopal chair of St Peter. A circle of flying angels surrounds a great halo of gilt stucco in the centre of which, providing the focal point of the whole church, is the Dove, set in the window above the throne.

Michelangelo's *Pietà*

The most famous sculpture in the church is **Michelangelo's *Pietà***, in the first chapel in the south aisle ❶. The artist made this exquisite work in 1499 at the age of 24 for the French ambassador, Cardinal Jean de Bilhères de Lagraulas. It is perhaps the most moving of all Michelangelo's sculptures and is the only one inscribed with his name (on the ribbon falling from the left shoulder of the Virgin). It is also one of the very few pieces that Michelangelo ever finished in his life, although the concept of '*non finito*' in his work remains an unresolved problem about which scholars have written copiously over the centuries. As an image, the *Pietà* is always to be seen as possessing

Michelangelo's celebrated *Pietà* (1499).

Ricci. It has a fine gate with the arms of Clement XIII, elegant classical stalls by Bernini, and two large organs. The altarpiece, after a painting by Pietro Bianchi, represents the *Immaculate Conception*. In the pavement is the simple tombstone of Clement XI, who died in 1721.

N **Baptistery:** The cover of a porphyry sarcophagus, placed upside-down, is used as the font. It formerly covered the tomb of the Emperor Otho II (973–83) in the Grottoes. The present metal cover is by Carlo Fontana.

O **Cappella della Colonna:** This, one of the domed corner chapels in the crossing, was decorated in 1757 with figures of angels carrying garlands and with symbols of the Virgin. Above the tomb of St Leo the Great (d. 461) is a splendid relief by Alessandro Algardi (1650), representing *Leo Arresting the Progress of Attila* with the help of St Peter and St Paul. On the altar to the left is an ancient and greatly venerated representation of the Virgin, painted on a column from the old basilica. In the middle of the chapel is the tombstone of Leo XII (d. 1829).

Altarpieces

Because of the huge scale of the church there are almost no paintings of note and most of the altarpieces are in miniature mosaic, using tiny tesserae of glass enamel instead of stone—copies of huge paintings, some of which once hung in the basilica. Among the best of these are the *Communion of St Jerome* after Domenichino above the effigy of John XXIII (**9**), and *St Petronilla* after Guercino (**15**). The mosaic of the *Transfiguration* (**16**) is a copy (enlarged four times) of Raphael's famous painting in the Vatican Picture Gallery (*see p. 464*). The mosaics in the baptistery also reproduce paintings.

The Treasury

The Treasury or Museo Storico Artistico (*for admission see p. 404 above*) is entered by the door under the monument to Pius VIII (**17**). In the vestibule is a large stone slab with the names of all the popes buried in the basilica. The treasury contents were plundered in 846 by the Saracens, and again during the Sack of Rome by Imperial troops in 1527, and it was impoverished by the provisions of the Treaty of Tolentino (1797), which Pius VI was forced to conclude with Napoleon. It was rearranged in 1975 in dark modern exhibition rooms (and the harsh illumination has been justly criticized). It still, however, contains objects of great value and interest.

Room I: The *Colonna Santa*, a 4th-century Byzantine spiral column, is one of 12 from the old basilica: eight decorate the balconies of the great piers of the dome in St Peter's, but the remaining three are lost. The column was once thought to be that against which Christ leaned when speaking with the doctors in the Temple of Jerusalem. The gilt-bronze cock (9th century) was used to decorate the top of the campanile of the old basilica (it evokes the cock which crowed when Peter denied Christ).

Room II (Sagrestia dei Beneficiati): The exquisite *Vatican Cross*, the most ancient possession of the treasury, dating from the 6th century, was the gift of the Emperor Justinian II. It is made of bronze and set with jewels. Also here is the so-called 'Dalmatic of Charlemagne', a beautiful work now usually considered to date from the 11th century or perhaps the early 15th. There are also Byzantine works (an enamelled cross and a fragment of an ivory diptych). The ancient *Cathedra of St Peter*, which Bernini incorporated in the decoration of the tribune of the basilica, can be seen here in a copy made in 1974.

Cappella della Sagrestia dei Beneficiati: The beautiful ciborium by Donatello (c. 1432) comes from the old basilica; it encloses a painting of the *Madonna della Febbre* (protectress of victims of malaria—once rife in the Roman Campagna). Over the chapel altar is *St Peter Receiving the Keys* by Girolamo Muziano. A plaster cast of Michelangelo's *Pietà* is also displayed here.

Room IV: The huge Monument of Sixtus IV is a masterpiece in bronze by Antonio Pollaiolo (1493). It can be seen to advantage from the raised platform. This pope is remembered as the builder of the Sistine Chapel (which is named after him), and for opening the Vatican Library to the public for the first time. He also donated some important Classical bronzes to the city of Rome. There is a bust of Henry Stuart, Cardinal York, by Canova.

Room V: Here are displayed the ceremonial ring of Sixtus IV (1471–84); a reliquary bust of St Luke the Evangelist (13th–14th century); and a wooden Crucifix probably dating from the 14th century.

Room VI: The display includes a Cross and candelabra by Sebastiano Torrigiani; a Crucifix and six candelabra (1581) made for Cardinal Alessandro Farnese and presented by him to the basilica in the following year; and two huge candelabra of the 16th century, traditionally attributed to the famous goldsmith Benvenuto Cellini.

Room VII: Here are displayed a 13th-century Slavonic icon in a jewelled silver frame, and reliquaries; and a model of an angel in clay by Bernini (1673), used for one of the angels flanking the ciborium in the Cappella del Sacramento.

Room VIII: The gold chalice set with diamonds (18th century) was bequeathed to the Vatican by Henry Stuart, Cardinal York. The platinum chalice, presented by Charles III of Spain to Pius VI, is interesting as the first recorded use of platinum for such a purpose. The gilt-bronze tiara was made in the 17th century for the seated statue of St Peter in the basilica, which on high festivals was attired in full pontificals.

Room IX: The superbly-carved sarcophagus of Junius Bassus, prefect of Rome in 359, which was was found near St Peter's in 1505, is shown here. With scenes from the Old and New Testaments, it is an extremely important example of early Christian art.

IMPORTANT POPES IN ROMAN HISTORY

Julius II (Giuliano della Rovere; 1503–13)
Born to a humble family in 1443, the ruthless and energetic Giuliano della Rovere
has gone down in history as the warrior pope, a man who led his armies into battle dressed in full armour, and who was satirized by Erasmus as the pontiff whom
St Peter balked at admitting to Paradise. When the grandiose funerary monument
planned for him by Michelangelo came to nothing (*see pp. 256–57*), Julius was
buried simply beneath the pavement of St Peter's.

Leo X (Giovanni de' Medici; 1513–21)
The second son of Lorenzo the Magnificent, Giovanni de' Medici was created cardinal when only thirteen. The celebrated portrait by Raphael (of whom Leo was an
enthusiastic patron) shows him to have been rather corpulent. He perspired a good
deal and during ecclesiastical functions was always wiping his face and hands, to
the distress of bystanders. Leo was a celebrated *bon viveur* and passionate hunter,
said to have exclaimed 'Since God has granted us the Papacy, let us enjoy it!'. His
bull *Exsurge Domine* of 1520 condemned 41 errors of Martin Luther. His tomb is
in Santa Maria sopra Minerva.

Clement VII (Giulio de' Medici; 1523–34)
The bastard nephew of Lorenzo the Magnificent, Giulio de' Medici was declared
legitimate and created cardinal in 1513. He had dark brown eyes, the left one
squinting. According to Benvenuto Cellini he had excellent taste—the beautiful but
faded portrait by Sebastiano del Piombo (Capodimonte, Naples) makes him look
vain and supercilious. Clement's bitter relations with the Emperor Charles V led to
the disastrous Sack of Rome in 1527 (*see p. 23*). Trapped for seven months in Castel
Sant'Angelo, he grew a beard as a sign of mourning. He refused to allow Henry VIII
to divorce Catherine of Aragon. He is buried in Santa Maria sopra Minerva.

Paul III (Alessandro Farnese; 1534–49)
As cardinal, Alessandro Farnese fathered four children, but he put away his mistress in 1514. His secular interests were not entirely abandoned, however. He loved
masked balls, fireworks, clowns and dwarfs, and in 1536 he revived the carnival,
when enormous floats were dragged through the streets of Rome by teams of buf-
falo. Yet he was a great reformer, and as well as his human children he fathered a
number of religious orders, most importantly the Jesuits, in 1540. Paul also established the Congregation of the Roman Inquisition, to extirpate heresy. When he
was elected, he claimed he had waited 30 years for Michelangelo—and promptly
commissioned the *Last Judgement* and the new layout of the Campidoglio. He is
buried in St Peter's in a beautiful tomb by Guglielmo della Porta.

Urban VIII (Maffeo Barberini; 1623–44)
Authoritarian, highly conscious of his own position, and a shameless nepotist, Urban was also learned and artistic. He wrote Latin verses (and indeed spoilt many hymns in the Breviary by rewriting them). Though an unpopular pope (there was unseemly rejoicing when he died), he gave Rome the art and architecture of Bernini, the young sculptor whom he made architect of the new St Peter's. The basilica was consecrated in 1626. Urban lies buried there, commemorated by a funeral monument designed by his brilliant protégé.

Innocent X (Giovan Battista Pamphilj; 1644–55)
Innocent was elected in 1644, after a stormy conclave (he was opposed by France), and consecrated on 4th October at a particularly splendid ceremony, when for the first time the *sanpietrini* lit up the dome of the basilica with flaming torches. His ugliness was noted by contemporaries, and Velázquez's famous portrait in the Palazzo Doria Pamphilj—which inspired several modern versions by Francis Bacon—has caught his disturbing, implacable gaze. His life was blameless, but he was irresolute and suspicious. Innocent died in January 1655 after a long agony; no one wanted to pay for his burial. Later a funerary monument was set up in the church of Sant'Agnese, which has a façade by his favourite architect, Borromini.

Pius VII (Luigi Barnaba Chiaramonti; 1800–23)
Elected in March 1800, Pius was constrained by political and military events to sign a concordat with Bonaparte in 1801. In 1804 he went to Paris to officiate at the emperor's coronation; he was rudely treated, and Napoleon placed the crown on his own head. In 1809 Pius was arrested by the French and interned. In 1814, after Bonaparte's fall, he returned to Rome amidst general rejoicing. Pius was magnanimous towards Napoleon's family. He died in 1823, after falling and breaking a leg. His funerary monument in St Peter's is by (the Protestant) Bertel Thorvaldsen.

Pius IX (Giovanni Maria Mastai-Ferretti; 1846–78)
Pius was politically maladroit, and to many his name is a byword for intransigence and arch-conservatism. Garibaldi despised him and named his horse 'Papa Mastai'; in Italian his regnal number (*Pio Nono*) sounds like a double negative, as though he were always saying 'No, no' to the radical reforms that were proposed to him—unsurprising, perhaps, since the radicals wanted his territories. Nationalist armies seized the Papal States in 1860 and Rome in 1870, confining papal authority to the Vatican. Pius was the last pope to hold temporal power. On the ecclesiastical level he was a very great pope, and even his enemies acknowledged his charm. In 1856 he defined the dogma of the Immaculate Conception; in 1870 he proclaimed the dogma of Papal Infallibility. After the longest reign in papal history he died in 1878, and lies buried in a simple tomb in San Lorenzo fuori le Mura.   M.R.

the Lateran Palace and Palazzo della Cancelleria. Miniature mosaics made in the Vatican workshops from the late 16th century onwards were particularly in vogue in the late 18th and early 19th centuries. This technique—which used tiny tesserae of glass enamel instead of stone—was used to reproduce large paintings in St Peter's and then to decorate boxes or precious objects often donated by the popes to their visitors.

To the left of the Chapel of St Pius V (*described on p. 446*) we enter the **Sobieski Room**, named after John Sobieski (John III of Poland), who liberated Vienna from a siege by the Turks in 1683. The decorations on the walls, carried out in 1883, depict the battle. The frescoes in the **Hall of the Immaculate Conception**, by Francesco Podesti, were painted to celebrate the definition and proclamation of the dogma of the Immaculate Conception of the Virgin pronounced by Pius IX on 8th December 1854. The floors of both rooms are inlaid with Roman mosaics from Ostia.

From here you can usually choose whether to continue through the Raphael Rooms to the Sistine Chapel or turn back through the Chapel of Pius V down the stairs directly to the Sistine Chapel. Note: if you decide the latter you cannot subsequently visit the Raphael Rooms unless you repeat the above itinerary from the Quattro Cancelli.

RAPHAEL ROOMS

The Raphael Rooms (*Stanze di Raffaello*) are a series of rooms built by Nicholas V as papal audience chambers, a library and a hall for the papal tribunal. The walls were originally painted by Andrea del Castagno, Piero della Francesca and Benedetto Bonfigli. Julius II employed a group of great artists to continue the decoration, including Luca Signorelli, Perugino, Sodoma, Bramantino, Baldassare Peruzzi, Lorenzo Lotto and the Flemish painter Jan Ruysch. But when in 1508, on Bramante's suggestion, the pope called Raphael from Urbino, he was so pleased with his work that he dismissed all the other painters, ordered their works to be destroyed, and commissioned Raphael to decorate the whole of this part of the Vatican.

The *Stanze* are the painter's masterpiece: they show the extraordinary development of his art during the years between his coming to Rome in 1508 and his death at the age of 37 in 1520. Rome was of the first importance during the High Renaissance, and when Raphael arrived he found the court of Julius II a stimulating intellectual centre. The College of Cardinals and the Curia included many celebrated savants, humanists and men of letters, and a crowd of artists, led by Bramante and Michelangelo, were at work in the city. In this highly cultured environment Raphael, who had great powers of assimilation, acquired an entirely new manner of painting.

Raphael painted a famous portrait of Julius II (now in the National Gallery in London) two years before the pope's death in 1513. The new Medici pope, Leo X, appointed Raphael head of the building works in St Peter's in 1514, and commissioned him to decorate the Vatican Loggia. In 1518 Raphael also painted Leo X, with two cardinals: this portrait is in the Uffizi. Leo appointed him commissioner of antiquities to ensure that

from the Quattro Cancelli and Gallery of Maps

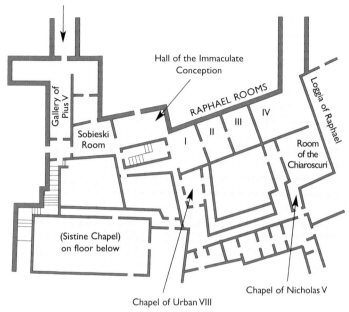

everything possible was done to preserve the ancient buildings of Rome. Raphael left the huge altarpiece of the *Transfiguration*, now in the Vatican Picture Gallery (*see p. 464*) incomplete and it was displayed above his coffin at his funeral in 1520. He is buried in the Pantheon.

Raphael began work in the Stanza della Segnatura (II), with the frescoes of Astronomy, Apollo, Adam and Eve, and the Judgement of Solomon, which were probably his trial works; he then carried out the other frescoes in this room. After this he decorated, successively, the Stanza d'Eliodoro (III), the Stanza dell'Incendio (I), and the Stanza di Costantino (IV). The entrance to the *Stanze* has been altered, so that the rooms now unfortunately have to be visited in reverse chronological order, as described below.

Room IV (Sala di Costantino): This room was painted almost entirely in the time of Clement VII (1523–34), after Raphael's death, by Giulio Romano with the assistance of Francesco Penni and Raffaellino del Colle. On the wall facing the window is the *Victory of Constantine over Maxentius near the Pons Milvius*, for which Raphael had made some sketches. The reddish tint which suffuses the picture is characteristic of Giulio Romano. To the right are the figures of St Urban with *Justice* and *Charity*; to the left, St Sylvester with *Faith* and *Religion*.

frescoes by Pinturicchio, his masterpiece. The room is divided by an arch into two cross-vaulted areas forming six lunettes. On the ceiling is the *Legend of Isis* and *Osiris and the Bull Apis* (a reference to the Borgia arms), with reliefs in gilded stucco. Above the door is a medallion with the *Madonna and Child with Saints*. Entrance wall, the *Visitation*; *St Paul the Hermit* and *St Anthony Abbot in the Desert*, on the right. The end wall shows the *Disputation between St Catherine of Alexandria and the Emperor Maximian*; the figure of the saint was once thought to be a portrait of Alexander VI's daughter, Lucrezia Borgia, or his mistress, Giulia Farnese. The figure behind the throne is a self-portrait by Pinturicchio, and in the background is the Arch of Constantine. The window wall shows the *Martyrdom of St Sebastian*, with a view of the Colosseum; and the exit wall, *Susanna and the Elders* and the *Legend of St Barbara*.

Room VI (Room of the Mysteries of the Faith): Frescoes partly by Pinturicchio represent the *Annunciation*, *Nativity*, *Adoration of the Magi*, *Resurrection* (the kneeling pontiff is Alexander VI), *Ascension*, *Pentecost* and *Assumption of the Virgin*. The last fresco includes a portrait of the donor, perhaps Francesco Borgia. In the ceiling are stuccoes and paintings of prophets.

Room VII (Room of the Popes): Formerly decorated with portraits of popes. The frescoes and stucco decoration of the splendid vaulted ceiling were commissioned by Leo X from Perino del Vaga and Giovanni da Udine.

Gallery of Modern Religious Art

This gallery was arranged in 1973 in the Borgia Apartments, and in 50 or so lavishly renovated rooms. The 540 works by some 250 artists from all over the world were presented to Pope Paul VI by invited artists, collectors and donors. The collection, arranged in no particular order but fully labelled, is disappointing despite the fact that it features some of the most important artists of the 20th century.

THE SISTINE CHAPEL

by Nigel McGilchrist

The Sistine Chapel is one of the most magnificently decorated spaces in the world, and represents the largest single concentration of Renaissance wall-paintings executed in pure fresco. The paintings are arranged in a complex programme illustrating Christian cosmology, and designed to reinforce the origins of papal authority. The chapel is the place where the cardinals gather to elect each pope in secret conclave: they deliberate their decision in the presence of a pictorial map of the whole of spiritual history.

The Renaissance Christian mind divided human existence into three epochs: *ante legem* (from the Creation up until the Law of Moses); *sub lege* (under the law of Moses) and *sub gratia* (the time 'of Grace' or Redemption following the teachings of Jesus Christ). The first of these periods is elaborated in images of the Creation and the life of

Noah, painted on the vault by Michelangelo between 1508 and 1512; the second—a series of scenes from the life of Moses, painted three decades earlier by a group of Italy's greatest Quattrocento painters—runs along the south wall; while the third—scenes from the life of Christ painted by the same group of artists—mirrors it on the north. The culmination of this sequence is a depiction of the ultimate destiny of all human history: the triumphal Second Coming on the Day of Judgement, painted by Michelangelo above the altar between 1536 and 1541. In the areas in between are images of those who bore witness: the Old Testament Prophets and the pagan Sibyls (interpreted as having fore-told the redemption of mankind through a saviour); the ancestors of Jesus of Nazareth in the lunettes; and the apostolic succession of popes in the spaces between the win-dows. Larger than almost any figure and directly above the altar, is the unusual *Jonah*, who in his willing self-sacrifice was seen to have foretold the Saviour's life, and in his return to the world after three days in the whale's belly, prefigured the Resurrection and all its consequences which are gloriously depicted on the wall below him. The Evangelists and Apostles are absent from much of the plan, although the tapestries which were to have hung along the walls at the lowest level and were executed on designs by Raphael (*see p. 431*), related scenes from the lives of St Peter and St Paul. The plan is in one sense universal, but in another, highly eclectic. Much of its elaboration, at least during the years of Julius II's pontificate, must be attributed to the elusive figure of Egidius of Viterbo, who was charged with formulating and refining Church doctrine.

Visiting the chapel

It is helpful to distinguish five separate campaigns of work: the building of the chapel itself (1475–80); the first series of wall paintings and decoration by Quattrocento mas-ters, on the east, north and south walls (1481–83); Michelangelo's painting of the ceil-ing (1508–12); Michelangelo's much later painting of the altar (west) wall with the *Last Judgement* (1536–41); the recent cleaning and conservation of the frescoes (1980–96).

The building

The building takes its name from Pope Sixtus IV, who commissioned the construction of the chapel in 1475 to provide a new and grander place for papal ceremony and for the convocation of the conclave which elected a new pope. The design, to plans drawn up by Baccio Pontelli, is unusually bare of architectural interest, with little natural illu-mination and a height which is disproportionate to its breadth. The ratios represented by its dimensions (40.5m by 13.2m, by 20.7m high) are those given for Solomon's tem-ple in *I Kings 6, v. 2*. It may also be significant that its appearance and dimensions recall the ancient Curia in the Roman Forum: this was the council chamber of the senators of ancient Rome, and Sixtus may have wished his chapel to be seen as a direct successor to it as the central building of a new world order: the congregational seat of the papal curia of the new Christian Empire which had replaced the former pagan one. Contemporary with the chapel's construction is the decorated floor—a fine example of *opus alexandrinum*. The choir loft and the delicate, carved marble transenna which divides the chapel are the work principally of Mino da Fiesole.

with grim humour in a sonnet in 1510. He concludes by protesting that his art 'was dead' and that he 'was no painter': his face was like a floor mosaic from the dripping paint, and his spine 'doubled back like a drawn bow'. We should not forget that fresco painting is a difficult technique, in which Michelangelo had had little or no experience since his apprenticeship: it requires speed and complete confidence, because it affords no possibility of correction during application.

The subject matter chosen for the ceiling paintings concentrates on the early chapters of Genesis. The exact programme would have been given to Michelangelo, probably by Egidius of Viterbo; but the artist's own genius emerges in the extraordinary clarity and processional dignity which he gives to the wide variety of subject matter. He encapsulates elusive concepts in simple and unforgettable images, and brilliantly articulates the huge expanse with the indispensable aid of a fictional architectural framework which both separates and unites the individual elements of the design. Clear primary colour is used in the main narrative scenes, while neutral tints define the architectural framework and its imaginary 'sculptural' decoration. Many of the nude male figures, in constantly varying poses, were inspired by the late Hellenistic *Belvedere Torso*, which was a centre-piece of Julius' collection of antiquities and is still to be seen in the Pio-Clementino Museum (*see p. 457*). Indeed, Michelangelo paints like a sculptor: close examination of the surface of his frescoes reveals how he often used his brush with rapid hatching strokes, as though it were his chisel working on stone. The celebrated scene of the *Creation of Adam*, is perhaps the greatest piece of sculpture ever created in paint. The reposed and idealized figure is based on the pose and type of the ancient Roman river divinity; but in the hands of Michelangelo it goes far beyond its ancient prototype to become a celebration of solitary and uncorrupted humanity, marvellously balanced by the large area of void before him. His dignified repose contrasts, too, with the concentrated dynamism in the features of the Almighty who reaches out towards him.

The *Last Judgement*

A changed world and a more pensive Michelangelo (now 61 years old) produced the depiction of the *Last Judgement* (1536–41) on the wall above the altar. In the interval between the two painting campaigns, the Sack of Rome of 1527 (*see p. 23*) had irrevocably altered the Church's perception of itself, and had left its scars upon the imagination of its artists—in particular one as devout as Michelangelo, who in any case was now facing the decay of his own life and the destiny of his soul. In his *Last Judgement*, however, there is no hint either of simplistic gloom or grating optimism. Where other artists had evoked contrasts of light and impenetrable dark, Michelangelo sets the whole against a unifying, unearthly, intense lapis blue: the huge empty spaces in the composition become thereby as eloquent as the groups of floating figures which they balance. Where many earlier painters had particularized the Judgement Day, dwelling upon the multifarious punishments of the wicked, Michelangelo has unified the event into a vast, single, cyclical motion, with the blessed rising to the left of the altar and the damned falling to the right. Everything else in the chapel has a linear direction: this alone is circular in sweep, radiating out from the magnificent gestures of Christ's arms. The beardless, youthful Christ, like a dynamized Apollo irrupting into the viewer's space, is in deliberate contrast to the reposed Adam at the centre of the ceiling.

The eye is drawn into the movement of the whole piece, passing from the central focus of Christ to the figure of his Mother beside him, turning away and partly drawing her veil in demure fear. Above, groups of angels and nude figures expand the scene outwards as they carry away the Cross and the column of the Flagellation to either side: there is a masterful audacity to some of these swirling figures, which are perceived from often bizarre angles as they somersault in the sky with a momentary glance towards us, which manifests itself in no more than a pair of eyes and nostrils emerging from beneath the bulk of a twisting abdomen. In the depths of Hades below, a few flourishing brushstrokes give form to a lurking soul, who, anxious of his fate, peers from partial darkness into the Eternal Future: the crazed glances, the floating figures, and the rapid and confident adumbrations of the master's technique, all seem to prefigure Goya's caricature by nearly 300 years. This is high bravura painting: urgent, restless, sometimes even playful, but a world away from the poise and balance of the earlier Michelangelo above.

The original nudity of the figures inevitably caused offence to some, and many of them were covered by Daniele da Volterra, at the request of Pope Pius IV, in 1565. (These draperies have—with the exception of the figure of St Catherine which has been repainted in fresco—been added to the surface in a soluble tempera, which could be removed: papal policy is currently to leave them in place.) Even while work was in progress on the painting the pope's master of ceremonies, Biagio da Cesena—according to Giorgio Vasari—was constantly chiding Michelangelo about the issue of nudity, irritating him to the point that he procured his revenge by painting Biagio prominently above the entrance-door to the right of the altar, as the figure of Minos with ass's ears on his head and a serpent wound around his body, poised with jaws open to detach his genitals. Michelangelo's other personalization in this great work is on a more sombre note. The gigantic figure of St Bartholomew (below and to the viewer's right of Christ) holds up, as was traditional, the attribute of his martyrdom: the knife with which he was flayed and the flayed skin itself. The tousled hair and broken nose scarcely visible on the face in the limp, hanging skin is a self-portrait of the artist. That so tortured an image should have suggested itself to Michelangelo as the way to sign his last great essay in painting speaks eloquently of his state of mind in these later years. He obdurately believed he was condemned to perdition.

The conservation and cleaning of the frescoes

What in the case of the ceiling alone took one man four years to paint single-handedly took eight restorers nine years to clean. All the fresco cycles in the Sistine Chapel have now been cleaned and conserved. The range of colour revealed is astonishing. It is now possible for the visitor to appreciate clearly the difference between the chromatic range of the Quattrocento paintings and the far bolder and more unorthodox brilliance of Michelangelo's palette. His virtuoso method of creating shadow—not by darker tints of the same colour, but by the juxtaposition of brilliant complementaries—gives an excitement to the work which was entirely lacking before the cleaning. As we see them now,

Sistine Hall: Named after its founder Sixtus V, this was built in 1587–89 by Domenico Fontana across the great Cortile del Belvedere, cutting it in two. The hall is divided into two vaulted aisles by seven columns, and is decorated with themes glorifying literature and the pontificate of Sixtus V, with interesting views of Rome. Exhibitions of the precious library possessions are sometimes held here. In the vestibule, above the doors, are paintings of the Lateran Palace, before and after its reconstruction by Domenico Fontana.

The Pauline Rooms: These two rooms were added by Paul V, and decorated in the Mannerist style in 1610–11.

The Alexandrine Room: This was adapted in 1690 by Alexander VIII, and decorated with scenes from the life of Pius VII.

The Clementine Gallery: The gallery was added to the library by Clement XII in 1732; in 1818, under Pius VII, it was decorated with paintings of scenes from the life of that pope. The last room has a bronze head of a Muse—a Roman copy of a Hellenistic original—and two bronze griffins of the Imperial period. Mithraic divinities flank the entrance.

A new staircase has been constructed in the last room, and you are obliged to use it. This means that the main hall of the **Museum of Pagan Antiquities of the Library** (*Museo Profano della Biblioteca*) beyond, is no longer accessible from here: it can only be reached from the Quattro Cancelli, but is described here since it forms part of the Library. It contains a collection begun by Clement XIII in 1767, with additions from excavations in 1809–15. It was completed in the time of Pius VI, and decorated by Luigi Valadier, with ceiling paintings symbolizing Time. In the niches on either side of the entrance wall are a head of Augustus (one of the best portraits of this emperor) and a bronze head of Nero. In the cupboards (*usually kept closed*) are carved Roman ivory, busts in semi-precious stones, a mosaic from Hadrian's Villa, Roman and Etruscan bronzes and the head and arm of a chryselephantine statue of Minerva, claimed to be a 5th-century BC Greek original.

The staircase leads down towards the exit, with a monumental double staircase built in 1932. From the hall you can also take one of the two delightful old-fashioned lifts down to the street level. To visit the museums described below, follow the signs.

EGYPTIAN MUSEUM

The Egyptian Museum (*marked on the plan on p. 454*) was founded by Gregory XVI in 1839 and was arranged by Father Luigi Maria Ungarelli, one of the first Italian Egyptologists, to continue the scientific research of Jean-François Champollion (1790–1832), the French archaeologist and founder of modern Egyptology. The rooms were decorated in the Egyptian style in the 19th century by Giuseppe de Fabris. The collection was beautifully rearranged in 1989 and is well labelled.

Room I: Funerary stelae and tomb reliefs are arranged in chronological order from c. 2600 BC–AD 600.

Room II: The room has wooden painted mummy cases (1000 BC); two marble sarcophagi (6th century BC); jewellery, ornaments and figurines found in tombs (1500–525 BC); canopic jars of the same date; a model of a boat (2000 BC); and funerary masks and a painted fabric from the Roman period.

Room III: Displays include the splendid sculptures from the Serapeum of the Canopus of the Egyptian Delta, built by Hadrian in his villa at Tivoli (*see p. 533*) after his journey to Egypt in 130–31, including Serapis, a colossal bust of Isis, and statues of Antinous.

Room IV: The colossal grey marble statue personifies the Nile (1st century AD); there are also two statues of Hapy, the god representing the Nile in flood; and works from the Serapeum in the Campus Martius.

Room V (the Hemicycle): The room follows the shape of the Niche of the Bronze Fir Cone (*described below*). The sandstone head of Mentuhotep II (who reigned from 2010–1998 BC) is displayed here. This is remarkable as the oldest portrait in the museum. The statues in black granite represent the lion-headed goddess Sekhmet (1390–1352 BC). The colossal statue of Queen Tuaa, mother of Rameses II, was brought to Rome by Caligula. Ptolemy Philadelphus (284–246 BC) and his wife Arsinoë are also represented in colossal granite statues. The black bust of Serapis dates from the 2nd century AD.

Room VI: Here is displayed the Grassi collection of small bronzes of sacred animals and gods, and ritual objects.

Room VII: The display comprises terracotta statuettes from Alexandria, and limestone funerary reliefs from Palmyra in Syria (2nd–3rd century AD).

Room VIII: Here are finds from Syria and Palestine from the Neolithic to the Roman period and cylinder seals from Mesopotamia.

Room IX: The exquisite bas-reliefs on display here are from Mesopotamia (884–626 BC).

From the landing outside Room IX stairs lead down to the Chiaramonti Museum, and a door into the large Cortile della Pigna (Courtyard of the Fir Cone), one of the three sections into which Bramante's Cortile del Belvedere was divided. At the north end is a niche where Paul V (1605–21) placed the colossal bronze fir cone (*pigna*), over 4m high, found near the Baths of Agrippa. There are tiny perforations in the cone's scales and it originally formed the centrepiece of a fountain beside the Temple of Isis, near the Pantheon, and gave its name to that district of the city, the *Quartiere della Pigna*. It was made by a certain Cincius Salvius in the 1st century AD. In the Middle Ages it was in the portico of Old St Peter's, together with the two gilt-bronze peacocks (here replaced by copies; the originals are in the New Wing) on either side of it. The fir cone was seen in the portico by Dante and is mentioned in his *Inferno* (*XXXI, 53*).

THE COLOUR OF ANCIENT MARBLE STATUES

When the *Augustus of Prima Porta* (*shown left*) was discovered it was famous since it still bore traces of colour: these have been recuperated after recent restoration work on the statue. It seems that the cloak of Augustus was a rich purple, and the reliefs on his breast-plate were picked out mostly in bright blue and purple. Soon after Winckelmann declared that a carved figure becomes more beautiful the whiter it is, in 1814 studies proved that the famous statue by Pheidias of Jove in Olympia was coloured. As exhibitions in Berlin and Chicago at the end of the 19th century showed, ancient Greek and Roman sculptures were normally coloured to intensify their effect and highlight their meaning, and also to provide greater legibility from afar. Studies are still being carried out to reconstruct the appearance of polychrome statues—it is difficult for us today to imagine these when we are so familiar with abstract and idealized pure white Classical works. However, just as over the centuries from the Etruscans onwards terracotta ornaments and friezes on temples were often enriched by colour, so marble statues were coloured and often also gilded. Thus they were made to fit their settings, where frequently the walls against which they stood were also brightly painted.

Just before the recess there is a statue of Titus (26). In the recess, near a statue of a Priestess of Isis (32), the **bust of Julius Caesar** (30) is one of the best examples to have survived of a posthumous portrait, dating from the time of Augustus. The two restored gilt-bronze Peacocks (30c–d) probably once stood at one of the entrance gates to Hadrian's Mausoleum. The six tombstones (30a, b, e–h) were found near the Mausoleum of Augustus; five of them belong to the Julian family and the sixth to that of Vespasian. Busts include one of Trajan (47), and a very fine **portrait of an unknown Roman** (53; 1st century AD). The sculpture of Selene (the Moon; 43) approaching the sleeping Endymion is a copy of a Hellenistic original of the 4th–3rd century; and the statue of a Tragic Poet (46; the head of Euripides does not belong), is a copy of a 4th-century original, perhaps of Aeschylus.

On the opposite wall is a very fine **statue of Demosthenes** (64). This is a replica of the original statue by Polyeuctus of Athens, set up in Athens in 280 BC to the memory of Demosthenes, the orator and statesman. The hands were originally joined, with the fingers crossed. The mouth plainly suggests the stutter from which the great Athenian suffered. Among the busts are Ptolemy of Numidia (65; 1st century AD); Hadrian (wearing armour; 74); two remarkable Roman portraits (80 and 112; 2nd and 1st century AD).

The **Wounded Amazon** (67) is a replica of one of the statues from the Temple of Diana at Ephesus, by Polyclitus. According to Pliny the Elder, this statue won the prize in a competition in which Polyclitus, Pheidias, Kresilas and Phradmon all entered. The arms and feet were restored by Bertel Thorvaldsen in the early 19th century. There is another statue of the same subject (37) on the wall opposite.

The statue of Hera (76) is a copy of a 5th-century original attributed to Alcamenes; that of Fortune (79—the head, though Roman, is from another figure, the oar and globe are Roman additions) and Artemis (85), are both copies of 4th-century originals. Instead the male figure (82) is thought to be a Greek portrait of the 4th century BC.

In the apse the splendid male bust dating from the late Republican era is thought by some scholars to be possibly a portrait of Mark Antony; it is displayed near a bust of Marcus Aurelius as a young man.

The huge **sculpture of the Nile** (106) is a fine Hellenistic work, found in 1513 near the Temple of Isis with a statue of the Tiber (now in the Louvre). The river-god, who reclines beside a sphinx and holds a horn of plenty, has the calm, benevolent expression of a benefactor who enjoys his munificence. The 16 children who frolic over him are supposed to symbolize the 16 cubits which the Nile rises when in flood. The plinth is decorated with characteristic scenes of life on the banks of the Nile.

The statue of Julia, daughter of Titus (108), is displayed near the famous **Giustiniani Athena** (111), after a Greek original of the 4th century BC, the best existing copy of an original in bronze attributed to Cephisodotus or to Euphranor; it portrays the goddess's twofold function as the divinity of the intellect and of arms. The statue of a man in a toga (114) was given a portrait head of Claudius, just as the statue of an athlete (120) was given the head of Lucius Verus. The delightful **Resting Satyr** (117) is one of several replicas of the famous statue by Praxiteles (others are in the Gallery of Statues; the Gregorian Museum of Pagan Antiquities and in the Musei Capitolini). Emperors portrayed in busts include Commodus (118) and Philip the Arabian (121). No less dignified is the head of a Dacian prisoner, found in Trajan's Forum. Domitian, instead, is here represented wearing a cuirass in a full-length statue. The **Doryphorus of Polyclitus** is one of numerous copies of the famous bronze statue of a young spear-bearer by Polyclitus, the greatest sculptor of the school of Argos and Sikyon, who made a careful study of the proportions of the human body.

It is now necessary to return through the Chiaramonti Museum to the landing outside the exit from the Egyptian Museum.

busts and statues (described from right of the entrance): *Jupiter of Otricoli*, a colossal head of majestic beauty, attributed to Bryaxis (4th century BC); *Antinous as Bacchus*, from a Greek prototype of the 4th century, the drapery, originally of bronze, restored in the early 19th century by Thorvaldsen; bust of Faustina the Elder (d. 141), wife of Antoninus Pius; a beautiful statue of a female divinity, perhaps Demeter, wearing the *peplos*, after a Greek original of the late 5th century BC; head of Hadrian, from his mausoleum; *Hercules*, a colossal statue in gilded bronze, an early Imperial copy of a work of the school of Skopas; bust of Antinous; Juno (the **Barberini Hera**), a Roman copy of a cult image in the manner of the late 5th century; head of a marine divinity (from Pozzuoli), believed to personify the Gulf of Baiae, an interesting example of the fusion of marine elements and human features; Nerva (or Galba), after a seated statue representing Jupiter; bust of Serapis, after a work by Bryaxis; *Claudius as Jupiter*; *Juno Sospita* from Lanuvium, dating from the Antonine period; head of Plotina (d 129), wife of Trajan; head of Julia Domna (d. 217), wife of Septimius Severus; Genius of Augustus; head of Pertinax.

Hall of the Greek Cross (*Sala a Croce Greca*): This is another Neoclassical room by Simonetti, dominated by two magnificent porphyry sarcophagi: that on the left belonged to St Helen, mother of Constantine, decorated with Roman horsemen, barbarian prisoners and fallen soldiers, and that on the right to Constantia, daughter of Constantine, decorated with vine-branches and children bearing Christian symbols of grapes, peacocks and a ram. It was moved here in 1791 from Santa Costanza (*see p. 482*). In the centre is a mosaic pavement with a shield decorated with the head of Minerva and surrounded by the phases of the moon. Between two granite Sphinxes is another exquisite mosaic representing a basket of flowers.

ETRUSCAN MUSEUM

The Etruscan Museum is on the upper floor, reached by the Simonetti Staircase from the landing outside the Room of the Biga (*described on p. 461*). At the top of the stairs, outside the entrance, is a beautiful krater in grey stone.

The museum, one of the most important collections of its kind in existence, was founded in 1837 by Gregory XVI. Many of the objects come from Southern Etruria, but there are also outstanding examples of Greek and Roman art, and a notable collection of Greek vases. In 1989 the Giacinto Guglielmi collection of finds from Vulci was acquired. The exhibits are well labelled (also in English). Apart from the first two rooms, the collection is subdivided according to material.

Room I: Early Iron Age material (9th–8th century BC): in the case on the left are finds from Etruria with Villanovan cinerary urns, and in the case on the right objects from *Latium Vetus* (south of the Tiber), including a reconstructed chariot and weapons of the late 8th century BC.

Room II: The room, decorated with frescoes by Federico Barocci and Taddeo Zuccari, and good stuccoes, contains objects found in 1836 in an Etruscan necropolis south of Cerveteri, where a small group of tumulus chamber-tombs was unearthed. The most important is the splendid **Regolini-Galassi Tomb**, named after its discoverers. Three important people were buried here in 650 BC, including a princess called Larthia, a warrior of high rank, and a priest-king who was cremated. Their funeral equipment includes gold jewellery (a superb gold clasp, with decorations in relief, necklaces and bracelets); ivories; cups; plates; silver ornaments of Graeco-Oriental provenance; a bronze libation bowl with six handles in the shape of animals; and a reconstructed throne. A beautiful cremation urn; a series of pottery statuettes; a bronze incense-burner in the shape of a wagon; a bronze stand with figures in relief; two five-handled jars; silverware including a drinking cup and jug; and small dishes of Eastern origin were also found in this tomb. The *biga* has been reconstructed, as well as a funeral carriage with a bronze bed and funeral couch. The two cases on the window wall contain finds from tombs in the immediate vicinity of the Regolini-Galassi Tomb, including *bucchero* vases in relief, and ceramics from another tomb in the necropolis.

Room III (bronze objects): Frescoed for Pius IV by Pomarancio and Santi di Tito, the room contains a rich collection of bronze objects in common use, including an incense-burner, tripod, buckles, jars, small throne and candelabra, and two statuettes of children. In the centre is the **Mars of Todi**, a very fine bronze statue of a man in armour dating from the beginning of the 4th century BC, but inspired by Greek art of the 5th century BC. The collection of mirrors includes a particularly fine one engraved with Heracles and Atlas, and another with Chalchas, the soothsayer—the designs of both of them are derived from Greek models of the 5th–4th century BC. The *cistae* come mostly from Palestrina, and include a fine oval one found at Vulci, decorated with a battle between Greeks and Amazons, with a handle formed by a satyr and a nymph riding on swans. Among the *paterae* is one with the figure of Eos (Aurora) carrying away Cephalus.

Room IV (works in stone): The two lions (late 6th century BC) used to guard a tomb at Vulci. The sarcophagus of Circeo has a polychrome relief of a procession from a tomb at Cerveteri (late 5th or early 4th century BC) with the deceased lying on the roof. Beyond some small inscribed funerary *cippi* of the Volsinii type (4th–3rd centuries BC) is a cippus from Todi with a bilingual inscription in Latin and Celtic on both sides. A sarcophagus from *Tuscania* has a relief of the battle of the Centaurs. Beyond is a seated female statue in sandstone, from Chiusi (3rd–2nd century BC), and *cippi* in the form of pine cones from Palestrina. A sarcophagus from *Tarquinia* (2nd century BC) shows the Thebans. The works from Vulci (4th century BC) include two horses' heads and a funerary cippus in the form of a capital.

VATICAN PICTURE GALLERY

The Vatican Picture Gallery (*Pinacoteca Vaticana*) is reached by the passageway from the open court beyond the Quattro Cancelli. It owes its origin to Pius VI, but under the Treaty of Tolentino (1797) he was forced to surrender the best works to Napoleon. Of these, 77 were recovered in 1815. The present building in the Lombard Renaissance style, by Luca Beltrami, was opened in 1932. The collection is devoted mostly to Italian painters, and the arrangement is chronological and by schools.

Room I: Displayed here are the earliest works, mostly 14th-century, including the oldest picture in the gallery, a very interesting *Last Judgement*, signed simply 'Giovanni' and 'Niccolò', painters at work in Rome in the late 11th century. The *Christ in Judgement* is by another Roman artist, dating from the following century. Other works are by 14th-century painters from Venice and Bologna not otherwise represented in Rome. There are two 13th-century portraits of St Francis by Giunta Pisano and Margaritone d'Arezzo. On the window wall, the 14th-century Tuscan works are by Giovanni del Biondo, Taddeo Gaddi, and Bernardo Daddi (a beautiful *Legend of St Stephen*). A *Madonna and Saints* is signed and dated 1371 by a certain Giovanni Bonsi, whose work is otherwise unknown.

Room II: In the centre is the **Stefaneschi Altarpiece**, one of the most important works in the collection, commissioned from Giotto for the confessio of Old St Peter's by Cardinal Jacopo Stefaneschi. The cardinal belonged to a patrician Roman family and was known as a patron of the arts (and he also commissioned the huge mosaic of the *Navicella* from Giotto for the atrium of the basilica; *see p. 408*). He lived many years in Avignon where he died in 1343. The polyptych is painted on both sides so that it could be seen at once by the congregation and by the prelates celebrating the service: on one side the central panel shows *Christ Enthroned*, surrounded by angels, with the donor Stefaneschi kneeling at the foot of the throne, with his cardinal's hat at his feet. On either side are two scenes of the *Crucifixion of St Peter* and the *Martyrdom of St Paul*. On the other side, the central panel depicts *St Peter Enthroned*, with St George presenting Stefaneschi to St Peter (Stefaneschi is kneeling and offers up an image of the altarpiece itself to Peter). Pope Celestine V is also shown kneeling making a gift of a codex to Peter (sometimes identified with the *St George Codex* which is still preserved in the Vatican library). The side panels show St James, St Paul, St Andrew and St John the Evangelist. The other Apostles are depicted in the predella panels below, together with the *Madonna and Child*.

Around the walls are some exquisite small paintings by Sienese and Florentine painters of the 14th and 15th centuries, most of whose works cannot be seen anywhere else in Rome: the Sienese school is represented by some of its greatest painters—Pietro Lorenzetti, Simone Martini, Sano di Pietro, Sassetta (*Vision of St Thomas Aquinas* and *Madonna and Child*), and Giovanni di

Paolo; and the Florentine school by Bernardo Daddi (*Madonna of the Magnificat*), and Mariotto di Nardo. There are also panels with stories from the lives of St Benedict and St Nicholas of Bari by Lorenzo Monaco and Gentile da Fabriano, both born around 1370, and the main protagonists of the International Gothic style.

Room III: Works here are by famous masters of the 15th-century Florentine school. The two beautiful panels by **Fra' Angelico**, with three scenes each from the life of St Nicholas of Bari, was part of a polyptych painted for the Dominicans for their church in Perugia around 1437. One panel shows the birth of St Nicholas; his calling to the Church as he stands listening to a sermon with a group of women seated on the grass in front of a pink church close to a bizarre circular building with a golden tower; and the saint delivering a bag of golden coins as a dowry for three poor girls (seen tucked up in bed) otherwise condemned by their father to prostitution. The other panel shows St Nicholas meeting a messenger from the emperor and his rescue of a galleon from shipwreck. Fra' Angelico frescoed a chapel in the Vatican for Nicholas V (*see p. 434*) some ten years after he painted these scenes (and he died in Rome in 1455). Benozzo Gozzoli, who collaborated with Fra' Angelico, is represented here with a painting of *St Thomas Receiving the Virgin's Girdle*. There is also a *Crucifixion*, and *Transition of the Virgin* by Masolino da Panicale, and a triptych of the *Coronation of the Virgin* by Filippo Lippi.

Room IV: Here are some of the most

important works of **Melozzo da Forlì**, who was a follower of Piero della Francesca and had an important influence on the course of painting in the late 15th century in Rome and central Italy. In 1480 he painted a splendid large fresco of the *Ascension* for the apse of Santi Apostoli in Rome. This was detached and the central part is now in the Quirinal, but its eight delightful Angel Musicians are displayed here. A few years earlier Melozzo was commissioned to paint another fresco for the Vatican Library: this has also been detached (and transferred to canvas) and is preserved here. It shows Sixtus IV conferring on the humanist Platina the librarianship of the Vatican in the presence of Giuliano della Rovere (afterwards Julius II), his brother Giovanni, and Girolamo and Raffaele Riario.

The beautiful *Madonna and Saints* is by Marco Palmezzano, who was a collaborator of Melozzo.

Room VI: Fine polyptychs by the late 15th-century **Venetian school**, including the brothers Carlo and Vittorio Crivelli, and Antonio Viviani, whose magnificent *Pesaro Polyptych* signed and dated 1469 (a late work) shows St Anthony Abbot (in relief) beneath Christ in *Pietà* surrounded by eight other saints. Also here are a *Crucifixion* and the *Polyptych of Montelparo* by the Umbrian painter Niccolò di Liberatore (L'Alunno).

Room VII: This room is devoted to works by the **Umbrian school**, the most famous member of whom was Perugino. He is represented by a number of works, including a beautiful *Madonna Enthroned with Saints*.

Room VIII: This, the largest room in the gallery, is devoted to **Raphael**. It contains three of his most famous paintings, as well as two exquisite predellas, and ten tapestries made from his original cartoons. The lovely *Coronation of the Virgin* was his first large composition, painted in Perugia in 1503 when he was just 20 years old. Its predella is exhibited in front in a showcase, with scenes of the *Annunciation*, *Adoration of the Magi*, and *Presentation in the Temple*. The magnificent *Madonna of Foligno* is a mature work painted about 1511. It was a votive offering by Sigismondo Conti in gratitude for his escape when a cannon ball fell on his house during the siege of Foligno. He is shown with St Jerome, and in the background is Foligno during the battle. The painting was kept in the Convent of Sant'Anna in Foligno from 1565 until it was stolen by Napoleon in 1797. The *Transfiguration* is Raphael's last work: the superb scene is shown above the dramatic episode of the healing of the young man possessed of a devil. It was commissioned in 1517 by Cardinal Giuliano de'Medici for the cathedral of Narbonne, but from 1523 to 1809 it hung in the Roman church of San Pietro in Montorio. It is not known how much of the painting had been finished by the time of Raphael's death in 1520, and although the composition is Raphael's, it seems likely that the lower part was completed by his pupils Giulio Romano and Francesco Penni.

The ten celebrated **'Acts of the Apostles' tapestries** were intended for the Sistine Chapel, where they were first exhibited in 1519. They were commissioned by Leo X and woven in Brussels by Pieter van Aelst from cartoons drawn by Raphael in 1515–16. Seven of the cartoons (the other three have been lost) are in the Victoria and Albert Museum, London, though some scholars believe that these seven, which were bought in 1630 by Charles I of England, are 17th-century copies and that all the originals have been lost. Other tapestries from the same cartoons are in Hampton Court Palace near London, in the Palazzo Ducale at Mantua, and in the Palazzo Apostolico at Loreto.

The tapestries have borders of grotesques and broad bases decorated with bronze-coloured designs; most of this work is by Giovanni da Udine. The subjects are: the *Blinding of Elymas* (the tapestry was cut in half during the Sack of Rome in 1527); the *Conversion of St Paul*; the *Stoning of St Stephen*; *St Peter Healing the Paralytic*; the *Death of Ananias*; *St Peter Receiving the Keys*; *The Miraculous Draught of Fishes*; *St Paul Preaching in Athens*; *The Inhabitants of Lystra Sacrificing to St Paul and St Barnabas*; and *St Paul in Prison at Philippi*. These tapestries belong to the so-called 'Old School' series. Ten of the 'New School' series are in the Gallery of Tapestries (*see p. 431*). Also displayed here is a 16th-century Flemish tapestry of the *Last Supper*, derived from Leonardo's famous fresco in Milan.

Room IX: One of the least famous but most memorable works by **Leonardo da Vinci**—his *St Jerome*—is hung here. An early work, dating from around 1480, it was probably painted in Florence, but was left unfinished (like his *Adoration of the Magi* in the Uffizi). It shows the aged penitent saint, the pose and head owing much to Hellenistic sculpture, with his lion with its magnificent tail lightly sketched at his feet, in a shadowy 'desert', which gives an extraordinary sense of space to the painting. As can be seen here, Leonardo's method of painting was to leave the foreground to the last.

Since the discovery in 1991 of an inventory of the possessions of Leonardo's helper and pupil Salaì, we know that he inherited this work along with the *Mona Lisa* and other paintings at Leonardo's death in France, and that he brought them all back with him to Milan. The next we hear of the *St Jerome* is when it was in Rome in the ownership of the painter Angelica Kauffmann. It subsequently passed into the collection of Napoleon's uncle Cardinal Fesch and was then acquired by Pius IX in the mid-19th century.

Another remarkable work here is **Giovanni Bellini's *Pietà***. This was the cimasa of a monumental altarpiece with the *Coronation of the Virgin* painted for the church of San Francesco in Pesaro (where its original frame is still preserved). Scholars have recently suggested the subject is the 'embalming' of the body of Christ.

Room X: Venetian works by Paolo Veronese, Moretto, and Paris Bordone and two paintings by **Titian**: the *Madonna of San Niccolò de'Frari*, and Doge Niccolò Marcello. The beautiful *Madonna of Monteluce* is by Raphael's pupils Giulio Romano and Francesco Penni.

Room XI: An important group of works by Federico Barocci—born in the Marche, but at work in Rome between 1561 and 1563—include a *Rest on the Flight into Egypt*, *Annunciation*, and the *Blessed Michelina*. The *Stoning of St Stephen* is by Vasari, whose famous patron, Cosimo I, is depicted in the marble bas-relief by Perino del Vaga in the centre of the room.

Room XII: The powerful and almost too dramatic *Descent from the Cross* (1602) by **Caravaggio**, which was copied by Rubens, is displayed in this room. Also here are works by his contemporaries Guido Reni, Domenichino and Guercino, all born in the last part of the 16th century and famous protagonists of the **Bolognese school** of painting, but all of whom worked also in Rome. Guercino's works include the *Incredulity of St Thomas, St Margaret of Cortona*, and *Mary Magdalene*. The *Communion of St Jerome,* signed and dated 1614 by Domenichino, was his first important work (and there is a copy of it in mosaic in St Peter's). The *Crucifixion of St Peter* was painted by Guido Reni in 1604–05 for the Roman church of San Paolo alle Tre Fontane, and shows the influence of Caravaggio's painting of the same subject in the church of Santa Maria del Popolo. Other works by this artist include *St Matthew* and a very fine *Virgin in Glory with Saints*. The *Martyrdom of St Processus and St Martinian* is by the less well-known French painter Valentin, who arrived in Rome around 1612 and was much admired by his contemporaries. He was to influence Nicolas Poussin, whose *Martyrdom of St Erasmus* is also hung here. The *Vision of St Romauld* (1631) is one of the most important works by Andrea Sacchi (*see p. 228*). From this room you can enjoy a fine view of the cupola of St Peter's.

Room XIII. The fine painting of *St Francis Xavier* was painted by Anthony van Dyck for the church of Gesù around 1622. Other artists represented here include Sassoferrato, Orazio Gentileschi and Pietro da Cortona.

Room XIV: 17th–18th-century Flemish, Dutch, German, and French painters among them Daniel Seghers, Matthias Stomer and van Bloemen.

Room XV: This room is devoted to portraits, perhaps the best of which is that of Clement IX by Carlo Maratta. Others include Gregory XII, an idealized portrait of the pope who abdicated in 1415, by Muziano; Pius VI by Pompeo Batoni (a painter known for his numerous portraits painted in the days of the Grand Tour); and Benedict XIV by Giuseppe Maria Crespi (painted while still a cardinal—the papal robes were added afterwards). There are also non-Italian works by Pieter Meert and David Teniers the Younger, and a portrait of George IV of England by Sir Thomas Lawrence (donated by the sitter to Pius VII).

Room XVI: Works by the little-known artist Wenceslao Peter (1742–1829).

Room XVII: Clay models by **Bernini**, including a *bozzetto* for the tabernacle of the Holy Sacrament in St Peter's and heads of Fathers of the Church and angels. The small inscription of 1638 commemorates the construction of one of the *campanili* of St Peter's which was later demolished.

Room XVIII: A very fine collection of 16th- and 17th-century Russian and Greek icons.

Gregorian Museum of Pagan Antiquities, Pio Christian Museum and Ethnological Missionary Museum

(*At the time of writing, the collections can only be visited by appointment.*) The striking building housing these museums was designed by a group of architects headed by Fausto and Lucio Passarelli, and opened in 1970, when the collections formerly housed in the Lateran Palace were moved here. The Gregorian Museum of Pagan Antiquities (*Museo Gregoriano Profano*) was founded by Gregory XVI (1831–46) to house the overflow of the Vatican Museums and the yields of excavations at Rome, Ostia, Veio and Cerveteri. It was enriched by further excavations up to 1870, and at the end of the 19th century by a collection of pagan inscriptions. It contains superb examples of Classical sculpture, including original Greek works and Roman copies, as well as mosaics and sarcophaghi. The Pio Christian Museum was founded by Pius IX in 1854 with objects found mainly in the catacombs, including a valuable collection of Christian sarcophagi of the 2nd–5th centuries, important for the study of early Christian iconography, and the largest and finest collection of Christian inscriptions in existence. The Ethnological Missionary Museum was established by Pius XI in 1927 as a development of the Vatican Missionary Exhibition of 1924–26. The primitive and more recent cultures of each country are arranged according to subject matter.

OUTSIDE THE ANCIENT WALLS

SAN LORENZO FUORI LE MURA
Map p. 617, 1C

Open 8–12.30 & 3–7.20. Best to visit in the afternoon since funerals are often held at 9.30, 10.15, 11 and 11.45. The huge, busy Piazza San Lorenzo is well served by public transport, including bus no. 71 from Piazza San Silvestro (map p. 622, 1C), and trams 19 and 3.

The basilica of San Lorenzo fuori le Mura is one of the seven pilgrimage churches of Rome. It has remarkable architectural features, including two storeys of ancient columns in the presbytery, superb Cosmati work, and extensive catacombs off the lovely cloister. Despite serious war damage it retains its venerable character. Although it is in an unattractive part of the city, it is a much more peaceful and friendly church to visit than some of the other major basilicas, for example San Paolo fuori le Mura and San Giovanni in Laterano.

St Lawrence is thought to have been a deacon under Pope Sixtus II, and despite the tradition that he was roasted alive on a gridiron (and the numerous paintings and sculptures which show the scene), he was probably in fact beheaded in 258. He was buried here in the Campo Verano (*see below*). He has always been venerated as one of the most important early Roman martyrs, and by the 4th century was considered one of the patron saints of the city, together with St Peter and St Paul.

The basilica consists of two churches placed end to end. Parallel to the 4th-century covered cemetery basilica built by Constantine in honour of St Lawrence, Pelagius II built a new church in 579. In 1216 Honorius III demolished the apse and built onto it another church, with a different orientation (placing the entrance at the opposite end). The churches were skilfully restored in 1864–70 by Virginio Vespignani.

San Lorenzo was the only church in Rome to suffer serious damage during the Second World War, when it was partly destroyed by Allied bombs (the target was meant to have been Tiburtina railway station close by): the façade and the south wall were carefully rebuilt in 1949.

The Exterior

The simple Romanesque campanile dates from the 12th century. The reconstructed 13th-century narthex of six antique Ionic columns has a carved cornice and a mosaic frieze. This is thought to be the work of the Vassalletto family (*see p. 479*). Inside are three Roman sarcophagi (the one with wine-harvest scenes is particularly interesting), and a monument (1954) by Giacomo Manzù to the statesman Alcide de Gasperi, the Christian Democrat who dominated Italian politics between 1943 and 1953. The 13th-century frescoes (restored in the 19th century and again after war damage) depict the lives of St Lawrence and St Stephen.

The Interior

The lovely light, basilican interior, with a raised chancel and no transept, retains its 13th-century appearance. Twenty-two Ionic columns of granite support an architrave, and the floor is paved with a 12th-century Cosmatesque mosaic. Near the entrance is the tomb of Cardinal Fieschi, a large Roman sarcophagus with a splendid relief of a marriage scene, converted to its present use in 1256; it was rebuilt from the original fragments after the war. In the nave on the right is a beautiful Cosmatesque ambone, with exquisite carvings and marble inlay, which incorporates a paschal candlestick with a twisted stem.

The lovely baldacchino in the choir is signed by Giovanni, Pietro, Angelo and Sasso, sons of a master mason called Paolo (1147); the upper part was restored in the 19th century. It has porphyry columns with exquisitely carved bases, surrounded by a miniature Cosmati pavement. Beneath are preserved the relics of St Lawrence and other martyrs. Steps lead up to the beautiful raised chancel, which incorporates the 6th-century church (except for its apse, which was demolished), on a slightly different axis. The Corinthian columns with magnificent huge capitals support a charming entablature constructed out of miscellaneous antique fragments mostly dating from the 1st century AD and, above, a delicate arcaded gallery with smaller columns and windows with transennae. The two large antique capitals at the west end of the chancel are decorated with trophies and winged Victories. From here can be seen the inner face of the triumphal arch, which bears a remarkable 6th-century mosaic (reset during the Byzantine revival) of Christ seated on a globe flanked by St Peter, St Paul, St Stephen, St Lawrence and St Hippolytus and Pope Pelagius II offering a model of the church. Beneath the two latticed windows are representations of Bethlehem and Jerusalem. On the arch is a beautiful mosaic inscription and, on the soffit, a ribbon charmingly decorated with fruit and flowers.

There are two long marble benches and at the east end the handsome 13th-century episcopal throne with a Cosmati screen of the same date.

The remains of the earliest church, cloister and catacombs are all shown on request at the sacristy. The lower level has some remains of the earliest basilica, including some of the original pillars, and in its narthex is the mausoleum of Pius IX (d. 1878; *see p. 421*), rebuilt by Raffaele Cattaneo in 1881 and decorated with mosaics by Ludovico Seitz. Beneath the chancel St Lawrence and two companions are buried.

The cloister and cemetery

The charming cloister with two storeys overlooking a little garden dates from 1187–91. The entrance to the extensive **Catacombs of St Cyriaca**, where the body of St Lawrence is said to have been placed after his death in 258, is here. They are on five levels, although only the middle one can be visited. Although lights have been installed, it is sometimes possible (on request) to visit them by candlelight. The catacombs, which have been known since earliest times, are now devoid of paintings and have only a few inscriptions: all the others have been removed and are now exhibited on the walls of the cloisters.

On the right of the church is the monastery, owned by Franciscan Capuchin friars since 1857. The entrance has four wide arches supported by Roman columns and a charming gallery above.

Also here is the entrance to the huge municipal cemetery, called **Campo Verano** since it is on the site of the estate of the Emperor Lucius Verus. It was designed by Giuseppe Valadier in 1807–12, with a chapel and quadriporticus by Virginio Vespignani. The four colossal allegorical figures at the entrance date from 1878. Among the tombs, in the first avenue to the left is that of the soldier-poet Goffredo Mameli (d. 1849; *see p. 390*). On the high ground beside Via Tiburtina is a memorial of the Battle of Mentana (1867), when the French and papal troops had a victory over Garibaldi.

The University

Piazza San Lorenzo, a busy traffic hub and bus and tram terminus, is traversed by Via Tiburtina, on the site of the ancient Roman road to *Tibur* (now Tivoli). Viale Regina Elena leads northwest between the Istituto Superiore di Sanità, with a research centre for chemical microbiology, and the Città Universitaria on the left, an interesting example of Fascist architecture. The faculty buildings and chapel were designed on a monumental scale by Marcello Piacentini and completed in 1935, in which year the seat of the University of Rome was transferred here from Palazzo della Sapienza. Numerous other buildings have been built in this century (some by Giovanni Michelucci, the rationalist architect (who, with others, designed Florence's main railway station) as the university has expanded. The entrance is in Piazzale Aldo Moro (*map p. 617, 1B*), near a bronze statue of Minerva by Arturo Martini. In the Rector's Palace there is a fresco by Mario Sironi, an artist of the 'Novecento' (*see p. 199*). The University Library was founded by Alexander VII and now has more than a million volumes. The scientific study collections are open by appointment (*see p. 545*). The Policlinico (*map p. 616, 4B*) is a large teaching hospital, designed by Giulio Podesti in 1893.

SOUTH OF PORTA SAN PAOLO
Map p. 621, 2–3A and p. 5

Underground line B from Termini and Colosseum stations runs to Piramide for Porta San Paolo and the Centrale Montemartini and to San Paolo for the basilica of San Paolo fuori le Mura. Bus no. 23 links Piazza Pia (Castel Sant'Angelo) via Trastevere with Porta San Paolo (Piazzale Ostiense). It continues via a request stop (the third from Piazzale Ostiense) for the Centrale Montemartini to San Paolo fuori le Mura.

The well-preserved Porta San Paolo (*map p. 621, 2A*) was the *Porta Ostiensis* of ancient Rome; its inner side is original, with two arches from the time of Aurelian. The outer face, rebuilt by Honorius in 402, has been restored. The gate houses the **Museo della**

able to make this journey on foot, but bus no. 23 follows the road to the basilica of San Paolo 2km away (get off at the third request stop from Piazzale Ostiense for the Centrale Montemartini). For bus and metro from the centre, see p. 469.

From Piazzale Ostiense the broad, uninteresting Via Ostiense leads almost due south through a depressing part of town. About halfway along, more or less opposite the Mercati Generali—the old wholesale food markets of Rome—and set back from the road on the right (not well signposted), is the Centrale Montemartini, with a superb display of Roman Classical statues from the Capitoline Museums.

Built in 1912, this was the first public electrical plant to be opened in Rome, and was named after its designer, Giovanni Montemartini. Operated by diesel and steam, it provided enough power to illuminate half the streets and *piazze* of the city. It continued to function throughout the Second World War and only fell into disuse in 1963. It was restored by the Rome water and electricity board (ACEA) in 1990 as a superb exhibition space and is also of the greatest interest as a monument of industrial archaeology.

Since 1997 some 400 Classical sculptures formerly kept in the Musei Capitolini have been exhibited here. They are beautifully displayed and labelled (also in English). Most of them were found in excavations in Rome at the end of the 19th or in the early 20th century, when many villas and gardens were destroyed to make room for new buildings, including the famous Villa Boncompagni-Ludovisi (*see pp. 225–26*) between the Pincian and Quirinal hills.

Palm trees and two elegant lamp posts designed by Duilio Cambellotti lead up to the fine façade.

Ground floor

Sala delle Colonne: This hall has exhibits from the earliest Archaic period: finds from the excavations around Sant'Omobono, near the foot of the Campidoglio; a fresco of the 3rd century BC with military scenes, found on the Esquiline Hill in 1873; finds from the tomb of the Cornelii discovered in Via Marco Polo in 1956; statues from the *area sacra* in Via Tiburtina; and the head of a girl in a helmet made out of *peperino* from the 2nd century BC, found near the Villa Aldobrandini on the Quirinal Hill.

At the end of the room is a fragment of a bed with very delicate inlaid decorations in bone, from Greece (late 1st cen-tury BC), and exquisite small mosaics from Via San Lorenzo in Panisperna, dating from the same century. There is a case of finds from a *domus* unearthed in Via del Babuino, and a bronze litter found on the Esquiline, known as the 'Lettiga Capitolina'.

Long Hall: Here are displayed statues and Republican heads including the well known **Togato Barberini**, the statue of a man in a toga carrying two busts, one of his father and one of his grandfather. In the hemicycle is an early portrait of Augustus (27–20 BC) found in Via del Mare. The headless *Aphrodite* is a replica of a statue by Callimachus (late 5th century BC). The turbines and tools used when the electrical plant was still functioning can also be seen here.

First floor

Sala Macchine (Engine Room): Here there is a superb display of Roman sculpture inspired by Greek masterpieces. At the end are five very fine statues of Athena: the colossal statue found in Via del Corso is inspired by a Greek original by Kresilas of 430 BC (the head is a cast from a statue now in the Louvre). In the centre of the hall by the stairs are exhibited sculpted heads and, on the right, *Young Athlete*, a head of Hercules; a beautiful head of an Amazon; a head of Dionysus; and a statue of a discus thrower. The statues in the centre of the room include a draped figure of Apollo (now damaged, but once portrayed as playing the *cetra*), two female figures wearing the *peplos*, and *Aphrodite* from a Greek original by Praxiteles. The two grey statues nearby are particularly interesting: that of a praying female figure has recently been identified as Agrippina the Younger, wife of Claudius. It is made out of basanite, a precious stone from the Egyptian desert, and was unearthed on the Caelian Hill: the original head was recently found in Copenhagen. The restored figure of the *Victory of Samothrace* is a Hellenistic work in *bigio antico*. Close by are statues and a metope of warriors. In front of the temple pediment (*see below*) are sculptures from other such pediments including a colossal figure of Jove and a female figure, both found near the Theatre of Marcellus and thought to date from the Augustan era.

Well displayed above steps is the reconstructed **pediment from the Temple of Apollo Sosianus**, dedicated to Apollo Medico in 433 BC and restored by the consul Sosius in 33 BC, three columns of which survive near the Theatre of Marcellus (*see p. 314*). The nine remarkably fine sculptural fragments represent a battle between Greeks and Amazons and are thought to date from 450–425 BC. At the end of the room, behind the pediment, are more fragments from the temple including a frieze with a triumphal procession, and the reconstructed *aedicula* of the cella of the temple. Sculpture found near the Capitoline Hill, including three colossal heads of Hercules and two female statues, dating from the 1st century BC, are also exhibited here. There follow finds from the temples in Largo Torre Argentina and the Theatre of Pompey, including a statue of a seated Muse, and fragments of a colossal statue of Fortuna—the head, arm and two feet show that it must have been some 8m high—attributed to a Greek artist working in Rome in 101 BC. The last two sections in the corridor behind the huge generator display reliefs from the time of Claudius, a pastoral scene with two cows, and Imperial portraits. Along the window wall are portrait heads and a statue of Icarus.

Sala delle Caldaie (Boiler Room): Sculptures which used to decorate private residences are exhibited here.

Many of those residences were the so-called *horti*, or grand villas with large gardens built on the hills of Rome and owned by the wealthiest citizens and members of the Imperial families. Finds from the Gardens of Maecenas on the Esquiline (*see p. 254*) include the so-called *Auriga* or charioteer, a copy of a 5th-century original. It was formerly attached to a statue of a horse, also displayed here, and is now thought to represent a hero, possibly Theseus, driving his chariot. The sculptures were found in 1874. The beautiful *Dancing Maenad*, in relief, is from an original by Callimachus, and the rhyton is a neo-Attic work signed by Pontius, and formerly used as a fountain. The statue of *Hercules in Combat* is from an original by Lysippus. Also from these gardens are the statues of Muses, a colossal statue of Demeter, and a very beautiful *Head of an Amazon*, a copy of a famous bronze work by Polyclitus.

Finds from the Gardens of Sallust (*see p. 550*) include a delicately carved fragment of a frieze, a kneeling statue of an Amazon from a temple pediment, and a herm of Hercules with a beard. The sculptures from the Gardens of Lamiani on the Esquiline include a funerary stele with the relief of a young girl holding a dove, a Greek original of 500–490 BC, and the head of a Centaur. Also here is the **Esquiline Venus**, the figure of a beautiful young girl probably connected with the cult of Isis, an eclectic work dating from the 1st century BC. Although the arms are missing,

we know that the girl was depicted tying up her hair before taking a swim. Nearby are two fine female statues, similar in style and date to the Venus. To the right is a large marble vase, beautifully decorated with garlands of acanthus, and on the left two handsome large kraters, one with Dionysiac scenes and the other with a relief of the marriage of Paris and Helen. Near the side wall is a fragment of an exquisite polychrome mosaic found near Santa Bibiana, with hunting scenes. The charming statue of a Muse—probably Polyhymnia—leaning on a pillar of rock, was found near the Variani Gardens. Close to the wall are statues found in the Gardens of Licinius (*see p. 552*), including a charming seated figure of a girl, a Hadrianic copy of a Hellenistic work, and *Dionysus with a Panther*. The three portraits of Hadrian, his wife Sabina, and mother-in-law Matidia were found in the Tauriani Gardens. On the window wall are the head of a Strategist, two statues of Pothos, and a headless statue of a Roman general found in a *domus* beneath Via Cavour. A series of small sculptures are displayed together since they were found near Porta San Lorenzo and once probably decorated a nymphaeum. They include *Wounded Satyr*, a fragment of a group of a giant fighting two satyrs, derived from the *gigantomachia* of Pergamon. Towards the end wall are a series of funerary monuments and two very fine sarcophagi.

Stairs lead up to a balcony with a good view of the mosaic with hunting scenes, where two cases display gilded bronze decoration and beautiful gems found in the Lamiani Gardens.

SAN PAOLO FUORI LE MURA

Open 7–6.30. Cloisters 9–1 & 3–6 (except Sun). Map p. 5. For public transport see p. 469 above.

San Paolo fuori le Mura, 2km from Porta San Paolo, is the largest church in Rome after St Peter's. It is one of the four great patriarchal basilicas of Rome, and one of the three which have the privilege of extraterritoriality. The church commemorates the martyrdom of St Paul and is believed to contain the Apostle's tomb.

According to Christian tradition, a Roman matron called Lucina buried the body of Paul in a vineyard on the site of the church. A small shrine existed here when, in 384, a large basilica was begun by Valentinian II and Theodosius the Great at the request of Pope Damasus. It was enlarged by Theodosius' son, Honorius, and decorated with mosaics at the expense of Galla Placidia, sister of Honorius. After the additions made by Leo III (pope 795–816), it became the largest and most beautiful church in Rome. In the 9th century it was pillaged by the Saracens and John VIII (872–82) enclosed it in a fortified village known as *Giovannipolis*. It was restored c. 1070 by Abbot Hildebrand, later Gregory VII. The façade, overlooking the Tiber, was preceded by a colonnaded quadriporticus. Before the Reformation, the king of England was *ex officio* a canon of San Paolo and the abbot, in return, was decorated with the Order of the Garter. This great basilica was almost entirely destroyed by fire on the night of 15th–16th July 1823.

Leo XII ordered the reconstruction, which was directed by Pasquale Belli, Pietro Bosio and Pietro Camporese, and afterwards by Luigi Poletti. In the rebuilding it was decided to use new materials instead of repairing the damaged structure, although in plan and dimensions, if not in spirit, the new basilica follows the old one almost exactly. The transept was consecrated by Gregory XVI in 1840 and the complete church by Pius IX in 1854. In 1891 an explosion in a neighbouring fort broke most of the stained glass, which was replaced by slabs of alabaster. In March 1966 a service was celebrated here by Pope Paul VI and the Archbishop of Canterbury, when they issued a joint declaration of amity.

The present frigid 19th-century reconstruction, 'which looks outside like a very ugly railway station' (Augustus Hare, *Walks in Rome*), has none of the atmosphere of the other ancient basilicas in Rome, and the sale of souvenirs in numerous parts of the church disturbs a visit.

The Exterior

The Romanesque campanile was pulled down to make way for the unattractive bell-tower by Luigi Poletti. Poletti was also responsible for the north portico, which incorporates 12 Hymettan marble columns from the old basilica. On one of the nearest columns, beneath the frieze, is a 4th-century inscription of Pope Siricius. The façade (right) is preceded by a great quadriporticus with 146 enormous monolithic granite columns, added by Guglielmo Calderini between 1892 and 1928. The elaborate frescoes on the façade date from 1885. The central bronze doors **1** are by Antonio

centre of the ceiling, which is richly decorated with stuccoes in white and gold, are the arms of Pius IX. The paintings between the windows, executed in the mid-19th century and depicting scenes from the life of St Paul, are by Pietro Gagliardi, Francesco Podesti, Guglielmo de Sanctis, Francesco Coghetti and Cesare Mariani; under these (and in the aisles), forming a frieze, are the portraits in mosaic of all the popes from St Peter to John Paul II. In the outermost aisles are niches with statues of the Apostles. The six huge alabaster columns beside the doors were presented by Mohammed Ali of Egypt. The statue of St Peter **3** is by Alberto Giacometti and that of St Paul **4** by Salvatore Revelli, both dating from the 19th century.

The triumphal arch, a relic of the old basilica, is supported by two colossal granite columns. Its much-restored mosaics represent Christ blessing in the Greek manner, with angels, symbols of the Evangelists, the Elders of the Apocalypse, and St Peter and St Paul. On the other face of the arch are the remains of early mosaics by Pietro Cavallini. Over the high altar, supported by four porphyry columns, is a splendid tabernacle **5** by Arnolfo di Cambio and his companion Pietro (Oderisi?, 1285). The huge 12th-century Paschal candlestick **6** is an exquisite work by Nicolò di Angelo and Pietro Vassalletto.

The **tomb of St Paul** is traditionally believed to be beneath the altar, where there is a 1st-century tomb surrounded by Christian and pagan burials. The inscription *paolo apostolo mart* dates from the time of Constantine.

The magnificent ceiling of the transept is decorated with the arms of Pius VII, Leo XII, Pius VIII and Gregory XVI, as well as with those of the basilica, an arm holding a sword. The walls are covered with rare marbles. The Corinthian pilasters are made up of fragments of the old columns. The great mosaic of the apse was executed c. 1220 by Venetian craftsmen sent by Doge Pietro Ziani at the request of Pope Honorius III. Although it was heavily restored after damage in the fire of 1823, it is a very beautiful work showing Christ blessing in the Greek manner, with St Peter, St Andrew, St Paul and St Luke; at the feet of Christ is Pope Honorius III; below this, a gem-studded Cross on the altar, with angels and apostles. On the outer face of the arch are the Virgin and Child with St John blessing Pope John XXII.

At either end of the transept is an altar of malachite and lapis lazuli, presented by Nicholas I of Russia: the mosaic **7** is a copy from the *Coronation of the Virgin* by Giulio Romano, and the *Conversion of St Paul* **8** is by Vincenzo Camuccini. The Chapel of St Stephen **9** has a statue of the saint by Rinaldo Rinaldi, and paintings of the *Expulsion from the Sanhedrin* by Francesco Coghetti, and the *Stoning of St Stephen* by Francesco Podesti. The Chapel of the Crucifix **10**, by Carlo Maderno, was the only chapel saved in the fire. On the altar is a crucifix attributed to Tino da Camaino. Also here are statues of St Bridget by Stefano Maderno, and of a saint in wood. In this chapel, in 1541, St Ignatius de Loyola and the first Jesuits took the corporate oaths that formally established their society as a religious order. The Chapel of the Choir, or of St Lawrence **11**, with choir stalls, is by Guglielmo Calderini. It contains a 15th-century marble triptych. The Chapel of St Benedict **12** is a sumptuous work by Luigi Poletti, with a reproduction of the cella of an ancient temple; the 12 fluted columns

are from Veio. The Sala del Martirologio, with 13th-century frescoes, is inappropri-
ately used for selling souvenirs.

The cloisters and baptistery

The cloisters (*open 9–1 & 3–6; closed Sun*) of the old Benedictine convent have coupled
colonnettes of different forms decorated with mosaics and tiny couchant animals—most
of which have now disappeared—between the columns. In the centre is a rose garden.
The cloisters were begun under Abbot Pietro da Capua (1193–1208) and finished after
1228, and are the work—at least in part—of the Vassalletti, a Roman family of sculptors who were active in the 12th and 13th centuries, and who also worked on the cloister of San Giovanni in Laterano. Pietro, who is known to have been at work between
1154 and 1186, was its best-known member. Along the walls are placed numerous
inscriptions and sculptured fragments, both Christian and pagan. In the walk to the
right is the statue of a Prophet; an inscription recording the suicide of Nero, probably a
17th-century forgery; a large sarcophagus which retains its lid and very worn reliefs
depicting the story of Apollo and Marsyas; and a seated statue of Boniface IX. Off the
cloister are the Chapel of Reliquaries, with a gilded silver cross, and the Pinacoteca, with
works by Antoniazzo Romano (*Madonna and Four Saints*) and Bramantino (*Flagellation*),
as well as old prints showing the damage caused by the fire.

The baptistery, designed by Arnaldo Foschini on a Greek-cross plan in 1930, leads
into the vestibule preceding the south door of the church, which contains a colossal
statue of Gregory XVI by Rinaldo Rinaldi, and 13th-century mosaics from the old
basilica.

ABBAZIA DELLE TRE FONTANE

About 1km east of the point where Via Cristoforo Colombo crosses Via delle Tre
Fontane, and reached by the latter and Via Laurentina, is the Abbazia delle Tre
Fontane (*map p. 5*). This was built on the traditional site of the martyrdom of St Paul,
whose severed head, rebounding three times, is supposed to have caused three fountains to spring up. A monastic community from Asia Minor was established here by
641. St Bernard is believed to have stayed here on his visit to Rome in 1138–40. Three
churches were built, but the locality was afterwards abandoned as malarial. In 1868
it was acquired by the Trappists, who drained the ground and planted large groves of
eucalyptus. A eucalyptus liqueur is distilled in the community. This and chocolate
made by the monks are on sale.

An ilex avenue leads to a medieval fortified gate with a frescoed vault. A small garden contains Classical fragments, and is filled with the sound of doves and a fountain.
Ahead is the porch of Santi Vincenzo ed Anastasio. It was founded by Honorius I
(625), rebuilt by Honorius III (1221), and restored by the Trappists. The plain, spacious interior preserves its marble windows. In the nave are poorly restored frescoes
of the Apostles (16th century).

On the right, on high ground, is Santa Maria Scala Coeli, an old church with an octagonal interior, rebuilt by Giacomo della Porta (1582). The design can best be appreciated from the outside. It owes its name to the legend that St Bernard, while celebrating Mass, saw in a vision the soul for which he was praying ascend by a ladder from purgatory to heaven. The Cosmatesque altar that was the scene of this miracle is still preserved in the crypt. The mosaics in the left-hand apse, of Saints with Clement VIII and his nephew Cardinal Pietro Aldobrandini, are by Francesco Zucchi from designs by Giovanni de' Vecchi.

From the left of this church an avenue leads to San Paolo alle Tre Fontane, a 5th-century church, rebuilt by della Porta in 1599, with a good façade. Inside to the right is the pillar to which St Paul is supposed to have been bound; on the floor are two Roman mosaic pavements from Ostia.

SANT'AGNESE FUORI LE MURA & DISTRICT

Express bus no. 60 along Via Nomentana from Piazza Venezia and Via Nazionale. Map p. 616, 2C.

At the beginning of the wide Via Nomentana, which runs northeast on the line of the ancient Roman consular road, traversing a residential district of the city with palaces and villas, many with beautiful gardens, stands **Porta Pia**. This was Michelangelo's last architectural work, commissioned by Pius IV in 1561 (the exterior face was added in 1868 by Virginio Vespignani). Porta Pia is famous in Italian history since it was here that the Italian troops under General Raffaele Cadorna entered Rome on 20th September 1870, and so brought to an end the temporal power of the popes. The breach was a few steps to the left of the gate, in Corso d'Italia, where there are commemorative inscriptions.

About 2km from Porta Pia, opposite a 19th-century fountain of the Acqua Marcia, stands the church of **Sant'Agnese fuori le Mura**, in an important group of early Christian buildings. According to a Christian tradition, St Agnes, having refused the advances of a praetor's son, was exposed in the Stadium of Domitian, where her nakedness was covered by the miraculous growth of her hair. She was then condemned to be burned at the stake, but the flames did not touch her, so that she was finally beheaded by Diocletian. The *pallium* or vestment worn by the pope is made of the wool of lambs blessed annually on the day of her festival, 21st January.

The buildings consist of the ruins of a large cemetery basilica built, probably after Constantine's death, by his elder daughter Constantia in 337–50 on her estate, next to the tomb where the martyred St Agnes had been buried in 304. Above the crypt sanctuary and catacombs Honorius I (625–38) built a second church, when the Constantinian basilica was already in ruins. Next to the basilica, with an entrance from its south aisle, Constantia built the mausoleum in which she and her sister Helena were buried. On the right of the court is a hall (originally a cellar) into which Pius IX and his entourage fell unharmed after the collapse of the floor of the room above in 1855.

The basilica

Open Tues–Sat 9–12 & 4–6; Sun 4–6; Mon 9–12; T: 06 861 0840. Map p. 616, 2C. The most direct entrance is through the garden on Via Sant'Agnese, but you can also enter through the gate of the convent of the Canonici Lateranensi on Via Nomentana.

Beyond a tower is the entrance to the 7th-century basilica, restored in 1479 by Giuliano della Rovere (later Julius II), by Cardinal Varallo after the sack of 1527, and by Pius IX in 1856. It is reached by a staircase of 45 white marble steps (1590), the walls of which are covered with inscriptions from the catacombs, including St Damasus' record of the martyrdom of St Agnes.

In the interior of the church (best light in the afternoon), the nave and aisles are separated by 14 ancient Roman columns of breccia and *pavonazzetto*, mottled and veined. There is a narthex for the catechumens, and a matroneum was built over the aisles and the west end in 620. The carved and gilded wood ceiling dates from 1606 but was restored in 1855. In the second chapel on the right, over a Cosmati altar, is a fine relief of St Stephen and St Lawrence by Andrea Bregno (1490), and a bust of Christ, probably the work of Nicolas Cordier after a lost work by Michelangelo. In the second chapel on the left there is a 15th-century fresco of the *Madonna and Child*. On the high altar, in which are preserved the relics of St Agnes and St Emerentiana, her foster-sister, is an antique torso of Oriental alabaster restored in 1600 as a statue of St Agnes, beneath a baldacchino (1614) supported on four porphyry columns. On the left of the altar is a fine candlestick, thought to be a neo-Attic work of the 2nd century. In the apse is the original plain marble decoration and an ancient episcopal throne. Above is a beautiful mosaic (625–38) representing St Agnes between Pope Symmachus and Pope Honorius I, two restorers of the basilica, a model of which is held by Honorius. The simplicity of the composition against a dull gold background is striking. The dedicatory inscription below records how much Honorius spent on the church.

The catacombs

The Catacombs of Sant'Agnese (entered from the left aisle) are the best-preserved and among the most interesting Roman catacombs. They were discovered in 1865–66. They are seldom visited by large groups, and the atmosphere offers a marked contrast to that in the more famous catacombs on the Via Appia. They are shown by a well-informed guide on a tour which normally takes about 40mins. They contain no paintings but there are numerous inscriptions and many of the *loculi* are intact and closed with marble or terracotta slabs. They may date from before 258, but certainly not later than 305; the oldest zone extends to the left of the basilica. A chapel was built where the body of St Agnes was found, and a silver coffer provided in 1615 by Pope Paul V.

SANTA COSTANZA

Open Tues–Sat 9–12 & 4–6; Sun 4–6; Mon 9–12. Map p. 616, 2C.
On the other side of the entrance court and garden a path leads to the round mau-

soleum of Constantia, known as the church of Santa Costanza since the 9th century. This was built by Constantia as a mausoleum for herself and her sister Helena, daughters of the Emperor Constantine, probably before 354. It is remarkably well preserved and in a lovely peaceful spot. The charming interior is annular in plan: 24 granite columns in pairs with beautiful Corinthian capitals and pulvinated imposts support the dome, which is 22.5m in diameter. There are 12 large windows with restored transennae beneath the dome. The pavement is in terracotta except between the columns where it is marble, and there are bare brick walls. On the barrel vaulting of the encircling ambulatory are remarkable very early Christian mosaics (4th century), pagan in character and designed in pairs on a white ground. They were restored by Vincenzo Camuccini in 1834–40. Those flanking the entrance have a geometric design, and the next a circular motif with animals and figures. Scenes of the wine harvest and vine tendrils with grapes follow, and the fourth pair have roundels with a leaf design, busts and figures. On either side of the sarcophagus are leaves, branches, amphorae and exotic birds. Over the sarcophagus only a fragment remains of a mosaic with a star design. The two side niches also have fine mosaics (5th or 7th century). The mosaics in the dome were destroyed when they were replaced by the frescoes in 1620. Constantia's magnificent porphyry sarcophagus was replaced here by a cast when it was removed to the Vatican in 1791 (*see p. 458*); Helena's sarcophagus was removed in 1606.

Two small gates on the right of the mausoleum lead into an overgrown garden and orchard with the remains of the huge Constantinian basilica, identified in 1954 and still being excavated. They include the outer walls with a round window in the apse, sustained on the outside by huge buttresses. In plan it was typical of the other early cemetery basilicas of Rome, such as San Lorenzo fuori le Mura and San Sebastiano.

THE CATACOMBS OF PRISCILLA

Open Tues–Sun 8.30–12.30 & 2.30–5; closed Mon, and in Jan; T: 06 8620 6272. Map p. 5. Visitors are taken in groups by an English-speaking nun or guide; the tour lasts about half an hour, and is easy under foot and well lit. Entrance at no. 430 Via Salaria. To get there, take bus no. 92 from Termini Station or no. 63 from Piazza Venezia (nearest stop, Via di Priscilla).

The catacombs of Priscilla, among the most important and interesting in Rome, are attached to a monastery of some 25 Benedictine nuns. Many popes were buried here between 309 and 555, and they were discovered in 1578. They extend for some 13km and it is estimated that there must have been about 40,000 burials here. They are on three levels, but only the uppermost level, dating from the 2nd century AD, is accessible. The first area shown is that of the '*arenario*', probably a *pozzolana* stone quarry, where the Cubiculum of the Velata has well-preserved late 3rd-century paintings, including a woman in prayer, representing the deceased who was buried here, between scenes of her marriage and her motherhood. In the pretty vault is the *Good*

Shepherd, surrounded by sheep, trees, peacocks and other birds. In the side lunettes are scenes from the Old Testament (three Hebrew youths being saved from fire by an angel, and the *Sacrifice of Abraham*). Above the entrance is a depiction of *Jonah and the Whale*. In the long corridors can be seen the burial places of both adults and children and fragments of the marble slabs carved with Christian symbols that once closed the tombs. Some tombs are preserved intact behind a wall dating from the 4th century. In another area of the catacombs, presumed to be near a martyr's tomb, there is a remarkable fragment of stucco decoration combined with painting, in a vault dating from 220 AD. The Good Shepherd is depicted again, flanked by two sheep amongst graceful trees. The figures of the Madonna and Child are the oldest known representations of this subject: next to the Virgin stands a prophet pointing up to a star.

The cryptoporticus, with cross-vaulting, was part of a villa of Priscilla's family, the Acilii, which probably stood above the cemetery and later became a chapel. There are photographs which help you to identify the frescoes in the so-called 'Greek Chapel', which is shown next. This funerary chapel, named after the Greek inscriptions found here, is interesting for its 3rd-century decorations in stucco and fresco. A banquet scene against a bright red ground, on the apse arch, includes the figure of a veiled woman (third from the right), and there are biblical scenes (the *Three Wise Men*, *Susanna and the Elders*, *Moses Striking the Rock*) as well as a pagan bust representing Summer.

THE VIA APPIA ANTICA
& THE CATACOMBS

The Via Appia originally began at *Porta Capena*, a gate in the Servian Walls near the Circus Maximus (*map p. 621, 1B*), but after Aurelian built his walls across it about 1.5km outside the Servian circle, this first stretch of the road was enclosed within the city limits and became known as its 'urban section'.

The first stretch described here, from Porta San Sebastiano to the church of Domine Quo Vadis, is still sadly unattractive and traffic-ridden, unpleasant to explore on foot except on Sundays, when it is officially (but not always) closed to traffic. Beyond the church the road, although very narrow (and you still have to beware of fast cars), becomes prettier. A short distance beyond the basilica of San Sebastiano are the Circus of Maxentius and the Tomb of Cecilia Metella, two very interesting Roman monuments. The most beautiful and characteristic section of the road is that beyond the Tomb of Cecilia Metella.

Since 1997 the road and the countryside close to it have been protected as a regional park which covers some 3,500 hectares (larger than the historic centre of Rome itself). Since 2000 the area has been beautifully restored and is now looked after by the wardens of the park. However, the project to eliminate through traffic has still not been implemented and this seriously damages the enjoyment of a visit.

Information
Parco Regionale dell'Appia Antica, 42 Via Appia Antica; T: 06 5212 6314. Information office, 60 Via Appia Antica.

Tours
Although the road is easy to explore on your own, there are also free guided Sunday visits (at other times these can be booked at the Park office, where bicycles can also be hired).

Getting there
Bus routes and timetables are subject to change, so telephone the park information office for up-to-date details. At present the special bus service from Termini station, called the Archeobus, can only be used by appointment. ATAC bus 118 runs every 20–40 mins from Piazzale Ostiense via the baths of Caracalla and Via di Porta San Sebastiano, along the Via Appia Antica as far as the Via Appia Pignatelli. On weekdays bus no. 218 from San Giovanni in Laterano runs via the outside of the Aurelian Walls to Porta San Sebastiano and then follows Via Appia Antica as far as Via Ardeatina, near the catacombs of San Callisto and Santa Domitilla.

The catacombs of San Sebastiano can also be reached by underground Line A from Piazza di Spagna and Termini stations to Colli Albani, from where (on weekdays) bus no. 660 takes Via Appia Pignatelli to the Appia Antica at the catacombs of San Sebastiano.

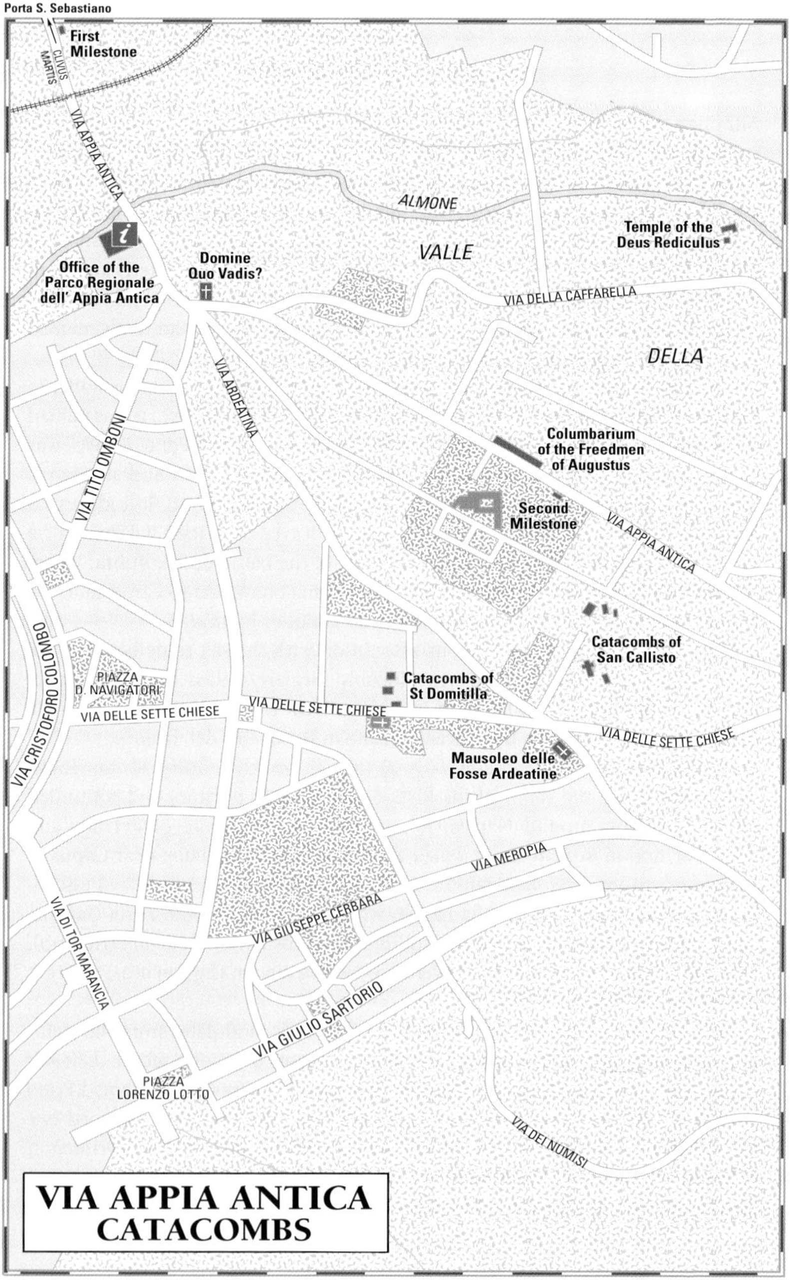

Porta S. Sebastiano

CLIVUS MARTIS

First
Milestone

VIA APPIA ANTICA

ALMONE

VALLE

Temple of the
Deus Rediculus

Office of the
Parco Regionale
dell' Appia Antica

Domine
Quo Vadis?

VIA DELLA CAFFARELLA

DELLA

VIA ARDEATINA

VIA TITO OMBONI

Columbarium
of the Freedmen
of Augustus

Second
Milestone

VIA APPIA ANTICA

Catacombs of
San Callisto

VIA CRISTOFORO COLOMBO

PIAZZA
D. NAVIGATORI

VIA DELLE SETTE CHIESE

Catacombs of
St Domitilla

VIA DELLE SETTE CHIESE

VIA DELLE SETTE CHIESE

Mausoleo delle
Fosse Ardeatine

VIA MEROPIA

VIA DI TOR MARANCIA

VIA GIUSEPPE CERBARA

VIA GIULIO SARTORIO

PIAZZA
LORENZO LOTTO

VIA DEI NUMISI

VIA APPIA ANTICA
CATACOMBS

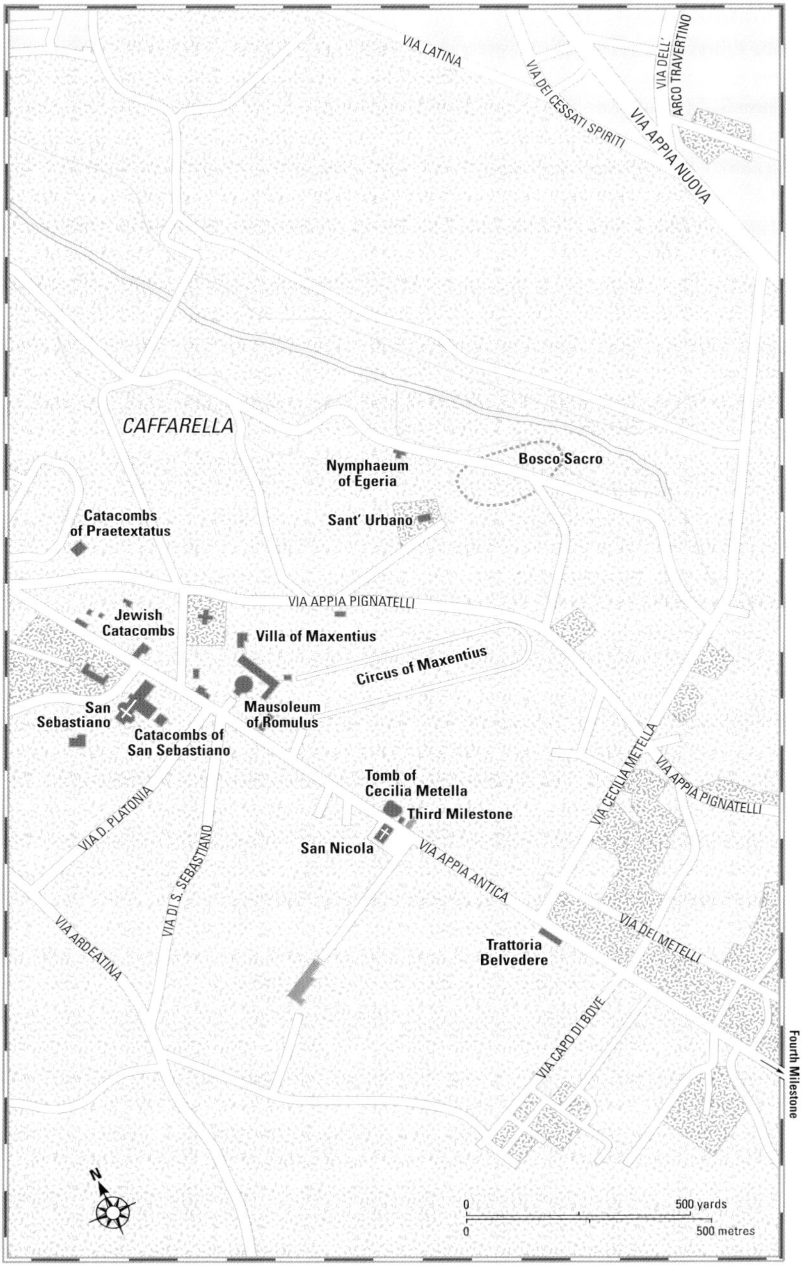

VIA LATINA

VIA DEI CESSATI SPIRITI

VIA DELL' ARCO TRAVERTINO

VIA APPIA NUOVA

CAFFARELLA

Nymphaeum of Egeria

Bosco Sacro

Catacombs of Praetextatus

Sant' Urbano

Jewish Catacombs

VIA APPIA PIGNATELLI

Villa of Maxentius

Circus of Maxentius

San Sebastiano

Mausoleum of Romulus

Catacombs of San Sebastiano

VIA CECILIA METELLA

VIA APPIA PIGNATELLI

Tomb of Cecilia Metella

Third Milestone

VIA D. PLATONIA

San Nicola

VIA APPIA ANTICA

VIA DI S. SEBASTIANO

VIA DEI METELLI

VIA ARDEATINA

Trattoria Belvedere

VIA CAPO DI BOVE

Fourth Milestone

N

0   500 yards

0   500 metres

end wall, *Christ Blessing*, with saints and angels; on the other walls, *Life of Jesus*, and the *Lives of St Cecilia and her Companions*, and *Life of St Vicolo*.

Sant'Urbano to the Catacombs

Sant'Urbano leads to Via Appia Pignatelli, a road opened in the late 17th century to link Via Appia Antica with Via Appia Nuova. It leads to the right past the entrance to the Catacombs of Praetextatus (*not regularly open; see p. 570*), with pagan burials above ground and Christian sarcophagi below—including those of the martyred companions of St Cecilia. The road rejoins the Appia Antica between the Catacombs of San Callisto and San Sebastiano. Beyond the church of Domine Quo Vadis the road goes uphill past a trattoria at no. 87, which incorporates remains of the Columbarium of the Freedmen of Augustus, where some 3,000 inscriptions were found. At no. 101 is the little Hypogeum of Vibia (*open 8.30–12 & 2.30–5 except Wed*), with pagan paintings of the 3rd century AD. Beyond, at no. 103, is the site of the second milestone. At no. 110, on the right, is the entrance to the Catacombs of San Callisto.

THE CATACOMBS

HISTORY OF THE CATACOMBS

The catacombs were used by the early Christians as underground cemeteries outside the walls, since burial within the city precinct was forbidden (pagan Romans were cremated). They were often situated on property donated by a wealthy individual, after whom the cemetery was named (i.e. Domitilla, Agnese, Priscilla and Commodilla). Easily quarried in the soft tufa, the catacombs provided space for the tombs of thousands of Christians. They were in use from the 1st to the early 5th centuries. Many martyrs were buried here and the early Christians chose to be buried close to them. Later they became places of pilgrimage until the martyrs' relics were transferred to churches. The catacombs were pillaged by the Goths (537) and the Lombards (755), and by the 9th century they were abandoned. They received their name *ad catacumbas* (literally, 'by the caves') from the stone quarries on the site of the cemetery of San Sebastiano.

In the 16th century the archaeologist Antonio Bosio explored the catacombs and his remarkable study of them was published posthumously in 1632. They were not systematically explored again until 1850, when Giovanni Battista de Rossi carried out excavations—at first at San Callisto—and the Pontificia Commissione di Archeologia Sacra was set up. Once opened to the public, they became one of the most famous sights of Rome, when visits by candlelight fired the romantic imagination of 19th-century travellers. The once popular belief that they were used as hiding places by the early Christians has been totally disproved.

Visiting the Catacombs

The catacombs are a system of galleries of different sizes, often arranged on as many as five levels, and sometimes extending for several kilometres. Simple rectangular niches (*loculi*), where the bodies were placed wrapped in a sheet, were cut in tiers in the walls. The openings were closed with slabs of marble or terracotta on which the names were inscribed (at first in Greek, later in Latin), sometimes with the date or the words '*in pace*' added: almost all of these have now disappeared. Terracotta lamps were hung above the tombs to provide illumination in the galleries. A more elaborate type of tomb was the *arcosolium*, which was a niche surmounted by an arch and often decorated. Small rooms or *cubicula* served as family vaults. The shallowest of the galleries are 7–8m beneath the surface, while the deepest are some 22m below ground level. Openings in the vaults, some of which survive, were used for the removal of earth during the excavations. Most of the tombs were rifled at some time over the centuries in the search for treasure and relics, but the inscriptions and paintings which survive are of the greatest interest.

NB: The catacombs tend to be very crowded with tour groups.

Catacombs of San Callisto

Open 8.30–12 & 2.30–5 or 5.30; closed Wed and in Feb; T: 06 5130 1580. Visitors are conducted by an English-speaking priest.

These, the first official cemetery of the early Christian community, are usually considered the most important of the Roman catacombs. They were named after St Calixtus (San Callisto), who was appointed to look after the cemetery by Pope St Zephyrinus (199–217), and who enlarged them when he himself became pope in 217. They were the official burial place of the bishops of Rome. First investigated in 1850 by Giovanni Battista de Rossi, they have not yet been fully explored.

The Oratory of St Sixtus and St Cecilia is a small basilica with three apses, where the dead were brought before burial. Here are inscriptions and sculptural fragments from the tombs, and a bust of de Rossi. Pope St Zephyrinus is generally believed to have been buried in the central apse.

The catacombs, excavated on five levels, are reached by an ancient staircase. The tour usually remains on the second level, from which several staircases can be seen descending to other levels. The remarkable papal crypt preserves the tombs with original Greek inscriptions of the martyred popes St Pontianus (230–35), St Anterus (236), St Fabian (236–50), St Lucius I (253–54) martyred under Valerian's persecution, St Stephen I (254–57), St Dionysius (259–68) and St Felix I (269–74). In honour of the martyred popes, Pope St Damasus I (366–84) set up the metrical inscription seen at the end of the crypt.

In the adjoining crypt is the **Cubiculum of St Cecilia**, where the body of the saint was supposedly buried after her martyrdom at her house in Trastevere in 230. It is thought that in 820 it was moved by Paschal I to the church built on the site of her house (*see p. 380*). A copy of Stefano Maderno's statue of the saint in the church has previous day of 32 German soldiers by the resistance movement in Via Rasella, the Germans shot 335 Italians. The victims, who had no connection with the killing of the German soldiers, included priests, officials, professional men, about a hundred Jews, a dozen foreigners, and a boy of 14. The Germans then buried the bodies here under an avalanche of sand artificially caused by exploding mines. Local inhabitants provided a legal and medical commission with the means of exhuming and identifying the bodies after the German retreat. The scene of the massacre, below a huge tufa cliff, now has cave chapels. The victims, reinterred after identification, are commemorated by a huge single concrete slab placed in 1949 over their mass grave, with a group of standing figures, in stone, by Francesco Coccia (1950).

Off the Via Ardeatina, in Via G. Aristide Sartorio, is the entrance to the **Tormarancia Estate** (*to book a visit, T: 06 5126314 or 06 84497206*), an area of 200 hectares of Roman Campagna which became part of the Appia Antica regional park in 2002. Since it is still mostly privately owned it is not yet open regularly to the public. There were plans in the early 1990s to use this agricultural land to build a new residential district, but it has been preserved as parkland through the valiant efforts of conservationists.

Catacombs of St Domitilla

Usually open 8.30–12 & 2.30–5 or 5.30; closed Tues, and in Jan. T: 06 511 0342. A friar conducts groups from the basilica to the catacombs. Entrance on Via delle Sette Chiese.
The Catacombs of St Domitilla, or Catacombs of St Nereus and St Achilleus, further along Via delle Sette Chiese, are among the most extensive in Rome and may be the most ancient Christian cemetery in existence. They contain more than 900 inscriptions. St Flavia Domitilla (niece of Flavia Domitilla, sister of Domitian) and her two Christian servants, Nereus and Achilleus, were buried here, as well as St Petronilla, another Christian patrician, perhaps the adopted daughter of St Peter.

At the foot of the entrance stairway is the aisled **Basilica of St Nereus and St Achilleus**, built in 390–95 over the tombs of the martyred saints. There are traces of a schola cantorum, and ancient columns probably from a pagan temple. The area below floor level has sarcophagi and tombs. By the altar is a rare small column, with scenes of the martyrdom of St Achilleus carved in relief. The adjoining **Chapel of St Petronilla** (shown during the tour of the catacombs), with a fresco of the saint, contained her sarcophagus until the 8th century, when it was removed to St Peter's.

The **catacombs** are excavated on two levels. The Cemetery of the Flavians (the family of Domitilla) had a separate entrance on the old Via Ardeatina. At this entrance is a vaulted vestibule probably designed as a meeting-place for the service of Intercession for the Dead, with a bench along the wall, and a well for water. A long gallery slopes down from here, with niches on either side decorated with 2nd-century frescoes of flowers and genii. From the original entrance a gallery leads to another hypogeum, with four large niches decorated with 2nd-century paintings (including *Daniel in the Lions' Den*). At the foot of a staircase is another ancient area; here is a cubicle with paintings of winged genii and the earliest known representation of the *Good Shepherd* (2nd century).

On the upper level is the Cubiculum of Ampliatus, with paintings in Classical style. Other areas contain more painted scenes including the *Madonna and Child with Four Magi*, *Christ and the Apostles*, and a scene of a cornmarket.

The Catacombs of Commodilla on the same street are not open regularly (*see p. 570*).

THE VIA APPIA BEYOND THE CATACOMBS

The Via Appia now leaves behind the area of the catacombs, and becomes more attractive and interesting for its Roman remains. On the left, in a hollow at no. 153, are the extensive ruins of the Villa of Maxentius (*open 9–1; closed Mon; T: 06 780 1324*). Built in 309 by the Emperor Maxentius, it included a palace, a circus and a mausoleum built in honour of his son Romulus (d. 307).

The **Circus of Maxentius** (open-air concerts are held here in summer) is the best-preserved of the Roman circuses, and one of the most romantic sites of ancient Rome. It has a good view of the Tomb of Cecilia Metella. The circus was excavated by Antonio Nibby in 1825 for the Torlonia family, and restored in the 1960s and 1970s. The stadium (c. 513m by 91m) was probably capable of holding some 10,000 spectators. The main entrance was on the west side with the 12 *carceres* or stalls for the chariots and *quadrigae*, and, on either side, two square towers with curved façades. Two arches, one of which has been restored, connected the towers to the long sides of the circus and provided side entrances. In the construction of the tiers of seats, amphorae were used to lighten the vaults, and these can still clearly be seen. In the centre of the left side is the conspicuous emperor's box, which was connected by a portico to his palace on the hill behind. At the far end was a triumphal arch where a fragment of a dedicatory inscription to Romulus, son of Maxentius, was found identifying the circus with Maxentius (it had previously been attributed to Caracalla). In the centre is the round *meta* and the *spina*, the low wall which divided the area longitudinally and where the obelisk of Domitian, now in Piazza Navona, originally stood. The course was seven laps around the spina. This and the *carceres* were both placed slightly obliquely to equalize, as far as possible, the chances of all competitors, although it is likely that the circus was never actually used since Maxentius fell from power in 312.

Fenced off on the hillside to the left, towards Via Appia Pignatelli, are the overgrown remains of the palace which include fragments of baths, a basilica and a cryptoporticus. The conspicuous high wall near the west end of the circus belongs to the quadriporticus around the Mausoleum of Romulus, which faces the Via Appia. Some of the pilasters of the quadriporticus survive, as well as much of the outer wall. In the centre is the circular tomb in front of which is a rectangular pronaos lying beneath a derelict house. The entrance is in front of a palm tree: beyond the pronaos is the mausoleum with niches in the outside wall for sarcophagi, and a huge pilaster in the centre also decorated with niches. The upper floor, probably covered with a cupola, has been destroyed. Nearby, beside the Via Appia, is the so-called Tomba dei Sempronii, probably dating from the Augustan era (*closed to the public while excavations are still in progress*).

are the ruins of the tepidarium. The best preserved of the thermal buildings is the frigidarium, a little to the east, which also retains its walls and its splendid pavement of polychrome marble in *opus sectile* (2nd century AD). The two *cipollino* columns were recently returned here (they were removed many years ago and later found their way to the Baths of Diocletian).

In front of the baths was an oval edifice built in the 2nd–3rd century AD (its shape can be seen clearly in the ground). This is usually called the Teatro Marittimo because of its similarity to a building at Hadrian's Villa in Tivoli (*see p. 530*), but its precise function is unknown; it may have been a small amphitheatre or simply a garden to take the air. The residential area was further east, on the edge of the hill. Near the reception rooms was a large open courtyard paved with white marble. The service areas and private quarters are marked by a high arch. There is another small thermal complex to the south, on the line of an aqueduct which descended past several cisterns from the nymphaeum at the top of the hill on the the Via Appia Antica at the original entrance to the villa. The nymphaeum was enclosed in a castle in the 15th century. Also in this area there was a garden, a hippodrome and a stadium.

Parco degli Acquedotti

Across the Via Appia Nuova a narrow road leads under two railway bridges to reach the **Parco degli Acquedotti**, a beautiful protected area of some 15 hectares, traversed by seven aqueducts and also forming part of the Park of the Appia Antica. Majestic long stretches of several aqueducts survive above ground (notably the Acqua Claudia) in open countryside where sheep are grazed. Beside an old farmhouse and group of pine trees (the Casale di Roma Vecchia) is a little public park with a pond fed by the Felice aqueduct, here channelled beneath a low vault. On a clear day there is a distant view of the dome of St Peter's.

The aqueducts in the park are supplied from springs in the upper valley of the Aniene beyond Tivoli, east of Rome, and in the Alban hills. The oldest aqueduct in the area of the park is that of the Anio Vetus (3rd century BC), but it is not visible here as it is almost totally underground. The most conspicuous aqueduct is the Acqua Claudia, long stretches of which survive above ground, carried on high arches. The lower arches belong to the Acqua Felice.

Area delle Tombe Latine

Off the Via Appia Nuova, at no. 151 Via Arco di Travertino near the Arco di Travertino underground stop, is the Area delle Tombe Latine (*open 9–1 & 2.30–5 except Sun; T: 06 3996 7700*). It includes a group of tombs dating from the 1st and 2nd centuries. Most of them are square and brick-built, with recesses on the outside and interior chambers with stucco ornamentation. The so-called Tomb of the Valeri (AD 160) is a subterranean chamber decorated with fine reliefs of nymphs, sea-monsters and nereids in stucco on a white ground, and the Tomb of the Pancrazi, of the same date, has landscape paintings, coloured stuccoes and four bas-reliefs of the *Judgement of Paris*, Admetus and Alcestis, Priam and Achilles, and Hercules playing a lyre with Bacchus and Minerva.

THE AQUEDUCTS OF ROME

Although a high proportion of the spring water brought to ancient Rome was channelled underground, stretches of aqueduct were also built above ground, and their magnificent arches crossing the Campagna used to be one of the most romantic sights for travellers approaching the city.

Like roads and bridges all over the Empire, some aqueducts still survive to demonstrate the skill of the Roman engineers. The first aqueduct of all, the Acqua Appia, was built c. 312 BC by Appius Claudius, the censor who also gave his name to the Via Appia. Some 16km in length, it entered Rome at the present Porta Maggiore, at a time when the city had around 200,000 inhabitants. Ten more aqueducts were constructed during the Republic and Empire. The Anio Vetus, the oldest aqueduct in the Parco degli Acquedotti, was built, mostly underground, between 272 and 269 BC, and supplies water from the valley of the Aniene, some 64km east of Rome. The Acqua Marcia, begun in 44 BC, reached from near Tivoli to the Campidoglio, a distance of some 91km. It ran underground until it emerged in the present area of the park (where it merges with the Acqua Tepula and Acqua Julia, both from the Alban hills). The Acqua Claudia and the Anio Novus also traverse the park. Begun by Caligula in AD 38, the Acqua Claudia was completed by Claudius in AD 42, and the Anio Novus in 52. The water of the Acqua Claudia came from two springs near *Sublaqueum* (Subiaco). The Anio Novus was the longest of all the aqueducts (95km) and the highest; some of its arches were 28m high. The last aqueduct of ancient Roman times was that by Alexander Severus c. AD 226.

A fascinating account of the waters of Rome, written in AD 97 by the head of the city's water works during the reigns of Nerva and Trajan, Sextus Julius Frontinus, was discovered in the 15th century. Frontinus helped to reorganize the supply, bringing water for the first time to the poorer districts of Rome. Many of the aqueducts leaked and frequently needed repair, but by AD 52, when nine aqueducts were in use, they were sufficient to supply nearly 1,000 litres a day for each of Rome's estimated one million inhabitants. No other city at any time has been supplied with so much water (the present supply is around 500 litres per family).

The aqueducts were cut by the Goths in 537, and it was not until the 16th century that attention was again paid to Rome's water supply, from then onwards under the care of the popes. The Acqua Vergine was restored by Pius V in 1570; Sixtus V built the new Acqua Felice in 1585; and Paul V restored the Acqua Traiana in 1611, calling it the Acqua Paola. These papal aqueducts are still functioning, but the water supply has had to be greatly increased. The Acqua Vergine Nuova was inaugurated in 1937, and the Peschiera-Capore aqueduct was constructed between 1938 and 1980. It uses abundant springs near Rieti never before brought to Rome, and supplies more water than all the other aqueducts put together. It claims to be the largest aqueduct in the world using only spring water.

two fish shops open onto the Decumanus. Behind them is the market place. Via Occidentale del Pomerio and Via del Tempio Rotondo, behind the Tempio Rotondo at the south end of the Forum, lead to the south continuation of the Cardo Maximus. On the right here is the **Domus di Giove Fulminatore**, a house of the Republican period remodelled in the 4th century, with a striking phallic 'doormat' mosaic. Priapus was often put in entrances to ward off intruders. In his dual role as god of gardens and of fertility he also functioned as a kind of divine scarecrow. Beside the house is the House of the Mosaic Niche (*Domus della Nicchia a Mosaico*), another Republican house, twice rebuilt. Adjoining is a nymphaeum, with a well-preserved marble floor and walls, and niches in which were found two copies of the *Eros* of Lysippus. The next building is the **House of the Columns** (*Domus delle Colonne*), a large corner house with façades on the Cardo Maximus and on Via della Caupona del Pavone to the right. In the centre of the courtyard is a stone basin with a double apse and short white marble columns; beyond is the large tablinum with its entrance between two columns. In the sidestreet is a wine-shop, the 3rd-century **Caupone del Pavone**. One of its rooms is decorated with paintings of flying Bacchanals and Muses; beyond is the bar, with a counter and small basins. On the opposite side of the street is the **House of the Fish** (*Domus dei Pesci*), evidently a Christian house (a vestibule has a mosaic showing a chalice and fish). A large room on the south side, with two marble columns, has a fine mosaic floor.

The route back to the entrance

The Cardo Maximus passes on the right the Portico dell'Ercole; opposite is a fulling mill. Adjoining are the **Terme del Faro**. In a floor of the frigidarium of the baths is a mosaic depicting fish, sea monsters and a lighthouse (*pharos*), after which the baths were named. One of the rooms has a white marble pool and frescoed walls in the 3rd-century style. A ramp leads from the Cardo to the triangular Campo della Magna Mater, one of the best-preserved sacred areas of the Roman world. At the west corner is the prostyle hexastyle Temple of Cybele. At the east corner the Sanctuary of Attis has an apse flanked by telamones in the shape of fauns. On the same side is the Temple of Bellona, the goddess of war, dating from the time of Marcus Aurelius, and, opposite, the Schola degli Hastiferes, seat of an association connected with the cult of Bellona. The sanctuary is close to the Porta Laurentina, which retains the tufa blocks of Sulla's circumvallation (c. 80 BC).

Some way south of Porta Laurentina, along the line of the ancient Via Laurentina, is the Cemetery of the Porta Laurentina, first excavated in 1865 and systematically explored in 1934–35. Many of the inscriptions relate to freedmen. Beyond the motorway, in the locality called Pianabella, excavations begun in 1976 revealed a necropolis and Christian basilica.

A short distance back along the Cardo Maximus, the Semita dei Cippi leads to the right (north). This street is flanked by two *cippi* and contains a 3rd-century *domus*, the Casa del Protiro, its reconstituted portal prettily flanked by cypresses. To the north a right turn leads into a street named after the **House of Fortuna Annonaria**, which has a garden in its peristyle. On the west side of the peristyle is a large room with three arches, columns and a nymphaeum. At the end of the street, on the right, is another Temple of Bona Dea, with a Mithraeum next door, notable for its mosaic pavement. Also in the street is the Domus Republicana, with four Doric columns; it is adjoined by the Edificio degli Augustali, the headquarters of the *Augustales*, those in charge of the imperial cult. This building has another entrance in Via degli Augustali, which leads to the Decumanus Maximus, and the main entrance.

MEDIEVAL OSTIA ANTICA

Across the road from the entrance to the excavations are a few houses outside the *borgo* of Ostia Antica, a fortified village whose walls are still standing, founded by Gregory IV in 830 and given the name of *Gregoriopolis*. The walls enclose a tiny picturesque hamlet of russet-coloured houses beside the castle, bishop's palace and church. The castle (*open 9–12.45; closed Mon; on Tues and Thur also 3–4.15; T. 06 5635 8024; excellent guided tours*) is a splendid building erected in 1483–86 by Baccio Pontelli for Julius II while he was still a cardinal.

From the courtyard there is access to a remarkable spiral stone staircase used by the guards, an old oven, a bath-house, and a room from which cannon were fired. A spiral ramp (designed for use by horses) leads up to the residential area with traces of frescoes by the school of Baldassare Peruzzi. From the battlements and terrace there are views towards Fiumicino and the present site of the Tiber (which formerly flowed beneath the castle walls). An old fortified tower which predates the castle can be seen from here, and the site of a drawbridge which connected it to the main building.

The church of Santa Aurea, by Baccio Pontelli or Meo del Caprina, contains the body of the martyred St Aurea (d. 268) and, in a side chapel, a fragment of the gravestone of St Augustine's mother, St Monica (*see p. 289*), who died at Ostia in 387. The Episcopal Palace, with fine monochrome frescoes on the first floor inspired by Trajan's Column in Rome, attributed to Baldassare Peruzzi (1508–13), is the residence of the Bishop of Ostia.

Lido di Ostia

Via del Mare continues to Lido di Ostia, now usually just called Ostia, on the coast. The lido became Rome's seaside resort after the First World War, and under the Fascist regime was planned as a district of the capital and connected to EUR (*see p. 553*) by a fast road, Via Cristoforo Colombo, in 1936. Ostia is now an ugly suburb of Rome, but is still used as a resort by thousands of Romans in summer. It has some monumental edifices erected in 1916–40, but has been ruined by indiscriminate new building. On the seafront, in Piazza Anco Marzio, a monument by Pietro Consagra was set up in 1993 to the writer and film director Pier Paolo Pasolini, found murdered on 2nd November 1975 at the Idroscalo, a former seaplane station near the mouth of the Tiber west of the esplanade (where another neglected monument stands). Nearby survives the Tor San Michele, built in 1568 by Nanni di Baccio Bigio to a design by Michelangelo.

HISTORY OF THE PORTS

When the harbour of Ostia, already inadequate for its trade, began to silt up with the action of the Tiber, Augustus planned a larger seaport. In AD 42 Claudius began operations. The work was completed in 54 by Nero, who issued commemorative coins stamped *Portus Augusti*. With an area of some 80 hectares, and a wharf frontage of 800m, it was the most important commercial port in the Mediterranean, and was connected to the Tiber by a canal. Part of the site is now covered by the airport buildings, and by the grassy fields near the museum, in which fragments of the quays and buildings can be seen. Still extant is part of the quay incorporating the form of Caligula's ship (104m by 20m), which brought from Egypt the obelisk now in Piazza San Pietro. The ship was sunk and used as the base of a huge four-storeyed lighthouse.

Even this harbour soon silted up, however, and in 103 Trajan constructed a hexagonal artificial basin, the Port of Trajan, further inland to the south and better protected. It was connected to the Port of Claudius by a series of docks. This is reached from the airport by Via Portuense, an ancient road which followed the right bank of the Tiber from Rome to the port. More than a hundred ships could be moored here at any one time, and it was surrounded by warehouses. (*The area is not yet regularly open to the public.*)

The remains of the Port of Trajan include the hexagonal basin (650m across), perfectly preserved, constructed with travertine blocks. It shows up excellently from the air when landing at Fiumicino, but is fenced off and can only be visited with permission or on guided tours (*for information T: 06 5635 8099*).

The area is still the private property of the Sforza Cesarini family, and is occupied by a safari park. Attempts have been made to expropriate it and save it from further destruction, and there are long-term plans to create a coastal archaeological park and nature reserve here. Excavations have unearthed the remains of granaries, a wall, a high arch in red brick and an underground passageway. To the west are more ruins, including a monumental portico, at present still overgrown and abandoned. Like Claudius, Trajan also dug canals in connection with the seaport. The *Fossa Traiana* (now the Canale di Fiumicino) survives as a navigable canal between the Tiber and the sea. Numerous marble columns and coloured marbles, imported from all over the Empire and destined for ancient Rome, have been found in the area.

The village of Porto, 2km from the airport on the Via Portuensis, takes its name from the ancient city of *Portus*, which grew up around the ports of Claudius and Trajan. It was favoured as a seaport by Constantine at the expense of Ostia; in 314 it had its own bishop and became known as *Civitas Constantina*. In the village are the rebuilt church of Santa Rufina (10th century), an old episcopal palace, and the Villa Torlonia. The suburbicarian see of Porto and Santa Rufina is one of the six held by the cardinal bishops.

TIVOLI & HADRIAN'S VILLA

TIVOLI

Tivoli, the Classical *Tibur*, is now a busy, noisy little town surrounded by ugly high-rise buildings. In the centre are the famous gardens of the Villa d'Este and the park of Villa Gregoriana, and below the hill, protected by a beautiful park, are the magnificent ruins of Hadrian's Villa, one of the most important archaeological sites in Italy. Tivoli was built in a delightful position on the lower slopes of the Sabine Hills at the end of the valley of the Aniene, the Classical *Anio*, which here narrows into a gorge and forms spectacular cascades. In Roman times its waters were carried to Rome by two aqueducts, the Anio Vetus (70km), begun in 273 BC, and the Anio Novus (95km) begun in AD 36.

Getting there by public transport
Tivoli is not a pleasant place to visit by public transport. It can be reached by the underground Line B from the Colosseum or Termini railway station to Ponte Mammolo (the stop before the terminus at Rebibbia) which is connected by a COTRAL bus service (c. every 20mins) to Tivoli (20km along Via Tiburtina, in c. 45mins). If you take this bus and wish to visit Hadrian's Villa before Tivoli, you can get off at a request stop at Via di Villa Adriano (but this is over one kilometre from the villa entrance). There is also a bus (c. every hour) from Ponte Mammolo along the Via Prenestina, which has a stop closer to the entrance of Hadrian's Villa.

There is a local bus service (no. 4) about every 30mins from Tivoli (with a stop outside the tourist office) to near the entrance of Hadrian's Villa.

By rail, there is a somewhat roundabout route (infrequent service) from Rome (Tiburtina) to Tivoli via Guidonia, but the journey time is usually shorter if you are travelling at the busiest times of day.

Getting there by car
Tivoli, 31km east of Rome, is reached by the ugly Via Tiburtina, now extremely busy with traffic, on the line of the old Roman road. It passes Bagni di Tivoli and a branch road (right), at Bivio Villa Adriano, for Hadrian's Villa.

Information
IAT office of the APT della Provincia di Roma, Largo Garibaldi: T: 0774 311 249.

Eating out
There are two good (medium-priced) restaurants in the central Via Giuliani: Antica Hostaria de' Carrettieri (T: 0774 330 159) run by Sardinians, and La Ronda (T: 0774 317 243), with a particularly imaginative menu. Near Hadrian's Villa is a large modern restaurant, La Tenuta di Rocca Bruna (T: 0774 535 985), which also has a pizzeria. The food is usually good and service efficient.

duces the dragons in his coat of arms), who was a guest at the villa in 1572. Continuing straight along the Viale, crossing the Scala dei Bollori (an ingenious water staircase designed in 1567 but at present dry), we come to the other side of the gardens and the bizarre Fontana della Civetta, which once used water power to produce birdsong interrupted by the screech of an owl. It was begun in 1565 by Giovanni del Duca, and finished by Raffaello Sangallo in 1569. Next to it is the Fontana di Proserpina (1570), which was used as an outside dining room.

In the lower gardens are three fishponds, from where there is a splendid view of unspoilt countryside. In the centre of the perimeter wall, decorated with climbing roses, is the Fontana della Madre Natura, with a statue of Diana of the Ephesians. Nearby is the Rotonda dei Cipressi, surrounded by some of the mightiest cypresses in Italy (three of them survive, albeit propped up, from the 17th century).

The interior of the villa

The *Appartamento Nobile* on the ground floor is a series of rooms off a long corridor, overlooking the gardens. The largest room is the *Salone* with the Fontana di Tivoli, a wall fountain in mosaic, begun by Curzio Maccarone and completed in 1568 by Paolo Calandrino. The frescoes are by the school of Girolamo Muziano and Federico Zuccari. On the walls are views of the garden painted by Matteo Neroni in 1568. The two rooms behind the fountain were decorated by Cesare Nebbia and assistants, and the rooms on the other side of the *Salone* have frescoes by Federico Zuccari and assistants. The *Sala della Caccia* has 17th-century frescoes. Stairs lead up to a series of rooms, part of the *Appartamento Vecchio*, with ceiling frescoes by Livio Agresti, and a balcony overlooking the gardens. The chapel was frescoed in 1572 by the workshop of Federico Zuccari.

Santa Maria Maggiore

In the piazza outside is the Romanesque church of Santa Maria Maggiore, with a fine rose window attributed to Angelo da Tivoli above a later Gothic narthex (which contains a 13th-century fresco of the *Madonna and Child*, in a fine tabernacle). The interior contains remains of the original floor at the east end. In the presbytery are two triptychs, the one on the right dates from the 16th century, and the one on the left is signed by Bartolomeo Bulgarini of Siena (14th century). Above the latter is a *Madonna and Child* by Iacopo Torriti. Over the high altar is a Byzantine *Madonna* (perhaps dating from the 12th century); in the right aisle there is a crucifix attributed to Baccio da Montelupo.

The town centre

The centre of town is Piazza del Plebiscito, with its daily market. Here is the church of San Biagio, founded in the 14th century. Rebuilt in 1887, the interior is a remarkable example of the neo-Gothic style, with three impressive stained-glass windows (replaced in 1950 after their destruction in the last war). On the second south altar is a good 15th-century painting of *San Vincenzo*. Behind the altar is a 15th-century detached fresco of the *Crucifixion*. Off the north side are interesting fresco fragments of the *Madonna Enthroned* and the *Glory of St Thomas*.

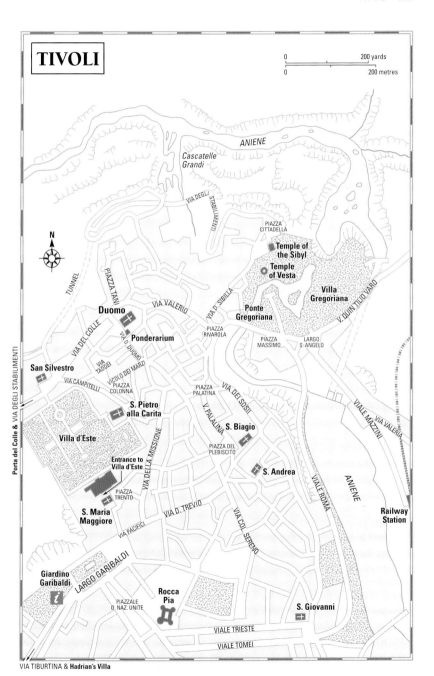

TIVOLI

0 _____ 200 yards
0 _____ 200 metres

ANIENE

Cascatelle
Grandi

VIA DEGLI STABILIMENTI

PIAZZA
CITTADELLA

Temple of
the Sibyl

Temple
of Vesta

Villa
Gregoriana

V. QUIN TILIO VARO

N

TUNNEL

PIAZZA TANI

VIA VALERIO

VIA D'SIBILLA

Duomo

Ponte
Gregoriana

PIAZZA
RIVAROLA

PIAZZA
MASSIMO

LARGO
S. ANGELO

VIA DEL COLLE

VIA D. DUOMO

Ponderarium

VIA TADDEI

VICOLO DEI MARZI

PIAZZA
COLONNA

PIAZZA
PALATINA

VIA DEI SOSII

VIALE MAZZINI

VIA VALERIA

San Silvestro

VIA CAMPITELLI

**S. Pietro
alla Carita**

V. PALATINA

S. Biagio

Villa d'Este

VIA DELLA MISSIONE

PIAZZA DEL
PLEBISCITO

S. Andrea

VIALE ROMA

ANIENE

Entrance to
Villa d'Este

PIAZZA
TRENTO

**S. Maria
Maggiore**

VIA D. TREVIO

VIA COL. SERENO

**Railway
Station**

VIA PACIFICI

Porta del Colle & VIA DEGLI STABILIMENTI

**Giardino
Garibaldi**

LARGO GARIBALDI

PIAZZALE
D. NAZ. UNITE

**Rocca
Pia**

S. Giovanni

VIALE TRIESTE

VIALE TOMEI

VIA TIBURTINA & **Hadrian's Villa**

HADRIAN'S VILLA

About 5km below the town of Tivoli, beyond a beautiful olive grove on the hillside, and reached from the Via Tiburtina, the main road to Rome, is Hadrian's Villa, the largest and richest Imperial villa in the Roman Empire. Hadrian became emperor on the death of Trajan in 117, and began the villa the following year, completing it ten years later. It is known that Hadrian prided himself on his abilities as an architect, and it is therefore presumed that this remarkably original complex was directly designed by him. It seems to have been used as a residence for the emperor and his court, particularly in the summer months: the buildings are spaciously laid out between gardens. Of all the surviving splendid monuments erected by Hadrian throughout the Empire, this is probably the most interesting. It is now one of the most evocative Classical sites to survive in Italy, protected by a beautiful park.

Opening times
Daily from 9–dusk; in winter it closes at 4; in Feb at 5; in March at 5.30; in April at 6; from May–Aug at 6.30; in Sept at 5.30, and in Oct at 5; T: 0774 453 0203. Closed 25 Dec, 1 Jan, and 1 March.

Getting there
The villa is not very easy to reach by public transport and it is mostly visited by coach tours. The road for the Villa leaves the Via Tiburtina (the main road from Rome to Tivoli) at the Bivio Villa Adriana, 28km from Rome, and 4km from Tivoli. From the turn an ugly byroad (1.5km) continues to the entrance. For transport from Rome and from Tivoli, see p. 521.

Eating out
At present there is no café, but the villa is a splendid place to picnic. For restaurant see p. 521.

Planing a visit

The general plan of the villa, which covers some 120 hectares, is capricious, although the buildings are grouped around four principal structures: the Pecile, the Imperial Palace, the Canopus and the Accademia (*numbered 1–4 on the plan overleaf*). Excavations and restorations are in progress on the hillside overlooking the Canopus. Recent studies suggest that the traditional interpretation of many of the buildings is probably wrong. All the ruins are labelled with explanatory diagrams (also in English). It is not easy to understand the connection between all the buildings since the order of the visit does not begin at the main entrance to the villa (only recently identified). A whole day is needed for a detailed visit to this vast site.

From the ticket entrance (with the car park), a short drive leads to a building which houses a model of the villa. On the far right an 18th-century villa is used as a museum with an excellent display on three floors, providing a useful introduction to the ruins. On the ground floor are models of various parts of the villa. The first floor illustrates its architecture, with fragments of friezes, capitals, and a Roman marble model of a stadium. The building techniques are illustrated, and the various brick stamps shown. The finds from the villa now in museums are recorded by photographs. On the second floor are engravings of the site (including copies of Piranesi's works) and examples of the various marbles used in the buildings. Fragments of floors, mosaics and painted plaster are displayed.

HISTORY OF HADRIAN'S VILLA

It is difficult to understand why Hadrian, with all the resources of the Empire at his disposal, should have chosen such an unprepossessing site for his magnificent estate. Though little over 5km from the scenic Roman health resort of Tivoli, the low-lying surroundings of the villa have no particular attraction. In the emperor's day the flat plain was not even healthy. One reason for the choice was probably the fact that the owner of the land was the Empress Sabina; another reason may have been the emperor's desire to keep himself apart from his courtiers, many of whom owned villas on the hills around Tivoli. Parts of a smaller country house of the 1st century BC, overlooking the Vale of Tempe, were incorporated into the emperor's villa.

Many of the buildings of the villa are derived from famous Classical monuments, some of which Hadrian saw during his prolonged travels in the Empire. These were the Lyceum, the Academy, the Prytaneion and the Stoa Poikile in Athens; the Canopus of the Egyptian Delta; and the Vale of Tempe in Thessaly. Hadrian also included a representation of Hades, as conceived by the Greek poets. An extensive system of underground passages (mostly now inaccessible), some mere corridors and others wide enough for a horse and carriage, exist beneath the villa; these were presumably service areas. Hadrian's successors enlarged the villa, but Constantine is supposed to have stolen some elements to decorate Byzantium. In the Middle Ages the site was plundered, and it later became a quarry for builders and lime-burners. Until the Renaissance the ruins continued to be neglected or abused.

The first excavations were ordered by Alexander VI and Cardinal Alessandro Farnese. Soon after he took up residence at the Villa d'Este in 1550, Cardinal Ippolito II d'Este employed Pirro Ligorio to continue excavations, but he took many of the finds to decorate his villa. Further excavations were carried out from the 17th to the 19th centuries. Piranesi drew a plan of the site, and made engravings of the buildings and sculptures (now in the Calcografia Nazionale in Rome). In 1730 Count Fede planted cypresses and pines among the ruins. In 1870 the Italian government acquired most of the site, and systematic excavations were begun (still far from complete). The works of art discovered in the villa (more than 260) are scattered in museums all over Europe, as well as in Rome (the Museo Nazionale Romano, and the Capitoline and Vatican Museums).

day to enter. This leads to the **Pavilion**, which overlooks a valley with a stream which is thought to have been landscaped by Hadrian to recreate the Vale of Tempe in Thessaly, famed for its beauty. The stream, now called the Pussiano, represented the ancient *Peneios*.

From here steps lead up to a path (south) which leads to the **Great Peristyle**, with a private library and other small rooms overlooking the Library Court. Also here is a well-proportioned room with two rows of small columns. Nearby, stairs lead underground to a cryptoporticus, with well-lit corridors. At the other end of this nucleus of the palace is the **Hall of the Doric Pilasters**, with a fine entablature, which connected the east and west parts of the villa. The so-called Firemen's Barracks, beyond the apse of the basilican hall (right), was more probably a storehouse near the kitchens. Beyond it is a **Quadriporticus**, with a pool and a portico of fluted Composite columns. This is now considered to be at the centre of the most important part of the Imperial Palace and the residence of Hadrian. The upper floors were supplied with heating systems. Beneath it is a well-preserved extensive cryptoporticus. Beyond it, on a lower level, is the large Nymphaeum (*described below*).

On the left is another nymphaeum, which had two round fountain basins, and from here a path leads to the **Piazza d'Oro**, a rectangular area at the southeast end of the palace. It was so named because excavations here yielded such rich finds. It is entered through the fine octagonal vestibule. The peristyle was formed of alternate columns of *cipollino* and granite in two rows. On the far side (southeast) is an intricate series of exedrae and nymphaea; the central one seems to have been a summer triclinium. This was an open courtyard with a remarkable Greek-cross plan, with alternate convex and concave sides. The plan of the portico recalls Greek gymnasia. It was formerly thought that this was used for banquets, but a recent interpretation is that it was in fact a stoa with libraries, similar to that which Hadrian had built in Athens in this period.

The baths

A path continues west past the back of the Firemen's Barracks (*Caserma dei Vigili*) and of the main nucleus of the palace, and descends to a clump of mighty cypresses and the **Small and Great Thermae**. The small baths are well preserved (they are visited from a wooden walkway) with a large rectangular hall, perhaps the frigidarium, and an octagonal hall with a domed vault. They were particularly elegant and refined, and may have been reserved for the use of the emperor alone. The large baths, on a simpler design, were probably used by court dignitaries and visitors. They include a circular hall, with cupola and skylight. The huge hall has an apse and a superb cross-vault, now mostly collapsed. Opposite is another cross-vaulted room decorated with exquisite stucco reliefs. On the east is a swimming-pool, bounded on the northwest by a cryptoporticus with, on its ruined walls, numerous graffiti of the 16th and 17th centuries. This gives access to the so-called Praetorium, a tall edifice which was divided into three storeys by wooden floors. It may have been used as a warehouse, or as a service wing.

The Canopus

Beyond a row of six huge ilexes is the celebrated **Canopus 3**, designed to imitate the famous Sanctuary of Serapis, which stood at the 15th milestone from Alexandria. Hadrian dug a hollow (185m by 75m), in which he constructed a basin, bordered on the east by a block of 20 rooms and a portico, and on the west by a heavy buttressed wall (238m long), against which were more rooms (some of them now used for the museum; *see below*). Around the curved north end of the canal, reproductions of statues found on the site have been set up between marble columns surmounted by an epistyle arched over alternate pillars. Along the west side are reproductions of colossal caryatids and telamones (the originals were found in the basin in the 1950s). At the south end is the so-called **Serapeum**, a monumental triclinium in the form of a Temple of Isis, with a half-dome formerly covered with mosaics above a semicircular banqueting table (reconstructed) from which the diners had a scenic view of the Canopus. Some scholars think this may have been intended as a symbolic representation of the Nile: a series of fountains represent its source (in the niche behind), the cataracts, and its delta (in the piscina in front). The basin would then have represented the Mediterranean, with Athens to the west (represented by the caryatids), and Ephesus to the east (represented by statues of Amazons). The Canopus may have been built by Hadrian in honour of his lover Antinous, a Bithynian boy born around 110 AD, who was renowned for his graceful beauty. When he accompanied the Emperor on his trip up the Nile in 130 he was drowned in the river in mysterious circumstances. Hadrian founded a city in Egypt in his memory, and ordered his deification so that his cult was celebrated all over the Empire. Numerous statues of him survive in the museums of Rome and elsewhere, and his full lips and dreamy eyes are instantly recognizable. He is often also represented as an Egyptian divinity (as in many of the works found here). Most of the Egyptian sculptures now in the Capitoline and Vatican museums come from here. Those in the Egyptian Museum (*see p. 449*) have recently been rearranged, according to the above interpretation.

The museum

There is a fine view of most of the villa from the hill behind. On the northwest side of the hollow is the museum, housing finds from excavations since 1950. The statues include a bust of Caracalla; *Venus*, copy of the *Aphrodite of Cnidos* by Praxiteles; wounded Amazons, one a mutilated copy of a Polyclitan original, the other a fine replica of the famous original by Pheidias; portrait of Verres; *Athena* and *Mars*, both from mid-5th-century originals; two Athletes; a Crocodile; tondo with the bas-relief of a Satyr; four marble Caryatids, copies of the 5th-century originals on the Erechtheion at Athens; and two Sileni.

A path leads west to the **Roccabruna Tower**, a belvedere which has square outer walls and is circular inside. This is possibly an imitation of the Tower of Timon of Athens, which stood near the Academy. It stands in an olive grove, famous for the size of its olive trees, one of them (the *Albero Bello*) claimed to be the largest in the Tivoli district.

uted to Mino da Fiesole and Giovanni Dalmata, and the tomb of Stefanus de Surdis (1303) is by Giovanni Cosmati.

Santa Bibiana

Map p. 617, 2B
Via Giovanni Giolitti.
A 5th-century church rebuilt by Bernini in 1625—his first architectural work—when the remains of St Bibiana (Vivian) were found here. It contains Bernini's expressive statue of the saint (set in an aedicule above the altar), which was his first commission for a church. The sensual figure of the martyr, with her eyes raised to heaven, shows the characteristics which were to become typical of the highly-charged religious fervour of the Counter-Reformation. Eight of the church's columns are from pagan temples, including, to the left of the entrance, that at which St Bibiana was supposedly flogged to death. On the architrave (on the left) are frescoes by Pietro da Cortona, early works in the same spirit as Bernini's statue (those on the right are by his contemporary Agostino Ciampelli).

Santa Caterina da Siena (a Magnanapoli)

Map p. 623, 2D
Largo Magnanapoli.
Approached by a double staircase, the façade was designed by Giovanni Battista Soria in 1641. The 17th-century high altarpiece of the *Ecstasy of St Teresa* is by Melchiorre Caffà.

Cristo Re

Map p. 5
Viale Mazzini.
Built in 1930 by Marcello Piacentini, with a sculpture by Arturo Martini over the central door. It contains frescoes by Achille Funi.

Santi Domenico e Sisto

Map p. 623, 2D
Via Panisperna. Admission sometimes grant-ed on request at the college next door (bell by the gate).
The tall façade is preceded by a theatrical staircase (1654) by Vincenzo della Greca. Inside is a huge fresco (1674–75) by the Bolognese painter Domenico Canuti, a sculptured group (*Noli me tangere*) by Antonio Raggi, and a *Madonna and Child* thought to be an early work by Antoniazzo Romano.

Sant'Eusebio

Map p. 617, 2A
Piazza Vittorio Emanuele, north corner.
Founded in the 4th century on the site of the house of a certain Eusebius, believed to have been a parish priest who was imprisoned for his beliefs. The cover of his tomb, carved in the 15th century, is preserved in the sacristy. The church was rebuilt twice in the 18th century, when Raphael Mengs provided the ceiling painting of the *Triumph of St Eusebius*. There are finely carved 16th-century stalls in the apse.

Sant'Eustachio

Map p. 622, 2B
Piazza Sant'Eustachio.
Of ancient foundation, it preserves its campanile of 1196. The pretty interior was designed by Antonio Canevari after 1724. The two large 18th-century altarpieces in the transepts are by the little-known artist Giacomo Zoboli.

Gesù e Maria

Map p. 620, 3B
Corso, opposite S. Giacomo in Augusta.
This small church was designed inside and out by Girolamo Rainaldi around 1675.

San Giacomo in Augusta

Map p. 620, 3B
Corso.
The façade is by Maderno. The church is also known as *San Giacomo degli Incurabili* from the adjoining hospital, but its present

name refers to the proximity of the Mausoleum of Augustus.

San Gioacchino
Map p. 618, 1D
Via Pompeo Magno.
Erected by Raffaele Inganni in 1890, with bronze capitals and an aluminium cupola painted inside to represent a star-strewn sky.

San Giovanni Decollato
Map p. 622, 3C
Via San Giovanni Decollato.
The interior has fine stucco and fresco decoration dating from 1580–90. The altarpiece of the *Beheading of St John* is by Giorgio Vasari. An oratory preserves remarkable frescoes by the 16th-century Roman Mannerists, including Jacopino del Conte, Francesco Salviati, and Pirro Ligorio. There is also a 16th-century cloister.

San Giovanni della Pigna
Map p. 622, 2C
Via della Pigna.
A Baroque church which has interesting tomb slabs inside the entrance wall.

San Girolamo degli Schiavoni
Map p. 622, 1B
Via di Ripetta.
The name 'Schiavoni' refers to the Serbs who came to live in this district as refugees after the battle of Kosovo polje in 1389. The church was rebuilt in 1587.

Sant'Isidoro
Map p. 620, 3C
Via degli Artisti, off Via Veneto.
Built by Antonio Casoni (1620), with a pink façade by Carlo Bizzaccheri (1704), it was attached to a college for Irish students founded by Luke Wadding (1588–1657), a distinguished Irish Franciscan who instigated the Irish rebellion of 1641 against the confiscation of Ulster. His tomb is in the church, which contains several works by Carlo Maratta, and a chapel designed by Bernini with sculptures attributed to his son Paolo.

San Lorenzo in Panisperna
Map p. 623, 2E
Via Panisperna.
This is the traditional site of the martyrdom of St Lawrence (depicted in a vast late 16th–century fresco by Pasquale Cati in the interior), although not his burial place (which is San Lorenzo fuori le Mura). The building is surrounded by a delightful court of old houses.

Madonna dei Monti
Map p. 623, 3D
Via dei Serpenti (off Via Cavour).
A fine church by Giacomo della Porta, who also designed the fountain nearby. The interior contains 17th-century stuccoes (by Ambrogio Buonvicino) and frescoes, including those in the first chapel on the south side by Giovanni da San Giovanni. The third chapel on this side has an altarpiece of *Christ Carrying the Cross* by Paris Nogari, dating from around the time when the dome was decorated (in 1599–1600) by Cesare Nebbia and Orazio Gentileschi. The prolific Nebbia also painted the altarpieces in two chapels on the north side, where an *Adoration of the Shepherds* by his master Girolamo Muziano is also hung. The *Annunciation* is by their contemporary Durante Alberti.

Santa Maria in Campo Marzio
Map p. 622, 1B
Via della Maddalena.
Of ancient foundation, but rebuilt in 1685 by Giovanni Antonio de Rossi on a Greek-cross plan, and with a good portico and court. Over the high altar is a *Madonna*, part of a triptych probably dating from the 12th–13th century. Since 1920 the church

torian and man of letters Mario Praz from 1969 until his death in 1982.

Although he was a Shakespeare scholar and wrote books on Charles Lamb and Lord Byron, Praz is perhaps best remembered for his *History of Interior Decoration* (1945). The apartment is filled with his remarkable collection of decorative arts, paintings, sculpture, drawings, miniatures, fans, wax portraits, porcelain and furniture, particularly representative of the Neoclassical period (late 18th and early 19th centuries), which up until his time had been out of vogue and largely ignored by scholars.

The nine rooms here, crowded with possessions and rather gloomy in atmosphere, give a clear idea of Praz's taste. Praz formed his collection while living in the more spacious Palazzo Ricci on Via Giulia, described in his autobiographical book *La Casa della Vita* (published in 1958; translated into English as *The House of Life* in 1964). The works of art include a marble statue of *Cupid* attributed to Adamo Tadolini, a portrait of Foscolo by François-Xavier Fabre, a French artist who lived for many years in Rome, and early 19th-century watercolours of period interiors.

Museo Napoleonico
Map p. 622, 1B
Via Giuseppe Zanardelli. Open 9–7, except Mon; T: 06 6880 6286.
On the ground floor of Palazzo Primoli, this was created and presented to the city of Rome in 1927 by Count Giuseppe Primoli (1851–1927), a descendant of Napoleon I who frequented the court of Napoleon III. This interesting collection illustrates the various periods of Napoleonic rule in Italy, but is particularly important as a record of the prolonged stays in Italy of Napoleon's numerous brothers and sisters and their descendants, and it documents the history of the Roman branch of the Bonaparte family. Although

Napoleon Bonaparte never came to Rome himself (his trip, planned in 1812, failed to take place), he led some brilliant military campaigns in northern Italy, and in 1798 French troops entered the city and remained here for a year. Rome was again occupied in 1808–09.

The 16th-century palace was acquired by the Primoli family in 1820–28, and reconstructed in 1901 by Raffaello Ojetti, who added the monumental entrance on Via Zanardelli and a new façade overlooking the Tiber. The interior arrangement has been left more or less as it was in Giuseppe Primoli's time (the majolica floors were made in Naples in the early 19th century).

Museo Nazionale d'Arte Orientale
Map p. 623, 3F
Largo Brancaccio (Via Merulana). Open 8.30–2; Sun, Tues, & Thur 8.30–7.30; closed first and third Mon of the month; T: 06 487 4415.
Housed in Palazzo Brancaccio, which was built for Mary Elizabeth Bradhurst Field by Gaetano Koch in 1879, and enlarged by Luca Carimini. The interior has decorations in the neo-Baroque style by Francesco Gai. Founded in 1957, this is the most important collection of Oriental art in Italy.

Museo Nazionale delle Arti e delle Tradizioni Popolari
Map p. 5
Piazza Marconi 8–10 (EUR). Open 9–6; Sat and Sun 9–8: closed Mon; T: 06 592 6148.
Illustrates with models and reconstructions various aspects of Italian life. On the ground floor are exhibits relating to transport. The sections on the upper floor include furniture from rural houses, toys, crib figures, carnival and theatrical costumes, musical instruments used during local festivals, and puppets. There is a large collection of 19th- and early 20th-century jewellery. A section on religious festivals includes ex-votos. On the stair

landing is a gondola of 1882. The great hall, with frescoes of 1941, exhibits arts and crafts, with reconstructions of artisans' workshops. The next section illustrates agricultural life. The sections on seafaring and pastoral life are closed for rearrangement.

Museo Nazionale delle Paste Alimentari
Map p. 622, 1C
Piazza Scanderbeg. Open 9.30–5.30; T: 06 699 1119.
Despite its name, this is a private museum. It illustrates the history of pasta.

Museo Nazionale Preistorico ed Etnografico Luigi Pigorini
Map p. 5
14 Piazza Marconi (EUR). Open 9–8 except Mon; T: 06 549 521.
The museum, one of the most important of its kind in the world, is derived from the collection formed in the late 17th century by Father Anastasius Kircher in the Collegio dei Gesuiti. From 1871 onwards it was greatly enlarged by Luigi Pigorini, and in 1876 it became the Museo Preistorico del Nuovo Regno d'Italia. After 1913 the protohistoric objects went to Villa Giulia; Classical and Christian antiquities to the Museo Nazionale Romano; and medieval exhibits to Palazzo di Venezia.

The museum is arranged geographically to indicate the way civilization developed regionally through the Stone, Bronze and Iron Ages. Most of the exhibits are Italian, of the prehistoric period. They include material from all parts of the peninsula, so that a complete idea may be obtained of the growth of its civilization and of the commercial and artistic influences of the East and of the countries bordering on the Aegean. The descriptive labels, maps and diagrams are very informative. The most interesting exhibits include material from cemeteries in the Lazio area; finds of the

Italian School in Crete; curious Sardinian statuettes of priests and warriors in bronze; a tomb from Golasecca, representative of the western civilization of northern Italy. The objects found in the cemeteries of western and southern Etruria (including Vetulonia, Tarquinia, Vulci, and Veio) are particularly interesting; among them are well-tombs (10th–8th centuries BC), with ossuaries resembling those of Villanova, closed with a flat lid or shaped like a house, and trench-tombs (8th–7th centuries BC) showing the influence of Greek commerce, especially on pottery.

The Ethnographic Collection includes material from the Americas, Africa, and Oceania. There is a pre-Columbian archaeological collection from Mexico and the Andes, and artefacts made by the Inuits of the Arctic Circle. The collections from Oceania and Africa are at present closed.

Museo Numismatico
Map p. 620, 3D
97 Via Venti Settembre. Open 9–12.30, except Mon and holidays; T: 06 4761 3317.
Displayed inside the colossal Treasury building by Raffaele Canevari (1870), this numismatic museum includes examples of coins minted from the 13th century to the present day (with some foreign works), a collection from the pontifical mint, and an interesting collection of wax seals by Benedetto Pistrucci, who designed the St George and dragon on the old English sovereign.

Museo di Roma
Map p. 622, 2B
10 Via di San Pantaleo. Open 9–7 except Mon; T: 06 6710 8346.
Housed in the huge Palazzo Braschi, which was built after 1792 by Cosimo Morelli, the museum was founded in 1930 to illustrate the history and life of Rome from the Middle Ages to the present day, but most of

the exhibits relate to the period between the 17th and 19th centuries.

At the foot of the staircase is a colossal sculptural group of the *Baptism of Christ* by Francesco Mochi. The magnificent staircase (1791–1804), by Cosimo Morelli, incorporates 18 antique columns of red granite. The ancient Roman statues decorating the staircase are the only works from the huge Braschi collection to have survived. The fine Neoclassical stuccoes are by Luigi Acquisti (perhaps on a design by Valadier).

First floor: Rooms 1 and 2 are devoted to Pius VI who commissioned Palazzo Braschi and died in exile in 1799. Room 3 has busts of popes and cardinals including works by Filippo della Valle and François Duquesnoy. Room 4 contains 17th-century portraits and scenes of tournaments in Rome. Beyond Room 8, with 18th-century views of celebrations in Piazza del Popolo, there are more paintings of 18th- and 19th-century Rome by Ippolito Caffi and Gaspar van Wittel in Room 9. From the window in Room 10 there is a splendid view over Piazza Navona. There is also a painted self-portrait by Canova (c. 1799) and a plaster model for a colossal self-portrait bust in marble he made for his own tomb (1811–12). The portrait of John Staples (1773) is by Pompeo Batoni. In Room 12 is a very fine ceiling fresco of the fable of Psyche by Cigoli (1610–13), detached from Palazzo Borghese on the Quirinal Hill.

Second floor: Remnants of collections once owned by the great patrician families of Rome are arranged on this floor. The last room has a fine collection of 19th-century photos. There are long-term plans to open more rooms to exhibit the rest of the collection.

The Gabinetto Comunale delle Stampe e Archivio Fotografico is housed in the same building (*admission by appointment; T: 06 6830 8393*).

Museo Storico dei Bersaglieri

Map p. 616, 4A
Porta Pia. Open by appointment; T: 06 486 723.
Documents the wars of independence, the African campaign, and the First World War.

Museo Storico delle Poste e delle Telecommunicazioni

Map p. 5
190 Viale Europa (EUR). Open Mon–Fri 9–1.
The postal display begins with a casket of 1300 used by the Pontifical Post Office of Urbino and 17th-century letter boxes, including a '*bocca di leone*', and there is a fine copy on tile of the Peutinger Table, an ancient map of the military roads of the Western Roman Empire. Later postal history—pioneer air-mail flights, Ethiopian military cancellers, etc—is well chosen. The electronic calculator invented by Enrico Fermi, made in 1956, is also displayed here. The history of telegraph and telephone is copiously illustrated by original appliances, including apparatus used by Marconi in his 1901 experiments between Cornwall and Newfoundland.

Raccolta Teatrale del Burcardo (Theatre Museum)

Map p. 622, 2B
44 Via del Sudario. Open Mon–Fri 9–1.30; T: 06 681 9471
Housed in the delightful little Palazzetto del Burcardo, which was built in 1503 for Strasbourg-born Bishop Hans Burckardt (or Burckhardt), who came to live in Rome in 1479. He called the house the Torre Argentina from the Latin name for Strasbourg (*Argentoratum*), which in turn became the name of the piazza and theatre (the back doors of which open onto the courtyard). Burckardt wrote a remarkable account of the papal court under Innocent VIII and Alexander VI. The well displayed museum illustrates the history of theatre with statuettes of characters

from the *commedia dell'arte*, puppets, costumes, autograph texts, prints, drawings, and paintings. On the first floor you can see frescoes which survive from Burckardt's time. The building also houses a library of some 40,000 volumes, the earliest of which date from the 16th century, including nearly all the editions of Carlo Goldoni's works, as well as a photographic archive, and is the seat of the Italian Authors and Publishers Society.

University Study Collections
Map p. 617, 1B–1C

Città Universitaria. Open by appointment only (www.uniroma1.it under 'musei'). These consist of some 19 museums, among the most important of which are the Museo delle Origini (founded in 1942), which illustrates the prehistory of Italy; the Museo dell'Arte Classica which has more than 1,000 casts of Greek and Hellenistic statuary; the Botanical Institute, which has an important herbarium; and the Museo della Matematica, a museum which illustrates the history of mathematics.

PALACES & VILLAS

Acquario Romano
Map p. 623, 2F
Via Rattazzi.
Built in 1887 as an aquarium by Ettore Bernich (with an interior in Pompeian style), and surrounded by a garden with remains of the Servian Wall, this has recently been restored as a space for exhibitions and theatrical productions.

Banca d'Italia
Map p. 623, 2D
Via Nazionale.
A huge Neoclassical building by Gaetano Koch (1886–1904), behind a row of palm trees and colossal lamp-posts. Famous as the headquarters of the Bank of Italy.

Casa dei Cavalieri di Rodi
Map p. 623, 2D
Piazza del Grillo.
The house was built over a Roman edifice at the end of the 12th century, and restored in 1467–70 by Cardinal Marco Balbo, nephew of Paul II. It has a well-preserved colonnaded atrium dating from the time of Augustus; the roof is a Renaissance addition. It is now used as a chapel by the Knights of St John (*open for*

services on Sun at 10.30). At the top of a flight of restored Roman stairs is a fine Renaissance hall (*not at present open as it is being restored; for information, T: 06 6710 2634*) off which are several contemporary rooms; one of these, the Sala del Balconcino, contains part of the attic storey of the portico of the Forum of Augustus, with caryatids. Stairs lead up to a loggia with restored frescoes and fine views over the Imperial Fora.

Collegio Romano
Map p. 622, 2C
Piazza del Collegio Romano.
A large building erected in 1585 by order of Gregory XIII for the Jesuits. The architect was probably the Jesuit Giuseppe Valeriani. It is now partly used by the Cultural Ministry. The Jesuit library founded here formed the nucleus of the Biblioteca Nazionale Centrale Vittorio Emanuele, which was moved to new premises near the Castro Pretorio in 1975. The Salone della Crociera, with its original bookcases, has been used to house part of the library of the Istituto Nazionale di Archeologia e Storia dell'Arte in Palazzo di Venezia.

altar. **Temple D**, in travertine, is the largest; it has not been completely excavated as part of it is under Via Florida, to the south. During the excavations the medieval Torre del Papito here was restored and isolated.

Since 1994 the large cat colony has been looked after by a voluntary association which has its headquarters in an underground shelter beside the temples and welcomes visitors. About 450 cats are abandoned every year in Rome and many of them find refuge here (*T: 06 687 2133; www.romancats.com*).

Auditorium of Maecenas
Map p. 617, 2A
Largo Leopardi.
Despite its name, this is thought to have been a nymphaeum in the Gardens of Maecenas, built in the Augustan period. The unusual apse has tiered seats in a semicircle. Although it has been restored, the traces of red landscape paintings in the apse and wall niches have all but disappeared. The building is adjoined by a stretch of the Servian Wall.

Castro Pretorio
Map p. 616, 4A–4B
Viale Castro Pretorio.
This huge site, now occupied by the Biblioteca Nazionale, was the barracks of the Praetorian Guard. The *Praetoriae Cohortes*, or emperor's bodyguard, originally nine or ten cohorts (9,000–10,000 men), were instituted by Augustus and concentrated into a permanent camp here by Sejanus, minister of Tiberius, in AD 23; some portions of his building survive. In later Imperial times the Praetorian Guard acquired undue influence in the conduct of affairs of state. Many an emperor had to bribe them on his accession with a 'donative'. On one occasion, after the death of Pertinax in 193, they put up the Roman Empire itself for sale by auction; it was bought by Didius Julianus, who enjoyed

his purchase for 66 days. Centuries later the Castro Pretorio passed into the hands of the Jesuits, who renamed it Macao after their most successful foreign mission. It was again used as barracks in the 20th century.

Gardens of Sallust
Map p. 620, 3D
Piazza Sallustio.
The Gardens of Sallust (*Horti Sallustiani*), laid out in 40 BC and once owned by Julius Caesar, received their name from the historian Gaius Sallustius Crispus, who lavished the wealth he had accumulated during his African governorship on embellishing them. All that remains of them today are fragments of a villa which once stood in their midst. Here, too, can be seen the foundations of the Trinità dei Monti obelisk, showing where it stood in the Middle Ages.

Ipogeo degli Aureli
Map p. 617, 3B
Near Via Luzzatti.
This early Christian tomb, which belonged to the freedmen of the *gens* Aurelia, has mosaics and well preserved wall-paintings (AD 200–250), suggesting a mixture of Christian and gnostic beliefs. It was discovered in 1919.

Mausoleum of Augustus
Map p. 620, 3A
Piazza Augusto Imperatore.
The Mausoleum of Augustus is the tomb of Augustus and of the principal members of his family, the *gens* Julia-Claudia. It was one of the most sacred monuments of ancient Rome. The last Roman emperor to be buried here was Nerva in AD 98. It dominated the north end of the Campus Martius and used to be surrounded in Roman days by a huge public park: it is now in an ugly piazza laid out by the Fascist regime in 1936–38. Erected in 28

BC, it is a circular structure 87m in diameter (330 Roman feet), the largest mausoleum known. The smaller cylinder above was originally surmounted by a tumulus of earth some 45m high, planted with cypresses and probably crowned with a bronze statue of the emperor.

In the Middle Ages the tomb was used as a fortress by the Colonna, a wealthy Roman family. Later it was pillaged to provide travertine for other buildings, and a wooden amphitheatre was built on top of it, where Goethe watched animal-baiting in 1787. In the 19th century a theatre was constructed on the site, which was used as a concert hall from 1908 to 1936. When these structures were demolished and excavations began it was left open to the sky.

Nowadays the mausoleum is rather neglected and the interior less interesting than it might be. The circular base, which incorporated a series of large niches, was built of *opus reticulatum* and was once faced with travertine. On either side of the entrance were two obelisks—one of which is now in Piazza del Quirinale, and the other in Piazza dell'Esquilino—and pilasters on which was inscribed in bronze lettering the official will of Augustus, a copy of which was found at Ankara in Turkey. A corridor leads to the centre of the building where the *opus reticulatum* walls can be seen. The numerous abandoned marble architectural fragments used to decorate the upper part of the mausoleum, and there are some finely carved fragments of inscriptions. The sepulchral cella in the centre had three niches, two of which can still be seen: that on the left preserves an inscription to Augustus' sister Octavia and his beloved nephew Marcellus, who was the first to be interred here in 23 BC; the other niches contained the cinerary urns of Augustus himself and of his wife Livia and his nephews Gaius and Lucius Caesar.

Necropoli Ostiense

Map p. 5
195 Via Ostiense. Admission by appointment; T: 06 6710 3819.
In the middle of the road just before San Paolo fuori le Mura is a small necropolis known as the Necropoli Ostiense, which contained pagan and perhaps Christian tombs. The site, seen through railings, extended over a wide area; another part is visible left of the road.

Ponte Milvio

Map p. 5
Via Flaminia.
This was the Ponte Molle (*Pons Milvius*), which once carried the Via Flaminia over the Tiber but is now used only by pedestrians. It was built by the censor Marcus Aemilius Scaurus in 109 BC. It was here that Cicero captured the emissaries of the Allobroges in 63 BC during the Catiline conspiracy; and it was from this bridge that the Emperor Maxentius was thrown into the Tiber and drowned after his defeat by his co-emperor Constantine on 28th October 312. Remodelled in the 15th century by Nicholas V, who added the watchtowers, it was restored in 1805 by Pius VII, who commissioned Giuseppe Valadier to erect the triumphal arch at the entrance. Blown up in 1849 by Garibaldi to arrest the advance of the French, it was again restored in 1850 by Pius IX.

Porta Tiburtina

Map p. 617, 2B
Via di Porta Tiburtina.
A gate in the Aurelian Walls built by Augustus and restored by Honorius in 403. The triple attic carried the waters of the Aquae Marcia, Tepula and Julia (*see p. 503*). There are more remains of ancient aqueducts nearby in Piazza Guglielmo Pepe, and Piazzale Sisto V, where an arch was built out of a section of the Aurelian Walls by Pius V and Sixtus V at the end of

covered by a fine rib-vaulted dome 100m in diameter, and seats 15,000 spectators. The well-designed Velodromo Olimpico, for cycling events, is nearby.

Foro Italico
Map p. 5
Along the Tiber at the foot of Monte Mario.
This ambitious sports centre built in 1928–31 by the former Accademia Fascista della Farnesina, is one of the most impressive building projects carried out by Mussolini in imitation of ancient Roman Imperial architecture. Designed by Enrico del Debbio, and finished by Luigi Moretti in 1936, it was altered during work on preparations for the World Cup in Italy in 1990. Facing the entrance is Ponte Duca d'Aosta (1939). A marble monolith, 17m high, inscribed *Mussolini Dux*, rises at the entrance in front of an imposing avenue paved with marble inlaid with mosaics designed by Gino Severini, Angelo Canevari and others. It ends in a piazza decorated with a fountain and with a huge marble sphere. On either side of the avenue are marble blocks, with inscriptions recording events in the history of Italy. At the end, beyond the piazza, is the Stadio Olimpico, finished for the Olympic Games in 1960, with accommodation for 100,000. It was reconstructed for the World Cup in 1990, with little respect for the setting. To the right is the Stadio dei Marmi, capable of seating 20,000 spectators, with 60 colossal statues of athletes. There are open-air and enclosed swimming-pools, the latter with mosaics by Giulio Rossi and Angelo Canevari. Another building has mosaics by Gino Severini. There are also lawn-tennis and basketball courts, running tracks, gymnasiums and fencing halls.

Mosque
Via di Ponte Salario (north edge of Villa Ada; map p. 5).
Rome's first mosque, built in 1984–93 and designed by Paolo Portoghesi, Vittorio Gigliotti and Sami Monsawi. The mosque, which can hold up to 3,000 people and is the largest in Europe, was financed by some 24 Arab countries. There is also a cultural centre and library here. It is at the foot of Monte Antenne, the site of the ancient Sabine town of *Antemnae*, said to have been founded by the Siculi, which had probably already disappeared by the time of the Roman kings.

Palazzetto dello Sport
Map p. 5
Via Flaminia.
An adventurous and striking construction by Pier Luigi Nervi and Annibale Vitellozzi, designed for the Olympic Games in 1960. Beyond is the Villaggio Olimpico, built to accommodate athletes in 1960, and now a residential district.

Ponte del Risorgimento
Map p. 620, 1A
Built in 1909–11, this was the first bridge to be built in the city in reinforced concrete, with a single span of 100m.

Stadio Flaminio
Map p. 5
Flaminio district. Address.
Designed in reinforced concrete by Pier Luigi and Antonio Nervi in 1959. A huge football stadium with other sports facilities. Earlier in the same decade Ponte Flaminio was built over the Tiber, as a monumental entrance to the city from the north.

PRACTICAL INFORMATION

PLANNING YOUR TRIP

When to go

The climate of Rome is usually very pleasant except in the height of summer and periodically in the winter. The best months to visit the city are November or March: the most crowded periods, to be avoided if at all possible, are Easter, May and June, September, October and Christmas. July and August have become less crowded in the last few years, but the summer is usually uncomfortably hot.

Websites on Rome

www.romaturismo.it	Azienda di Promozione Turistica di Roma
www.comune.roma.it	Municipality (Comune di Roma)
www.informaroma.it	Municipality (Comune di Roma)
www.romapreview.com	Municipality (Comune di Roma)
www.vatican.va	Vatican
www.capitolium.org	Excavations in the Imperial Fora
www.romeguide.it	General website to Rome

Disabled travellers

All new public buildings are obliged by law to provide access and facilities for the disabled. In the annual list of hotels in Rome published by the APT, hotels which are able to provide hospitality for the disabled are indicated. Airports and railway stations in Italy provide assistance and certain trains are equipped to transport wheelchairs. The seats at the front of city buses are reserved for disabled passengers, as is ATAC bus no. 590. In the list of current opening times of museums and galleries available from the APT, those which are accessible to wheelchairs are indicated. The historic centre of Rome, however, remains a very difficult place to traverse in a wheelchair.

Travellers can contact Co.In (Consorzio Cooperative Integrate), T: 06 2326 7504, Mon–Fri 9.30–5, for a guide to Rome for the disabled in English. Another organisation with information is ANTHAI T: 06 6821 9168; www.tour-web.com/accessibleitaly

GETTING AROUND

Airports

Fiumicino (also called Leonardo da Vinci; T: 06 65951, www.adr.it), 26km southwest of Rome, is the airport for both international and domestic air services. Non-stop trains run from Stazione Termini every half hour from about 7am–9.15pm (30mins) and underground trains every 15mins from Stazione Roma Tiburtina via Ostiense and Trastevere from about 5am–11pm (41mins). There are also night bus services between Stazione Tiburtina and the airport. If you arrive late at night, however, it is usually best to take a taxi. Taxis cost standard meter charges plus an airport supplement, or a price by agreement in advance.

Ciampino (T: 06 794 941, www.adr.it), 13km southeast of Rome, is a subsidiary airport used mainly for domestic flights, international charter flights and low-cost airlines. It can be reached by underground Line A from Stazione Termini to Anagnina station, and from there by COTRAL airport bus from 6am–10pm (every 30mins), but this journey is not very convenient and most visitors prefer to take a taxi, for standard meter charges plus an airport supplement.

Railway stations

Stazione Termini, Piazza dei Cinquecento, is the main station for all services of the state railways and for the underground (*la metropolitana*). It has left-luggage deposit facilities and a supermarket open 24hrs.

Stazione Roma Tiburtina, less central than Termini, is used by some trains which do not stop at the main station. It is well served by buses, and is on Line B of the underground, four stops from Termini. The stations of Ostiense and Trastevere are on the line to Fiumicino airport.

Local tourist offices

The official tourist agency for Rome is the APT (Azienda di Promozione Turistica di Roma), whose offices supply a list of hotels, a map (when available), a brief guide to the city and up-to-date opening times:

APT: 5 Via Parigi, T: 06 488 991, daily except Sun 8.15–7;

Tourist Information Service: T: 06 3600 4399;

Fiumicino airport: daily 7.45–7.

There are also a number of tourist information kiosks, in the centre of the city, open daily 9–6: Via del Corso (Largo Goldoni), the Fori Imperiali, Castel Sant'Angelo, Piazza San Giovanni in Laterano, Trastevere (Piazza Sonnino), Via Marco Minghetti (Fontana di Trevi), Via Nazionale (Palazzo delle Esposizioni), and Via dell'Olmata (Santa Maria Maggiore).

Buses and trams

Rome is well served by a fairly efficient bus and tram service, since most of the centre of the city has been closed to private traffic. The service of orange buses is run by ATAC (Azienda Tramvie e Autobus del Comune di Roma; www.atac.roma.it). Free maps of the principal routes (one for day-time services, and one for the night services) are usually available from the ATAC information kiosk on Piazza dei Cinquecento in front of Stazione Termini (open Mon–Sat 8–8).

Tickets are sold at tobacconists, bars and newspaper kiosks, as well as at ATAC booths and by automatic machines at many bus stops and metro stations. They are valid for 75mins on any number of lines and for one journey on the metro. They have to be stamped at automatic machines on board the vehicle. Those found travelling without a valid ticket are liable to a heavy fine.

It is usually worth purchasing a one-day ticket, a BIG (*biglietto giornaliero*), which expires at midnight of the day it was purchased. Available from the usual outlets, it must be stamped once on board. A seven-day ticket or CIS (*carta settimanale*) expires at midnight of the seventh day. Season tickets valid for one calendar month are also available.

Blue electric mini-bus services (nos. 116 and 117) operate a circular route through some of the most beautiful districts in the centre of town on weekdays. Express buses (*espressi*) make fewer stops than the other lines: one of these is no. 60 which provides a fast service between Piazza della Repubblica, Piazza Venezia, the Colosseum and Porta San Paolo (Piramide). The most convenient bus for St Peter's and the Vatican is no. 64 from the Stazione Termini via Piazza Venezia. There are usually no bus or underground services in Rome on 1st May or on the afternoon of Christmas Day, and services are limited on other holidays. Night bus services operate from ten past midnight to 5.30am; the numbers on these routes are followed by 'N'. Because of one-way streets, return journeys do not always follow the same route as the outward journey.

The few tramlines which survive (particularly useful for the Galleria Nazionale d'Arte Moderna) are charmingly old-fashioned and slow, but are more comfortable than the buses. A new line runs to Trastevere from Largo Torre Argentina.

The underground

There are two lines in Rome's underground (*metropolitana*), although if you want to visit the centre of the city, you are almost always better off taking a bus. The only really useful parts of the system if you are staying in the centre are from Stazione Termini to Piazza di Spagna, and from Stazione Termini to the Colosseum. The service begins at 5.30am and ends at 11.30pm; on Sat the last train is at half past midnight.

Line A runs from Battistini in the western suburbs to Via Ottaviano near the Vatican. From here it runs beneath the centre of Rome with stations at Piazzale Flaminio (Piazza del Popolo), Piazza di Spagna, Piazza Barberini, Piazza della Repubblica and Stazione Termini. It continues to San Giovanni in Laterano and traverses the southern suburbs of Rome along the Via Appia Nuova and Via Tuscolana to terminate beyond Cinecittà at Anagnina. It runs underground for the whole of its 14km length except for the bridge across the Tiber.

Line B runs southwest from Stazione Termini to Porta San Paolo, in Piazzale Ostiense, where it comes to the surface just beyond Ostiense station, running from there alongside the Rome–Lido railway as far as Magliana, beyond the Basilica of San Paolo fuori le Mura. It then runs underground northeast to terminate at Tre Fontane (Laurentina) in EUR. The intermediate stops most useful to visitors serving the centre of Rome south of Termini station are Via Cavour, Colosseo, Circo Massimo, and Piramide (Porta San Paolo).

Bicycles and scooters

Bicycles can be hired at stands in Piazza del Popolo, Piazza San Silvestro, Piazza di Spagna and Piazza Augusto Imperatore. Both bicycles and scooters can be hired from:

Scoot-a-long: 302 Via Cavour, T: 06 678 0206, map p. 623, 3E.
Scooters for Rent: 84 Via della Purificazione, T: 06 488 5485, map p. 623, 1D.
St Peter's Moto: 7 Fosse di Castello (before Lg. Castello, T: 06 687 5714, map p. 620, 2D.

Taxis

Taxis (white or yellow in colour) are provided with an identification name and number, the emblem of the municipality of Rome, and a meter; you should always make sure the latter is operational before hiring a taxi. The fare includes service, so tipping is not necessary. Licensed taxis are hired from ranks; there are no cruising taxis, and it is never advisable to accept rides from non-authorized taxis at the airports or train stations. There are additional charges for travel at night (10pm–7am), on Sun and for each piece of luggage. To call a taxi, T: 06 3570; T: 06 4994; or T: 06 8822: you will be given the approximate arrival time and the number of the taxi.

HOTELS & ACCOMMODATION

Rome offers some good, medium-sized hotels, often run with close involvement of the owning family. Most of the big chains are also represented with flagship hotels, and clean, cheap, central accommodation is provided by nuns whose convents are now emptier of novices than they once were. The following is just a selection: hotels which are specially recommended are marked (■). Details on Blue Guides recommended hotels and restaurants are on www.blueguides.com. A full listing of accommodation in all categories is available from Roma Turismo at 11 Via Parigi (map p. 623, 1E) or on its website www.romaturismo.it. Contact hotels directly for seasonal changes or special offers. The prices below are a guideline only for a double room in high season:

€€€	€300+
€€	€200–300
€	below €200

€€€ **Albergo del Senato**. *73 Piazza della Rotonda, T: 06 678 4343, www. albergodelsenato.it. 57 rooms. Map p. 622, 2B.* Rooms and a terrace overlooking the Pantheon, elegant lobby, a 19th-century building. The roof terrace is a wonderful place to sit, with tables, wrought iron chairs, and a breathtaking view.
€€€ **Bernini Bristol**. *23 Piazza Barberini, T: 06 488 931, www. berninibristol.com. 127 rooms. Map p. 623, 1D.* A restored 19th-century palazzo

overlooking Bernini's Fontana del Tritone on Piazza Barberini. Its L'Olimpo restaurant and roof garden on the top floor of the hotel has spectacular views across Rome and of the dome of St. Peter's.
€€€ **Boscolo Exedra**. *47 Piazza della Repubblica, T: 06 489 38000, www. boscolohotels.com. 240 rooms. Map p. 623, 1E.* A grand luxury five-star hotel, with imposing curving colonnades on the Piazza della Repubblica. The location, close to Termini station, is not tradi-

tionally sought-after, but it is very central. Classical features of the hotel incorporate modern stonework, sheet glass, steel and a myriad coloured marbles. There are some splendid rooms in the adjoining property originally used by the Vatican's Istituto San Michele to store grain. They retain the massive timbers in the roof and are a rustic contrast to the main section of the hotel. There is an open-air restaurant on the roof terrace (Sensus); the restaurant on the ground floor (Tazio) serves the seemingly obligatory Asian-fusion cuisine. The main restaurant, La Frusta, inspired by Fellini's *Otto e mezzo* is styled in stark modern black and white, but softened by good lighting.

€€€ **Hassler Hotel** and €€ **Il Palazzetto**. ▪ *6 Piazza Trinità dei Monti, T: 06 699 34730, www.hotelhassler.it. Hassler 99 rooms; Palazzetto 4 rooms. Map p. 620, 3B.* The Hassler is one of the most famous of Rome's luxury hotels, at the top of the Spanish Steps, with magnificent views from the rooms, terraces and rooftop restaurant. It has a delightful secret, in the form of a tiny 15th-century palazzetto on the other side of Piazza Trinità dei Monti. It was acquired in 1999 by Roberto Wirth, owner and General Manager of the Hassler Hotel, and refurbished by his wife Astrid to provide four elegant rooms overlooking the Spanish Steps. It is home to the International Wine Academy of Rome, with tasting rooms, wine salon, outdoor garden and Il Palazzetto Restaurant.

€€€ **Hotel Forum**. ▪ *25–30 Via Tor de' Conti, T: 06 679 2446. www. hotel forumrome.com. 80 rooms. Map p. 623, 3D.* Originally built in the 18th century and previously a convent for the neighbouring church. Relaxed and comfortable. The views of the Forum and Capitoline Hill, seen from some of the bedrooms as well as the rooftop restaurant, are spectacular.

€€€ **Hotel d'Inghilterra**. ▪ *14 Via Bocca di Leone, T: 06 699 811. www.hotel dinghilterraroma.it. 98 rooms. Map p. 622, 1C.* A club atmosphere and a loyal following with many guests returning year after year. A former favourite of Gregory Peck during the filming of *Roman Holiday*, as well as of Elizabeth Taylor, Richard Burton and Ernest Hemingway. Though close to the Spanish Steps and choicest shopping streets, its location is discreet and secluded. The small English-style bar, frequented by locals as well as hotel guests, is renowned for its excellent Martinis and Bloody Marys. The chambermaids are all extremely friendly.

€€€ **The Inn at the Spanish Steps**. ▪ *85 Via Condotti, T: 06 699 25657. www.atspanishsteps.com. 24 rooms. Map p. 622, 1C.* Next to the Caffè Greco on Via Condotti, this is one of the most popular townhouse hotels in the area, with a tiny but extremely friendly reception up a flight of stairs from an unobtrusive entrance. Individual, distinctively styled rooms are by the Roman interior furnishings firm Tenco (whose work includes elements of the nearby Hotel de Russie). The breakfast room on the top floor leads onto a large terrace with wrought iron tables under large square sun shades, and an abundance of flowering plants. From here you can watch the shoppers and sightseers down below, either before you set off after breakfast to join them, or in the evening accompanied by a glass of wine and canapés (both are included in the room rate). The hotel also has four exquisitely decorated serviced rooms and a suite with two bedrooms and two bathrooms on an upper floor of the next-door building at the end of Via Condotti, all looking over the Spanish Steps (rates on request). Advisable to book well in advance.

€€€ **Intercontinental de la Ville**. *69 Via Sistina, T: 06 67331,www.interconti. com. 192 rooms. Map p. 623, 1D.* A fine Neoclassical building at the top of the Spanish Steps designed in 1925 by Hungarian architect József Vágó (who also designed the League of Nations building in Geneva). Classical rooms, some special suites with large terraces covered with bougainvillea, jasmine and lemon trees, and panoramas across the Roman rooftops. The piano bar serves aperitifs and after-dinner drinks.

€€€ **Grand Hotel Parco dei Principi**. *5 Via G. Frescobaldi, T: 06 854 421, www.parcodeiprincipi.com. 180 rooms. Map p. 620, 1C.* Designed by Giò Ponti in 1964 and renovated in 2002, with elegant public areas and replicas of paintings from the nearby Galleria Borghese. All the rooms have a balcony, and most overlook the Villa Borghese park. An olympic-size swimming pool, together with gym and fitness centre gives the Parco dei Principi the feeling of a resort hotel, particularly during the summer months. Since the summer of 2005, the Italian Sommelier Institute has made its home here.

€€€ **Raphael**. ■ *2 Largo Febo (Piazza Navona), T: 06 682831, www.raphael hotel.com. 56 rooms. Map p. 622, 2B.* Tucked away behind the Piazza Navona, this ivy-clad 18th-century palazzo is one

of the most charming and finest hotels in Rome, within easy walking distance of the Pantheon, Campo dei Fiori, and Via del Corso. Original Picasso plates, pre-Columbian Mayan pottery and contemporary paintings are all part of the decoration. The multi-level roof terrace has a superb view including the dome of St Peter's in the distance and Santa Maria della Pace in the next street. The Bramante Bar is one of the most romantic spots in town for a glass of Prosecco.

€€€ **Hotel de Russie**. *9 Via del Babuino. T: 06 32 88 81. www.roccoforte hotels.com. 94 rooms. Map p. 620, 2B.* Part of the Rocco Forte Hotels Group, it attracts a glamorous crowd to its Jardin de Russie courtyard restaurant and extensive terraced gardens behind.

€€€ **St Regis Grand Hotel**. *3 Via Vittorio Emanuele Orlando, T: 06 47091, www.stregis.com/grandrome. 161 rooms. Map p. 623, 1E.* A truly Grand Hotel, opened by Cesar Ritz in 1894, the first hotel in Rome with private baths and electric light. Elegant salons, glass ceilings, trompe l'oeil designs, and a magnificent ballroom all contribute to the *belle époque* atmosphere. Some rooms overlook the Piazza della Repubblica. Part of the Starwood group.

€€€ **Hotel Splendide Royal**. *14 Via di Porta Pinciana, T: 06 421689, www.splendideroyal.com. 52 rooms. Map p. 620, 2C.* Luxurious five-star hotel with the famous Mirabelle Restaurant, managed by Bruno Borghesi. The roof terrace offers a stunning panorama of both the city and the Borghese gardens.

€€€ (Scheduled to open in Jan 2006) **Salvatore Ferragamo Hotel**. Above the Salvatore Ferragamo shop in Via Condotti, the hotel will have 14 suites in the style of the other Ferragamo-owned Lungarno Hotels in Florence.

€€ **Albergo Cesari**. *89a Via di Pietra. T: 06 674 9701. www.albergocesari.it. 47 rooms. Map p. 622, 2C.* A well-managed 3-star hotel in a great location between the Trevi Fountain and the Pantheon. It opened as a hotel in 1787, and guests have included Stendhal and Giuseppe Mazzini. The rooms are classically simple, and public areas include a small salon and breakfast room. No restaurant, but plenty in the immediate vicinity.

€€ **Albergo Santa Chiara**. *21 Via Santa Chiara. T: 06 687 2979. www.albergosantachiara.com. 100 rooms. Map p. 622, 2B.* Following a period of extensive refurbishment, the hotel will re-open in early 2006. A welcoming place, with a loyal clientele. Good value for money considering location, quality and service.

€€ **Albergo del Sole al Pantheon**. ◾ *63 Piazza della Rotonda, T: 06 678 0441, www.hotelsolealpantheon.com. 31 rooms plus 5 additional suites in the building across the street. Map p. 622, 2B.* Possibly the oldest hotel in Rome, built in 1467. Guests have included Frederick III of Austria (who gives his name to one of the suites), Jean-Paul Sartre, Ariosto, who may have written his *Orlando Furioso* in what is now room 110, and Mascagni, who celebrated the première of *Cavalleria Rusticana* here (room 210). Gracious rooms have white walls, tiled floors and rich fabrics. Eight rooms have views of the Pantheon. In the labyrinth of corridors and stairways are numerous architectural details and stone reliefs. The breakfast room, off an inner courtyard where you can sit out in warm weather, serves one of the best breakfast buffets in the city.

€€ **Hotel Art**. *56 Via Margutta, T: 06 360 03995, www.hotelart.it. 46 rooms. Map p. 620, 3B.* One of the few modern style hotels in Rome, this contemporary hotel in an older building stands on the Via Margutta, the street of artists (*see p. 169*). The building was originally a church, evident still from the lobby ceilings. The reception by contrast consists of two separate 'pods' (which look remarkably similar to giant white plastic motorcycle helmets). Media types come and go, all presumably on a mission of importance in the world of creativity and fashion. Each of the three floors has its own neon colour scheme: yellow, orange or blue. Rooms are not large, but well planned, with dark wood floors, polished concrete walls and excellent lighting. If a contemporary alternative to the classical Roman style is your preference, the Art is probably the pick of a relatively small but expanding bunch of modern hotels, and in an excellent location. No restaurant.

€€ **Aventino S. Anselmo Hotels**. *19 Via Santa Melania, T: 06 574 5231, www.aventinohotels.com. Hotel Villa S. Pio 78 rooms, Hotel Aventino 21 rooms. Map p. 621, 2A.* Three charming late-Baroque villas all within minutes of each other, in the peaceful Aventino district. Villa San Pio consists of three separate buildings connected by covered paths set in lush gardens. Each room is different, with hand-painted country-style furniture, parquet flooring, fine fabrics and linen. The bathrooms are marble, mostly with showers, and cleverly designed (if a little on the small side in some cases). Special rooms include 531 and 529, the former with a full bath, and both with private terrace. Room 255 is a tiny house on its

Hostels, apartments and convents

A number of convents offer well-located, well-priced accommodation: the website of the American Catholic Church in Rome has a list (www.santasusanna.org/coming ToRome/convents.html). Alternatively there is www.hospites.it, an Italian website for religious houses across the country, partially in English but harder to navigate. If considering a stay in a convent, you need to be aware of each establishment's curfew to avoid being locked out for the night. The Suore di Santa Elisabetta convent in Via dell'Olmata just off Piazza Santa Maria di Maggiore (map p. 623, 2F) has double rooms with bath and breakfast for €75 for two, and without bath for €58. T: 06 488 4066. ist.it.s.elisabetta@libero.it

Hotel Campo de'Fiori has 15 apartments, all with one bedroom, living room and kitchen, accommodating up to four people with sofa bed and/or rollaway. Breakfast is included in the rates, which range from €100–€240 depending on season and number of guests. T: 06 688 06865. www.campodefiori.com. Also www.apartmentsapart.com, with a dozen or so apartments in the centre of Rome.

Hostels Alessandro has been operating in Rome for over ten years, and has three properties, all close to the Termini Station: the Alessandro Palace Hostel, the Alessandro Downtown and Alessandro Legends. All have a selection of double, triple, quad and dorms with up to ten beds, segregated for male and female travellers. The rates include breakfast, linen, free maps. T: 06 446 1958. www.hostelsalessandro.com

RESTAURANTS

The best guide to eating in Rome is *Roma del Gambero Rosso*, published annually (only in Italian). A selection of a few restaurants—grouped according to location and divided into four categories according to price per person for dinner, with wine—is given below. Blue Guides recommended restaurants are marked (■).

€€€€	around € 125
€€€	around € 80
€€	around€ 30–40
€	under € 30

NB: smoking is forbidden inside all restaurants.

Pantheon, Piazza Navona and Campo dei Fiori

€€€€

La Rosetta. *8 Via della Rosetta, T: 06 686 1002. Closed Sun. Map p. 622, 2B. A handsome restaurant a few steps from* the Pantheon, La Rosetta is widely held to be the top fish restaurant in Rome. Preparations are gracefully simple and accentuate rather than disguise the flavour of wonderfully fresh fish and seafood. Excellent list of wines and champagne.

€€€

Il Convivio Troiani. *31 Vicolo dei Soldati, T: 06 686 9432. Closed Sun. Map p. 622, 1B.* A very good, small restaurant with cooking that begins with traditional ingredients but is particularly imaginative. It has an excellent *menù degustazione*—a many-course set menu—that changes weekly. Professional service.

€€

L'Eau Vive. *85 Via Monterone, T: 06 6880 1095. Closed Sun. Map p. 622, 2B.* A long-established restaurant inside a 15th century palace. The French nuns who run the restaurant for charity provide traditional French cuisine.

Fortunato al Pantheon. *55 Via del Pantheon, T: 06 679 2788. Closed Sun. Map p. 622, 2B.* An efficiently run traditional Roman restaurant with particularly high-quality food. Frequented by politicians and businessmen. Seasonal fare and good fish.

Settimio. *117 Via del Pellegrino, T: 06 6880 1978. Closed Wed. Map p. 622, 2A.* A simple restaurant with a limited selection of wines but high quality traditional Roman cuisine.

€

Cul de Sac 1. *73 Piazza Pasquino, T: 06 6880 1094. Closed Mon lunchtime. Map p. 280.* The first wine bar in Rome. Long and narrow, warm and friendly, this place makes a pleasant change from pizza whenever an informal or frugal meal is required. Cheeses, cold meat, vegetable quiches, but also hearty lentil soup in wintertime. There are over 700 wine labels to choose from.

Montecarlo. *12 Vicolo Savelli, T: 06 686 1877. Closed Mon. Map p. 622, 2A.* No credit cards. A good place to eat a pizza or simple meal, with crowded old-fashioned tables, and a bustling atmosphere without any pretension, typical of Rome. Good simple local dishes (including the desserts).

Piazza di Spagna

€€€–€€

Dal Bolognese. ◼ *1/2 Piazza del Popolo, T: 06 361 1426. Closed Mon. Map p. 620, 2A.* In a wonderful position, with elegant clientele and professional service. As the name suggests, the cuisine is from Bologna, with excellent fresh pasta.

Via Veneto and the Parioli

€€€€

La Terrazza dell'Hotel Eden. *49 Via Ludovisi, T: 06 478 121. Open every day. Map p. 620, 3C.* Having the best view in the city tends to distract attention from the food, but the modern interpretations of Italian classics are expertly prepared and beautifully presented.

€€€–€€

Al Ceppo. *2 Via Panama, T: 06 841 9696. Closed Mon. Map p. 616, 1A.* A favourite with locals in the quiet Parioli quarter, Al Ceppo has been here for more than 30 years. The menu always features specialities from the Marche region, and the grilled meats are especially good.

Le Colline Emiliane. ◼ *22 Via degli Avignonesi, T: 06 4817538. Closed Sun eve and Mon. Map p. 623, 1D.* An elegant, classic-style Roman restaurant with good service. The food includes Emilian specialities such as a pasta dish with squash (*tortelli di zucca*) and good meat dishes.

Papà Baccus. *36 Via Toscana, T: 06 4274 2808. Closed Sun. Map p. 620, 3C.* A fairly priced restaurant not far from Via Veneto, serving light Italian food, mostly Tuscan in origin. Professional yet friendly service. Very good desserts and wines.

Ghetto

€€

Piperno. ▪ *9 Monte dei Cenci, T: 06 6880 6629. Closed Sun eve and Mon. Map p. 622, 3B.* Small and cosy with a panelled dado and green baize above, Piperno serves home-cooked specialities, simple but delicious. Oxtail, sweetbreads and tripe all feature on the menu: this is real food. But there are plenty of other choices too, including fish. The Jewish-style artichokes are excellent, as is the light, refreshing house Frascati.

€

Giggetto al Portico d'Ottavia. *21 Via del Portico d'Ottavia, T: 06 686 1105. Closed Mon. Map p. 622, 3B.* Good pasta dishes, and traditional Roman fare including lamb (*abbacchio*) and *fritto di fiori di zucca* (courgette flowers stuffed with mozzarella cheese and salted anchovies, dipped in egg and fried). An excellent choice, and you can eat outside in summer.

Trastevere

€€€€

Alberto Ciarla. *40 Piazza San Cosimato, T: 06 581 8668. Open evenings only; closed Sun. Map p. 622, 4A.* Mostly fish on this menu, which is always beautifully prepared. Several set menus as well as à la carte, and a good wine selection. A very well run old-established restaurant.

€€

Paris. *7a Piazza San Callisto, T: 06 581 5378. Closed Sun eve and Mon. Map p. 622, 3A.* A comfortable restaurant near Piazza Santa Maria in Trastevere, Paris offers many good Roman dishes such as fried courgette flowers stuffed with mozzarella and anchovies and *zuppa di arzilla* (fish soup with broccoli). Excellent wine list.

Checco er Carettiere. *10 Via Benedetta, T: 06 581 7018. Closed Sun eve. Map p. 622, 3A.* An extremely popular and noisy family-run restaurant offering traditional Roman dishes, such as *coda alla vaccinara* (oxtail stewed in a tomato and celery sauce), as well as lighter food, such as simple grilled fish. Home-made desserts. **Sora Lella**. *16 Via di Ponte dei Quattro Capi, T: 06 686 1601. Closed Sun. Map p. 622, 3B.* A small, neat, family-run trattoria located on Isola Tiberina. Traditional Roman cooking, such as *amatriciana* (pasta in a tomato sauce with chunks of cured pork), oxtail, artichokes *alla romana* (stewed with mint) or *alla giudia* (deep-fried); home-made desserts. **Dar Poeta**. *45 Vicolo del Bologna, T: 06 588 0516. Open evenings only. Map p. 622, 3A.* One of the best *pizzerie* in Rome, always crowded.

Termini

€€–€

Trimani. *37b Via Cernaia, T: 06 446 9630. Closed Sun. Map p. 623, 1F.* Located near Stazione Termini, Trimani is one of the oldest wine shops in Rome, with a friendly wine bar round the corner. Excellent wine list. The menu includes a few hot dishes, such as soups, quiches, grilled beef and seasonal vegetables, as well as a tempting selection of cheeses, smoked fish and cured pork. Good desserts. Friendly service.

Piramide and Testaccio

€€€

Checchino dal 1887. *30 Via di Monte Testaccio, T: 06 574 3816. Closed Sun and Mon. Map p. 621, 3A*. Literally carved out of Monte Testaccio and run by the same family for over a hundred years, Checchino serves the most traditional Roman cuisine. Simple decor and good wine list (also available by the glass).

€€

La Sella del Diavolo. *102 Via Ostiense, T: 06 578 1260. Map p. 5*. Right beside the Centrale Montemartini, a splendid gallery with works from the Musei Capitolini (*see p. 471*). Spacious rooms frequented by Italians who work nearby. Particularly good for fish and Sardinian specialities. Efficient, professional service.

€

Da Oio a casa mia. ◼ *43 Via N. Galvani, T: 06 5782680. Map p. 621, 2A. Closed Sun*. A simple Roman trattoria run by a family who once owned a successful butchers' shop, with excellent traditional dishes including *coda alla vaccinara* (oxtail in a celery and tomato sauce), and an unusual version of spaghetti carbonara with '*glicia*' (salt pork), pecorino cheese and black pepper (but without egg).

Snacks

For a slice of pizza and other good hot snacks go to a *rosticceria* or *tavola calda*; some of these have no seating and sell food to take away or eat on the spot. They often sell sliced *porchetta* (roast suckling pig) and other hot snacks including *supplì* (fried rice balls with mozzarella), *arancini* (fried rice balls with tomato), *calzoni* (a pizza 'roll' usually filled with ham and mozzarella) and *crocchette* (minced meat or potato croquettes).

Cafés and bars

Cafés are open all day. Most customers eat the excellent refreshments they serve standing up. You pay the cashier first, and show the receipt to the barman in order to get served. In almost all bars, if you sit at a table you are charged considerably more—at least double—and are given waiter service (you should not pay first).

Well-known cafés in the city, all of which have tables (some outside), include **Caffè Greco**, a famous café (*see p. 174*), 86 Via Condotti, map p. 622, 1C; **Babington**, English tearooms, Piazza di Spagna, map p. 620, 3B; **Rosati**, 4 Piazza del Popolo, map p. 620, 2A; **Tre Scalini**, noted for its ices, including *tartufi* (truffles), 31 Piazza Navona, map p. 622, 2B; **Camilloni a Sant'Eustachio**, Piazza Sant'Eustachio, map p. 622, 2B; **Doney** and **Caffè de Paris**, 90 and 145 Via Veneto, map p. 622, 1D; **Pascucci**, justly famous for its fresh fruit milk-shakes, Via di Torre Argentina, map p. 622, 2B; **La Casa del Caffè**, Via degli Orfani, and **Il Caffe**, Piazza Sant'Eustachio (both near the Pantheon) serve particularly good coffee, map p. 622, 2B; **Vanni**, good snacks and a yogurt bar, in Via Frattina (corner of Via Belsiana), map p. 622, 1C.

MUSEUMS, GALLERIES & MONUMENTS

Hours of admission to museums, collections and monuments in Rome are given in the text. Specialist museums or those not of the first importance, and Roman archaeological sites not normally open to the public without booking, or at present closed, are listed in the Appendix at the back of the book. Opening times vary and often change without warning; those given in this guide should therefore be accepted with reserve. An up-to-date list of opening times is always available at APT information offices and the information kiosks of the municipality, but even this can be inaccurate. To make certain the times are correct, it is worth telephoning first. The opening hours for Sundays given here usually apply also to public holidays. All museums are usually closed on the main public holidays in Rome: Easter Sunday, 29th June and 15th August. Monday remains the most usual closing day for the state museums and those owned by the municipality. The closing times given in the text indicate when the ticket office closes, which is usually 30–60mins before the actual closing time. Most opening times change between summer and winter. More and more museums are introducing longer opening hours: the major museums—except for the Vatican—are often open in summer after dark.

British citizens under the age of 18 and over the age of 65 are entitled to free admission to state-owned museums and monuments, and all members of EU countries between the ages of 18 and 25 are entitled to a half-price ticket for all state-owned museums in Italy (you must show proof of nationality). The same terms apply in Rome to all the museums and monuments owned by the municipality. There is a student discount for the Vatican museums.

An inclusive ticket, called the **Roma Archaeologia Card**, valid for 7 days, allows entrance to the main state-owned archaeological sites and museums in Rome. There is also a 7-day inclusive ticket for the four museums run by the Museo Nazionale Romano; for information T: 06 3996 7700. Up-to-date information on state museums is also available at www. beniculturali.it. For information on the archaeological sites owned by the municipality, T: 06 6710 2070.

Lecture tours of museums and villas (sometimes otherwise closed to the public) are organized by various cultural associations: these are advertised in the local press. *La Settimana dei Musei Italiani* (Museum Week) has now become established as an annual event, usually held in March or April. Entrance to most museums is free during the week, and some have longer opening hours. Some private collections and monuments not generally accessible are normally opened at this time.

The office of the Monumenti Antichi e Scavi Archeologici of the Comune of Rome is at 29 Via Portico d'Ottavia (map p. 622, 3C).

CHURCHES & CATACOMBS

Catholic basilicas and churches

The four great patriarchal basilicas are San Giovanni in Laterano (St John Lateran), the cathedral and mother church of the world, San Pietro in Vaticano (St Peter's), San Paolo fuori le Mura and Santa Maria Maggiore. These, with the three basilicas of San Lorenzo fuori le Mura, Santa Croce in Gerusalemme and San Sebastiano, comprise the Seven Churches of Rome. Among minor basilicas rank Sant'Agnese fuori le Mura, Santi Apostoli, Santa Cecilia, San Clemente and Santa Maria in Trastevere.

Some churches, including several of importance, are open only for a short time in the morning and evening (opening times have been given where possible in the text, but might vary). St Peter's and the other three great basilicas are open all day 7–7; 7–6 in winter. Other churches are closed between 12 and 3.30, 4 or 5, but most of them open early in the morning (around 7). Most churches now ask that sightseers do not visit the church during a service. Many pictures and frescoes are difficult to see without lights, which often have to be operated with coins. When visiting churches it is always useful to carry a torch and a pair of binoculars. Churches in Rome are very often not orientated. In the text the terms north and south refer to the liturgical north (left) and south (right), taking the high altar as at the east end.

Dress: If you are wearing shorts or a mini skirt or have bare shoulders you can be stopped from entering some churches, including St Peter's.

Roman Catholic services The ringing of the evening Ave Maria or Angelus bell at sunset is an important event in Rome, where it signifies the end of the day and the beginning of night. The hour varies according to the season. On Sunday and, in the principal churches, often on weekdays, Mass is celebrated until 1 and from 5–8. High Mass, with music, is celebrated in the basilicas on Sunday at 9.30 or 10.30 (the latter in St Peter's). The choir of St Peter's sings on Sunday at High Mass and at vespers at 5. The Sistine Chapel choir sings in St Peter's on 29th June and whenever the pope celebrates Mass.

Roman Catholic services in English take place in San Silvestro in Capite, Piazza San Silvestro (map p. 622, 1C); San Clemente, 95 Via Labicana (map p. 623, 3E); and Santa Susanna, 15 Via Venti Settembre (map p. 623, 1E); services in Irish are at St Patrick's, 31 Via Boncompagni (map p. 620, 3D); and also at Sant'Isidoro; San Clemente; and Sant'Agata dei Goti. Confessions are heard in English in the four main basilicas and in the Gesù, Santa Maria sopra Minerva, Sant'Anselmo, Sant'Ignazio, and Santa Sabina.

Church festivals: On saints' days Mass and vespers with music are celebrated in the churches dedicated to the saints concerned. The Octave of the Epiphany is held at Sant'Andrea della Valle. The Blessing of the Lambs takes place at Sant'Agnese fuori le Mura on 21st January around 10.30. On the evening of 6th January there is a procession with the *Santo Bambino* at Santa Maria in Aracoeli (the statue is a copy of the one stolen in 1994). The singing of the *Te Deum* annually on 31st December in the church of the *Gesù* is a magnificent traditional ceremony. In San Giovanni in Laterano a choral Mass is held on 24th June, in commemoration of the service held here on 24th June 1929 by Pius XI, and the pope attends the Maundy Thursday celebrations in the basilica when he gives his benediction from the loggia on the façade. On 5th August the leg-

The Lion Bookshop, 33 Via dei Greci. Open 10–7.30; Mon 3.30–7.30. The shop also has a reading room and tea and coffee are available. Map p. 620, 3B.

Markets

Open-air markets are open Mon–Sat 8–1. These include excellent food markets at Campo dei Fiori; near Piazza Vittorio Emanuele II (with North African and Middle Eastern products); Via Andrea Doria and Testaccio. New and second-hand clothes are sold in Via Sannio (Porta San Giovanni), and old prints and books at the Mercato delle Stampe, Largo della Fontanella di Borghese. Porta Portese is a huge, chaotic flea market between Via Portuense and Viale Trastevere, open Sun 7–1.

ADDITIONAL INFORMATION

Banking services

Banks are usually open Mon–Fri 8.30–1.30, and for one hour in the afternoon, usually 2.30 or 3–3.30 or 4; closed Sat, Sun and holidays. A few banks are now open on Saturday mornings, including the Banca di Roma in Piazza di Spagna, and the Banca Nazionale del Lavoro at 266 Via del Corso. All banks close early (about 11am) on days preceding national holidays.

Crime and personal security

For all emergencies, dial 113 or 112.

As in large towns everywhere, pickpocketing is a problem in Rome; it is always advisable not to carry valuables, and to be particularly careful on public transport.

Cash, documents and valuables can be left in hotel safes. It is a good idea to make photocopies of all important documents in case of loss. Particular care should be taken when using a credit card to draw cash from an ATM.

There are three categories of policemen in Italy: *Vigili Urbani*, municipal police who wear blue uniforms in winter and white during the summer, and have hats similar to those of London policemen; *Carabinieri*, military police who wear black uniforms with a red stripe down the side of their trousers; and the *Polizia di Stato*, state police who wear dark-blue jackets and light-blue trousers. The central police station of the Polizia di Stato is at 15 Via San Vitale, map p. 623, 2E, T: 06 4686; foreigners' office, T: 06 4686 2102.

Municipal police	T: 06 67691
Carabinieri	T: 112
Traffic police	T: 55441
Railway police	T: 06 481 9561

Crime should be reported at once, theft to either the Polizia di Stato or the Carabinieri. A detailed statement has to be given in order to get an official document confirming loss or damage (*denunzia di smarrimento*), which is essential for insurance claims. Interpreters are usually provided.

To report the loss or theft of a credit card, call:

Visa   T: 800 822056
Mastercard   T: 800 872 050
American Express   T: 06 7228 0371

Emergency services

For all emergencies, T: 113: the switchboard will coordinate the help you need.

First aid services (*pronto soccorso*) are available at all hospitals, railway stations and airports. San Giovanni, in Piazza San Giovanni in Laterano, is the central hospital for road accidents and other emergencies: for first aid, T: 06 7705 5297. The American Hospital in Rome, 69 Via Emilio Longoni, T: 06 225 5290, is a private English-speaking hospital which accepts most American insurance plans. The International Medical Centre will refer callers to English-speaking doctors: T: 06 488 2371, nights and weekends T: 06 488 4051.

First-aid and ambulance service   T: 118
Red Cross ambulance service   T: 5510
Fire brigade   T: 115
Road assistance   T: 116

For all other emergencies, see under 'Crime' above.

Pharmacies

Pharmacies are usually open Mon–Sat 9–1 & 4–7.30 or 8. Some are open 24hrs a day, including the one outside Stazione Termini on Piazza dei Cinquecento. A few are open on Sundays and holidays, and at night: these are listed on the door of every chemist, and in the daily newspapers.

Public holidays and annual festivals

The main holidays in Rome, when offices and shops are closed, are as follows:

1st January (New Year's Day)	1st November (All Saints' Day)
25th April (Liberation Day)	1st December (Immaculate Conception)
Easter Monday	25th December (Christmas Day)
1st May (Labour Day)	26th December (St Stephen)
15th August (Assumption)	

In addition, the festival of the patron saints of Rome, Peter and Paul, is celebrated on 29th June as a local holiday in the city.

Museums are usually closed on 29th June, Easter Sunday and 15th August, and there is usually no public transport on 1st May and the afternoon of Christmas Day.

Annual festivals

5th–6th January: Epiphany (*Befana*), celebrated at night in Piazza Navona
Shrove Tuesday: Carnival is celebrated in the streets and squares
19th March: *Festa di San Giuseppe*, in the Trionfale district (north of the Vatican)
21st April: Anniversary of the birth of Rome, celebrated on the Campidoglio

Carceres, openings in the barriers through which the competing chariots entered the circus

Cardo, the main street of a Roman town, at right angles to the Decumanus

Cartoon, from *cartone*, meaning large sheet of paper. A full-size preparatory drawing for a painting or fresco

Caryatid, female figure used as a supporting column

Cavea, the part of a theatre or amphitheatre occupied by the row of seats

Cella, sanctuary of a temple, usually in the centre of the building

Chiaroscuro, distribution of light and shade in a painting

Chiton, linen tunic worn by the ancient Greeks

Ciborium, casket or tabernacle containing the Host

Cipollino, a greyish marble with streaks of white or green

Cippus, sepulchral monument in the form of an altar

Cista, casket, usually of bronze and cylindrical in shape, to hold jewels, toilet articles, etc, and decorated with mythological subjects

Clerestory, upper part of the nave of a church above the side aisles, with windows, usually a feature of Gothic architecture

Cloisonné, type of enamel decoration divided by narrow strips of metal, typical of Byzantine craftsmanship

Columbarium, a building (usually subterranean) with niches to hold urns containing the ashes of the dead

Confessio, crypt beneath the high altar and raised choir of a church, usually containing the relics of a saint

Corbel, a projecting block, usually of stone, to support an arch or beam

Cornice, topmost part of a temple entablature; any projecting ornamental moulding at the top of a building beneath the roof

Cosmatesque (or *Cosmati*), inlaid marble work using mosaic and coloured glass and stone to decorate pavements, pulpits, choir screens, columns, cloisters, etc.

Cryptoporticus, vaulted subterranean corridor

Cuneus, wedge-shaped block of seats in an antique theatre

Cyclopean, the term applied to walls of unmortared masonry, older than the Etruscan civilization, and attributed by the ancients to the giant Cyclopes

Decumanus, main street of a Roman town, running parallel to its longer axis

Diaconia, early Christian charitable institution

Dipteral, temple surrounded by a double peristyle

Diptych, painting or ivory tablet in two sections

Engaged columns, columns which partially retreat into the wall

Entablature, upper part of a temple above the columns, made up of an architrave, frieze, and cornice

Ephebus, Greek youth under training (military or university)

Exedra, semicircular recess

Ex-voto, tablet or small painting expressing gratitude to a saint

Flavian, of the emperors Vespasian, Titus, Domitian, Nerva and Trajan; or of the period of their rule

Forum, open space in a town serving as a market or meeting-place

Fresco, (in Italian, *affresco*), painting

executed on wet plaster. On the wall beneath is sketched the sinopia, and the cartoon is transferred onto the fresh plaster (intonaco) before the fresco is begun, either by pricking the outline with small holes over which a powder is dusted, or by means of a stylus which leaves an incised line on the wet plaster. In recent years many frescoes have been detached from the walls on which they were executed

Frieze, strip of decoration usually along the upper part of a wall; in a temple this refers to the horizontal feature above the columns between the architrave and the cornice

Frigidarium, room for cold baths in a Roman bath

Gens, Roman clan or group of families linked by a common name

Giallo antico, red-veined yellow marble from Numidia

Gigantomachia, contest between giants

Gonfalone banner of a medieval guild or commune

Graffiti, design on a wall made with an iron tool on a prepared surface, the design showing in white. Also used loosely to describe scratched designs or words on walls

Greek cross, cross with all four arms of equal length

Grisaille, painting in various tones of grey

Grotesque (or *grottesche*), painting or stucco decoration based on the style of the ancient Romans found during the Renaissance in the Domus Aurea (then underground, hence the name, from 'grotto'). The delicate ornamental decoration usually includes patterns of flowers, sphinxes, birds and human figures, against a light ground

Herm (pl. *hermae*), quadrangular pillar decreasing in girth towards the ground, surmounted by a head

Hexastyle, temple with a portico of six columns at the end

Hydria, a vessel for water

Hypogeum, subterranean excavation for the interment of the dead (usually Etruscan)

Impasto, early Etruscan ware made of inferior clay

Imperial period, Period of ancient Roman history under the Roman emperors (27 BC–476 AD)

Impluvium, pool or cistern in the centre of an atrium in a Roman house, into which rainwater falls

Insula (pl. *insulae*), tenement house

Intarsia (or *tarsia*), inlay of wood, marble or metal

Intercolumniations, the space between the columns in a colonnade

Intonaco, plaster

Krater, antique mixing-bowl, conical in shape with a rounded base

Kylix, wide shallow vase with two handles and short stem

Laconicum, room for vapour baths in a Roman bath

Latin cross, cross where the vertical arm is longer than the horizontal

Loggia, covered gallery or balcony, usually preceding a larger building

Lunette, semicircular space in a vault or above a door or window, often decorated with a painting or relief

Maenad, female participant in the orgiastic rites of Dionysus

Matroneum, gallery reserved for women in early Christian churches

Meta, conical turning-post for chariot races in a circus or stadium

Metope, panel between two triglyphs

Stele, upright stone bearing a monumental inscription

Stemma, coat of arms or heraldic device

Stereobate, basement of a temple or other building

Stoa, a long, narrow colonnaded building, used as a meeting hall or for public gatherings

Strigil, bronze scraper used by the Romans to remove the oil with which they had anointed themselves

Stylobate, basement of a columned temple or other building

Tablinum, the reception or family room in a Roman house

Telamones, (see *Atlantes*)

Temenos, a sacred enclosure

Tepidarium, room for warm baths in a Roman bath

Tessera (*pl. tesserae*), a small cube of marble, glass etc, used in mosaic work

Tetrastyle, having four columns at the end

Thermae, originally simply baths, later elaborate complexes with libraries, assembly rooms and gymnasia

Tholos, a circular building

Tondo, round painting or bas-relief

Trabeated, construction where the apertures (doors, windows) have vertical supports and horizontal lintels as opposed to arches

Transenna, open grille or screen, usually of marble, in an early Christian church

Travertine, tufa quarried near Tivoli; the commonest of Roman building materials

Tribune, raised platform or gallery, for watching a spectacle or addressing an audience or crowd

Triclinium, dining-room and reception-room of a Roman house

Triglyph, small panel of a Doric frieze raised slightly and carved with three vertical channels

Triptych, painting or tablet in three sections

Trompe l'oeil, literally a deception of the eye. Used to describe illusionist decoration, painted architectural perspectives, etc.

Tropaion (or Trophy), a victory monument

Tumulus, a burial mound

Velarium, canvas sheet supported by masts to protect the spectators in an open theatre from the sun

Verde antico, green marble from Tessaglia

Volute, scroll-like decoration at the corners of an Ionic capital; also typically present console-style on the façades of Baroque churches

Zoöphorus, frieze of a Doric temple, so-called because the metopes were often decorated with figures of animals

RULERS OF ANCIENT ROME

Kings of Rome

Romulus	753–716 BC	Tarquinius Priscus	616–579 BC
Numa Pompilius	716–673 BC	Servius Tullius	579–534 BC
Tullus Hostilius	673–640 BC	Tarquinius Superbus	534–509 BC
Ancus Martius	640–616 BC		

Roman Republic (509–27 BC)

Sulla (dictator)	82–78 BC	Julius Caesar (dictator)	45–44 BC
First Triumvirate (Julius Caesar,		Second Triumvirate (Mark Antony,	
Crassus, Pompey)	60–53 BC	Lepidus, Octavian)	43–27 BC
Pompey (dictator)	52–47 BC		

Roman Empire (27 BC–AD 395)

Augustus		Pertinax	193
(formerly Octavian)	27 BC–AD 14	Didius Julianus	193
Tiberius	14–37		
Caligula	37–41	**Severans**	
Claudius	41–54	Septimius Severus	193–211
Nero	54–68	Caracalla	211–217
Galba	68–69	Geta (co-emperor)	211–212
Otho	69	Macrinus	217–218
Vitellius	69	Elagabalus	218–222
		Alexander Severus	222–235
Flavians		Maximinus Thrax	235–238
Vespasian	69–79	Gordian I	238
Titus	79–81	Gordian II	238
Domitian	81–96	Pupienus	238
Nerva	96–98	Balbinus (co-emperor)	238
Trajan	98–117	Gordian III	238–244
		Philip I	244–247
Antonines		Philip II	247–249
Hadrian	117–138	Decius	249–251
Antoninus Pius	138–161	Gallus and Volusian	251–253
Marcus Aurelius	161–180	Aemilianus	253
Lucius Verus (co-emperor)	161–169	Valerian	253–260
Commodus	180–192	Gallienus	260–268

Claudius II	268–270	Maxentius	306–312
Quintillus	270	Constantine the Great	
Aurelian	270–275	(reunites empire)	306–337
Tacitus	275–276	Constantine II	337–340
Florian	276	Constans (co-emperor)	337–350
Probus	276–282	Constantius II (co-emperor)	337–361
Carus	282–283	Magnentius (co-emperor)	350–353
Carinus	282–285	Julian the Apostate	361–363
Numerian (co-emperor)	283–284	Jovian	363–364
Diocletian (institutes tetrarchy)	285–305	Valentinian I (in West)	364–375
Maximian (co-emperor)	286–305	Valens (in East)	364–378
Constantius Chlorus	305–306	Gratian	367–383
Galerius	305–310	Valentinian II (usurper)	375–392
Licinius	308–324	Theodosius I	378–395
Flavius Severus	306–307		

Western Empire (395–476)

Honorius	395–423	Anthemius	467–472
Valentinian III	425–55	Olybrius	472
Petronius Maximus	455	Glycerius	473
Avitus	455–456	Julius Nepos	474–475
Majorian	457–461	Romulus Augustulus	475–476
Libius Severus	461–465		

POPES

Antipopes, usurpers or otherwise unlawful occupants of the pontifical throne are given in square brackets.

1. **St Peter**; martyr; 42–67
2. **St Linus**, of Tuscia (Volterra?); martyr; 67–78
3. **St Anacletus I**, of Rome; martyr; 78–90 (?)
4. **St Clement I**, of the Roman Flavian *gens*; M.; 90–99 (?)
5. **St Evaristus**, of Greece (or of Bethlehem); martyr; 99–105 (?)
6. **St Alexander I**, of Rome; martyr; 105–115 (?)
7. **St Sixtus I**, of Rome; martyr; 115–125 (?)
8. **St Telesphorus**, of Greece; martyr; 125–136 (?)
9. **St Iginus**, of Greece; martyr; 136–140 (?)
10. **St Pius I**, of Italy; martyr; 140–155 (?)
11. **St Anicetus**, of Syria; martyr; 155–166 (?)
12. **St Soter**, of Campania (Fundi?); martyr; 166–175 (?)
13. **St Eleutherus**, of Epirus (Nicopolis?); martyr; 175–189
14. **St Victor I**, of Africa; martyr; 189–199
15. **St Zephyrinus**, of Rome; martyr; 199–217
16. **St Calixtus**, of Rome; martyr; 217–222
    [Hippolytus, 217–235]
17. **St Urban I**, of Rome; martyr; 222–230
18. **St Pontianus**, of Rome; martyr; 21 July 230–28 Sept 235
19. **St Anterus**, of Greece; martyr; 21 Nov 235–3 Jan 236
20. **St Fabian**, of Rome; martyr; 10 Jan 236–20 Jan 250
21. **St Cornelius**, of Rome; martyr; March 251–June 253
    [Novatian, 251–258]
22. **St Lucius I**, of Rome; martyr; 25 June 253–5 March 254
23. **St Stephen I**, of Rome; martyr; 12 May 254–2 Aug 257
24. **St Sixtus II**, of Greece (?); martyr; 30 Aug 257–6 Aug 258
25. **St Dionysius**, of Magna Graecia (?); martyr; 22 July 259–26 Dec 268
26. **St Felix I**, of Rome; martyr; 5 Jan 269–30 Dec 274
27. **St Eutychianus**, of Luni; martyr; 4 Jan 275–7 Dec 283
28. **St Gaius**, of Dalmatia (Salona?); martyr; 17 Dec 283–22 April 296
29. **St Marcellinus**, of Rome; martyr; 30 June 296–25 Oct 304
30. **St Marcellus I**, of Rome; martyr; 27 May 308–16 Jan 30931.
31. **St Eusebius**, of Greece; martyr; 18 April 309–17 Aug 309 or 310
32. **St Melchiades or Miltiades**, of Africa; martyr; 2 July 311–11 Jan 314
33. **St Sylvester I**, of Rome; 31 Jan 314–31 Dec 335
34. **St Mark**, of Rome; 18 Jan 336–7 Oct 336
35. **St Julius I**, of Rome; 6 Feb 337–12 April 352
36. **Liberius**, of Rome; 17 May 352–22 Sept 366
    [St Felix II, 355–22 Nov 365]
37. **St Damasus I**, of Spain; 1 Oct 366–11 Dec 384
    [Ursinus, 366–367]
38. **St Siricius**, of Rome; 15 Dec 384–26 Nov 399

39. St **Anastasius I**, of Rome; 27 Nov 399–19 Dec 401
40. St **Innocent I**, of Albano; 22 Dec 401–12 March 417
41. St **Zosimus**, of Greece; 18 March 417–26 Dec 418
42. St **Boniface I**, of Rome; 29 Dec 418–4 Sept 422
   [**Eulalius**, 27 Dec 418–3 April 419]
43. St **Caelestinus I**, of Campania; 10 Sept 422–27 July 432
44. St **Sixtus III**, of Rome; 3 July (?) 432–19 Aug 440
45. St **Leo I the Great**, of Tusculum; 29 Sept 440–10 Nov 461
46. St **Hilarius**, of Sardinia; 19 Nov 461–29 Feb 468
47. St **Simplicius**, of Tivoli; 3 March 468–10 March 483
48. St **Felix III** (II), of Rome, of the gens Anicia; 13 March 483–1 March 492
49. St **Gelasius I**, of Africa; 1 March 492–21 Nov 496
50. St **Anastasius II**, of Rome; 24 Nov 496–19 Nov 498
51. St **Symmachus**, of Sardinia; 22 Nov 498–19 July 514
   [**Laurentius**, Nov 498–505]
52. St **Hormisdas**, of Frosinone; 20 July 514–6 Aug 523
53. St **John I**, of Tusculum; martyr; 13 Aug 523–18 May 526. Died at Ravenna
54. St **Felix IV (III)**, of Samnium (Benevento?); 12 July 526–22 Sept 530
55. **Boniface II**, of Rome; 22 Sept 530–7 Oct 532
   [**Dioscurus**, 22 Sept 530–14 Oct 530]
56. **John II**, of Rome; 2 Jan 533–8 May 535
57. St **Agapitus I**, of Rome; 13 May 535–22 April 536. Died at Constantinople
58. St **Silverius**, of Frosinone; martyr; 8 June 536–deposed 11 March 537. Died in exile on the island of Ponza 538 (?)
59. **Vigilius**, of Rome; June 538 (?)–7 June 555 (but elected 29 March 537). Died at Syracuse
60. **Pelagius I**, of Rome; 16 April 556–4 March 561
61. **John III**, of Rome; 17 July 561–13 July 574
62. **Benedict I**, of Rome; 2 June 575–30 July 579
63. **Pelagius II**, of Rome; 26 Nov 579–7 Feb 590
64. St **Gregory I the Great**, of Rome, of the gens Anicia; 3 Sept 590–13 March 604
65. **Sabinianus**, of Tusculum; 13 Sept 604–22 Feb 606
66. **Boniface III**, of Rome; 19 Feb 607–12 Nov 607
67. St **Boniface IV**, of Valeria de' Marsi; 25 Aug 608–8 May 615
68. St **Deusdedit I**, of Rome; 19 Oct 615–8 Nov 618
69. **Boniface V**, of Naples; 23 Dec 619–25 Oct 625
70. **Honorius I**, of Campania; 27 Oct 625–12 Oct 638
71. **Severinus**, of Rome; 28 May 640–2 Aug 640
72. **John IV**, of Dalmatia; 24 Dec 640–12 Oct 642
73. **Theodore I**, of Jerusalem (? or Greece); 24 Nov 642–14 May 649
74. St **Martin I**, of Todi; martyr; 21 July 649–exiled 18 June 653–16 Sept 655. Died at Sebastopol
75. St **Eugenius I**, of Rome; 16 Sept 655–2 June 657
76. St **Vitalian**, of Segni; 30 July 657–27 Jan 672
77. **Deusdedit II**, of Rome; 11 April 672–17 June 676
78. **Donus**, of Rome; 2 Nov 676–11 April 678
79. St **Agatho**, of Sicily; 27 June 678–10 Jan 681

80. **St Leo II**, of Sicily; 17 Aug 682–3 July 683

81. **St Benedict II**, of Rome; 26 June 684–8 May 685

82. **John V**, of Antioch; 23 July 685–2 Aug 686

83. **Conon**, of Thrace; 21 Oct 686–21 Sept 687
    [**Theodore**, 22 Sept 687–Oct 687]
    [**Paschal**, 687]

84. **St Sergius I**, of Palermo; 15 Dec 687–8 Sept 701

85. **John VI**, of Greece; 30 Oct 701–11 Jan 705

86. **John VII**, of Greece; 1 March 705–18 Oct 707

87. **Sisinnius**, of Syria; 15 Jan 708–4 Feb 708

88. **Constantine**, of Syria; 25 March 708–9 April 715

89. **St Gregory II**, of Rome; 19 May 715–11 Feb 731

90. **St Gregory III**, of Syria; 18 March 731–10 Dec 741

91. **St Zacharias**, of Greece; 10 Dec 741–22 March 752

92. **Stephen II**, of Rome; 23 March 752–25 March 752

93. **St Stephen III**, of Rome; 26 March 752–26 April 757

94. **St Paul I**, of Rome; 29 May 757–28 June 767
    [**Constantine II**, 5 July 767–murdered 769]
    [**Philip**, elected 31 July 768–abdicated 768]

95. **Stephen IV**, of Sicily; 7 Aug 768–3 Feb 772

96. **Hadrian I**, of Rome; 9 Feb 772–26 Dec 795

97. **St Leo III**, of Rome; 27 Dec 795–12 June 816

98. **St Stephen V**, of Rome; 22 June 816–14 Jan 817

99. **St Paschal I**, of Rome; 25 Jan 817–11 Feb 824

100. **Eugenius II**, of Rome; 21 Feb 824–27 Aug 827

101. **Valentine**, of Rome; Aug (?) 827–Sept (?) 827

102. **Gregory IV**, of Rome; Oct 827–25 Jan 844

103. **Sergius II**, of Rome; Jan 844–27 Jan 847
    [**John**, 844]

104. **St Leo IV**, of Rome; 10 April 847–17 July 855

105. **St Benedict III**, of Rome; 6 Oct 855–17 April 858
    [**Anastasius**, 29 Sept 855–20 Oct 855]

106. **St Nicholas I the Great**, of Rome; 24 April 858–13 Nov 867

107. **Hadrian II**, of Rome; 14 Dec 867–14 Dec 872

108. **John VIII**, of Rome, 14 Dec 872–16 Dec 882

109. **Marinus I** (Martin II) of Gallesium; 16 Dec 882–15 May 884

110. **St Hadrian III**, of Rome; 17 May 884–17 Sept 885

111. **Stephen VI**, of Rome; Sept 885–Sept 891

112. **Formosus**, bishop of Porto; 6 Oct 891–4 April 896

113. **Boniface VI**, of Gallesium; April 896

114. **Stephen VII**, of Rome; May 896–Aug 897. Strangled in prison

115. **Romanus**, of Gallesium; Aug 897–end of Nov 897

116. **Theodore II**, of Rome; Dec 897

117. **John IX**, of Tivoli; Jan 898–Jan 900

118. **Benedict IV**, of Rome; Jan 900–end July 903

119. **Leo V**, of Ardea; end of July 903–Sept 903. Deposed and imprisoned
    [**Christopher**, of Rome; 903, deposed in Jan 904]

120. **Sergius III**, of Rome; 29 Jan 904–14 April 911

121. **Anastasius III**, of Rome; April 911–June 913

122. **Lando**, of Sabina; end of July 913–Feb 914

123. **John X**, of Ravenna; March 914–May 928. Strangled in prison

124. **Leo VI**, of Rome; May 928–Dec 928

125. **Stephen VIII**, of Rome; Jan 929–Feb 931

126. **John XI**, of Rome; son of Pope Sergius III and Marozia; March 931–Dec 935. Died in prison

127. **Leo VII**; 3 (?) Jan 936–13 (?) July 939

128. **Stephen IX**, of Germany (?); 14 (?) July 939–end of Oct 942

129. **Marinus II** (Martin III), of Rome; 30 (?) Oct 942–May 946

130. **Agapitus II**, of Rome; 10 May 946–Dec 955

131. **John XII**, Ottaviano, of the family of the Counts of Tusculum, aged 19; 16 (?) Dec 955–deposed 14th May 964

132. **Leo VIII**, of Rome, 4 Nov 963–1 March 965

133. **Benedict V**, Grammatico, of Rome; 22 (?) May 964–expelled from the pontifical see 23 June 964; died at Bremen 4 July 966

134. **John XIII**, of Rome; 1 Oct 965–5 Sept 972

135. **Benedict VI**, of Rome; 19 Jan 973–June 974. Strangled in prison
    [**Boniface VII**, Francone, of Rome; June–July 974 for the first time]

136. **Benedict VII**, of the family of the Counts of Tusculum, of Rome; Oct 974–10 July 983

137. **John XIV**, of Pavia; Dec 983–20 Aug 984; killed by Francone (Boniface VII)
    [**Boniface VII**, Francone; for the second time, Aug 984–murdered July 985]

138. **John XV**, of Rome; Aug 985–March 996

139. **Gregory V**, Bruno, of the family of the Counts of Carinthia; 3 May 996–18 Feb 999
    [**John XVI**, John Philagathus, of Greece; March 997–Feb 998]

140. **Sylvester II**, Gerbert of Aurillc, Auvergne; 2 April 999–12 May 1003

141. **John XVII**, Sicco, of Rome; June (?) 1003–6 Nov 1003

142. **John XVIII**, of Rapagnano; Jan (?) 1004–July (?) 1009

143. **Sergius IV**, of Rome; 31 July 1009–12 May 1012

144. **Benedict VIII**, John, of the family of the Counts of Tusculum, of Rome; 18 May 1012–9 April 1024
    [**Gregory**, 1012]

145. **John XIX**, of Rome, brother of Benedict VIII; April 1024–1032

146. **Benedict IX**, Theophylact, of the family of the Counts of Tusculum; elected (aged 15) for the first time in 1032–deposed in Dec 1044; elected for the second time 10 March 1045–deposed 1 May 1045; elected for the third time 8 Nov 1047– deposed 17 July 1048

147. **Sylvester III**, John, bishop of Sabina; 20 Jan 1045–deposed 10 March 1045

148. **Gregory VI**, Gratian, of Rome; 5 May 1045–banished 20 Dec 1046; died 1047

149. **Clement II**, Suidger, bishop of Bamberg; 25 Dec 1046–died at Pesaro 9 Oct 1047

150. **Damasus II**, Poppo, bishop of Bressanone, of Bavaria; 17 July 1048–9 Aug 1048. Died at Palestrina

151. **St Leo IX**, Bruno, of Germany, bishop of Toul; 12 Feb 1049–19 April 1054

152. **Victor II**, Gebhard, of Germany, bishop of Eichstätt; 16 April 1055–28 July 1057. Died at Arezzo

153. **Stephen X**, Frédéric, of the family of the Dukes of Lorraine; 3 Aug

1057–29 March 1058
[**Benedict X**, of Rome; 5 April
1058–deposed 24 Jan 1059]

154. **Nicholas II**, Gérard de Bourgogne;
24 Jan 1059–27 (?) July 1061

155. **Alexander II**, Anselmo of Milan;
30 Sept 1061–21 April 1073
[**Honorius II**, appointed by
Imperial Diet of Basle 1061–1072]

156. **St Gregory VII**, Hildebrand di
Bonizio Aldobrandeschi, of
Sovana; 22 April 1073–25 May
1085
[**Clement III**, Ghiberto; 25 Jan
1080–Sept 1100]

157. **Bl. Victor III**, Desiderio Epifani, of
Benevento; elected 24 May 1086,
consecrated 9 May 1087–16 Sept
1087

158. **Bl. Urban II**, of Reims; 12 March
1088–29 July 1099

159. **Paschal II**, Rainiero, of Breda; 14
Aug 1099–21 Jan 1118
[**Theodoric**, Sept–Dec 1100]
[**Albert**, Feb–March 1102]
[**Sylvester IV**, 18 Nov 1105–12
April 1111]

160. **Gelasius II**, Giov. Caetani, of
Gaeta; 24 Jan 1118–28 Jan 1119
[**Gregory VIII**, Maurice Bourdain,
of Limoges, 8 March 1118–
deposed April 1121]

161. **Calixtus II**, Gui de Bourgogne,
of Quingey; 2 Feb 1119–13 Dec
1124

162. **Honorius II**, Lamberto
Scannabecchi, of Fanano
(Modena); 15 Dec 1124–13 Feb
1130

163. **Innocent II**, Gregorio Papareschi,
of Trastevere; 14 Feb 1130–24
Sept 1143
[**Anacletus II**, Pierleone, a converted Jew; 14 Feb 1130–25 Jan
1138]
[**Victor IV**, Gregorio da Monticelli,
elected 15 March 1138, abdicated
29 May 1138]

164. **Celestine II**, Guido, of Città di
Castello; 26 Sept 1143–8 March
1144

165. **Lucius II**, Gerardo Caccianemici
dell'Orso, of Bologna; 12 March
1144–15 Feb 1145

166. **Bl. Eugenius III**, Bernardo
Paganelli, of Montemagno (Pisa);
15 Feb 1145–8 July 1153

167. **Anastasius IV**, Corrado, of the
Suburra, Rome; 12 July 1153–3
Dec 1154

168. **Hadrian IV**, Nicholas Breakspeare,
of Bedmond (Hertfordshire,
England); 4 Dec 1154–1 Sept
1159. Died at Anagni

169. **Alexander III**, Rolando Bandinelli,
of Siena; 7 Sept 1159–30 Aug
1181. Died at Civita Castellana
[**Victor IV** (V), Ottaviano; 7 Oct
1159–20 April 1164]
[**Paschal III**, Guido da Crema;
22 April 1164–20 Sept 1168]
[**Calixtus III**, John of Strumio,
a Hungarian, Sept 1168, abdicated
29 Aug 1178]
[**Innocent III**, Lando Frangipane
of Sezze, elected 29 Sept 1179,
deposed in Jan 1180]

170. **Lucius III**, Ubaldo Allucingoli,
of Lucca; 1 Sept 1181–25 Nov
1185. Died in exile at Verona

171. **Urban III**, Uberto Crivelli, of
Milan; 25 Nov 1185–20 Oct 1187.
Died at Ferrara

172. **Gregory VIII**, Alberto di Morra, of
Benevento; 21 Oct 1187–17 Dec
1187

173. **Clement III**, Paolino Scolare, of
Rome; 19 Dec 1187–Mar 1191

174. **Celestine III**, Giacinto Bobone
Orsini, of Rome; 30 March 1191–8
Jan 1198

175. **Innocent III**, Lotario dei Conti di
Segni, of Anagni; 8 Jan 1198–16
July 1216. Died at Perugia

176. **Honorius III**, Cencio Savelli, of
Rome; elected in Perugia, 18 July

1216– died at Rome, 18 March 1227

177. **Gregory IX**, Ugolino dei Conti di Segni, of Anagni; elected at the age of 86; 19 March 1227–22 Aug 1241

178. **Celestine IV**, Castiglione, of Milan; 25 Oct 1241–10 Nov 1241

179. **Innocent IV**, Sinibaldo Fieschi of Genoa; 25 June 1243–7 Dec 1254. Died at Naples

180. **Alexander IV**, Orlando dei Conti di Segni, of Anagni; 12 Dec 1254–25 May 1261. Died at Viterbo

181. **Urban IV**, Hyacinthe Pantaléon, of Troyes; elected at Viterbo 29 Aug 1261; died at Perugia 2 Oct 1264

182. **Clement IV**, Gui Foulques Le Gros, of St-Gilles; elected at Viterbo 5 Feb 1265–died at Viterbo 29 Nov 1268

183. **Gregory X**, Teobaldo Visconti of Piacenza; elected at Viterbo 1 Sept 1271–died at Arezzo 10 Jan 1276

184. **Innocent V**, Pierre de Champagny, of the Tarentaise; 21 Jan 1276–22 June 1276

185. **Hadrian V**, Ottobono de' Fieschi, of Genoa; elected at Rome 11 July 1276–18 Aug 1276

186. **John XXI**, Pedro Juliao, of Lisbon; elected at Viterbo 8 Sept 1276–20 May 1277

187. **Nicholas III**, Giov. Gaetano Orsini, of Rome; elected at Viterbo 25 Nov 1277–died at Soriano nel Cimino 22 Aug 1280

188. **Martin IV**, Simon de Brion, of Montpincé in Brie; elected at Viterbo 22 Feb 1281–died at Perugia 28 March 1285

189. **Honorius IV**, Iacopo Savelli, of Rome; elected at Perugia 2 April 1285–3 April 1287

190. **Nicholas IV**, Girolamo Masci, of Lisciano di Ascoli; 15 Feb 1288–4 April 1292

191. **St Celestine V**, Pietro Angeleri da Morrone, of Isérnia; 5 July 1294– abdicated 13 Dec 1294. Died in the Castello di Fumone near Alatri 19 May 1296

192. **Boniface VIII**, Benedetto Gaetani, of Anagni; 24 Dec 1294–11 or 12 Oct 1303

193. **Bl. Benedict XI**, Niccolò Boccasini, of Treviso; 22 Oct 1303–died at Perugia 7 July 1304

194. **Clement V**, Bertrand de Got, of Villandraut, near Bordeaux; elected at Perugia 5 June 1305–died at Roquemaure 14 April 1314

195. **John XXII**, Jacques d'Euse, of Cahors; elected at Avignon 7 Aug 1316–died at Avignon 4 Dec 1334 [**Nicholas V**, Pietro da Corvara, 12 May 1328–30 Aug 1330]

196. **Benedict XII**, Jacques Fournier, of Saverdun, near Toulouse; 20 Dec 1334–25 April 1342

197. **Clement VI**, Pierre Roger de Beaufort, of Château Maumont, near Limoges; 7 May 1342–6 Dec 1352

198. **Innocent VI**, Etienne d'Aubert, of Mont, near Limoges; 18 Dec 1352–12 Sept 1362

199. **Urban V**, Guillaume de Grimoard, of Grisac, near Mende in Languedoc; 16 Oct 1362–19 Dec 1370

200. **Gregory XI**, Pierre Roger de Beaufort, nephew of Clement VI, of Château Maumont, near Limoges; elected at Avignon 30 Dec 1370–died at Rome 27 March 1378

201. **Urban VI**, Bart. Prigano, of Naples; 9 April 1378–15 Oct 1389

202. **Boniface IX**, Pietro Tomacelli, of Naples; 2 Nov 1389–1 Oct 1404

203. **Innocent VII**, Cosimo de'Migliorati, of Sulmona; 17 Oct 1404–6 Nov 1406.

204. **Gregory XII**, Angelo Correr, of

Venice; 30 Nov 1406–abdicated 4 June 1415–died at Recanati 17 Oct 1417

ANTIPOPES

Clement VII, Robert of Savoy, of Geneva; elected at Fondi 20 Sept 1378–16 Sept 1394
Benedict XIII, Pedro de Luna, of Aragon; 28 Sept 1394–23 May 1423
Clement VIII, Gil Sanchez Muñoz, of Barcelona; 10 June 1423–16 July 1429
Benedict XIV, Bernard Garnier; 12 Nov 1425–1430 (?)
Alexander V, Pietro Filargis, of Candia; 26 June 1409–3 May 1410
John XXIII, Baldassarre Cossa, of Naples; 17 May 1410, deposed 29 May 1415–died at Florence 23 Dec 1419

205. **Martin V**, Oddone Colonna, of Genazzano; elected (aged 50) at Constance, 11 Nov 1417–20 Feb 1431
206. **Eugenius IV**, Gabriele Condulmero of Venice; elected (aged 48) 3 March 1431–23 Feb 1447
[**Felix V**, Amadeus, duke of Savoy; 5 Nov 1439–7 April 1449; died 1451 at the Château de Ripaille on the Lake of Geneva]
207. **Nicholas V**, Tommaso Parentucelli, of Sarzana; electe (aged 49) 6 March 1447–24 March 1455
208. **Calixtus III**, Alfonso Borgia, of Xativa, in Spain; elected (aged 78) 8 April 1455–6 Aug 1458
209. **Pius II**, Aeneas Silvius Piccolomini, of Corsignano (Pienza); elected (aged 53) 19 Aug 1458–15 Aug 1464

210. **Paul II**, Pietro Barbo, of Venice; elected (aged 48) 30 Aug 1464–26 July 1471
211. **Sixtus IV**, Fr. della Rovere, of Savona; elected (aged 57) 9 Aug 1471–12 Aug 1484
212. **Innocent VIII**, G. B. Cibo, of Genoa; elected (aged 52) 29 Aug 1484–25 July 1492
213. **Alexander VI**, Roderigo Lenzuoli-Borgia, of Valencia, Spain; elected (aged 62) 11 Aug 1492–18 Aug 1503
214. **Pius III**, Fr. Todeschini Piccolomini, of Siena; elected (aged 64) 22 Sept 1503–18 Oct 1503
215. **Julius II**, Giuliano della Rovere, of Savona; elected (aged 60) 31 Oct 1503–21 Feb 1513
216. **Leo X**, Giov. de' Medici, of Florence; elected (aged 38) 9 March 1513–1 Dec 1521
217. **Adrian VI**, Adrian Florisz. Dedel, of Utrecht; elected (aged 63) 9 Jan 1522–14 Sept 1523
218. **Clement VII**. Giulio de' Medici, of Florence; elected (aged 45) 19 Nov 1523–25 Sept 1534
219. **Paul III**, Aless. Farnese, of Camino (Rome) or of Viterbo (?), elected (aged 66) 13 Oct 1534–10 Nov 1549
220. **Julius III**, Giov. Maria Ciocchi del Monte, of Monte San Savino, near Arezzo; elected (aged 63) 7 Feb 1550–23 March 1555
221. **Marcellus II**, Marcello Cervini, of Montefano (Macerata); elected (aged 54) 9 April 1555–30 April 1555
222. **Paul IV**, Giov. Pietro Caraffa, of Capriglio, Avellino; elected (aged 79) 23 May 1555–18 Aug 1559
223. **Pius IV**, Giov. Angelo de'Medici, of Milan; elected (aged 60) 26 Dec 1559–9 Dec 1565
224. **St Pius V**, Ant. Ghislieri, of Bosco

INDEX

Explanatory or more detailed references (where there are many), or references to places where an artist's work is best represented, are given in bold. Numbers in italics are picture references. Dates are given for all artists, architects and sculptors. Conjectural attributions to artists and sculptors are not indexed.

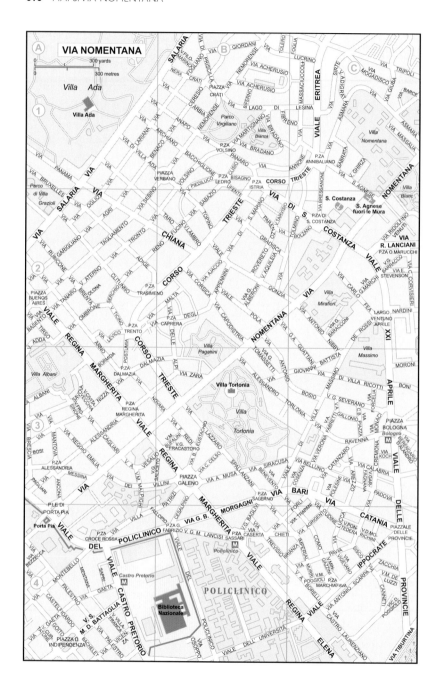

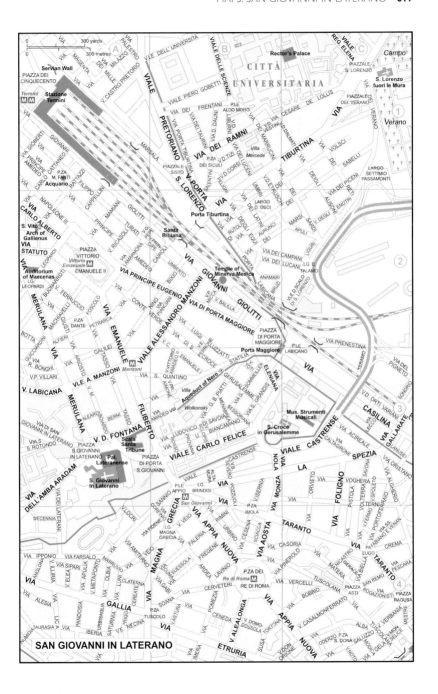

SAN GIOVANNI IN LATERANO

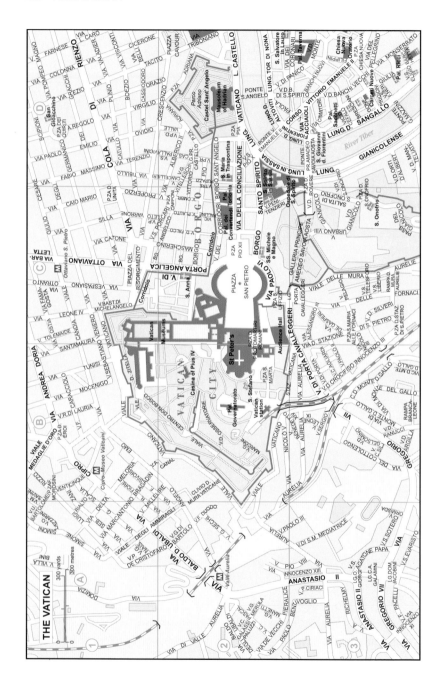

THE VATICAN

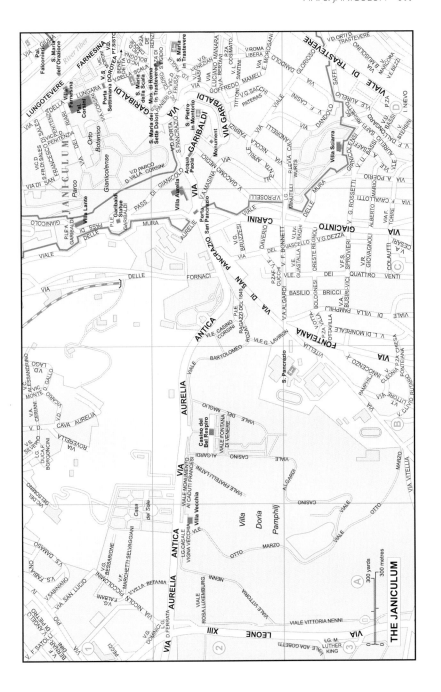

THE JANICULUM

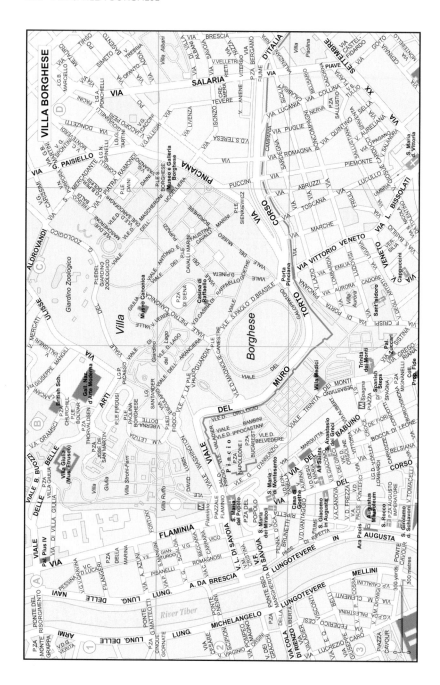

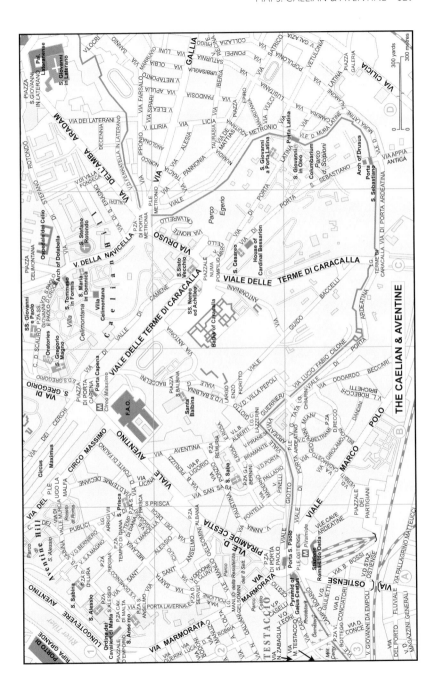

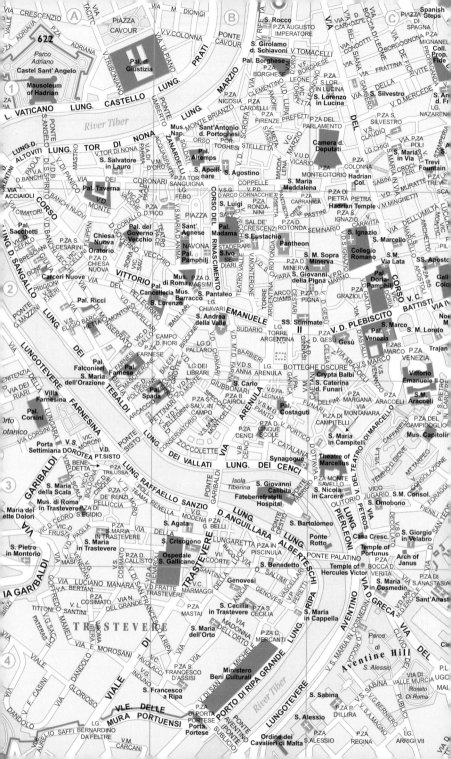

CENTRAL ROME 623

Editor-in-Chief: Annabel Barber
Assistant editor: Judy Tither

Editorial Board: Charles Freeman, Nigel McGilchrist
Hotels adviser: Rebecca Orde (with thanks to Antonio del Balzo, Marco Manetti,
Gianluca Novarini, Maurizio Papiri, Martin Stanford, Bertina & Giorgio Vaglio)

Design: Anikó Kuzmich
Maps by Dimap Bt
Architectural elevations: Michael Mansell RIBA & Gabriella Juhász
Floor plans and watercolours: Imre Bába
Diagrams and other artwork (except as below) © Blue Guides Limited

Photo Editor: Róbert Szabó Benke
Photographs by Róbert Szabó Benke: pp. 47, 83, 105, 129, 133, 151, 153, 157,
173, 175, 216, 256, 262, 269, 295, 299, 300, 343, 344, 359, 393, 413;
Phil Robinson: pp. 60, 115, 174, 190, 210, 218, 316, 319, 327, 328, 331, 334, 357, 365, 484
Other photographs by Arion (p. 452), Annabel Barber (pp. 36, 251, 382),
Helen McGrath (p. 102) and Jon Smith (p. 394)
Artworks are reproduced by kind permission of: Archivio Fotografico dei Musei Capitolini/Musei
Capitolini (p. 49); Archivio Fotografico dei Musei Capitolini/Pinacoteca Capitolina (p. 45);
Archivio Fotografico Soprintendenza Speciale per il Polo Museale Romano (pp. 126, 161, 162,
164, 184, 188, 221, 222, 224, 374); Arti Doria Pamphilj (pp. 138, 142); the Irish Dominican
Fathers of San Clemente (pp. 348, 351); Soprintendenza Archeologica di Roma (pp. 92, 94)

Acknowledgements
Special thanks are due to Alessandro Padula, from whom the author received much help during
numerous visits to Rome; also to Richard Robinson and Professor Luigi de Simone Niquesa

Printed in Hungary by Dürer Nyomda Kft, Gyula

ISBN 1–905131–11–9